WICKED THEORY, NAKED PRACTICE

Wicked Theory,

A FRED HO READER

Naked Practice

FRED HO

EDITED BY Diane C. Fujino
FOREWORD BY Robin D. G. Kelley
AFTERWORD BY Bill V. Mullen

University of Minnesota Press

MINNEAPOLIS / LONDON

Copyright 2009 by the Regents of the University of Minnesota

Published by the University of Minnesota Press
111 Third Avenue South, Suite 290
Minneapolis, MN 55401-2520
http://www.upress.umn.edu

Library of Congress Cataloging-in-Publication Data

Ho, Fred Wei-han.
    Wicked theory, naked practice : A Fred Ho reader / Fred Ho ; edited by Diane C. Fujino ; foreword by Robin D. G. Kelley ; afterword by Bill V. Mullen.
        p. cm.
Includes bibliographical references and index.
    ISBN 978-0-8166-5684-4 (hc : alk. paper)—ISBN 978-0-8166-5685-1 (pb : alk. paper)
    1. Jazz—History and criticism. 2. Music—Social aspects. 3. Asian American musicians. 4. Asian Americans—Social conditions. I. Fujino, Diane Carol. II. Title. III. Title: Fred Ho reader.
ML60.H68 2009
781.65—dc22   2008038195

Printed in the United States of America on acid-free paper

The University of Minnesota is an equal-opportunity educator and employer.

Produced by Wilsted & Taylor Publishing Services
Copy editing by Nancy Evans
Text design by Susan E. Kelly

18 17 16 15 14 13 12 11 10 09   10 9 8 7 6 5 4 3 2 1

CONTENTS

ACKNOWLEDGMENTS

MANY THANK-YOUS must be given to people who have not only made this collection possible but who have also stood by me during stormy and uncertain times for the past thirty years at critical crossroads in my personal, political, and professional development.

   First, for this anthology, Bill Mullen and Diane Fujino, two terrific friends and brilliant scholar-activist comrades. Bill agreed to write the Afterword, and his pioneering work *Afro-Orientalism* (published by the University of Minnesota Press in 2005) put me into the consciousness of Douglas Armato, director and editor of the University of Minnesota Press. That Diane Fujino's powerful political biography of veteran Japanese American radical activist Yuri Kochiyama, *Heartbeat of Struggle: The Revolutionary Life of Yuri Kochiyama* (again, the University of Minnesota Press, 2005) has sold so well and been so well received across the United States was also a plus for the editors at the Press to consider publishing someone like myself. Others who encouraged the publication and support of this anthology in particular, and my overall work in general, are Roger Buckley and Angela Rola at the University of Connecticut–Storrs (where the Fred Ho Collection on Asian American Politics and Culture is housed in the Special Collections of the university's prestigious Thomas J. Dodd Center); Samantha Smart, who helped with the typing of the original manuscript; Shawn Wong, who gave me encouragement to continue to pursue publication of this collection; and of course to preeminent historian and cultural scholar Robin D. G. Kelley, a fan of my musical and intellectual work, who enthusiastically cheered me on and agreed to write the Foreword.

Back in the mid-1990s, my collaboration with Ron Sakolsky on my first published book, *Sounding Off! Music as Subversion/Resistance/Revolution,* an anthology on music and social change that won the American Book Award in 1996, turned me on to writing, editing, and publishing books that could be radical tools. The publisher of this first book, Jim Fleming of Autonomedia, continues to be a friend and positive person. Autonomedia published my second project, a popular radical calendar of Sheroes/Womyn Warriors that came out annually from 1998 to 2005. (In 2007, the calendar continued under the publishing auspices of the Gustavus Myers Center for the Study of Bigotry and Human Rights at Simmons College, under the helm of Loretta J. Williams.) Ron later introduced me to AK Press, which published my third book, the anthology *Legacy to Liberation: Politics and Culture of Revolutionary Asian Pacific America* (2000), a collection of essays and creative writing.

The following people have had major influence on my creative and political thinking: Amiri Baraka, Bill Fletcher, Romulus Franceschini, Magdalena Gomez, Marilyn Lewis, Ngũgĩ wa Thiong'o, Max Roach, Sonia Sanchez, Archie Shepp, and the many younger radical activists I have had the pleasure to struggle with during the 1990s in the dark days after the collapse of the League of Revolutionary Struggle who were part of revolutionary study groups I initiated at my former duplex loft in Brooklyn.

Other people have been patrons, supporters, opportunity-givers. The ones that "discovered" me were those who responded and acted immediately, without hesitation, in genuine excitement about my creative work. Myra Mayman, the first director of the Harvard-Radcliffe Office of the Arts, now retired, gave me my first grant of two hundred dollars to write big band arrangements. She later validated my talent even further by conferring on me the Peter Ivers Visiting Artist Fellowship at Harvard in 1987—my first really better-paying gig. In December 1983, I received an exciting phone message from Giovanni Bonandrini, the owner-producer of Black Saint/Soul Note Records in Milan, Italy, inviting me to record my first album for his label. Jack Chen, who died in the early 1990s, was my first real patron; as founder of the Pear Garden in the West, a Chinese American

performing arts consortium, he presented my first large-scale productions, often with only a tiny budget. Jack's passion and belief in
my work inspired me to learn how to produce as a guerrilla entrepre-
neur. The great composer Charles Wuorinen and manager Howard
Stokar have been terrific friends and connectors. They introduced
me to Mary Sharp Cronson, one of America's great supporters of contemporary performing arts, who became my second major patron.
She introduced me and my work to Harvey Lichtenstein, visionary
impresario and creator of the Next Wave Festival at the Brooklyn
Academy of Music. Acting from his gut, Harvey placed my work *Journey Beyond the West: The New Adventures of Monkey!* in the 1997 Next
Wave Festival and so put me on a very big stage in contemporary
performance. Joseph Franklin, former executive and artistic director
of the New Music group Relâche, was introduced to me via the great
Cal Massey collaborator, arranger-composer, and socialist Romulus
Franceschini, and commissioned my first work beyond my own ensembles. Joseph would interest the music management guru Marty
Khan to connect with me. My discussions with Marty have offered
confirmation and constant insight and counsel. In recent years, the
freshest, most brilliant impresario of contemporary music and performance, Thaddeus Squire of Peregrine Arts, Inc., has become a true
friend and producing/presenting partner of all my new work.

I have had the fantastic experience of working with visionary collaborators: writers Ann T. Greene and Ruth Margraff; directors So-
noko Kawahara, Mira Kingsley, and Christopher Mattaliano; martial
artists George Crayton III, Kathleen Cruz, Jose Figueroa, Tsuyoshi
Kaseda, Robert Scott Parker, Sekou (Ronald Williams), Ron Wheeler,
and the many performers in my shows since 1997; and a host of musicians credited in numerous programs and recordings of mine.

I have sought the power of ideas, the guiding role of theory, and
the analysis of struggle and organizing experience on the role of
culture and the arts in the very difficult challenges of radical social
change. Some works had profound impact on my direction: many
of Amiri Baraka's writings, Ngũgĩ's *Decolonising the Mind,* and the
very first book that changed my life: *The Autobiography of Malcolm
X.* These are books. Equally profoundly impactful have been recordings: Charles Mingus's *The Black Saint and the Sinner Lady;* Archie
Shepp's *Blasé, Attica Blues,* and *The Cry of My People*; Duke Ellington's

A Tone Parallel to Harlem and *The Liberian Suite*; the many records of the Thad Jones/Mel Lewis Orchestra; the great recordings by Eddie Palmieri; every recording made by John Coltrane as leader or sideman; and so many more. And then the live performances, unforgettable, life-changing: Sun Ra and his Arkestra, the marathon power of Rahsaan Roland Kirk, Max Roach and M'Boom, Kazue Sawai's all-female Koto Ensemble—these have been most memorable. And the poets who rocked my world: Amiri, Magdalena Gomez, Esther Iverem, Genny Lim, Tony Medina, Janice Mirikitani, Kalamu ya Salaam, Raul Salinas, Quincy Troupe . . .

I am grateful for the support and guidance of my editor, Adam Brunner, at the University of Minnesota Press. He is a person of integrity and diligence.

Lastly, there are people in my life who accept me unconditionally (though they care about me enough to challenge me when I need it). My mother, Frances Lu Houn, sacrificed and gave so much so that I could be who I am and do what I do. My sister Flora, her husband Steve, and my two nieces, Emma Lu and Julia, are big fans whom I love to see at my shows. Florence, her husband Mark, and my nephew, Ethan, have made their home always open to me.

Finally, to my soul mate, who refers to me as her "avant-garde man," I dedicate this collection.

Tomorrow Is Now!

Robin D. G. Kelley

"YOU'VE GOT TO HEAR THIS!" My sister Makani, flushed with
excitement, pulled a bright-colored album out of her bag. I remember chuckling over the cover art: the colors of the rainbow breaking
through storm clouds like sun rays, forming what could have been a
metaphoric vagina à la Georgia O'Keeffe or Judy Chicago. I laughed
because it was near the end of 1985 or early 1986, and we both had
been active in Jesse Jackson's Rainbow Coalition campaign two years
earlier—my sister more than I. Back then we thought the rainbow
coalitions we were building had the power to move back the storm
we knew as the American Empire. Once the needle hit the vinyl, I
realized this was no laughing matter. The band was the Afro Asian
Music Ensemble, and the leader and founder was a young baritone
sax player named Fred Wei-han Houn—today known as Fred Ho. The
music was swinging, reminiscent of the best of Charles Mingus, Sun
Ra, Archie Shepp, Max Roach, Frank Foster's *The Loud Minority,* Gary
Bartz, and infused with fleeting moments of Asian improv.

And it had politics. *Tomorrow Is Now!* was not your garden-vari-
ety liberal protest politics put to music. It was revolutionary to the
core, from its politically inspired Afro-Asian fusions and its radical
lyrics and poetry, to the liner notes by none other than Amiri Baraka.
The movements in Ho's *Tomorrow Is Now Suite* were calls to action:
"You've Got to Overthrow the Big Bourgeoisie" and do so "A.F.A.P."
(as fast as possible). And they were assertions of a new movement:
"History Crying for a Change" and the lovely "A Blk Woman Speaks,"

which includes a portion of Sonia Sanchez's poem of the same title. We heard tunes like "Blues to the Freedom Fighters" and "Ganbaro!" (a Japanese expression for "the spirit of perseverance, determination, and struggle"), which swung hard and incorporated scales associated with Asian music.

We needed this album. We felt thoroughly embattled: apartheid in South Africa; death squads in Central America; the defense of revolution in Nicaragua; the U.S. invasions of Grenada and Panama; police brutality; antiblack and anti-Asian violence; and a second term for Ronald Reagan. Makani and I were especially sensitive to issues of Black–Asian unity, since we were both students at UCLA, where the Third World Coalition built strong ties between African American, Asian, and Latino students. And we were members of the Communist Workers Party, an outgrowth of the Workers Viewpoint Organization, with strong roots in the Asian American and Black Liberation movements. We were as concerned about the racist murder of Vincent Chin as we were with the murders of Michael Stewart and Eleanor Bumpurs. But by 1986, we were feeling thoroughly defeated. The Jesse Jackson campaign was supposed to be the Left's great moment to build a radical grassroots movement, but the cult of Jackson, his own egocentrism, and our utter failure to sustain the momentum derailed our agenda. Then the CWP imploded, shedding its Marxist base and reinventing itself as the New Democratic Movement in 1985. The Party adopted the line that "knowledge workers," or left-of-liberal technocrats, were the movement's future. Makani and I didn't stay much longer.

So here we were, feeling exhausted and a bit dejected, and out of nowhere comes this hip Chinese American composer/baritone saxophonist, reminding us of the radical traditions that brought us to the movement and *to the music.* Two decades and numerous recordings, performances, books, essays, films, operas, poems, plays, calendars, collaborations, injunctions, pronouncements, and manifestos later, listening to or reading Fred Ho still has the same effect. *Wicked Theory, Naked Practice* is the literary version of his greatest hits—and I don't use "hits" lightly. These are fighting words, and Ho comes out swinging every time. The essays he and Diane Fujino gathered together in this volume not only tell the story of Fred Ho's trajectory from Third World nationalist to Marxist-Leninist to Matriarchal

Socialist, but they also render transparent the relationship between theory and practice. What makes Fred Ho unique is that he actually *struggles* with cultural theory as a framework for practice, not simply as a mode of analysis. It is not enough to ask what is revolutionary art: in these pages he is grappling with the question of how to create it.

At the heart of all of his writings is the question of power: how is oppression reproduced, and what will it take to overturn it? How do social relations under patriarchy and racial capitalism actually shape cultural and artistic production? How does one create meaningful art that is both rooted in tradition and transcendent, that illuminates and moves without speaking "down" to people? These are the book's most fundamental questions. For example, in this age of postmodernism, when pastiche and hybridity are celebrated uncritically, Ho makes a clear distinction between the politics of appropriation or cultural imperialism and "kreolization." He reminds us that the politically engaged cultural exchange among oppressed nationalities in the service of resistance, liberation, and solidarity is a form of revolutionary internationalism. Understanding this distinction is crucial, for what Ho does differs dramatically from the way composers of the dominant class scoured folk traditions or so-called jazz in order to create high art for the concert hall. Ho not only theorizes the relationship between cross-cultural work and power but he is also one of the premiere practitioners of this work. All of his music and multimedia works, from *A Chinaman's Chance* and *A Song for Manong* to *Warrior Sisters: The New Adventures of African and Asian Womyn Warriors* and *All Power to the People! The Black Panther Suite,* expose the limits of terms such as multiculturalism. Drawing on a vast musical well, from spirituals to Chinese opera, blues to Filipino kulintang, Ho's radical assemblages are a far cry from "world beat." He refuses to appropriate traditions out of their context and instead strives for a real synthesis that is transformative and encourages cross-cultural respect and communication. Consider his explorations of trickster figures in Chinese and African American folk cultures. His suite *Journey Beyond the West: The New Adventures of Monkey!* (1995) emphasizes the power of the trickster to challenge a violent ruling class and unite the oppressed.

But Ho is not merely concerned about *his* practice. On the con-

‹ 3

trary, he is offering a framework for revolutionary practice in general: ideas, insights, and histories that can inform current and future struggles for social justice and transformation. In doing so, he also delivers blistering critiques of other political and cultural movements. He trains his critical sights on Asian American writers and so-called jazz musicians and critics, as well as prominent figures in the Black Arts movement. (His stunning essay on composer Cal Massey is worth the price of the book.) And his assessments are often harsh, direct, and honest. Ho's "take no prisoners" approach may be a bit unnerving for young readers who came of age in a world of extreme cultural relativism where everyone's opinion deserves equal respect and criticism is treated as a personal affront. But Ho is a product of oppressed nationality movements, the antirevisionist Left, and other political formations, where "unity and struggle" is the order of the day. His world believes in honest criticism and self-criticism, always leveled with love. He is not interested in hagiography or romanticizing past movements; he wants to figure out where we succeeded and where we failed, and how to move forward.

4 ›

Ho walks a fine line between scholar and propagandist—a term I do not use derisively. On the contrary, he writes, speaks, and plays in order to persuade and inspire, to expose the crimes of the ruling class and to challenge the status quo so that we might imagine a different future. In his essay "Matriarchy: The First and Final Communism" (this volume), he describes his own work as a "combination of scientific argumentation as well as advocacy, i.e., a political stand motivated by the premise to eliminate all inequality, injustice, exploitation, and oppression and to create a new society." He can be harsh, as in his sweeping attack on cultural studies and mainstream academia, or in his stinging rebukes of Leftists who backpedaled from the national question or anti-imperialism in the wake of the September 11 attacks. At the same time, his critical responses operate on different registers, whether he is offering a scholarly reading of Japanese tanka poetry or the musical traditions of female sugarcane plantation workers in Hawaii, or giving a rousing speech on the importance of Mao Zedong thought for the Black Liberation movement. Ho's scholarship must be read as being both inside and outside academia. He is not only indebted to ethnic studies but also reminds us that ethnic studies (Black studies, Asian/Pacific American studies, Latina/o studies, and Native American studies) owes a debt to the revolutionary movements of which Ho was a part. He understands that ethnic studies was a product of student and community-based protest, that it was meant to establish an institutional presence in oppressed nationality communities, and that liberation, not more tenured positions, was the primary goal.

Wicked Theory, Naked Practice is a real gift. Fred Ho has given us a huge body of work; its full political and cultural implications have yet to be fully realized and will be studied for years to come. Study it well, for if we do we will see that the point of Ho's nearly four-decade odyssey swimming the cultural and political waters of the African and Asian diasporas has been to change the Earth, to end all forms of oppression everywhere, and to create an art that can turn our pain into power.

I can't wait to give this book to my sister.

Revolutionary Dreaming and New Dawns

Diane C. Fujino

Principled people in an unprincipled world always confront problems that seem too complex to solve, they always find themselves pitted against powers that seem too strong to defeat. But the very seriousness of the situation contains the seeds of a solution.... We stand in this life at midnight, always on the verge of a new dawn.

—George Lipsitz, *American Studies in a Moment of Danger*

‹ 7

IN 1989, FRED HO faced a moment of crisis. He had been working closely, intensively with fellow musicians to develop an Asian American jazz movement for several years. But the revolutionary political organization that had been his home for more than a decade was growing increasingly moderate ideologically and requiring its artists to create "accessible" works (meaning, to Ho, "tailing the familiar and conventional").[1] The decision was not entirely his—the group ejected him—but it was his choice to publicly oppose the political and aesthetic direction of the organization. This left him isolated (organizationally, socially, and personally), abandoned by many of his closest friends, comrades, and fellow musicians. Like Malcolm X, whose forced departure from his beloved Nation of Islam left him feeling as if his head were bleeding from the inside, Ho nonetheless had faith in "poetic knowledge"—Robin Kelley's reference for the ability to "imagine a new society," to "transport us to another place," to "see the future in the present."[2] Ho had faith in the importance of a revolutionary vision, and in the power of his music, his words, his practice, and his ideas to transform not only society, but also the alienation of his midnight hour.[3]

The Sociological and Other Imaginations

In *The Sociological Imagination* (1959), C. Wright Mills discusses the need "to grasp the interplay between man [*sic*] and society, of biography and history, of self and world."[4] Fred Ho discusses his own life as a dialectical relationship between the personal and the historical. He came of age in the 1970s as an Asian American immersed in the Black Power and Black Arts movements, turned to activism in the era of Third World radicalism, was active in the Asian American Movement, and helped to develop the Asian American jazz movement. As a radical activist devoted to collaborative struggle and societal change, his music making and activism have also been a continuous struggle between asserting individuality and working collectively. Influenced by the ideas of Malcolm X in what Amiri Baraka calls the "roaring sixties," but born a decade later than most 1960s activists, Ho is actually a 1970s activist. This shifting of decades is important. By the late 1960s, the beloved community, interracial, and reconciliatory politics of the Civil Rights and early New Left movements gave way to the militancy and radicalism of the Black Power and Third World liberation movements. While many social movement scholars, notably Todd Gitlin, lament this change, activists like Ho and activist-writers like Max Elbaum celebrate the radicalness of this vision and its possibilities for liberatory change.[5] In *Freedom Dreams*, Robin Kelley states that when critics dismiss revolutionary movements for failing to achieve their far-reaching goals, they miss "what these movements might tell us about how black people have imagined real freedom."[6] There is power in revolutionary dreaming.

The story of Fred Ho, like so many other biographical narratives, fits the general parameters of a conversion story. Born in 1957 as Fred Wei-han Houn, Ho grew up in Amherst, Massachusetts, where his father worked as a university professor.[7] Ho's own narration, told years after becoming a revolutionary activist, emphasizes the

impact of White racism on his ethnic identity. His use of the deroga-
tory term "banana" (yellow on the outside, White on the inside) in
self-reference not only describes the ways he sought after Whiteness
as a strategy for acceptance in a predominantly White college town,
but also, significantly, heightens his later conversion to racial pride
and radical politics. The political milieu of the late 1960s and early
1970s shaped Ho's political conversion. Black activists demanded the
hiring of Black teachers. The first Black teacher hired at his junior
high school initiated the first Black studies class. With her "big Afro"
and "militant black pride," she introduced Ho to *The Autobiography of
Malcolm X* and other transformative writings and sparked his political awakening. The acquisition of a saxophone from his school band
at age fourteen allowed Ho a creative outlet for his growing critical
consciousness. The most influential course Ho, then an advanced
high school student, took at the University of Massachusetts, Amherst, was taught by jazz saxophonist Archie Shepp. Shepp not only
taught Ho technique and provided opportunities to play professional
gigs, but he was also among the jazz musicians who created a political free jazz movement.[8]

‹ 9

As a teenager, Ho gravitated toward cultural nationalism, drawn by
its appeal of racial pride and the satisfaction of "hating Whitey." At
the time, he saw the source of his personal oppression as the racism of
White people. But he rather quickly moved to a social structural analysis of oppression, one that linked race, class, and gender oppression
and identified capitalism as the major source of oppression. After embracing Marxism-Leninism—another political conversion—he joined
the Asian American revolutionary group I Wor Kuen (IWK) in Boston,
at age nineteen. When IWK merged with a predominantly Chicano
organization to form the League of Revolutionary Struggle (LRS), Ho
found himself in one of the largest New Communist organizations
and one unique for its majority "oppressed nationality" membership
and leadership and its women's leadership. Ho and other artists in
the LRS pushed the organization to incorporate cultural resistance,
and LRS, in turn, provided an institutional venue for its activist-
artists to develop an Asian American jazz movement. For Ho, it is no
exaggeration to say that his music and politics are mutually linked;
his music is a creative expression of his revolutionary politics and

his political activism is constantly, though by no means exclusively, focused on building a revolutionary art movement.[9]

In the early 1990s, Wei-hua Zhang wrote: "Fred Wei-han Ho is only 35, but has already gone through a long personal, political, and musical journey. Although he is regarded as one of the leading figures in the Asian-American jazz movement, he considers himself more than a jazz musician."[10] Zhang alludes not only to Ho's multiple conversions, but also to his significant achievements. Ho has more than fifteen recordings as a leader, has composed numerous scores, and is or has been the leader of the Afro Asian Music Ensemble, Monkey Orchestra, Brooklyn Sax Quartet, and Caliente! Circle around the Sun, with poets Magdalena Gomez and the late Raul Salinas. He is the subject of several scholarly works, the author of numerous articles, and the editor of three books, in addition to the present volume: *Sounding Off! Music as Subversion/Resistance/Revolution* (with Ron Sakolsky, Autonomedia, 1995); the first anthology on the revolutionary Asian American Movement, *Legacy to Liberation: Politics and Culture of Revolutionary Asian Pacific America* (AK Press, 2000); and *Afro Asia: Revolutionary Political and Cultural Connections between African Americans and Asian Americans* (with Bill Mullen, Duke University Press, 2008).[11]

Ho is an award-winning artist: his distinctions include six Rockefeller fellowships; two National Endowment for the Arts fellowships; three New York Foundation for the Arts fellowships; the 1996 American Book Award (for *Sounding Off!*); and the Duke Ellington Distinguished Artist Lifetime Achievement Award at the Seventeenth Annual Black Musicians Conference, which he was the youngest person to receive. At the 2007 world premiere of the documentary *Urban Dragons,* by Kamau Hunter and Jose Figueroa, which explores Black and Latino masters of Chinese martial arts, Ho was honored as "the ultimate Urban Dragon" for his "genius revelations of the true international face of martial arts," because "his revolutionary and creative force on meshing Chinese martial arts with jazz in theater is without peer," and for "his overwhelming dedication to righting injustices with the heart of a warrior, the intellect of a philosopher, and the righteousness of the spiritual."[12] Journalist Arthur Song proclaimed: "A soulful saxophonic storyteller in his solo improvisations, with *huge* technique (I mean, six octaves on that horn), Fred Ho has encyclopedic knowledge on a range of topics from Asian American radical activism, to 'jazz,' to clothing design, and of course his own inimitable brand of searing radical politics."[13]

Creating Asian American Jazz

Countering the binary construction of jazz as predominantly Black or White music, a group of Asian American musicians worked to create a new musical aesthetic. Russel Baba, Anthony Brown, Fred Ho, Glenn Horiuchi, Mark Izu, Jon Jang, Gerald Oshita, Francis Wong, and Paul Yamazaki, though largely unknown among jazz aficionados, were instrumental in developing an Asian American free jazz movement as it emerged in the late 1970s, primarily in the San Francisco Bay Area. All of them were committed to Asian American activism, collaborated with African American jazz musicians, and recorded with independent labels working to give power to Asian American artists and expression to Asian American arts.[14] With these activist-musicians, Ho sought to address a theoretical question that continues to be raised by musicians and ethnomusicologists today: What is Asian American music? Even more basic, is there such a thing as Asian American music? Many reject the ethnic labeling of their music, as when jazz musician Francis Wong contested the introduction of his music as "Asian American music," preferring to see it simply as music.[15] Certainly there are "historical, cultural, economic, and music reasons why the term Asian American music should be rejected," notes musicologist Joseph Lam.[16] The very term "Asian American," as a relatively new category of panethnicity emerging in the Asian American Movement of the late 1960s, often does not describe the social identities of many, who instead use self-referential terms such as Chinese, Korean, or Vietnamese American. The diverse histories and demographics of Asian Americans further render it difficult to create any recognizable style or sound. Moreover, "the categorization is limiting because Asian Americans have little presence in musical-commercial America" as producers, distributors (there's no Asian American section at record stores), or consumers (at least through a visible and unified market), thus reducing economic incentives to claim an "Asian American music."[17]

While accepting Wong's right to self-definition, Lam argues that

‹ 11

"the term Asian American music is needed to provide a theoretical and historical point of reference so that we can contrast and compare diverse musical works of Asian Americans, examine their musical creativity and artistry, and understand their expressions of living in America as individuals and as members of ethnic groups."[18] Lam's rationale for the designation "Asian American music(s)" is not to homogenize the music or to develop a singular recognizable sound or style. Instead, Lam offers a three-part "heuristic device"—examining themes, musical structures and performative contexts, and social and historical contexts—to begin a discussion of the category of Asian American music. As musicologist Oliver Wang explained, to Lam, "Asian American music is *not* dependent on the text (e.g., lyrics, images, even melody, timbre, rhythm) or even a tradition of musical practices. Instead, Asian American music is so designated based on the context of production (who makes the music and why) as well as reception (how is the music used, how is it understood?)."[19] Here, Lam's broad and inclusive framework would include Francis Wong's music as Asian American music. This is not surprising. To many, Wong's music is closely connected to the development of Asian American jazz: AsianImprov[20] produced and distributed his CDs; the liner notes for his *Great Wall* CD state that he aims "to participate in the jazz/creative music tradition and to contribute to an Asian American voice." Wong's contradictions show the tensions that exist between a desire to promote an Asian American musical aesthetic and a desire to appeal to a universal sound and audience that transcends ethnic boundaries.[21]

Ho, by contrast, is unambiguous about his desire to create an Asian American music. As an artist and activist, his goal is not to create a theoretical framework (or a space, for that matter) inclusive of multiple forms of Asian American music. Instead, he has sought to develop a new Asian American musical form, to integrate incisive political content, to challenge the politics of music production, and, ultimately, to create a music that helps transform humanity and society in the interest of social justice. He explains: "The lessons I drew from my study and involvement in 'jazz' about the role of art and music in revolutionary social transformation extended far beyond the simple expression of political views through song lyrics or titles and their subsequent use in social movements, which has composed the primary discourse about music and social change. Rather, I saw the 'politics' of music in musical aesthetics, in ways of music making and in building alternatives to the music industry."[22] He saw himself in the 1980s as a proponent of an Asian American jazz movement that inspired a critical social consciousness and "combined actual Asian traditional instrumentation and Asian-inspired or -influenced stylistic elements with predominantly 'free' or modal improvisation in the African American avant-garde 'jazz' context."[23] These two elements—traditional Asian instrumentation and "free jazz"—are the key elements in the efforts of Ho and his musician-comrades to create a new and distinctive Asian American music.

Ho has not only contributed to the development of Asian American jazz as a musician and composer, but he has also, it seems, written more about this politicized Asian American jazz movement than any other musician.[24] His generation's effort to integrate a new musical form with politically transgressive content is rooted in a continuum of Asian American musics. The music of early Asian immigrants, including the Cantonese operas, suggested themes of cultural hybridity, speaking to the hardships, struggles, and contradictions of their life in America. The *hole hole bushi*—a hybrid term combining sugarcane fieldwork (*hole hole*) with Japanese folk tune (*bushi*)—"were both personal and collectively shared critiques of plantation society and expressions of personal opposition and rebellion."[25] Despite the blending of two cultures represented in early immigrant music, Ho observes that the music was largely rooted in traditional Asian form. By contrast, the children of Asian immigrants developed music that drew primarily from American styles, including jazz. Paul Yamazaki notes: "Most of my parents' generation . . . [came of age] in the '30s and '40s; a large number of them were interested in jazz. [T]here was enough interest that by . . . World War II, almost every camp had its own dance, jazz bands."[26] Some Asian American musicians even gained a measure of commercial success (at least in racially segregated venues) playing in Chinese nightclubs, Filipino taxi dance halls, and Japanese American concentration camps. But, asserts Ho, "in all cases, these Asian American players and groups were imitations of the commercially popular jazz and dance bands, making no distinctive or unique artistic contribution."[27]

The Asian American Movement, emerging in the late 1960s,

sparked an explosion of Asian American politically transgressive art and inspired new hybrid musical forms.[28] The most widely known Asian American Movement band was the folk trio of Chris Iijima, Joanne Nobuko Miyamoto, and Charlie Chin, known as A Grain of Sand.[29] In a 1983 review of a new release by former band members, Ho proclaims their significance, despite his differences with their musical style: "In 1973 the release of A Grain of Sand (Paredon P-1020) established the presence of Asian American Music."[30] Given that the term "Asian American" has its etiological roots in the Asian American Movement, it is not entirely surprising that the very concept and etiology of "Asian American music" also developed through this movement.[31] Formed in the early 1970s, A Grain of Sand asserted their political critique mainly through powerful lyrics. The songs on this album reveal the group's Pan-Asian focus: "Yellow Pearl" inverts the pejorative Yellow Peril; their most famous song, "We Are the Children," connects the "offspring" of the Filipino "migrant worker," Japanese American "concentration camps," and Chinese immigrant "railroad builder." Other song titles invoke themes of Third World solidarity and anti-imperialist struggles, including "Imperialism Is Another Word for Hunger," "Jonathan Jackson," and "Warriors of the Rainbow."[32] The folk form of their music added to their rebelliousness by invoking themes of protest in the antiwar activist style of Pete Seeger, Bob Dylan, and Joan Baez. But aesthetically, Ho explains, the band did not create any new musical style.[33] In fact, he asserts that most of the widely known musicians who identified with "Asian American music" were "mostly Western in form and source."[34]

By the mid-1970s, other groups began to create hybrid music that integrated traditional Asian instrumentation and styles with American music. The best known and most commercially successful of these is the jazz-fusion group Hiroshima, whose many achievements include being signed with Epic and Arista and having a Grammy-nominated album. The band demonstrates an awareness of how to cater to mainstream tastes and commercial success. Hiroshima co-founder and classically trained koto player June Kuramoto acknowledges her need to return to the classical koto repertoire as a source of inspiration after playing the less demanding structure and technique of pop music. Given Ho's radical politics and commitments to autonomy in music making, one could predict his criticism of Hiroshima's tendency to be "commercially 'slickened'" and "over-orchestrat[ed]." While the band holds the responsibility of choice, Ho also recognizes the presence of a dominating power: the pressures placed on musicians "by the capitalist recording industry to conform to 'hit formulas.'" Ho views Hiroshima's significance as their "innovative and stylistically unique" "use of *taiko* (Japanese drums), *fue* (Japanese bamboo flute), *koto* with electric guitar, bass, piano, [and] trap drums." For Johnny Mori, Hiroshima's lead drummer, playing the taiko drums became not only an expression of a unique, hybrid identity, but also the means for transforming the taiko from a Japanese musical form to an Asian American one. Ho's review of Hiroshima's second album captures this musical innovation: "*Odori* possesses a clear and continuous thematic concept: the development of the Asian American musical identity in combination with a strong rhythm 'n blues base. The title piece, *Odori*, is my favorite—conjuring the ritualistic rhythms of traditional *Bon* dancing. The graceful flute melody and deft rhythms can really get you up on your feet and *sway* with the group. Peter Hata's guitar solos are succulent. The use of traditional *shamisen* strumming (which is a-rhythmical) against the duple meter (two or duplicates of two beats per measure) is an exciting contrast."[35]

‹ 15

Ho's own efforts to produce a hybrid Asian American music are influenced less by Hiroshima and more by the context of his political work, particularly in I Wor Kuen (IWK), the first national Asian American revolutionary organization. IWK, composed of radical students, workers, and working-class youth, first formed in New York City in 1969. In 1971, around the time Ho acquired his first saxophone, IWK merged with the Red Guard Party, a San Francisco Chinatown street-youth group closely patterned after the Black Panther Party in ideology and membership. Reflecting the dominance of student intellectuals over the lumpenproletariat in the movement in general, the new national formation took on the name IWK.[36] IWK created a twelve-point platform and program, modeled after the Black Panther Party's, but expressing a heightened radicalism. IWK's politics were both Pan-Asian and Third Worldist, demanding "self determination for all Asian Americans" and "for all Asians" and the "liberation of all Third World peoples and other oppressed peoples." Like the Black Panthers, they desired human rights and provided "serve the people" programs, including healthcare, housing, and food, to the Asian working-class immigrant communities. Extending beyond the Panthers' platform, IWK demanded "an end to male chauvinism and sexual exploitation" and "a socialist society."[37]

In opposition to the mainstream historiography that claims the demise of social movements by the early to mid-1970s, Max Elbaum shows that in this same period, many revolutionary nationalist and New Left organizations were adopting Marxism-Leninism, merging to form multinational organizations, and creating a New Communist movement (a subset of which Laura Pulido calls the Third World Left and Cynthia Young calls the U.S. Third World Left).[38] IWK was part of this motion. By 1974, IWK adopted Marxism-Leninism, and by 1976, Ho had done the same. Around 1977, at the age of nineteen, Ho joined IWK in Boston, where he was a student at Harvard University.[39]

Around the time Ho joined, IWK took the position that "Asian American art and culture necessitates a link to traditional Asian cultural forms."[40] This tenet, combined with Ho's interactions with the working-class community in Boston's Chinatown, motivated him to begin an intensive study of the folk traditions of Asian American culture. He notes: "It became clear to me that a working-class, even revolutionary, tradition exists in APA cultures. Such a tradition includes the first immigrant cultural forms: Cantonese opera, the wood-fish head chants, the talk-story traditions, the folk ballads and syllabic verses of the Chinese immigrant laborers, the Japanese American female plantation labor songs (*hole hole buŝhi*), the Angel Island poetry, the Filipino rondalla and folk ballads of the manongs (Filipino immigrant bachelor workers), Japanese American tanka (syllabic verse) poetry, etc."[41] When IWK merged with the predominantly Chicana/o August Twenty-Ninth Movement in 1978 to form the largest majority-oppressed nationality New Communist formation, the League of Revolutionary Struggle, Ho and his LRS comrades continued to develop the Asian American jazz movement.[42]

Ho identified three styles of Asian American jazz. Besides this "free jazz" movement, there were also "a 'jazz fusion' scene with its most prominent Los Angeles-based band, Hiroshima, along with Deems

Tsutakawa in Seattle, and others" and "a mainstream straight-ahead 'jazz' group, mostly older generation players such as Filipino pianist Bobby Enriquez, pianist Toshiko Akiyoshi, alto saxophonist Gabe Baltazar." With the exception of the "straight-ahead" players, virtually all of the Asian American jazz musicians of the 1970s and 1980s were connected, in varying ways, to the politics of the Asian American Movement.[43]

Jazz as Revolutionary Music: Black Power, Black Arts, and Afro-Asian Solidarities

By asking, in the title of one of his articles, "What Makes 'Jazz' the Revolutionary Music of the Twentieth Century?" (this volume), Ho is asserting his views on the relationship between music and social change. To Ho, the lowly status accorded jazz—as pop music lacking in artistic value or as music performed in nightclubs, dives, and brothels—exerted a dialectical effect: "[D]ue to national oppression, 'jazz' was, ironically, spared the canonization and institutionalization that the concert music of Western Europe underwent.... [T]he music resisted the calcification and ossification that 'classical' music had undergone." Instead, jazz was able to develop with tremendous flexibility and to challenge the structures and boundaries of music making. The "entire history" of Black music, asserts Ho, "has been the freeing of time, pitch, and harmony from fixed, regulated, predictable standards. Every major innovation in the history of the music has been from the struggle of musicians to attain greater and greater levels of expressive freedom through liberating the two basic fundamentals of music: time (meter) and sound (pitch/temperament/harmony)."[44] The improvisational form of jazz freed artists to think and play imaginatively.

‹ 17

Ho's reference to "the music" follows the efforts by musicians and activists to liberate jazz from its pejorative connotations as sexual music played in houses of prostitution or other sordid contexts. Ho writes: "I do not use the term 'jazz,' as I do not use such terms as *Negro, Oriental,* or *Hispanic....* The struggle to redefine and reimage our existence involves the struggle to reject the stereotyping, distortions, and devaluation embodied in the classifications of conquerors and racists."[45] More pointedly, saxophonist Archie Shepp said, "If we continue to call our music jazz, we must continue to be called niggers."[46] As a practice in self-definition, and in the absence of any satisfactory replacement term, beginning in the mid-1960s, musicians began to develop a new vocabulary: "free jazz," "avant-garde jazz," "the New Thing," "the New Black Music," or, as the musicians themselves call it, "The Music."[47]

This new form of jazz came to life in the "roaring sixties," a music that both reflected and forwarded the nascent Black Power and Black Arts movements that influenced Ho.[48] Frank Kofsky makes the claim that "the jazz musician . . . , of any identifiable group of blacks, ha[s] been the first to be converted and to espouse the tenets of black nationalism."[49] Kofsky presents a history of the development of jazz linked to changes in political economy and ideological frameworks. "Hard bop" emerged to reject "cool jazz" and its "bleaching" (i.e., domination by White musicians) and the mellowing of jazz in the early Cold War period. Hard bop, emerging as early as the mid-1950s, sought to reclaim the Black roots of jazz music, reviving the "bebop" of the 1940s and the blues and gospel before that.[50] "The Music" was consciously political. It strove to arouse a critical social consciousness and provoke protest not only through its textual content (titles, lyrics), but also through its "freeing of time, pitch and harmony" and, by the advent of "free jazz," its disturbing sounds and style. As Archie Shepp articulated:

> The Negro musician is a reflection of the Negro people as a social phenomenon. His purpose ought to be to liberate America aesthetically and socially from its inhumanity. The inhumanity of the white American to the black American, as well as the inhumanity of the white American to the white American, is not basic to America and can be exorcised. I think the Negro people through the force of their struggles are the only hope of saving America, the political or cultural America.[51]

It was Archie Shepp, daring to dream of a liberated society, who exerted the greatest influence on Ho's music. Ho came to be taught by and on occasion play with Shepp when Shepp joined the faculty at the University of Massachusetts, Amherst, in Ho's hometown. In the early 1970s, Ho, then a high school student, began attending Shepp's university classes. Even before meeting him, Shepp was "larger than life to me," recounted Ho. "I voraciously read everything about him and interviews of him. I bought all of his recordings I could, sought out imports when I traveled down to New York City (which had better record stores), and regularly scouted the bins for new releases."[52] By then, Shepp had already performed with John Coltrane, been picked up by Impulse! Records through the influence of Coltrane and Cecil Taylor, and recorded his famous tribute to the New York prison uprising, "Attica Blues" (1972). At the time Ho met Shepp, he had recently acquired a second-hand baritone saxophone from his high school band and, having been influenced by the revolutionary nationalist upsurges of the late 1960s, had begun to seriously investigate African American music, particularly its more radical or "avant-garde" forms. "I was searching for a creative expression that would give voice to my exploding radicalism, my hatred of oppression, and my burning commitment to revolutionary struggle," noted Ho.[53] Shepp had made statements about jazz: "[Jazz is] one of the most meaningful social, aesthetic contributions to America. It is that certain people accept it for what it is, that it is a meaningful, profound contribution to America—it is antiwar; it is opposed to Viet Nam; it is for Cuba; it is for the liberation of all people. That is the nature of jazz. That's not far-fetched. Why is that so? Because jazz is a music itself born out of oppression, born out of the enslavement of my people. It is precisely that."[54] Certainly not all, jazz musicians or others, would agree with Shepp's characterization of jazz as antiwar or pro-Cuba. But for Ho, Shepp was the kind of militant, outspoken activist-musician for whom he was searching as he formed his "exploding radicalism."

‹ 19

Ho could not have found a more musically and politically revolutionary mentor than Shepp. This was the case in spite of Shepp's "intensely contradictory character," which Ho discusses candidly in "An Asian American Tribute to the Black Arts Movement" (this volume). Beyond boldly speaking his mind, Shepp was engaged in Leftist politics, "identify[ing] himself with Marxism" more than just about "any of the other prominent downtown [New York] black artists and intellectuals."[55] Ho explained: "What fascinated me about Archie was the combination of his outspoken militant political views, fused with Marxist influences (I later learned he participated in Marxist study circles when he lived in New York City), and his soulful and incendiary tenor saxophone playing."[56] Through Shepp and others in the avant-garde scene, Ho came to identify with jazz as music of resistance, "with its pro-oppressed, anti-oppressor character: with the militancy the musicians displayed, with its social history of rebellion and revolt, and with its musical defiance to not kow-tow to, but challenge and contest, Western European 'classical' music and co-opted, diluted, eviscerated commercialized forms that became American pop music."[57]

Ho was not alone among Asian American musicians in his fascination and solidarity with the music and politics of the Black Arts and Black Power movements.[58] He drew inspiration from Japanese American bassist Mark Izu for his leadership in developing a hybrid traditional Asian and African American jazz music. In the 1970s in San Francisco's club scene, Izu met African American saxophonist Lewis Jordan. By 1977, Izu and Jordan had formed Marron, an African and Asian American ensemble, and later their own recording company, RPM, to fill the vacuum of production sites for free jazz music.[59]

One of Ho's closest jazz and political collaborators and friends in the 1980s was Jon Jang. The Black Power and Black jazz movements of the 1970s, particularly John Coltrane, who "liberated me on a humanistic, spiritual, and political level," inspired Jang's transformation from a conservatory-trained pianist to a free jazz musician.[60] Stirred by the work songs of African Americans, as discussed by LeRoi Jones (now Amiri Baraka) in *Blues People* (1963), Jang searched for and discovered a Chinese blues equivalent in the Cantonese opera. Jang was also influenced by the ways Black and Asian American musicians incorporated Asian and Black forms and instrumentation. In the mid-1980s, he expressed: "Playing the koto and producing 'Koto' harp-like gestures on the piano to create new textures, McCoy Tyner was contributing an Asian sound in an African American context. In Fred Houn's [now Fred Ho] Asian American Art Ensemble, I hear[d] Asian music influencing African American music in an Asian American context. . . . In one of Houn's recorded works, *Ganbaro!*, dedicated to the Japanese American working class, I found extensive usage of different kinds of Japanese pentatonic scales. . . . [H]ow Fred Houn uses them is more in the context of the blues; not in the superficial and mechanical observation of pentatonic scales, but in the feeling and its function as an expression of life."[61]

The Politics of Production and the Production of Politics

The inequities in the music industry are abundantly clear to Black musicians. Amiri Baraka (then LeRoi Jones) begins his book *Black Music*: "Most jazz critics have been white Americans, but most important jazz musicians have not been."[62] Archie Shepp stated succinctly, "You own the music and we make it."[63] Even without any racial signifiers, most people understood to whom "you" and "we" referred. In the language of the 1960s and 1970s, the music industry reproduced a colonial relationship between Black musicians, who owned nothing but their talent, and the White music industry, which controlled production, distribution, clubs, radio time, and, ultimately, profits. The Black Power Movement, with its promotion of self-determination, encouraged the development of independent Black recording companies, emulated by Asian American musicians. In her article addressing the politics of production, ethnomusicologist Deborah Wong discussed two small, independent Asian American recording companies that consciously promote Asian American identities, artists, and audiences.[64]

‹ 21

Jon Jang and Francis Wong founded AsianImprov Records in 1987. Listening to the music of Mark Izu at the first Asian American Jazz Festival in San Francisco in 1981, Jang realized that "my dream of creating a music so personal and powerful could become a reality." Yet, "[w]ith the exception of Fred Houn, all of us have had to produce our music on our own label," Jang noted. It was this lack of recording venues for Asian American independent artists, especially those producing politically transgressive music, that motivated the formation of AsianImprov. As Francis Wong explained, "[we were] trying to bring the African American tradition of improvised music and jazz together with our Asian roots."[65]

With different goals and motivations, AARisings (for Asian Americans Rising), founded in 1990, seeks commercial profits, focuses on popular music, and strives to generally promote any Asian American artist. AARisings cofounder Nelson Wong explains: "[We at AARisings] are trying to sell our stuff to as many people as we can, because that's the way we make money. [At AsianImprov], they're doing it more . . . as a vehicle to promote their beliefs, their art." Still, he sees similarities in that both recording companies seek to "get more visibility for Asian Americans in art, in music."[66] Deborah Wong, as an academic musicologist, is interested in showing the diversity of goals and ideas about Asian American music making; in fact, she includes in her study a third Asian American recording company that denies any effort to promote anything Asian American, preferring to market the universal appeal and mainstream sound of their nevertheless mainly Filipino artists.

By contrast, Ho, as an independent artist and radical activist, consciously takes a stand—clearly, articulately, and forcefully:

> I polemicized against the white assimilationist notion of the petty bourgeois Asian American artist that anything by an Asian American artist makes it Asian American. While also rejective of being proscriptive or essentialist, I do maintain that the Asian Americanness of an artistic work lies in more than content, and is rooted and linked to cultural traditions and forms. Along with expressing aspects of the "Asian American experience," the music itself would draw from or reflect aspects of traditional Asian music influences. Yo-Yo Ma is a cellist who happens to be Chinese/Asian American, not a Chinese/Asian American musician. John Kaizan Neptune is a white American virtuosic *shakuhachi* (traditional Japanese vertical flute) player, but he is not playing Japanese/Asian American music because he is not intending to express or reflect a Japanese/Asian American identity.[67]

Ho argues for the development of an Asian American music and not simply for the promotion of any artist who is Asian American. Many would disagree with Ho's ideas, including musicologist Joseph Lam, whose broad heuristic device would include artists as musically and demographically diverse as Ma and Neptune within the rubric of Asian American music making. But this is the significance of Ho's writings. He is not afraid to articulate his ideas, however controversial. His ideas are generative; they provoke discussion and debate.

His are not simply unsubstantiated "opinions"; instead, he demands logical thinking and/or evidence to support his arguments. He himself is critical of scholarly writing for failing to take a stand (see "A Voice Is a Voice, but What Is It Saying?," this volume).

His position as an outsider to both the academy and the music industry brings a certain freedom to speak his mind, to advocate for his radical positions, to promote a particular political ideology. Of course, his outspoken radicalism has not been without cost. As a Harvard graduate and possessing a brilliant mind, had Ho chosen the path of mainstream music or scholarship, he likely would have had a more "successful" career, at least by mainstream standards of fame and financial reward. Harder to bear have been the splits within the political and artistic Asian American Movement. Ho had worked closely with several of the AsianImprov artists, particularly Jon Jang. Jang himself stated in the mid-1980s, "Fred Houn has been the most influential Asian American creative music force in my development as an Asian American creative musician."[68] In the late 1980s, Ho broke with AsianImprov Records and later the LRS. Political differences between Ho's and Jang's views on music became apparent. Weihua Zhang wrote: "Unlike Fred Ho, who is an unswerving Marxist and openly claims himself a political revolutionary, Jang considers himself [to be] an artist/musician first. Jang does not like to be labeled a political artist because he thinks that all artists are political. Jang feels that music is an expression of his life; the message and expression he tries to convey is the basic truth of humanity."[69] The breaks were painful to Ho, with the loss of not only a space to create and produce radical Asian American music, but also his closest friends and political-artistic community. Time has not healed this rupture, with Ho being written out of the history of AsianImprov Records.[70]

‹ 23

Political Theorizing

Martin Luther King, Jr., expresses the symbolism of midnights and dawns in Black culture: "Our eternal message of hope is that dawn will come. . . . Even the most starless midnight may herald the dawn of great fulfillment."[71] For Ho, the upheavals, confusion, and pain contained in the midnight hour also generate the possibilities of new insights, new opportunities, new formations, new philosophies, and new dawns. It was Ho's break with his friends, comrades, and fellow artists in the Asian American jazz movement and the LRS that provoked a major aesthetical and political turning point in his life. He explains:

> Politically, I had become increasingly alienated from the rightist, reformist decline of the LRS.... Part of the rightism ... involved a political directive that required music and art to be "accessible" (which became a codeword for culturally mainstream and politically reformist). In internal gatherings, I rose to challenge this position as tailist (obsequious to mainstream acceptance) and accommodationist. As revolutionaries, I argued, the goal of our work must be the raising of both consciousness and cultural and artistic levels and standards, as well as the popularization of innovative, oppositional, transgressive, radical work.[72]

24 ›

Ho was "ejected" from the LRS a year before its September 1990 vote to dissolve itself. The organization's dissolution statement explained: "[A] majority of us wish to move beyond the Marxist-Leninist framework, and do not feel that today's movement is best served by a Marxist-Leninist organizational form." This is based on three major disagreements with Marxist-Leninist theory: (1) "[We] do not believe that Marxism-Leninism is the sole or leading ideology for fundamental social change, nor that Marxism-Leninism or any other ideology should have hegemony"; (2) opposition to vanguard party formation—"[we] do not believe that a single party can or should determine the direction, strategy and tactics of the struggle"; and (3) disagreement "with the goal of the 'dictatorship of the proletariat,' and believe instead in multi-party democracy and free elections."[73] The LRS majority was articulating the philosophy of the "new social movements." The collapse of the Soviet Union seemed to signal the failure of activist efforts to create liberated zones, collectives, community control of cities, or national liberation up against the overwhelming hegemonic power of global capital. Instead, for new social movements in the postcolonial period, "cultural expressions are based in the experiences of people and communities, rather than on the master narratives of the nation state," explains George Lipsitz. "They foreground questions of cultural and social identity, rather

than direct struggles for political power. They are pragmatic, immediate, and non-ideological, seeking to change life but putting forth
no single blueprint for the future."[74] In short, activists in the 1990s
participated in "what Gramsci called the war of position (an effort to
build a counter-hegemonic alliance) rather than what he termed the
war of maneuver (the effort to seize state power)."[75]

By contrast, Ho (and the LRS minority) continued to believe in the
need to seize state power and in the correctness of Marxist-Leninist
theories, even in today's globalized and postcolonial society, despite
some incorrect applications in practice.[76] While recognizing the
phenomenon of globalization, Ho would argue that the nation-state
remains an important site of power and resistance. The unilateral
move by the United States to intervene in Iraq, despite strong opposition by the United Nations, is one example of the continuing power
of the nation-state. Venezuela's supply of oil, at below market prices
or sometimes without charge, to various nations, including to U.S.
cities, offers an example of how national policies create global networks and connections. If the nation-state remains an important
site of power and resistance, then, to Ho, the question of national liberation remains critical. His response is contained within his essay
"Notes on the National Question: Oppressed Nations and Liberation
Struggles within the U.S.A." (this volume). Based on years of study
in the IWK and LRS, Ho argues that national oppression, rather than
racism alone, characterizes the oppression of "people of color" in the
United States and throughout the world. Such an analysis allows for
the crucial discussion of power, extends the political solution beyond integrationism, and emphasizes the right to claim a land base.
By presenting a major political theory of the Third World Left and
Marxism-Leninism, Ho's writings facilitate debates with scholars
today who posit a new thinking about place and space, less in terms
of physical territoriality and more in terms of global movement, connections, and disjunctures.[77]

While Ho retains some theories created in earlier periods, these
have also been rearticulated into new political and artistic ideas.
Ho's efforts to develop what he calls "Afro Asian New American Multicultural Music"—an unwieldy term that has not caught on—was
already under way from the mid-1980s, but became solidified with

his departure from the LRS. Ho's "new" music incorporates many of the elements of his Asian American jazz period—integration of traditional Asian instrumentation with African American music and Asian American political themes. So what's new? Ho stated: "I was continuously struggling with the question of what makes Chinese American music Chinese American? What would comprise an Asian American musical content and form that could transform American music in general rather than simply be subsumed in one or another American musical genre such as 'jazz'?"[78] Certainly, he felt the confines of a single musical genre were constricting his creative expression. Ho's music "synthesize[s] different musical styles and genres," including "West African, Latin, reggae rhythms, Chinese and Korean instruments, Arabic and Japanese modes"[79] as well as Chinese opera, martial arts, and ballet performances. Moreover, being freed from the pressures of the LRS to produce "accessible" and "conventional" art enabled him to become more committed to avant-gardism, more aesthetically sophisticated, and more politically complicated. One theater owner commented: "Fred play[ed] the role of the angry yellow man. . . . His new music is much more interesting on the musical level. There he speaks to his Asian Americanness much more eloquently rather than taking a hammer, hitting you on the head and saying, 'I am pissed off.' Now it's a real fusion, a blend of East and West."[80]

In "Beyond Asian American 'Jazz'" (this volume), Ho explains his efforts at synthesis, while being critical of celebratory multiculturalism or "bureaucratic multiculturalism" (Vijay Prashad's term for limiting antiracist struggles to the promotion of diversity[81]):

> I wanted my compositional process to be a real synthesis, and not a pastiche or juxtaposition of contrasting cultural styles. Most "world beat" or intercultural collaborative efforts, in my view, are limited in the extent to which they manifest real and truly "new" synthesis. These efforts are, at best, exoticism when proffered by culturally imperialistic whites and "chop-sueyism" when presented superficially by people of color.
>
> In opposing cultural imperialism, a genuine multicultural synthesis embodies revolutionary internationalism in music: rather than co-opting different cultures, musicians and composers achieve

revolutionary transformation predicated upon anti-imperialism in terms of both musical respect and integrity as well as a practical political economic commitment to equality between peoples.[82]

In his *Journey Beyond the West,* for example, Ho sought, as musicologist Wei-hua Zhang explains, to make "Chinese instruments . . . an integral part of the orchestra in sections of collective improvisation as well as in the notated scores" and "not just used for special effects. Besides the Chinese and jazz sources, electric percussion is used for 'hip-hop' effects, and oboe sometimes double[s on] sona. Chinese instruments are often given prominent melodic roles in the ensemble."[83] In addition, Ho gives an unusual interpretation to the Monkey King, the popular character found in Chinese stories and operas. Instead of the common signifier as a trickster, "Ho interprets the Monkey as a social revolutionary and leader of the oppressed."[84]

One other important change for Ho in his post-LRS years was the development of his ideas on "matriarchal socialism." As he explains, being organizationally isolated, "I began to associate with the new, young generation of activists emerging in the early 1990s, which included anarchists, Trotskyites, and others. Many of these younger activists, though inexperienced and lacking in actual understanding of the Left of which I was a part, nonetheless had made their own analyses and summations of the problems and failures of my movement, albeit some of them very sketchy and often inaccurate. A major critique of our movement by this 1990s generation involved sexism, the continuation of patriarchy, and homophobia. The young 1990s activists also emphasized 'personal' politics, struggling with me about my meat-eating, about environmentalism, about the need for attention to 'democratic' process in political work, etc."[85] From early on, Ho had addressed the oppression of Asian and Asian American women in his music. These works included *Bound Feet* (1985), addressing feudal Chinese beauty practices; *Soran (hole hole) Bushi* (1989), a solo baritone saxophone work based on Japanese American women workers' songs; *Home Is Where the Violence Is* (1992), addressing violence against women, including his mother's abuse at the hands of his father; and *I'm Sorry* (1988), his own self-criticism about womanizing.[86] Given the repeated criticisms of Ho as a womanizer, it has been important to Ho to affirm his opposition to sexism and

‹ 27

support for what he calls "matriarchal socialism." Ho articulates a Marxist analysis of the historic subjugation of women and offers a vision for a "revolutionary matriarchal socialist society" (see "Matriarchy: The First and Final Communism," this volume).[87]

Publishing *Wicked Theory, Naked Practice*

I became actively involved in this project when, in August 2006, Ho announced that he had just been diagnosed with colon cancer, with surgery to follow within two weeks, and asked me to get his writings published.[88] I felt the urgency of Fred's request and believed in the importance of his ideas, the seriousness of his political and cultural work, and the strength of his writings. Fred had already submitted his manuscript to the University of Minnesota Press, based on Bill Mullen's recommendation and my own positive experiences with the Press.[89] But there had been no response for quite some time. I, with either Bill or Fred, was able to meet with editors from the Press at a couple of conferences, which helped to move the manuscript forward. The Press handed me the task of turning a very large manuscript into a publishable book and invited me to serve as its editor. Fred's writings augment my own work to uncover the hidden histories of Asian American social movements, Asian American radicalism, and Afro-Asian solidarities, while allowing me to explore the world of revolutionary music making. Like those of Yuri Kochiyama, Grace Lee Boggs, Richard Aoki, Mo Nishida, Guy Kurose, Mike Tagawa, and other Asian American activists, Fred Ho's political ideas and practice have been shaped by the revolutionary Black movement.[90]

Fred Ho's writings will be read in different ways by diverse readerships. Some will use his writings as primary source documents that give insight into the political thinking and artistic endeavors of a radical Asian American activist-musician-composer-writer. Some will be curious about the ideas and practices of the Third World Left, the revolutionary Asian American Movement, the Asian American jazz movement, and/or Afro-Asian solidarities. Some will vehemently disagree with his ideas or his methods.[91] Others will be inspired by his efforts to remain committed to revolutionary goals and to independence in creating music. Still others will view his writings as theoretical and practical guides, of course with their own adaptations, to creating social justice today in both their own local sites and globally. Those with interests in history, social movements, musicology, cultural studies, American studies, ethnic studies, Asian American studies, on-the-ground activism, and independent music making will all find something of use in these pages.

Wicked Theory, Naked Practice presents a selection of Fred Ho's writings from 1984 to 2006, mostly from his post-LRS period, to illuminate his ideas about political theory and activist transformations, art and music as transgressive forces unleashing the imagination, and the integration of intense activist practices and creative expressions into an ever expanding and committed life. My organization of the book builds on Ho's original ideas.

Because ideas develop in material contexts, the first section, "The Movement and the Self," attends to biography as well as the socio-political-economic context generative of Ho's ideas. The section integrates politics and culture, since the two are intricately linked and mutually influential in Ho's life. As Ho states: "When people ask me, How long have you been playing the saxophone? I tell them, As long as I've been in the struggle. When activists ask me, How long have you been in the movement? I tell them, As long as I've been playing the saxophone."[92] Though many of the essays in this book speak to biographical themes, this book is not primarily biographical. So this section is brief, but still a substantive introduction to Ho's political and cultural development.

‹ 29

The second section, "Music, Aesthetics, and Cultural Production," centers on the ways cultural work and revolutionary political ideas are mutually constitutive. "What Makes 'Jazz' the Revolutionary Music of the Twentieth Century ... ?" argues for a view of jazz as political. The form of jazz—improvisational, experimental, complex, and free from fixed, predictable standards—suggests the kind of creativity and fluidity necessary in political movements. But jazz is also about practice, discipline, and training. Jazz, like political movements, is both improvisational and compositional. In Ho's essay on Calvin Massey, "The Damned Don't Cry," we not only learn about a little-known jazz composer-musician who influenced Ho through his extended suites with their "thematically epic historical scope, Fanonic titles ..., soulful melodies, complex and rich harmonies, [and] Afrocentric rhythms," but we also become witness to Ho's astute analytic and research skills.[93] This section contains several other important themes. For Ho, the ideas of hybridity, fusion, and "kreolization" are key to understanding his efforts to create a new synthesis of African American and Asian American music (see "Musical Borrowings, Exchanges, and Fusions" and "Kreolization and the Hybridity of Resistance vs. Cultural Imperialism"). He also offers insightful and refreshingly practical guidelines to working as an independent artist in "How to Sell but Not Sell Out" and about establishing an independent production company in "Big Red Media, Inc., a Composer/Musician-Driven Production Company"(see www .bigredmediainc.com). Finally, Ho's discussion of Ken Burns's super-marketed, widely watched, and highly acclaimed documentary series *Jazz* offers a critique not just of Burns's interpretation of jazz, but of American society itself. Ho states: "Rather than characterize the music as resistance to oppression . . . or as a music that sounds the aspirations for freedom . . . , the integrationist-imperialist position proclaims 'we are all Americans' and that the 'music' is consistent with . . . the values espoused and practiced by this social system."[94] Scholar George Lipsitz offers similar objections: *Jazz* is "not just a film *about* history, this production *makes* history"—a history that promotes the master narrative of heroic individualism and bureaucratic multiculturalism and reduces the need to protest problems with American democracy and racism.[95]

In the third section, "Asian Pacific American Cultural Theory and Criticism," Ho discusses his efforts to create an Asian American musical aesthetic, one that for Ho is linked to his political vision and commitments (see "Asian American Music and Empowerment" and "Interview with Amy Ling"). This section begins with the important essay "An Asian American Tribute to the Black Arts Movement" as a way of making Afro-Asian linkages between the two sections and of illuminating Ho's musical development. This essay is appropriately as much autobiographical as it is about the Black Arts Movement and its influence on Asian American cultural work. In "Bamboo That Snaps Back!," Ho turns on its head a common representation of Asian American culture. By symbolizing bending with adversity, the bamboo metaphor is used to applaud Asian Americans for, as the model minority story goes, enduring hardship and discrimination with stoicism, patience, and, significantly, without protest. But Ho creates an oppositional symbolism. "If bamboo is bent back too far," he warns, "it will either break or snap back and hit an opponent in the face." It is this image of resistance and these Asian Americans who have "snapped back" that Ho analyzes in his essays in this section on Asian American literature, poetry, and other artistic expressions.

Ho's political ideas and activities are contained in the fourth section, "Wicked Theory, Naked Practice." This section begins with "The Inspiration of Mao . . ." as a way to segue from Asian American culture to Asian American politics and as a way to connect Asian and African political movements. In "Notes on the National Question" and "Matriarchy," Ho articulate his ideas, rooted in a Marxist-Leninist historical materialist analysis and his own study and practice in the Third World Left, about the nature of national oppression, racism linked to capitalist and imperialist development, and the historic subordination of women, as well as his vision for a liberated society and strategies for societal and individual transformation. These two essays are the key to understanding Ho's political ideas. His speech "Momentum for Change," on the history of the East Coast Asian Student Union, a group he co-founded, presents a practical manifestation of his politics and shows some flexibility in speaking to a less political audience. The book ends with "Flags, Falsehoods, and Fascism," which applies Ho's ideas to the current post–September 11 environment.

‹ 31

Today, Ho faces another moment of crisis. His most urgent, darkest hour is now upon him as he fights a horrendous battle against cancer. When I heard his phone message, I worried about his psychological ability to fight back against a second round of cancer, which had returned only months after he finished a grueling six-month regimen of chemotherapy. But when I called, I was met with the same steadfast determination and optimism necessary to be a long-term activist. Though the battle for one's very life is different in many ways than the battle for a liberated society, Ho sees many connections—not just in the ways that capitalist strivings for profit have eroded the environment and undermined healthcare (his partial analysis of cancer), but also in the necessity for fighting back and for living and struggling in community. One might not expect a hardcore revolutionary to espouse "love" as the best cure for cancer in the body and cancer in society, unless one believes in Che Guevara's famous quote, "At the risk of seeming ridiculous, let me say that the true revolutionary is guided by great feelings of love."[96] Ho understands the importance of "poetic knowledge," of dreaming of a new body and a new society. So, "we stand in this life at midnight, always on the verge of a new dawn."[97]

NOTES

1   Ho, "Beyond Asian American 'Jazz,'" this volume.

2   Robin D. G. Kelley, *Freedom Dreams: The Black Radical Imagination* (Boston: Beacon Press, 2002), 9.

3   Malcolm X with Alex Haley, *The Autobiography of Malcolm X* (New York: Grove Press, 1965), 190.

4   C. Wright Mills, *The Sociological Imagination* (Oxford: Oxford University Press, 1959), 4.

5   Todd Gitlin, *The Sixties: Years of Hope, Days of Rage* (New York: Bantam Books, 1987); Todd Gitlin, *The Twilight of Common Dreams: Why America Is Wracked by Culture Wars* (New York: Henry Holt, 1995); Max Elbaum, *Revolution in the Air: Radicals Turn to Lenin, Mao, and Che* (London: Verso, 2002).

6   Kelley, *Freedom Dreams*, 16.

7   In the fall of 1988, Ho legally changed his last name from Houn to Ho, "phoneticizing a problematic spelling of Houn, which was always pronounced Ho" (Ho, "An Asian American Tribute to the Black Arts Movement," note 9).

8   Ho, "From Banana to Third World Marxist," this volume.

9   Ho, "From Banana to Third World Marxist"; Ho, "Beyond Asian American 'Jazz.'"

10 Wei-hua Zhang, "Fred Wei-han Ho: Case Study of a Chinese-American Creative Musician," *Asian Music* 25 (1993–94): 81.

11 Roger Buckley is editing an oeuvre book project on Ho. Fred Ho's papers are located at the Archives and Special Collections at the Thomas J. Dodd Research Center at the University of Connecticut, Storrs.

12 Stephan Berwick, "Urban Dragons: Black and Latino Masters of Chinese Martial Arts," *Kungfu Magazine*, February 29, 2008; see www.kungfumagazine.com.

13 Arthur Song, interview with Fred Ho, March 3, 2000, Brooklyn, New York.

14 Deborah Wong, *Speak It Louder: Asian Americans Making Music* (New York: Routledge, 2004), 172; Susan M. Asai, "Cultural Politics: The African American Connection in Asian American Jazz-based Music," *Asian Music* 36 (2005): 87-108; Ho, "Beyond Asian American 'Jazz.'"

15 Joseph Lam, "Embracing 'Asian American Music' as an Heuristic Device," *Journal of Asian American Studies* 2 (1999): 34.

16 Lam, "Embracing 'Asian American Music,'" 35.

17 Lam, "Embracing 'Asian American Music,'" 36. On panethnicity, see Yen Le Espiritu, *Asian American Panethnicity: Bridging Institutions and Identities* (Philadelphia: Temple University Press, 1992).

18 Lam, "Embracing 'Asian American Music,'" 30.

19 Oliver Wang, "Between the Notes: Finding Asian America in Popular Music," *American Music* 19 (2001): 441-42.

20 AsianImprov appears to have been spelled as one word during the 1980s when Ho worked with them; this is the spelling Ho uses (see Jon Jang, response in *Yellow Light: The Flowering of Asian American Arts*, edited by Amy Ling [Philadelphia: Temple University Press, 1999], 342). Today, Asian Improv is more often spelled as two words (see www.asianimprov. org); Wong, *Speak It Louder*; Ho, "Beyond Asian American 'Jazz.'"

21 When the Asian American hip-hop group Mountain Brothers entered and won the 1996 national competition for a Sprite commercial, they consciously made no ethnic self-referential statements in words, music, or otherwise. Not only were they seeking mainstream success, but they also believed any reference to their Asian American identities would hinder their success in the hip-hop world (Deborah Wong, "Just Being There: Making Asian American Space in the Recording Industry," in *Musics of Multicultural America,* edited by Kip Lornell and Anne Rasmussen [New York: Schirmer Books, 1997]: 287-316).

22 Ho, "Beyond Asian American 'Jazz.'"

23 Ho, "Beyond Asian American 'Jazz.'"

24 Peter Kiang writes: "musician/writer/activist Fred Houn deserves credit for establishing, at the very least, an unequivocal viewpoint in his reviews of Asian American poetry and music" in "Transformation: The Challenge Facing the Asian American Artist in the '80s," *East Wind* 4, no. 1 (Winter/Spring 1985): 33.

25 Susan Asai and Fred Ho, "*Hole Hole Bushi*: Cultural/Musical Resistance by Japanese Women Plantation Workers in Early Twentieth-Century Hawaii," this volume.

26 Brian Auerbach, "Asian-American Jazz: An Oral History with Paul Yamazaki," *Option* 3-4 (March/April 1985): 37-39.

27 Fred Wei-han Houn, "Asian American Music and Empowerment: Is There Such a Thing as 'Asian American Jazz'?," this volume.

28 On the Asian American Movement, see William Wei, *The Asian American Movement* (Philadelphia: Temple University Press, 1993); *Legacy to Liberation: Politics and Culture of Revolutionary Asian Pacific America*, edited by Fred Ho, with Carolyn Antonio, Diane C. Fujino, and Steve Yip (San Francisco: AK Press, 2000); *Asian Americans: The Movement and the Moment*, edited by Steve Louie and Glenn Omatsu (Los Angeles: UCLA Asian American Studies Center Press, 2001); Diane C. Fujino, "Who Studies the Asian American Movement? A Historiographical Analysis," *Journal of Asian American Studies* 11 (2008): 127-69.

29 A Grain of Sand is one of the most widely studied Asian American musical groups. See, among others, Susan M. Asai, "*Sansei* Voices in the Community: Japanese American Musicians in California," in Lornell and Rasmussen, eds., *Musics of Multicultural America*, 257-85; Ling, ed., *Yellow Light*; and Wong, *Speak It Louder*.

30 Fred Houn, "Songs to Warm Your Soul: Record Review of 'Back to Back' by Charlie Chin and Chris Iijima," *Sampan* (February 1983): 27. This review was also published as "Asian American Music Moves with Chin, Iijima," in *East/West* (January 26, 1983): 8.

31 One of the earliest documented uses of the term is in an interview by Norman Jayo and Paul Yamazaki, "Searching for an Asian American Music: Robert Kikuchi-Yngojo," *East Wind* 5, no. 1 (1986): 10-12; see also Lam, "Embracing 'Asian American Music,'" 56. This special issue was edited by Fred Wei-han Houn and published by the League of Revolutionary Struggle.

32 Liner notes, *A Grain of Sand: Songs from the Birth of Asian America*, 1973, re-released 1997.

33 Offering remarks far more candid than other discussions of A Grain of Sand, band member Chris Iijima, in an interview by Fred Ho, discusses how the urgency of the times necessitated their music, despite its artistic limitations. Iijima recounted that Nobuko Miyamoto, a professionally trained dancer and musician, "always felt more artistically constrained by what we were doing. And understandably. We never rehearsed. We never really sat down and worked out arrangements. It was, I got a phone call, they want us to come to Boston, let's go." Interview with Chris Iijima, by Fred Ho, in *Legacy to Liberation*, 245.

34 Ho, "Asian American Music and Empowerment."

35 Fred Houn, "The Traditional and Modern in Asian American Music," *Unity* newspaper, March 20, 1981; Wang, "Between the Notes," 453-54; Asai, "*Sansei* Voices in the Community," 278-81; *Cruisin J-Town,* directed by Alan Kondo, CrossCurrents Media, 1976.

36 After merging with the IWK, a small group of former Red Guard members wrote a paper denouncing the militaristic tendencies of the Red Guard ("A History of Red Guard Party," *Getting Together*, n.d.).

37 I Wor Kuen, "12-point Platform and Program."

38 Elbaum, *Revolution in the Air*; Laura Pulido, *Black Brown Yellow and Left: Radical Activism in Los Angeles* (Berkeley and Los Angeles: University of California Press, 2006); Cynthia A. Young, *Soul Power: Culture, Radicalism, and the Making of a U.S. Third World Left* (Durham, N.C.: Duke University Press, 2006).

39 Ambiguities often surround membership, as is the case for when Ho joined IWK. Ho has stated three different dates: late 1976/early 1977 ("An Asian American Tribute to the Black Arts Movement," this volume); late 1977 (Ho, *Legacy to Liberation*, 5); or early 1978 (Fred Wei-han Ho, "Marxism and Asian Americans: The Struggle Continues!," *Forward Motion* 11 [1992]: 66–71).

40 Ho, "Beyond Asian American 'Jazz,'" 46; also Kiang, "Transformation," 31–33.

41 Ho, "Beyond Asian American 'Jazz,'" 46; also Fred Houn, "Revolutionary Asian American Art: Tradition and Change, Inheritance and Innovation, Not Imitation!" in Ho, *Legacy to Liberation*, 383–88.

42 African American (Amiri Baraka's Revolutionary Communist League, formerly the Congress of Afrikan Peoples), Puerto Rican, Dominican, and other Asian (East Wind) and Chicano groups later joined the LRS, making it one of the largest New Communist organizations.

43 Ho, "An Asian American Tribute to the Black Arts Movement." The program notes to the 1991 Asian American Jazz Festival stated that in the 1980s, "Asian American jazz was taking off in two directions. One direction was being defined by Hiroshima and Visions, another LA-based group. The other direction is being defined by Jon Jang and Fred Ho. By incorporating politics and music, they are following the jazz tradition founded by African American musicians" (Nelson Nagai, "50 Years of Asian American Jazz," program, Asian American Jazz Festival, 1991).

44 Ho, "What Makes 'Jazz' the Revolutionary Music of the Twentieth Century, and Will It Be Revolutionary for the Twenty-first Century?," this volume.

45 Ho, "What Makes 'Jazz' the Revolutionary Music of the Twentieth Century?"; also Valerie Wilmer, *As Serious as Your Life: The Story of the New Jazz* (London: Allison and Busby, 1977), 22–24.

46 Wilmer, *As Serious as Your Life*, 23.

47 Wilmer, *As Serious as Your Life*, 22; John D. Baskerville, "Free Jazz: A Reflection of Black Power Ideology," *Journal of Black Studies* 24 (1994): 484. Given the absence of a satisfactory replacement term, I will continue to use the term "jazz" in this essay. Today, in a different political climate, Archie Shepp, a world-renowned jazz musician and university professor, now uses the phrase "jazz musician" (without quotes) as the primary identifier on his Web site, www.archieshepp.com.

‹ 35

48 For an excellent study of the Black Arts Movement, one that draws genealogical linkages with the Old Left, see James Edward Smethurst, *The Black Arts Movement: Literary Nationalism in the 1960s and 1970s* (Chapel Hill: University of North Carolina Press, 2005).

49 Frank Kofsky, *Black Nationalism and the Revolution in Music* (New York: Pathfinder Press, 1970), 27.

50 Kofsky, *Black Nationalism and the Revolution in Music*, 27-35; LeRoi Jones (Amiri Baraka), *Blues People* (New York: Perennial, 2002/1963).

51 Kofsky, *Black Nationalism and the Revolution in Music*, 9.

52 Ho, "An Asian American Tribute to the Black Arts Movement."

53 Ho, "Beyond Asian American 'Jazz.'"

54 Shepp is quoted in *Down Beat Music*, 1966, 20, cited in Kofsky, *Black Nationalism and the Revolution in Music*, 64.

55 Smethurst, *The Black Arts Movement*, 142.

56 Ho, "An Asian American Tribute to the Black Arts Movement."

57 Ho, "What Makes 'Jazz' the Revolutionary Music of the Twentieth Century?"

58 A number of Asian American free jazz musicians who had grown up in middle- or upper-middle-class White suburbs, including Ho, cite feelings of alienation as motivating their attraction to Black music (Zhang, "Fred Wei-han Ho," 110).

59 Asai, "*Sansei* Voices in the Community," 272-78; Asai, "Cultural Politics," 101-2; Ho, "Beyond Asian American 'Jazz.'" Jon Jang explains that *marron* is "a Caribbean term for slaves who, instead of running away for their own safety, would stay underground and help other slaves escape" ("We All Don't Sound Alike," *Views on Black American Music 3* [1985-88]: 35).

60 Jang, response in Ling, ed., *Yellow Light,* 340.

61 Jang, "We All Don't Sound Alike," 37-38; Jang, response in Ling, ed., *Yellow Light*, 340-44.

62 LeRoi Jones, *Black Music* (New York: Morrow, 1967), 11.

63 Kofsky, *Black Nationalism and the Revolution in Music*, 12.

64 Wong, "Just Being There."

65 Jang, "We All Don't Sound Alike," 34, 35; Jang, in Ling, ed., *Yellow Light*, 340-41; Wong, "Just Being There," 297-99.

66 Wong, "Just Being There," 299-300.

67 · Ho, "Beyond Asian American 'Jazz.'"

68 Jang, "We All Don't Sound Alike," 37; also Wei-hua Zhang, "Fred Ho and Jon Jang: Profiles of Two Chinese American Jazz Musicians," in *Chinese America: History and Perspectives* (San Francisco: Chinese Historical Society of America, 1994), 175-99.

69 Zhang, "Fred Ho and Jon Jang," 191-92, based on Jang, interview with San Francisco television station KQED, July 17, 1991.

70 Ho's name does not appear on a list of "Asian Improv Artist's Bio's/ Discography" (www.asianimprov.com/artists.asp; accessed February 6, 2008). On the "Asian Improv Records: A Checklist," there is a blank next to 003, where Ho's "A Song for a Manong" should be listed (www.dpo .uab.edu/~moudry/discog/asianimp; accessed February 6, 2008).

71 Martin Luther King, Jr., "A Knock at Midnight," in *Strength to Love* (New York: Pocket Books, 1964), 59, 60.

72 Ho, "Beyond Asian American 'Jazz.' "

73 The LRS majority remained optimistic about the possibilities for social change via collective struggle. They affirmed, in their dissolution statement, their belief "that jobs, education, health care, and housing are rights, and not privileges" and their critique of capitalism—"that society must be reorganized to put human needs before profit." League of Revolutionary Struggle, "Statement on the Dissolution of the League of Revolutionary Struggle," circa 1990.

74 George Lipsitz, *Dangerous Crossroads: Popular Music, Postmodernism, and the Poetics of Place* (London: Verso, 1994), 32.

75 Lipsitz, *Dangerous Crossroads*, 35; Antonio Gramsci, *Selections from the Prison Notebooks* (New York: International Publishers, 1971), 206-9, 229-39.

76 Ho views Marxism-Leninism "not [as] a dogma or fixed truths, but [as] a science that is tested and transformed continually as a 'work in progress' capable of self-criticism to strengthen its revolutionary practice and service to the liberation of all humanity" (Ho, "Matriarchy: The First and Final Communism," this volume).

77 Arjun Appadurai, "Disjuncture and Difference in the Global Cultural Economy," *Public Culture* 2 (1990): 1-24.

78 Ho, "Beyond Asian American 'Jazz.' "

79 Zhang, "Fred Wei-han Ho," 96.

80 Bendrew Jong, interview with Wei-hua Zhang, February 21, 1991, cited in Zhang, "Fred Ho and Jon Jang," 193.

81 Vijay Prashad, foreword, *AfroAsian Encounters: Culture, History, Politics*, edited by Heike Raphael-Hernandez and Shannon Steen (New York: New York University Press, 2006), xvi.

82 Ho, "Beyond Asian American 'Jazz.' "

83 Zhang, "Fred Wei-han Ho," 100.

84 Zhang, "Fred Wei-han Ho," 98; see also Bill V. Mullen, "Making Monkey Signify: Fred Ho's Revolutionary Vision Quest," in *Afro-Orientalism* (Minneapolis: University of Minnesota Press, 2004), 163-204.

85 Ho, "Beyond Asian American 'Jazz.'"

86 Ho, "Beyond Asian American 'Jazz.'"

87 Ho rejects the term "feminism" because of its close association with the mainstream or bourgeois women's movement. Drawing on ideas of feminists of color, Ho asserts: "Feminist sisterhood doesn't extend to ending imperialism and the privileges of white settler-colonial society. Feminism seeks equality with white bourgeois men, to reform capitalism and to include white womyn as equal participants along with white men in the system of imperialist privilege and power" (Ho, "Matriarchy: The First and Final Communism").

88 Fred Ho, e-mail to Diane Fujino, Billy Jennings, and Bill Mullen (subject: "fred ho: emergency"), August 5, 2006.

89 Bill V. Mullen, *Afro-Orientalism* (Minneapolis: University of Minnesota Press, 2004); Diane C. Fujino, *Heartbeat of Struggle: The Revolutionary Life of Yuri Kochiyama* (Minneapolis: University of Minnesota Press, 2005).

90 Grace Lee Boggs, *Living for Change: An Autobiography* (Minneapolis: University of Minnesota Press, 1998); Eric Nakamura and Martin Wong, "Yellow Power," *Giant Robot* (1998): 61–81; Diane C. Fujino, "The Black Liberation Movement and Japanese American Activism: The Radical Activism of Richard Aoki and Yuri Kochiyama," in *Afro Asia: Revolutionary Political and Cultural Connections between African Americans and Asian Americans*, edited by Fred Ho and Bill V. Mullen (Durham, N.C.: Duke University Press, 2008); Diane C. Fujino, "Race, Place, Space, and Political Development: Japanese American Radicalism in the 'Pre-Movement' 1960s," *Social Justice,* forthcoming; Fujino, "Who Studies the Asian American Movement? A Historiographical Analysis."

91 I myself disagree with the harshness of some of Ho's criticisms, but my job as editor is not to censure Ho's words, so these remain in the text.

92 Ho, "How to Sell but Not Sell Out," this volume.

93 Ho, "Beyond Asian American 'Jazz.'"

94 Ho, "Highlights in the History of 'Jazz' *Not* Covered by Ken Burns: A Request from Ishmael Reed," this volume.

95 George Lipsitz, "Jazz: The Hidden History of Nationalist Multiculturalism," in *Footsteps in the Dark: Hidden Histories of Popular Music* (Minneapolis: University of Minnesota Press, 2007), 81, 79–106.

96 Che Guevara, "Socialism and Man in Cuba," in *Che Guevara and the Cuban Revolution* (Sydney, Australia: Pathfinder, 1987), 258–59.

97 George Lipsitz, *American Studies in a Moment of Danger* (Minneapolis: University of Minnesota Press, 2001), 30.

hat I can remember was my first pain with white racism. At a preschool program, I remem
andbox being segregated, how the white schoolteacher (at that time, white, black or Asian/
had no meaning) deliberately told the other kids (all white) not to play with me. But the feelin
olation and avoidance by the other kids, and the pain I felt from this one particular teacher
ling me out, would remain with me for the rest of my life. ¶ Around the time I started element
ol, I became aware that I was Chinese. Again, racism provoked a self-awareness of difference wh
other school kids (except for one other Chinese boy) made fun of and laughed at me for eat
nch a Chinese *bao* (or steamed flower-shaped bun). The kids pointed at my favorite snack a
uled me/it: "Yecch, he's eating play dough!" From then on, a feeling of shame for being Chin
d take hold, even though I loved the foods my mom prepared. The *char sui* (Chinese roast po
heong (Chinese sausage), *bing bing* and various other *baos* (fried and steamed buns) were my
es, more so than American spaghetti or hamburgers (which I blamed my mom for not know
to make authentically). My mother tells me that before entering public school I spoke and
tood more Chinese than English, but after a few months of first grade, and the painful feeling
g different, I actively tried to give up everything to do with being Chinese. I wanted to be lik
accepted, to do well and be respected. ¶ "White got the might / White is right / Might as well
e . . ." It wasn't until years later that I became clear about the pressures of white assimilation, s
al, and self-hatred. By turning away from my Chinese American identity, I became a banana (yell

he outside, white on the inside): actively disavowing my heritage while desperately identifying w
ppressor *in toto* (physical appearance, politics, values, etc.). ¶ My parents didn't want me to lose
ese heritage and pride. They never understood what my form of "Americanization," or what I m
"whitification." They were immigrants. My father, a university professor, was seemingly bicultu
as fluent in both Chinese and English (although he always had an accent), a tenured professor w
ht Chinese political science. But he was actually culturally schizophrenic: he self-identified a
ucian scholar who had to culturally lower himself to function in white academia, frustrated
rofessional/career politics required to advance. While he was the most published of all the sen
ty members in his department, he was the least paid. He would take out his frustration with
which included white students making fun of him for his accent) and be a Chinese feudal patria
ome. We—my mom, myself, and my two sisters—were the victims of his fulminations and viol
ination. He battered my mom for her inability to speak English, for her wanting the independe
she perceived white middle-class wives possessed. One of my first revolutionary insurrecti
when, at the age of seventeen, I opposed my father's physical abuse of my mother. To get him
hitting her, I fist-fought him, giving him two black eyes. I remember the next day he went into w
ing dark sunglasses, not wanting to miss giving a lecture as the dutiful teacher. ¶ Because
e life was so awful, it was very important to be accepted at school by my peers in a white colle
. I parted my hair, tried to put in a wave. I tried to become a fan of white popular music. Strang
Star Trek came on network TV in the mid-to-late 1960s, I came to identify with Mr. Spock,
Vulcan, half-human first officer—the "alien." Spock was good in math and science; so was I. Sp
ed to suppress his emotions (his human side), and so did I. And Vulcans and Asians bore a si
hysical resemblance. For two or three Halloweens, I just wore a blue turtleneck shirt bearin
fleet insignia I had made with crayons and cardboard. When the other kids shouted "trick or tre
e a Vulcan hand salute and stoically proclaimed, "Live long and prosper." Only a few white nei
asked me, "What are you supposed to be?" (Interestingly, I never identified with Sulu, the Asian
how; I think because he was so token, his Asian-ness completely peripheral or nonexistent, unl
ov or Scotty, who spoke with accents to identify their cultural/national heritages, or Uhura, w
sionally dressed in African garb or who viewers knew spoke Swahili. Sulu was completely cult

From Banana to Third World Marxist

MY EARLY CHILDHOOD MEMORIES begin at around the age of three. The second experience in life that I can remember was my first pain with white racism. At a preschool program, I remember my sandbox being segregated, how the white schoolteacher (at that time, white, black or Asian/yellow had no meaning) deliberately told the other kids (all white) not to play with me. But the feelings of isolation and avoidance by the other kids, and the pain I felt from this one particular teacher for singling me out, would remain with me for the rest of my life.

Around the time I started elementary school, I became aware that I was Chinese. Again, racism provoked a self-awareness of difference when the other school kids (except for one other Chinese boy) made fun of and laughed at me for eating at lunch a Chinese *bao* (or steamed flower-shaped bun). The kids pointed at my favorite snack and ridiculed me/it: "Yecch, he's eating play dough!" From then on, a feeling of shame for being Chinese would take hold, even though I loved the foods my mom prepared. The *char sui* (Chinese roast pork), *lop cheong* (Chinese sausage), *bing bing* and various other *baos* (fried and steamed buns) were my favorites, more so than American spaghetti or hamburgers (which I blamed my mom for not knowing how to make authentically). My mother tells me that before entering

Published in *Boyhood, Growing Up Male: A Multicultural Anthology,* edited by Franklin Abbott (Freedom, Calif.: Crossing Press, 1993).

public school I spoke and understood more Chinese than English, but after a few months of first grade, and the painful feeling of being different, I actively tried to give up everything to do with being Chinese. I wanted to be liked, to be accepted, to do well and be respected.

"White got the might / White is right / Might as well be White ..." It wasn't until years later that I became clear about the pressures of white assimilation, self-denial, and self-hatred. By turning away from my Chinese American identity, I became a banana (yellow on the outside, white on the inside): actively disavowing my heritage and people and identifying with the oppressor *in toto* (physical appearance, politics, values, etc.).

My parents didn't want me to lose my Chinese heritage and pride. They never understood what they termed "Americanization," or what I now call "whitification." They were immigrants. My father, a university professor, was seemingly bicultural: he was fluent in both Chinese and English (although he always had an accent), a tenured professor who taught Chinese political science. But he was actually culturally schizophrenic: he self-identified as a Confucian scholar who had to culturally lower himself to function in white academia, frustrated by the professional/career politics required to advance. While he was the most published of all the senior faculty members in his department, he was the least paid. He would take out his frustration with the job (which included white students making fun of him for his accent) and be a Chinese feudal patriarch at home. We—my mom, myself, and my two sisters—were the victims of his fulminations and violent domination. He battered my mom for her inability to speak English, for her wanting the independence that she perceived white middle-class wives possessed. One of my first revolutionary insurrections was when, at the age of seventeen, I opposed my father's physical abuse of my mother. To get him to stop hitting her, I fist-fought him, giving him two black eyes. I remember the next day he went into work wearing dark sunglasses, not wanting to miss giving a lecture as the dutiful teacher.

Because my home life was so awful, it was very important to be accepted at school by my peers in a white college town. I parted my hair, tried to put in a wave. I tried to become a fan of white popular music. Strangely, when *Star Trek* came on network TV in the mid-to-late 1960s, I came to identify with Mr. Spock, the half-Vulcan, half-human first officer—the "alien." Spock was good in math and science; so was I. Spock tended to suppress his emotions (his human side), and so did I. And Vulcans and Asians bore a similar physical resemblance. For two or three Halloweens, I just wore a blue turtleneck shirt bearing a Starfleet insignia I had made with crayons and cardboard. When the other kids shouted "trick or treat," I gave a Vulcan hand salute and stoically proclaimed, "Live long and prosper." Only a few white neighbors asked me, "What are you supposed to be?" (Interestingly, I never identified with Sulu, the Asian on the show; I think because he was so token, his Asian-ness completely peripheral or nonexistent, unlike Chekov or Scotty, who spoke with accents to identify their cultural/national heritages, or Uhura, who occasionally dressed in African garb or who viewers knew spoke Swahili. Sulu was completely culturally de-ethnicized.)

All the other Asian males on TV were pathetic stereotypes: comic relief servant/sidekick types like Fuji and Hop Sing, or evil inscrutables like *Hawaii Five-O*'s nemesis, the red commie Wo Fat (never played by an Asian). I tried to be like David Carradine as Kwai Chang Caine in *Kung Fu*, but the fake martial arts couldn't make up for the even more slant eyes and yellow skin makeup (the racist Hollywood/American entertainment tradition of yellow-face).

The one exception on TV while growing up was Bruce Lee as Kato on *The Green Hornet*. Kato had a thick Cantonese accent, even in his common one-liner: "Whele to, Boss?" (Chinese makes "r" sounds come out like "l.") Raised in the boys-will-be-boys heterosexual socialization of male aggressiveness and heroism, I craved an action-adventure character like Kato, who could really kick ass. I always secretly wondered why Kato wasn't the boss instead of the Green Hornet. But after all, I still hadn't begun to question the notion of the white man's world.

My sexual awareness started to take off at age eight when my family drove cross-country from Massachusetts to California. Bored from hours of simply seeing highway, when we stopped at stores to get supplies, I took off for the magazine stands. At first I was simply looking for new comics, but I quickly noticed "girlie" magazines. Of course, all the sexy women were white, busty, and mostly blonde. After we got to California and had stayed in the Bay Area for a year, I noticed that there were many more Asians, and that Safeway supermarkets sold tofu, and, of course, the openly run ads for top-less bars in newspapers. Chinatown was right next to the topless red-light district of North Beach in San Francisco. There was a lot for an eight-year-old boy to ogle.

I didn't like Asian girls. I was deeply entrenched in my banana-ness. My dad kept trying to match me up with this Chinese American girl my age who lived right across the street. I had always lived and gone to school in overwhelmingly white communities where there were only a handful of Asian girls; your sisters and the others, who were like cousins because our parents socialized together. Romance couldn't be racially anonymous when it came to Asian girls. And be-sides, all that society upheld and promoted as desirable and attrac-tive was white images.

Two significant factors worked to rid me of the white/banana syndrome: first, no matter how hard I tried to be racially effacing, I couldn't escape from racism at all levels: from jeers and taunting to outright restrictions—starting with the segregated sandbox. Second, the social changes of the late 1960s brought the first African Ameri-can teacher to my junior high. She wore a big Afro, projected militant black pride, and brought about the first "Black Experience" class that exposed me to African American literature, including *The Auto-biography of Malcolm X*. It was Malcolm X's life and ideas that awak-ened my political consciousness: that I/we are victims of a system of white supremacy and racism. For the first time, I began to theo-rize my personal experience to the level of social analysis and radi-cal political concepts; it never could remain at the level of feel-good politics or "identity politics." More and more as I struggled to change myself through changing the social environment around me, I came to understand the structural and systematic roots of the oppression of "people of color," but also of the world's majority: the oppression of women, workers of all nationalities, entire peoples. The high level of political debate and struggle in the "movement" of the United States at this period eventually brought me into Marxism as I discarded my anti-white nationalism or "Third-World consciousness" for a more dialectical and thus scientific analysis. I am not anti-white, but anti-white supremacy. I am pro-liberation for women, gays, or oppressed nationalities (what I prefer to call "people of color" as it specifically locates our political condition as oppressed, thus belying notions of "reverse discrimination," etc.), and I'm for socialism. I reject the homophobia, racism, and sexism that also have infected parts of the American Left and the socialist movements around the world. While I believe that ultimately our struggle is for political and economic structural or systemic changes, I also uphold the critical importance of cultural change: creating new values and human relations and expressions. In my present position as composer/baritone saxophonist and bandleader of the Afro Asian Music Ensemble, I insist upon and work toward an audience that is *not* majority white. This is integral to revolutionary change.

While I think it's possible to love anyone, as an oppressed nationality leader in the political and cultural liberation struggle, my sexual/intimate preferences are for oppressed nationality women (I choose to personally be heterosexual). But more importantly, such a lover and intimate partner must also possess radical political consciousness, be committed to the struggle, be personally intelligent, passionate, generous and mature, and strive to uphold the highest standards of excellence and responsibility.

The struggle for all of us who are serious about changing the world is to unite our personal, political, and professional lives toward this work/goal.

Beyond Asian American Jazz:
My Musical and Political Changes
in the Asian American Movement

I HAVE BEEN a professional baritone saxophonist, composer/arranger, bandleader, writer, activist and (more recently) producer in New York City for almost two decades. Some regard me as "successful" since I am able to make a living solely from my music, have paid off my mortgage to a great duplex loft at the age of thirty-seven, have earned several awards[1] and manage to somehow get all my opera and music/theater works produced (primarily through my own resources). I consider my "success" not in mainstream bourgeois terms of "fame and fortune" but in the fact that I have been able to unite my career, my art, and my revolutionary politics.

My music has developed in parallel with and been shaped by my history of political struggle and activism. Today, at the age of forty-two, I am still a revolutionary Marxist even though much of the originally Marxist-Leninist political movement of which I have been a part has collapsed into reformism and the opportunism of maneuvering within the system.

Revolutionary Yellow Nationalism and Resistance: 1971–1976

My biographical and political history has been discussed in other articles.[2] Growing up, I experienced oppression from both domestic violence and white racist violence. As a young teenager, I was influ-

Published in *Leonardo Music Journal* 9 (1999).

enced by the revolutionary nationalist upsurges of the late 1960s and early 1970s in the United States and, through the influence of Malcolm X, became what I termed a "yellow revolutionary nationalist." I was attracted to the Nation of Islam for their self-reliant independence from white American institutions. I distrusted nationalists who mouthed Yellow/Black/Brown pride and/or anti-white diatribes but took paychecks from white institutions. At the age of fourteen, I acquired a second-hand baritone saxophone from my public school band and began seriously to investigate African American music, especially its more radical and "avant-garde" forms, the so-called Free Music of the 1960s. I searched for a creative expression that would give voice to my exploding radicalism, my hatred of oppression, and my burning commitment to revolutionary struggle.

It was the music of little-known composer Cal Massey in particular (as performed and recorded by Archie Shepp) that had a major impact upon me.[3] Massey's extended suites, such as *The Black Liberation Movement Suite* (which he wrote for fundraising concerts for the Black Panther Party), strongly appealed to me with their thematically epic historical scope, Fanonic titles (e.g., "The Damned Don't Cry"), soulful melodies, complex and rich harmonies, Afrocentric rhythms (i.e., more African-inspired or African American interpreted than actually traditional African). It was the music of liberation and revolution (connected to the "jazz tradition," simultaneously swinging and radical); one could hear the Black Panthers marching inside the music itself.

‹ 47

My cultural awakening and entrance into revolutionary politics occurred in the mid-1970s. In previously published articles and interviews, I have discussed the major inspirations and influence of the Black Power and Black Arts movements upon my political consciousness and artistic development. The lessons I drew from my study and involvement in "jazz" about the role of art and music in revolutionary social transformation extended far beyond the simple expression of political views through song lyrics or titles and their subsequent use in social movements, which has composed the primary discourse about music and social change. Rather, I saw the "politics" of music in musical aesthetics, in ways of music making and in building alternatives to the music industry.[4]

During this time, I joined an Asian American counterpart to the

Black Panthers, I Wor Kuen (IWK). By the mid-1970s, most Asian American revolutionaries had become Marxist-Leninist (M-L) and belonged to one of several national M-L organizations: I Wor Kuen/ League of Revolutionary Struggle (LRS), Workers Viewpoint Organization/Communist Workers Party, Wei Min She/Revolutionary Communist Party, Katipunan Demokratik Pilipino/Line of March, etc.[5]

I was one of the younger activists of that generation. Much of the sociopolitical and cultural advances in today's Asian Pacific American (APA) communities—social services and legal aid programs, Asian American studies and art/cultural organizations—were products of struggles waged by APA revolutionaries and militants of this period. Many communists and revolutionaries initiated and founded organizations (albeit presently devoid of their original militancy) such as Visual Communications, Japantown Art and Media, Kearny Street Workshop, and Asian CineVision. Other APA cultural organizations that have since ceased operations include the Community Asian American Mural Project (CAAMP) in Oakland/Bay Area, *Bridge* magazine, *East Wind* magazine, Basement Workshop, Ating Tao, Kalayan, Dragon Thunder Arts Forum, etc.[6] APA communists were even members of many Japanese American taiko (drum) groups on both coasts, which tended to attract ex-activists and ex-communists who wanted taiko to be "cultural" or apolitical as they were both burned out from and negative toward radical activism.

Lenin pointed out that there could be no revolutionary movement without revolutionary theory. Similarly, the character and development of revolutionary art and music is oriented by the revolutionary movement and theory that guide such creative work.

Being from a middle-class intellectual background, belonging to IWK/LRS reoriented me toward the proletariat or working class. I did my political work as a cultural organizer in Boston's Chinatown, an immigrant and working-class community. Fresh out of college activism, I agreed to a political assignment to organize the Asian American Resource Workshop (AARW), a fledgling educational and cultural group in the community. In the AARW, we started the first Asian American poetry readings in the community, organized a biweekly and monthly summer coffeehouse series that featured agitprop theater ("skits") in both Chinese and English, and other bilingual cultural performances. I and other IWK/LRS cadres led the

AARW Chinese folksinging ensemble; I began to learn and draw inspiration from the rich heritage of Chinese folk songs.

As a cadre of IWK/LRS, the AARW operated on the political directive, or "line," to unite immigrant and American-born Asians and to integrate with the working class. Significantly, this shaped my view of Asian American culture not solely or primarily as the expression of the college-educated, English-speaking, middle-class, American-born Asians, but as a continuum that spanned and embraced the earliest Cantonese opera traditions of nineteenth-century Chinese laborers along with the most experimental contemporary works. We worked to build a Pan-Asian identity that would amalgamate the diverse national cultures, languages, and histories of the Asian/Pacific nationalities in the United States.

Guided by this general political direction, I embarked upon a serious and extensive research into the folk traditions and roots of Asian American culture. It became clear to me that a working-class, even revolutionary tradition exists in APA cultures. Such a tradition includes the first immigrant cultural forms: Cantonese opera, the wood-fish head chants, the talk-story traditions, the folk ballads and syllabic verses of the Chinese immigrant laborers, the Japanese American female plantation labor songs (*hole hole bushi*), the Angel Island poetry, the Filipino rondalla and folk ballads of the manongs (Filipino immigrant bachelor workers), Japanese American tanka (syllabic verse) poetry, etc.[7]

It also became evident to me that a huge gulf has existed between this rich traditional heritage of the immigrants and the highly Western-imitative cultural expressions of the American-born. In the late 1970s, IWK put forward a published position that Asian American art and culture necessitates a link to traditional Asian cultural forms. During this time, the APA movement was attempting to address the question of what makes Asian American art/cultural expression Asian American?

By and large, these attempts at a revolutionary theory of APA art and culture simply reiterated standard M-L views (mostly from Mao's Yenan talks on art, literature, and revolution) on the political and class nature of art, the propaganda value of folk and popular forms, the question of aesthetic form and its dialectical, yet subordinate, relationship to revolutionary proletarian content. This theoretical shallowness was reflected in an equally shallow early Asian American Movement music—a derivative of both white folk and leftist styles à la Bob Dylan and Pete Seeger or African American gospel, soul, and rhythm and blues idioms. The major limitation of the American Left's theory and practice in cultural work has stemmed from the influence of socialist realism (the Zhdanov policies of the Soviet Union[8]), commonly regarded as "agitprop." This theory regards art solely for its utilitarian value as a vehicle for propaganda. With the advancement of both my professional artistic career and my personal understanding of the complex relationship between ideology, the arts, and struggle would come frustrating and conflictual struggles with LRS political leadership around these issues, including the validity of "Asian American jazz."

"Asian American Jazz": 1982–1989

Self-described "Asian American jazz" emerged during the period of the late 1970s/early 1980s, primarily from a small group of Bay Area/West Coast musicians. These "Asian American jazz" musicians included saxophonist Russel Baba, bassist Mark Izu, bass clarinetist Paul Yamazaki, and New York violinist Jason Kao Hwang, among others, including myself.

This grouping represented some of the more imaginative contemporary efforts toward forging a distinctive Asian American music. These instrumentalists/composers combined actual Asian traditional instrumentation and Asian-inspired or -influenced stylistic elements with predominantly "free" or modal improvisation in the African American avant-garde "jazz" context. Indeed, much of their music had more to do with the developments within the 1960s African American "jazz" avant-garde of Ornette Coleman, John Coltrane, Archie Shepp, and others than a substantial cultural grounding within traditional Asian music. However, the identification with the musical radicalism of the 1960s often reflected a concomitant ideological radicalism. Clearly, we were aligned with the most militant of the African American music of the 1960s.

During the 1980s, I emerged as one of the leading "Asian American jazz" artists on both coasts. I was constantly writing reviews and (often polemical) essays that argued for an Asian American culture

and artistic expression rooted to immigrant and working-class traditions.[9] I sought to clarify—for other Asian American artists and for
my own artistic creation—a revolutionary Asian American art/music
that embraces tradition and change and that would not be imitative
of Eurocentric and white pop forms but innovative by inheriting and
expanding upon the continuum of Asian Pacific American cultures.

Beyond rejecting "art for art's sake," I polemicized against the
white assimilationist notion of the petty bourgeois Asian American artist that anything by an Asian American artist makes it Asian
American. While also rejective of being proscriptive or essentialist,
I do maintain that the Asian American-ness of an artistic work lies
in more than content, and is rooted and linked to cultural traditions
and forms. Along with expressing aspects of the "Asian American
experience," the music itself would draw from or reflect aspects of
traditional Asian music influences. Yo-Yo Ma is a cellist who happens
to be Chinese/Asian American, not a Chinese/Asian American musician. John Kaizan Neptune is a white American virtuosic *shakuhachi*
(traditional Japanese vertical flute) player, but he is not playing Japa-
nese/Asian American music because he is not intending to express
or reflect a Japanese/Asian American identity. While Asian American music may very well be cross-cultural, we in the "Asian American
jazz" movement saw as the focus of our music/cultural work to help
catalyze Asian American consciousness about our oppression and
need to struggle for liberation. The very identity and term "Asian
American" in our sobriquet "Asian American jazz or music" is a political signifier.

By the late 1980s, I was musically and ideologically evolving away
from "Asian American jazz." (And as further discussed below, I was
also moving away from the growing political rightism of the LRS, reflected in its "line" on cultural work of producing work that would
be "accessible"—in my view, tailing the familiar and conventional.)
As "Asian American jazz," my first four recordings as a leader of
my Afro Asian Music Ensemble and now-defunct Asian American
Art Ensemble featured compositions that spoke to the Asian American struggle and celebrated the resistance of Asian workers in the
United States. I also consciously collaborated with and brought together other progressive Asian American artists and featured them
in my performances and recordings, including Janice Mirikitani,

musicians Francis Wong and Jon Jang (the one artist featured on all my first four recordings), San Francisco Kulintang Arts, and visual artists Yong Soon Min, Santiago Bose, and others doing album cover art. An "Asian American jazz" movement—coalesced via the Asian-Improv Records (AIR) label initiated by Jang and including myself, Wong, Glenn Horiuchi and other then-LRS cadres—was beginning to bloom. However, in the late 1980s, both musical/aesthetical and political changes would result in differences that would later lead me to break from AIR (with whom I had been recording) and then eventually with the LRS.

Afro Asian New American Multicultural Music: 1989–Present

Heretofore, I would characterize my music as "jazz" with Asian American thematic and musical references. But 1986 was a major aesthetical turning point for me. I was continuously struggling with the question of what makes Chinese American music Chinese American? What would comprise an Asian American musical content and form that could transform American music in general rather than simply be subsumed in one or another American musical genre such as "jazz"?

I began to embark upon a course that I articulated as creating "an Afro Asian new American multicultural music." Taking Mark Izu's significant leadership in the incorporation of traditional Asian instrumentation (in his case, mostly in improvised or incidental approaches), I began to explore such an incorporation in a composed, orchestrated manner. With no desire to be a Sinophile or traditional Asian music academic, yet recognizing the importance of studying and drawing from traditional formal structures, I wanted to evoke the spirit of folk music in both (solo and ensemble) performance and in composition.

As early as 1985, in my multimedia work *Bound Feet* (led by then-Asian American Art Ensemble member/actress/vocalist Jodi Long), I incorporated the Chinese double-reed *sona* and the Chinese two-stringed vertical violin, *erhu,* with Western woodwinds, contrabass, and multiple percussion. I wrote the *sona* and *erhu* parts in Chinese notation, an ability I had acquired from the days leading the Boston AARW's Chinese folksinging group during the late 1970s/early

1980s. In *Bound Feet* I became excited about the musical results of this embryonic integration of Eastern non-tempered and Western tempered instruments. While employing my own "jazz" voicing in the harmonization of the parts, I had struck upon some new, fresh, and unusual timbral qualities from this combination. This synthesis of Chinese and African American components seemed to be a musical analogy for the Chinese American identity or, even further, something Afro Asian in sensibility.

In 1986 and 1987, I embarked upon composing what was to become the first modern Chinese American opera, *A Chinaman's Chance*. I wanted this new opera to be an extension of the traditional Chinese opera in America that was once so flourishing in the Chinatown communities before World War II. My concept was to utilize the wood-fish head and syllabic verse chants as episodic narration. Less a conventional plot/story than a historical suite, *A Chinaman's Chance* is about the transformation of the Chinese to becoming Chinese American. In April 1989, a one-time stage production was presented at the Brooklyn Academy of Music's Majestic Theatre. I considered this first opera of mine to be an experimentation for me in working out an extended Chinese American music/theatre form, and was satisfied with neither the work as a whole or its staging. Out of this first effort, I became committed to putting the music ensemble onstage as part of the theatrical setting rather than buried in a subterranean orchestra pit. In future staged music/theatre and opera productions, I plan for the music ensemble to be elevated 10 feet off stage in the air, to be part of the "heavens."

New lessons and new directions flowed from these experiments in my efforts to create a true multicultural synthesis. The integration of two vastly different musical traditions requires bi- or multicultural musicians and artists willing to stretch beyond their traditional roles and musical understanding. As such, experimental works sorely lack financial resources, and it is hard to sustain the years of rehearsal and interfacing needed to forge such an interactive musical dialogue and exchange. The process of forging my multicultural music has taken many years of efforts through such projects, working with a stable core of musicians who have come to understand (albeit unevenly) the concepts toward which I am striving.

The Chinese artists with whom I work are not only master

musicians within their own traditions and contexts, but are also open to playing my music, which they call "*jen chi gwai*" (literally, "very strange"). Their initial skepticism toward combining Chinese and "jazz" music has since given way to genuine excitement and commitment.

I wanted my compositional process to be a real synthesis, and not a pastiche or juxtaposition of contrasting cultural styles. Most "world beat" or intercultural collaborative efforts, in my view, are limited in the extent to which they manifest real and truly "new" synthesis. These efforts are, at best, exoticism when proffered by culturally imperialistic whites and "chop-sueyism" when presented superficially by people of color.

In opposing cultural imperialism, a genuine multicultural synthesis embodies revolutionary internationalism in music: rather than co-opting different cultures, musicians and composers achieve revolutionary transformation predicated upon anti-imperialism in terms of both musical respect and integrity as well as a practical political economic commitment to equality between peoples.[10]

Nineteen eighty-nine was a watershed year. Artistically, I was moving away from "Asian American jazz" toward "Afro Asian new American multicultural music." Politically, I had become increasingly alienated from the rightist, reformist decline of the LRS. In the spring of 1989, a majority of the leadership moved to "question" Marxism, socialism, and revolution and soon split into a reformist majority and a socialist minority. Interestingly (and what requires further analysis and explanation) the overwhelming majority of Asians in the LRS went along with the rightist liquidation of revolutionary influence. This included the Asian American jazz cadres with whom I had worked closely for years to build AIR and an Asian American jazz movement. After I was ejected in July 1989 for challenging the unprincipled and opportunist liquidation, by mid-1990 the majority of the LRS had jettisoned socialism, Marxism, and revolution, opting to become Democratic Party hacks and brokers and changing the name of the organization to the Unity Organizing Committee (which soon quickly faded away).

Part of the rightism of this period of the LRS involved a political directive that required music and art to be "accessible" (which became a codeword for culturally mainstream and politically reformist). In internal gatherings, I rose to challenge this position as tailist (obsequious to mainstream acceptance) and accommodationist. As revolutionaries, I argued, the goal of our work must be the raising of both consciousness and cultural and artistic levels and standards, as well as the popularization of innovative, oppositional, transgressive, radical work.

The LRS split turned into a good thing for me, though it politically was a major setback to the U.S. Left and a personal loss since the organization was my life for over a decade. By challenging the liqui-dationism, I not only reaffirmed my understanding of and commit-ment to Marxism, but also struggled to move forward, correct errors, discard old baggage, and seek unity with other Leftist movements.

Realizing that I might never be signed to a major label or become the celebrity darling of establishment curators and gatekeepers, or even be signed to high-powered management or agents, I knew that I would continue to be primarily a self-producing artist trying to forge alternatives to the corporate or nonprofit institutions via guerrilla cultural production and distribution approaches. As the LRS had self-destructed and the sufficient unity needed for me to join another Left group did not seem to exist, I developed an individual strategy of maintaining independence while making short-term incursions into the mainstream and spending mostly my own personal earnings to fund productions. The challenge to unite my career and revolution-ary cultural work requires the same skills and qualities needed to build revolutionary organization: commitment, clarity, creativity, and competence. Musically, I disassociated myself with the rest of "Asian American jazz."

‹ 55

Upon my severance from the LRS, in the fall of 1989, I was then commissioned by the late Jack Chen, then octogenarian president of the Bay Area–based Pear Garden in the West, to compose the music for an episode extracted from the Chinese serial adventure classic, *Journey to the West*. This project began my formation of the Monkey Orchestra, a unique chamber ensemble combining traditional Chi-nese and Western "jazz" instrumentation and a Chinese-language vocalist. It also motivated me to develop my new music/theater, opera, and ballet forms. In its premiere as a 25-minute "pilot" epi-sode, "Monkey Meets the Spider-Spirit Vampires" not only became the first Chinese American opera ballet with a libretto sung totally in Mandarin Chinese, but, more significantly, it also created a music score that was a unique and unusual hybrid of Chinese and "jazz" music. Throughout the early 1990s, catalyzed by this episodic piece, I incorporated additional episodes that became a four-act, serial action-adventure music/theater piece (or opera-martial arts/dance ballet), *Journey Beyond the West: The New Adventures of Monkey!* Two acts of *Journey...* were eventually fully staged and the first act presented in concert version during the 1997 Brooklyn Academy of Music's Next Wave Festival.

Matriarchal Socialism: 1992–Present

As the 1990s began, the majority of LRS members had rejected socialism, revolution, and Marxism, opting for reformist, Democratic Party-type politics of multicultural political brokering. In general, much of the U.S. Marxist-Leninist Left that had emerged in the mid-1970s had collapsed from a combination of the overall international crisis in socialism (fall of the U.S.S.R., Tiananmen Square) and an aggressive right-wing capitalist fundamentalism. There was only a scattering of still-committed revolutionary socialists from my former movement, not enough to sustain, much less rebuild, a national organization.

I had emerged from this split and destruction of a movement of which I had been a part for over a decade with even more commitment to the cause of revolutionary socialist ideology and politics. I also (for the first time) began to primarily make a living from my art/music. Without an organized movement, I was trying to understand how my music would support the revolutionary struggle beyond the aesthetical and ideological.

I began to associate with the new, young generation of activists emerging in the early 1990s, which included anarchists, Trotskyites, and others. Many of these younger activists, though inexperienced and lacking in actual understanding of the Left of which I was a part, nonetheless had made their own analyses and summations of the problems and failures of my movement, albeit some of them very sketchy and often inaccurate. A major critique of our movement by this 1990s generation involved sexism, the continuation of patriarchy, and homophobia. The young 1990s activists also emphasized "personal" politics, struggling with me about my meat-eating, about environmentalism, about the need for attention to "democratic" process in political work, and so on.

Since the earliest stages of my professional cultural work, I have been one of the few Asian American male artists to consistently deal with the oppression of Asian and Asian American womyn.[11] A list of my works up to 1993 includes *Bound Feet* (1985), a text/dance/music piece that addressed the oppressive feudal Chinese feminine beauty practice; "What's a Girl to Do?" and "(The Earth Is) Rockin' in Revolution/Drowning in the Yellow River" (both 1984), based on Janice Mirikitani's poetry; "Lan Hua Hua" (1990), a reworking of a traditional Chinese folk song that was a protest of arranged marriages; "Soran (hole hole) Bushi" (1989), a solo baritone sax work based on a Japanese American womyn's plantation worker song; "I'm Sorry" (1988), a self-criticism for womanizing; "Song of the Slave Girl" (1989), the extended aria of a nineteenth-century Chinatown prostitute; "Home Is Where the Violence Is" (1992), an extended work that deals with violence against womyn, commissioned by WHAM! (Women's Health Action and Mobilization) and BWARE (Brooklyn Women's Anti-Rape Exchange). My mother is a survivor of domestic violence, and as a young teenager, I physically fought my father to stop him beating her. I see this as my first revolutionary insurrection and challenge of patriarchal authority.

Many twenty-something womyn activists educated me about the question of patriarchy. I began a very extensive Marxist and radical feminist study of patriarchy as rooted in the very beginning of class society, the overthrow of womyn's matriarchy, the rise of the state as an instrument of patriarchal class rule, and the cultural and social domination, oppression, and exploitation of gender. I briefly joined an interesting collective, ORSSASM (Organization of Revolutionary Socialist Sisters and Some Men), made up of revolutionary anarchists, socialist and radical feminists, and Marxists. The collective was majority-oppressed nationalities (so-called "people of color"), majority womyn, and younger than me. It engaged in an interesting and significant project, the Womyn Warriors/Sheroes Calendar, which featured information and history on an important womyn revolutionary or rebel for each of the 365 days of the year.[12] Working as an editor on the project brought home to me personally that there can be no real revolution without the revolution of womyn; that womyn have been the first, largest, and longest-standing class; that class division is fundamentally a gender division; that patriarchal socialism in unacceptable; and that the opposite of white supremacist, Eurocentric, patriarchal capitalism must be multicultural, internationalist matriarchal socialism. As a male revolutionary artist, intellectual, and activist, I had come to assert my identity as a revolutionary matriarchal socialist.

With this new political understanding, I began a new opera in collaboration with Ann T. Greene, *Warrior Sisters: The New Adventures of African and Asian Womyn Warriors*–an action-adventure opera about the escape from a New Jersey prison of Black Liberation Army leader Assata Shakur told as a myth-epic.[13] I wanted to write an opera that broke all the conventions of, at least, Western European opera. First, the characters feature strong warrior womyn. The entire principal cast were womyn of African and Asian descent, heretofore unprecedented in Western operatic history. The singers were to be a mix of trained (Western) opera and pop-soul singers. In my vision and practice of radical cross-cultural, nontraditional casting, I had singers of African descent perform Asian roles and singers of Asian descent perform African roles. I reject "blackfacing" and "yellowfacing"–the racist practice of whites playing "people of color" roles; I encouraged a "Third World" cross-cultural casting, hoping to encourage greater "Third World" consciousness and solidarity.

Second, in the music and staging concept, I wanted to continue mixing African and Chinese influences in the musical score to be performed not by a standard Western European–style orchestra, but by my Afro Asian Music Ensemble. I wanted to offer work to singers not necessarily trained in Western European opera music. I also incorporated elements of Chinese martial arts, West African dance, African American popular dance, and Chinese opera.

In the 1990s, I have been consciously trying to make all my staged productions appeal to an audience of two years and up, and incorporate both martial arts and fantasy-action adventure in the context of bringing strong political messages about gender and national liberation and the fight against capitalism and imperialism. I am trying to create a new American opera that appeals to today's youth–particularly inner-city youth–who think of opera as something conservative and exclusionary. I want my operas and musical theatre works to go up against the Ninja Turtles, the Mighty Morphin Power Rangers, the fake kung fu of David Carradine, Mortal Kombat, Xena, etc. I do not have the budgets and marketing dollars of these commercial shows, but I at least want my artistic/theatrical concept to be more exciting and captivating, and for the martial arts to demolish the aesthetics of grade-B action films, boring Broadway, and moribund modern dance.

Warrior Sisters is a multicultural new American opera that does not kowtow to European cultural conventions, but generates its own forms and styles and subject matter that come from the African American and Asian American heritages. This opera is politically matriarchal socialist, musically new Afro Asian, and theatrically an action-adventure epic.

My newest opera, *Night Vision: A New Third to First World Vampyre Opera* (with libretto by Ruth E. Margraff), features a two-thousand-year-old female vampire pop superstar singer as the protagonist against the Spin Doctor, a human male character, failed televangelist, "public relations genius, the DJ of her supersonic (supernatural) sound design ... a snake-oil creature, balding masterminding Renfield antagonist who spins vampyre's hype...."[14] Musically, I blend pop musical styles but often in odd meters, in unconventional harmony, and with live digital mixing and editing to blur the lines between live performance and electronic manipulation. The staging concept also blurs the lines between past and present and reality and virtual reality via the use of interactive live video mixing and editing. Politically, this work is my most apocalyptic vision of capitalism; it is also my most adventuresome foray into music/video technology.

Artistically, I still compose acoustic music with very little electronic processing. I believe that musicians have only scratched the surface of all the sonic/creative possibilities of acoustic instrumentation. While it may take a musician twenty years to master a certain esoteric technique that electronics can simulate at the touch of a button or key, the journey of discipline is intrinsically more spiritualizing. I still maintain that electronics tend to mute the human personality, to dehumanize rather than spiritualize. Live performance is still the best and most satisfying way to experience music as long as the work is boldly radical in its artistry and politics.

However, I have begun to utilize multimedia technology in my operas and musicals as a more economic substitute for scenic design and old-hat theatrical special effects. While much of the twentieth-century Left's artistic tradition is heavily dominated by "socialist" or "critical" realism (the common working man or peasant as hero/protagonist), my work is revolutionary fantasy or vision-quests. I reject socialist heroes, but I do populate my theatrical landscapes with tricksters, womyn warrior sheroes, and supernatural beings. I draw from tall-tale trickster and martial Chinese opera stories to create a neo-mythology of a world beyond this one that unleashes the imagination enough for a two-year-old child (my biggest critic) to be both spellbound and revolutionized.

Big Red Media—Revolutionary New American Opera, Musical Theater Epics, and Chinese American Martial Arts Ballets: 1997–Present

While I identify with the "jazz" tradition, much of "jazz" has become occupied with reactionaries and their sociocultural domination of the art, not only as gatekeepers of establishment cultural citadels, but also of prescribed ideology and style. For the first time in the music's history, twenty-something musicians are stuck playing a style that predates their birth. Others have characterized this current period as "business-suited" music, "neo-conservative," "retrograde," etc. I stopped playing nightclubs in the United States in 1987 to extricate myself from a carcinogenic environment and a cycle of exploitation. Some people do not view me as a part of "jazz" anymore: to be honest, if what they consider "jazz" is not innovative, radical or inclusive, that is true. But I believe that the tradition is embodied in all of my works, many of which extend far beyond what the "jazz" herd is doing.

I have composed and am mounting a martial arts ballet (*Once upon a Time in Chinese America ... A Martial Arts/Music/Theatre Epic*), a multimedia Black Panther ballet (*All Power to the People!*), a trickster/music theatre epic (*Journey Beyond the West: The New Adventures of Monkey!*), and a matriarchalist opera (*Warrior Sisters*). I lead one of the most unique "jazz" chamber orchestras, the Monkey Orchestra, a twelve-piece bug band of Chinese and Western instruments with vocals in Chinese. I have had to become a self-producing artist because of my unusual and radical musical, artistic, theatrical, and political vision, which cannot "fit" into conventional producing and presenting modes as they are presently configured. Fortunately, my political organizing skills have helped me as a producer-artist. But more than that, the movement's politics have informed and developed my own unique musical identity, voice, and vision.

The ultimate goal of revolutionary cultural work is to control our means of cultural production so that we do not have to appease funders nor compromise our integrity and principles to the corporate music industry or establishment arts institutions. In the absence of a revolutionary national organization or movement, I have finally been able to form my own production company, Big Red Media, Inc. (BRM).[15] It is not a collective as it might have been two decades ago because I have frankly not found sufficient ideological and political unity with enough professional artists to make feasible the combination of collective decision-making and shared economic risk venture. BRM is what I call a "guerrilla enterprise," of which I am the sole owner, although I employ and collaborate with many artists on the creation and presentation of my work, and with consultants who help support the business operations. BRM's mission is to produce revolutionary performances, recordings, publications, videos, and digital media. In its start-up phase, BRM primarily focuses on my work.

‹ 61

I have not begun to develop a strategy for alternative radical distribution, which will be key to busting the hegemony of the corporate media octopus. In many ways, such a distribution system will require the building of nationwide and international organization and networks that I as an artist cannot primarily do. I am always seeking skilled and radical organizers, but due to the general weakness of radicalism today, it is hard to expect people to devote their lives to such an enterprise with near-zero resources.

I still sell my recordings person-to-person at performances as I sold newspapers and publications when I was in a Leftist organization. Revolutionary ideological boldness and political activism continue to be essential to me, although figuring out how to survive and progress in a period when the movement is weak poses continual challenges. I have tried to sum up some of my key experiences in revolutionary cultural work. Hopefully, this discussion and analysis of my musical/political development offers lessons and clarity to both the struggle to create revolutionary art and to change the relations of cultural production, all of which, I have tried to argue, is shaped by and shapes the movement.

NOTES

1 National Endowment for the Arts Music Composition (1992) and Opera/Musical-Theater (1994) fellowships, and the 1988 Duke Ellington Distinguished Lifetime Achievement Award for the 17th Annual Black Musicians Conference, among others.

2 Fred Ho, "From Banana to Third World Marxist," in *Boyhood, Growing Up Male: A Multicultural Anthology*, edited by Franklin Abbott (Freedom, Calif.: Crossing Press, 1993), 195–99; and Fred Ho, "Marxism and Asian Americans," *Forward Motion: A Socialist Magazine* 11, no. 3 (July 1992): 66–72.

3 Recordings by Archie Shepp on the Impulse! label in the early 1970s, such as *Things Have Got to Change, Attica Blues,* and *The Cry of My People*, featured Cal Massey's work.

4 Ron Sakolsky and Fred Ho, *Sounding Off! Music as Subversion/Resistance/Revolution* (Brooklyn, N.Y.: Autonomedia, 1995).

5 Fred Ho, *Legacy to Liberation: Politics and Culture of Revolutionary Asian Pacific America* (San Francisco, Calif.: AK Press, 2000).

6 For more on these organizations, see Ho, *Legacy to Liberation.*

7 For more on these cultural forms, see Ho, *Legacy to Liberation.*

8 Maynard Solomon, "Zhdanovism," in *Marxism and Art* (Detroit: Wayne State University Press, 1979), 235–41.

9 Fred Houn, "Revolutionary Asian American Art: Tradition and Change, Inheritance and Innovation, Not Imitation!" *East Wind* 4, no. 1 (Spring/Summer 1986): 4–8. (Before fall 1988, I was known as Fred Houn.)

10 Sakolsky and Ho, *Sounding Off!*

11 Spelled with a "y" to take the "men" out.

12 Fred Ho and Carol Genetti, *Womyn Warriors/Sheroes* (Brooklyn, N.Y.: Autonomedia, 1998 and 1999).

13 See Assata Shakur, *Assata: An Autobiography* (New York: Lawrence Hill, 1988). The Black Liberation Army, an outgrowth of the Black Panthers, was the clandestine armed movement of the Black Liberation struggle in the United States.

14 From our own press material descriptions of *Night Vision: A New Third to First World Vampyre Opera.*

15 The Big Red Media Web site is accessible at http://www.bigredmediainc .com.

Interview with Chris Mitchell

FRED HO: That was a piece entitled *All Power to the People! The Black Panther Suite,* which we performed with my Afro Asian Music Ensemble in August 1999 at the Walker Art Center. That title was actually taken from a slogan raised by one of the founders of the Black Panther Party for Self-Defense, Huey P. Newton, as a way to popularize the concept of socialism. So, "All Power to the People" became a kind of anthemic slogan for that whole period of time, and continues to be one, in terms of the people taking control of everything.

RADICAL RADIO: *Excellent. Would you like to introduce yourself and say a bit about what you are doing here in the Twin Cities?*

I am concluding a residency that was funded by the McKnight Foundation and American Composers Forum to work with activists. In the first half of this residency I worked with Local 17 of the Hotel Employees and Restaurant Employees [International] Union. We put on a workers' cultural banquet at the Cedar Cultural Center back in February. I have been working this week on support work for the political prisoner on death row, Mumia Abu-Jamal. I am a composer, baritone saxophonist, bandleader of the Afro Asian Music Ensemble

Interview conducted by Chris Mitchell of Radical Radio at Macalester College, St. Paul, Minnesota, February 2001.

and the Monkey Orchestra, also a writer, producer, cultural activist, and activist in support of political prisoners.

Excellent, and you have something going tonight?

I am performing a solo baritone saxophone along with some local improvisers at a program at the Nobles [eXperimental] interMedia Studio, which is an experimental space in St. Paul.

We would like to continue on with the discussion we started last night on security culture, when it is healthy and when it isn't. You spoke here at Mac [Macalester College], [on] how to deal with it, basically.

I think that the real question that Krista was asking was how do we distinguish between real security and false security. Real security, because every movement has to protect itself, if we have a proper analysis of the state as an instrument of repression and class rule, and that the ultimate use of the state is to imprison, incarcerate, and actually kill and subdue movements for social change. Real security is based on having a strong position and support among the masses of people. When the escape of Assata Shakur took place and she went underground for four or five years, it was only because the people themselves believed in and supported Assata, that she could avoid an extensive woman hunt, manhunt, whatever you want to use if you want to be gender-neutral. In that case they were trying to capture Assata and she eluded capture for those years because of the support that the masses of people had for her and because of the physical organization that was set up. So, really, that is the nexus of it all that people don't understand, that true security can only be based upon how much mass and popular support you have and how much people are willing to protect you and defend you by any means necessary. So that is the real issue of support. People who are playing at being guerrillas get caught up into things like coded names, and elusive phone messages and ways of communication, and secrecy, and all these things. Those are really secondary measures that don't amount to a hill of beans if you don't have mass support. All revolutionary movements that have succeeded have done so because of that, because the people themselves will give you support, they will protect you, they will feed you, clothe you, and they will look after you and defend you. That is really the critical definition of what is true security, real security. All these other things are precautions that need to be done, however. I think that even in terms of those measures, they are simply minimal efforts. I think the greatest effort is that you have to have a very clear and united, politically and ideologically, group of people. They have to understand what the political strategy and the line is, that they have to be disciplined and both able to function creatively within the context of their political program and directives, and they have to be able to defend and articulate and promote the political line—in other words, what they are trying to achieve—in a very disciplined and creative fashion. So all these other little playthings at security are secondary to having consolidated political and ideological unity, clear direction, clear organization, and mass support. Once you have those things, then everything else falls within that context. So all these other things are really superficial and somewhat infantile measures. When you look at the sophistication of the state and the enemy that you are up against, they have much more sophistication, apparatus, training than almost any of us, per se. But when you look at what we have, we have clarity, we have a commitment, we have discipline, we have organization, and we have strategic vision. That is the problem, I think, with modern-day organizing and today's younger movements, that the question of ideology and political line seems to be very pushed to the side. Really, the key thing in order to ensure the longevity and security of a movement is that you have to have ideology. You have to have a framework in which you analyze things, in which, even if you don't know someone, if they are on the same page with you logically, you are able to critique and analyze things, you are able to solve problems together creatively, yet with unity. That is critical, and also understanding the political line. What is it that we are strategically doing, and how does everything fit within that? How do we discern who is an ally and who isn't? How all that fits in. Those things have been neglected. Largely in reaction to some of the errors my generation committed, over bureaucracy, commandism, over centralization, cult of personality, some of those mistakes. But the thing is not to throw the baby out with the bath

66 ›

water. The thing is to find what is useful and correct and effective and to build upon that.

I think that one thing you talked about last night, and one way in which you set up your talks, is to set up some ground rules. It seems that is a very healthy way of maintaining an organization. A lot of us on the left are pretty hesitant about setting rules and things like that. It seems like it is really important. I would like to recap some of those: being nonviolent with each other, being civil with each other. Is there anything else you would suggest?

I think the problem with younger activists is that you are getting your training from schools and professors who never were at the front lines, so to speak. You need to study the programs of revolutionary organizations: for example, you need to study the Black Panther Party, the Young Lords, I Wor Kuen. You look at their rules of membership and their rules of discipline, they enumerate certain things: for example, never to steal even a needle and thread from the people. A lot of people today glorify shoplifting or vandalism and those sorts of things. Those should only be done if they are politically directed and authorized to do so in a collective sense. To just do that randomly or as an individual act of rebellion serves nothing, in fact it really tends to alienate people who potentially could be supporters; even if they may not be direct activists, they could provide material resources, donate food, space, give cash, even free advertising at different points. I think we need to study these different rules of discipline. We had rules: for example, there was not to be use of any kind of intoxicants while doing political work. All money raised had to be turned in immediately to the district officer. All cadres had to carry the literature and be ready to recite the program instantaneously to people. These are the rules that made for effective political work. So, for example, when we had public events, for me it was important that debate and disagreement [were] encouraged, but that no one should play a disruptive role or monopolize that, particularly if you didn't organize the event, you are coming there to leech off of it, to soapbox at it, that is a wrong sort of thing, because you didn't do the work to build the event. So the people who organized and built the event have the authority, and I know that word doesn't sound good to many anarchists, but they actually do have the authority to establish the rules for the event, otherwise their work isn't respected. So then, everyone is a parasite and a leech. We have this libertarian sort of view that we don't have to do the work but we can come pimp off of it or we can leech off of it, and push our own things and grandstand and get on our soapbox, but don't respect the labor that others have done. Really, if you have any kind of respect for the working class, you know that it takes work to do these things. So, organizing is an activity of labor. You have to respect the work that people do, and the people who organize events have the right to establish the ground rules for these events. You do want to have feedback, you do want to have discussion, you do want to have polemics, but you want to be able to set a standard so that people's conduct doesn't attack someone, doesn't assault someone, but encourages people to think creatively and to disagree but to disagree in a way that helps to enhance the movement. We need to promote a culture in which respect and civility [are] the general norm and standard, but at the same time, not diminish ideological struggle. Ideological struggle oftentimes is circumvented by anarchistic-minded people simply by manipulating the agenda, or the people who can stay the latest at a meeting. You know, we can continue to debate into the wee hours of the night. You know working-class people have to go to bed and go to work the next morning. So, it is just a reflection of a certain kind of class privilege that needs to be recognized and struggled against. You can have disciplined agendas and so forth, and encourage controversy, polemics, debate, and discussion, but it has to be in a politically organized framework and be useful for everyone there.

That makes a lot of sense. In meetings, disregarding the fact of going long and discriminating against those who have to get up early in the morning. I think it is just disrespect for time, whether or not someone has to get up in the morning, no one wants to sit through a three- or four-hour meeting listening to one person talking about a certain issue or monopolizing the discussion and dragging things along. One thing that we have been discussing is dealing with state violence and how to protect ourselves from it. You gave a really good overview of how to insulate yourself from that by drawing support from the community. By drawing

lessons from the 1960s and 1970s, there is a model of armed resistance.
A friend of mine, for instance, in Virginia, an anarchist, has recently ap-
plied for a concealed-weapons permit and taken a pistol safety training
course. He feels more secure carrying a weapon around. My own view
tends to be that that is more likely to get you in trouble. I was wondering
what you think about that?

My personal feeling is that guns are for cowards. That is why the
state is doomed to fail, because it is run by a bunch of cowards who
can only maintain their hegemony, control, and rule simply because
of the monopolization of firearms. Not because of any moral righteousness, any ideological or intellectual depth, or security, but because they control all the guns. So, guns are essentially for cowards.
People who know that they would be swept off the face of history mo-
mentarily if the masses of people themselves, if they didn't have the
guns, the masses of people could recognize that and move forward.
Surge forward. I think that these kinds of things are secondary issues. I think the greatest security or strength one has is with political and ideological clarity, courage and commitment, good methods
of organization so that people respect you; they don't have to agree
with you, but they will defend you. They will defend your right to be
who you are, even if they don't agree with you, but because they know
that through your practice you stand for the interests of the people, that you are willing to sacrifice yourself for justice and for these
principles.

‹ 69

So, essentially, it is more about collective self-defense than individual
self-defense, it seems.

Partly, but even the issue of self-defense has to be looked at as a political one. In the sense of, you have to have political support for who
you are, first and foremost. For other issues that deal with the techniques of self-defense, I think a lot of that comes from being able
to discipline and train oneself to avoid unnecessary conflicts, and
be able to politically choose the battles that you want to fight. Obviously, in the face of armed assault, one has to be not naïve or pacifist
about it, but realize that turning the other cheek will only get you
two sore cheeks, and that you don't want to get your ass creamed,

so that you need to make all the necessary preparations to be able to take on the kind of assault that you are about to face. So, it is really being able to politically be able to read and analyze where your struggle is at, where the forces [are] that oppose you, where they are at, and be able to make the necessary preparations, but at the same time never neglect the need to politically prepare support for yourself, that people have to come and rally around you. That is the key way to fight armed repression.

I think that we will take a break here. This is from Fred Ho's Warrior Sisters. *We hope that you enjoy it.*

. . . .

We had a caller during the break; she wanted to ask Fred how he felt about ELF's tactics, which would be the Earth Liberation Front, and whether he would characterize their tactics as infantile or as productive.

I don't have direct experience with the Earth Liberation Front, so I will talk about this more generally and answer this from a general perspective. All tactics are evaluated based on a strategy of what you are trying to accomplish. The key thing is to be able to accomplish greater political support and mobilization for what you believe in, your principles. So I think all actions have to be based on evaluating their effectiveness, in terms of being able to generate much more political awareness and support for your goals. So, in that context, you evaluate particular actions. I think that there is always going to be a dual necessity for aboveground and underground activism going on. Obviously, you need to have an underground component because the state is a constant threat to both disrupt as well as squash the movement. However, the underground is only as strong as the aboveground. To what degree large numbers of people can be rallied, mobilized to support your overall political objectives. So, it is very important to have a program that is popularized and that people understand what it is, and your tactics have to fit that program, in terms of accomplishing what you are trying to achieve, illustrating concretely to people why certain steps are necessary in terms of their political development and why it is necessary to do this in order to get to a higher level of political engagement. I think it is wrong to presume that just because one has a consciousness oneself as an individual, that that somehow can be ignited through an act of martyrdom or an act of disruption against a corporation or government institution.... People ... involved in the long-haul revolutionary process, willing to die for their struggle, are willing to commit themselves to build, even more than just dying for it. The arduous task of the rebuilding of a new kind of society and figuring that out from scratch requires a process of transformation that is going to require patience, ground building, education, [and] ideological and political development. I think that any display of impatience, of the single spark kind of thing, that doesn't have political groundwork or preparation laid, is infantile and idealist in the sense that it somehow expects people to wake up because of an action that is done that may be outrageous. I think that it is a very romantic view of how revolution happens. Revolution happens person by person, and it is a wave that has to be built. Usually, it is not the act of individuals that would spark, but incidents—for example, the Rodney King verdict, when it came down, was the spark that ignited one of the biggest urban rebellions in America. It is not usually the individual actions of a small group of people that are the spark; it is the result of coming together of certain sociohistorical events.

‹ 71

One of the things that caught my eye, and this is a question of if maybe sometimes, effective small-scale, non-symbolic, but also maybe not contributing toward the overall revolutionary picture, if those actions are helpful. I think it was ELF that took credit for it recently. There is a large expansion of these neighborhoods moving away from the city, suburban sprawl, and recently I think there was a new construction area, they had just finished building seventeen new luxury homes, and ELF burned them all down. Is that sort of action effective at all and helpful, in your mind?

Depending on what the objective is; for example, if it was just to stop one housing development, it may have worked temporarily, but all housing developments are products of capitalist land speculation and the commodification of housing. So, unless you deal with some of these systemic issues that are going to require mass movements of tenants, of homeless people, of workers themselves that are involved in the construction trade. Unless there is going to be more long-term social transformation happening, then basically you are just dealing with symptoms. That is why, when Mao talks about how ultra-leftism is fundamentally rightism, meaning that adventurous kinds of acts contribute to the strengthening of the right because, (1) It alienates popular support; (2) It allows sections of the movement to become targets; (3) It strengthens the repressive forces and the justification of the use of repression by the state. So, we have to analyze things from the point of view of the balance sheets of political forces. The political sophistication of our movement needs to be bumped up quite a bit in terms of understanding that allies need to be built and that social change, revolution, is not a putschist, or guerrilla, small band activity, but is a mass movement. That is why, when we look at revolutions, in particular revolutions in the Third World, even though they have been led by vanguard parties, they have had mass support in order to be victorious, in order to overcome a superior force, that has lost moral as well as any kind of political support. I think we have to look at this as a long-term strategy of how do you build social change, support for ending these atrocities against nature, against human beings, and for people to come to accept that we are going to eventually need revolution. I think that winning people over to the concept of revolution is the key thing in terms of what tactics to use. If it doesn't win people over to that, then we have actually strengthened the state.

One thing I think about a lot, though, that short-term alienation sometimes is necessary to wake people up. It's a very elitist, arrogant view in some ways, but I will just use an example here at Macalester. About two years ago, the United States commenced Operation Desert Fox against Iraq, and initiated the heaviest bombing since the Gulf War, and while bombing is nowhere near as destructive to the Iraqi people as the sanctions are, it was still a catalyst that turned a lot of people at Macalester out. What we did, a number of us got involved in a lot of really radical actions that really pissed off a lot of people in the Macalester community. One of the things we did was to chain shut the doors of the administration building. People were saying that that was the wrong target, that we should be chaining shut the doors of the foreign policy makers in D.C. One of the other things that we did was to slip a piece of paper under people's doors saying that finals had been cancelled; it was the day of finals. It was a very provocative act that really upset a lot of people, and at the same time, others and I defended those actions because I felt they were necessary. When you look at what happened in the end, even though people were upset with us as individuals in the short run, by the next semester, everybody knew what was happening in Iraq and when people looked at the situation, a lot of them began realizing that the U.S. government was by its nature acting in a beyond unfair, in an imperialistic and destructive manner. While that knowledge may not be changing anything, I think it is definitely a step. I think that short-term alienation can be effective.

Well, it has to be coupled with a broader plan and use of strategy and tactics. Just that alone is not enough, because somebody else will have to do the preparation and do the education and the defense work. I think these tactics are part of a mixed approach of struggle and I think that the problem is, that, if I may use postmodern language, privileging one form of tactics over another, in the sense that a broad use of tactics is going to be necessary to win over different kinds of people and to produce different kinds of results among different kinds of people at different levels of consciousness. So, the whole thing, however, is that coordination of the use of tactics based upon a strategic view needs to be done and we don't have that. We don't have the presence of professional revolutionaries or cadres coordinating the use of these tactics so that we can gain maximum effectiveness out of them. Unfortunately, sometimes they are done in isolation, oftentimes fragmented and disconnected from each other. The consequence of that is that the state is capable of attacking us on many levels and many fronts, obviously through outright repression, through the police, through the courts, putting us on probation, through intellectual media slanders and those sorts of things. Our approach has to be multifaceted as well, and work on many levels and many fronts, the more sophisticated the development of revolutionary organization. For example, I feel that the environmental ecology radicals need to unite with the social justice and the oppressed nationality radicals, and that it's part of what it means to develop a revolutionary party, if you will, so that all these various social movements come under joint leadership, and can be more effective in their coordination and their allocation of resources and forces and be able, at a moment's notice, to shift, change, and readjust as the struggle goes through twists and turns. The whole thing is to be able to develop a higher level of political sophistication and organizational operation and to be able to understand that struggle happens on many fronts and at different levels. To be self-righteous and to say that only one is going to work or that only one is the true way to do things is just to be immature and wrong, immature and incorrect.

We are going to hear another selection from your CD, The Underground Railroad to My Heart.

This is a piece sung in Chinese called "Lan Hua Hua," which in Mandarin means "blue flower." It is an early folk song that was introduced to me by the singer on this recording, Cindy Zuoxin Wang, that came from eighth-century China, and was a protest against arranged marriages, which were part of the oppression of women in feudal China. It is a part of my own investigation of peasant and working-class songs of resistance, as part of my developing a radical new Asian American culture.

I have a question about what we can do as students, how we can get outside of the classroom, to learn what we believe in, how we can get involved, what activists are doing, and how we can build a base for the rest of our lives.

Theory and practice need to be developed simultaneously, and one of the advantages that students have, in being in colleges and universities, is the ability to study. Not to take that lightly, particularly study that helps build revolutionary consciousness and the ability to analyze the world around you. That doesn't necessarily mean going to all the classes and so forth, but it does mean that where you can, in the sense that there aren't professors and classes suitable for the kind of studies that you want to do, that you set up independent study, for credit or not for credit. You must be able to use the intellectual resources here, as well as funding, to promote revolutionary education and consciousness. Second, I think it is important not to be isolated but to develop links, ties, and alliances with many groups outside of the campus community, in the larger community, [with] the struggles of other social movements and organizations that may not be on campus. To be able to help them out, help students get outside of campus to work with these groups, that kind of exchange is very important. Third, I think it is important while you are students to struggle with one another about what you are going to do with your lives, what it means to make a commitment, what it means to stay in the struggle for the long haul, to figure out these questions, to argue and debate with one another. You are part of a generation that must struggle to define its mission, and, as Franz Fanon put forward, choose to either fulfill it or betray it. You need to discuss what your worldview is and what you want to do, what kinds of organizations you want to build and be a part of when you finish school, how you can still stay a part of the movement for social change in America and the world. I think these are some of the things that can be done.

‹ 75

For people who haven't really gotten off the campus and they don't really know how to get involved, sometimes it's kind of hard to find a niche and how to be active when you really want to be active. Do you have any suggestions about certain ways or certain groups that you can suggest?

Well, I am not from the Twin Cities; I am from New York and I can give you lots of suggestions there. However, just from the time I have been here in the Twin Cities, there are certain things, progressive, alternative outlets that people can go to, like Arise Bookstore and Mayday Books. People can also follow the mainstream media and see what are the struggles that are out there and go to programs, to demonstrations, events, fundraisers, and so forth, and learn more about what is going on in the surrounding community. It is part of being attuned to and in touch with the social environment we are in and not being cloistered on campuses. Whereas, I think that the main responsibility for students, while you are on campus, is that you should be organizing on campus and raising consciousness.

During last night's discussion, you said that you were a proponent of matriarchal socialism, and I was wondering why matriarchal, instead of socialism based only on equality?

Well, equality is matriarchy, if you want to look at true social justice. If women are the majority of the world's population, they bear 100 percent of the world's children, they do 70 percent of the world's work, grow 60 percent of the world's food, but only have 10 percent of the world's income and own less than 1 percent of the world's property, then true fundamental social change will be a radical transformation of the condition and position of women throughout the world. That will mean a considerable amount of power going to women because of their historical and ongoing social identity, in the sense of being producers, and doing the majority of the work and growing most of the world's food. That would mean a rightful and just return of the resources and benefits from that activity that has been unrewarded, unrecognized, devalued, denigrated, marginalized, excluded, neglected; it would be a return of what is rightfully theirs. To me, what most people are unfamiliar with, and some people are uncomfortable with, is that adjective, matriarchal socialism. To me that is what socialism is. Or, communism, actually, where [there is] true equality and the elimination of classes, where each person gets according to what they need, based on a rightful distribution of what one contributes; then women will hold the majority of the world's resources and power. I am not an anarchist; I am a socialist, a revolutionary socialist. I believe that we are still going to need to have states. So, how do we have noncoercive, nonhierarchical, nonmilitaristic states? We have never had a military in human history, except in a few isolated instances, of matriarchal armies. In fact, in one of my operas, *Warrior Sisters: The New Adventures of African and Asian Womyn Warriors,* it kind of explores that whole question of developing matriarchal guerrilla armies. If women held all the guns, do you think there would be violence against women? Do you think domestic violence would continue? Do you think the inferior treatment of women would continue? Do you think sexism would continue? That is different from a patriarchal army that integrates women into it, as women join the U.S. military in large numbers and are recruited. That is different because we are talking about a fundamentally different kind of social power. To me, patriarchal socialism is completely unacceptable and is an oxymoron. That is not what we are struggling for. What we are struggling for is true gender equality, but true gender equality does not exist in the abstract. It means returning to women all that they have been denied and deprived of and disempowered from, including the use of force. So that is what matriarchal socialism is about. It is a wild concept for many people, but I think if you do serious reflection and analysis, and come to understand that women were the first and the longest class, that the overthrow of women—as Marx and Engels talked about the origin of the family, the state, and private property—that women were the first class to be overthrown. The male monopolization of the means of violence institutionalized the state, institutionalizes patriarchy, and institutionalizes class division.

I am really interested in the dynamic of gender in the Black Panther Party. A lot of us at Macalester don't know much about the Black Panther Party, and you have had first-hand experience. It seems to be that the talk was always good at the top levels of the organization, at least Huey P. Newton seemed very much against patriarchy, but it seems like there was also a large movement within the Panthers that was also macho, masculine, and very patriarchal.

‹ 77

Well, the danger, and I want to address it head on, the danger with this discussion is that it has been framed by academicians who weren't there, who weren't part of that historical process, part of the struggle. People like bell hooks, like Michelle Wallace, I consider to be frauds, because they are trying to make a critique when they themselves took no responsibility, were not participants themselves, and are trying to apply a late-twentieth-century academic feminism to a social movement that was of tremendous upheaval, figuring out things as it was going along, in the heat of struggle and fierce repression. So, the Black Panther Party Central Committee had one woman, Kathleen Neal Cleaver, who was an actual participant and has right to "First Voice," meaning that we should respect people who are actually part of the struggle and engaged in it, and their analysis should be studied very seriously. She has a brilliant article about gender and the Black Panther Party in the journal called *New Political Science*. The journal is devoted to the subject of the Black Panther Party. The article looks at it in the correct context, in the sense that the Black Panther Movement and the Black Liberation struggle brought in thousands upon thousands of women who never were politicized before; revolutionized gender roles for women who were expected to become housewives, get married, take menial secretarial jobs; and brought them into revolutionary political life on the order of tens of thousands and many of them became fierce leaders. We can talk about Assata Shakur, Safiya Bukhari: these are sisters who are leaders and faced severe repression, incarcerated, and, in the case of Assata, put in maximum-security prison and is now in exile, a fugitive, if you will, in Cuba.

The Black Panther Party, the Black Liberation struggle reflected the contradictions of society, but at the same time endeavored to come up with revolutionary solutions to those contradictions. It didn't solve everything; obviously the movement was crushed, largely by the state. It had its own errors, its own failings, and its own mistakes. However, through the lessons and analysis drawn by people like Kathleen Cleaver, we begin to understand that more women were revolutionized and gender roles were massively transformed, than had ever happened before. The fact is that it didn't go as far as one would like in terms of how one measures it today, but one only measures what has happened today as a result of the foundations that were laid through that upsurge. So that to dismiss the movement as male-centered or macho is an irresponsible criticism that doesn't look at the proper context of how things were unfolding and developing and changing dramatically. For example, black women were no longer straightening their hair: the whole concept of the Afro was highly publicized by the Black Liberation struggle and the Panthers; the image of women carrying guns, for instance, or grandmothers packing pistols, the images that were popularized in the cartoons of Emory Douglas and so forth, are radically different images.

Today, this young generation, no matter how it likes to posture about being militant, can't even match. The fact that women from all walks of life, particularly poor, working-class women, were radicalized and brought into political life and activity is a testament to how tremendous the legacy of the Panthers has been. I think it's a problem in terms of these armchair academic feminists who want to try to apply their criteria to a movement that none of them actually contributed to or participated in, and didn't understand the day-to-day struggles one had to do to change people who were conditioned by society from years and years of conventions, of expectations, of family roles, and so forth. It was a huge undertaking, and it was quite dramatic in terms of what happened. That doesn't excuse or mean that we should not take the struggle for gender transformation or equality even further than what has happened before. I think the main thing is that one has to give history a proper and objective assessment, and not a prejudiced and biased one. Overall, women's roles were radically transformed and changed and developed, and tens of thousands of women were brought into radical political activism as a result of it, so it was overwhelmingly positive, with some errors and mistakes and things that needed to be corrected. Nonetheless, it was a revolutionary leap from what had happened before. These same academics never credit the women warriors who do come forward, because they are so self-serving; they want themselves to be the glamour, in the center, in the limelight all the time. They don't look at, for example, the women who are discussed in my Womyn Warriors and Sheroes calendar that comes out every year, where we celebrate 365 women, one woman for every day of the year, who are transgressors, rebels, and revolutionaries who challenged the prevailing society, broke the molds, fought foreign aggression, and exacted tremendous sacrifices, including assassination.

I have a question. When we were in Washington D.C. for the inauguration, there was a lot of hype about the New Black Panther Party. Is that in any way related to the Black Panther Party?

Well, there are offshoots from the Black Panther Party out there now. The best thing is to go to this Web site and subscribe to the newsletter, "It's About Time"; the Web site is www.itsabouttimebpp.com. It's an attempt to look at all the activism that is going on among former Panthers as well as offshoots of the Panther tradition going on nationally. It is a fairly ecumenical, nonsectarian journal. I am going to meet a lot of these people in Sacramento. I am doing a benefit for them. I think it bodes well. The revolutionary legacy of the Panthers, particularly as more political prisoners come out, as Geronimo Pratt was released, he punches right into activism again. And then you also have these celebrity ones who get book deals and put on fancy speaking tours; I think you have to take them with a grain of salt. Or all these performers who try to do these one-man bio shows, and deal with the Panther leaders as sociopaths and not as revolutionaries. We are all, by nature of being human beings, flawed people. But the thing is really to understand and study the history of the Panthers. It was a young movement, young people your age in their twenties, some of them teenagers, fighting day-to-day with a tremendous amount of aggression against them, trying to figure out how to move forward in very hostile circumstances. Many mistakes were made, but at the same time many victories and triumphs were made. But just think of the toll, thirty Panthers killed, over one thousand put in jail; most of the ranks of political prisoners today in jail came from the ranks of the Black Panther Movement.

I always think that being part of a cultural event helps to humanize and provide some kind of aesthetics to our activism, and we can hopefully come to appreciate the many colors of human expression and appreciate the beauties expressed in all these different forms, especially through music.

We are going to be talking now about the politics of race in revolutionary movements. Last night you commented that there are few white political prisoners now. Perhaps you can comment on that.

Well, there are fewer now, fortunately, with the conditional amnesty that was granted to people like Susan Rosenberg, Linda Evans, and my good friend Laura Whitehorn, so people have been released, fortunately, along with the five Puerto Rican activists, released, I think, in the summer of 1999. Those are all welcome developments. Any political prisoner is too many. The brunt of repression was faced by the oppressed nationality revolutionaries, African Americans, Latinos, and their white anti-imperialist North American comrades. All political prisoners need our support and need to be freed because they are suffering from sentences that are unduly harsh and extended primarily because of their political beliefs and activism. In the case of Leonard Peltier, we need to do our utmost to work for his freedom, and especially for Mumia Abu-Jamal, because he is the only political prisoner facing the death sentence, for what I believe is a crime he did not commit. His right to due process and the evidence and the whole circumstance around his trial were completely unfair and unjust. I am also completely against capital punishment and the death penalty. It is interesting that capital punishment has never been used for capitalists.

That is an astute observation. It is interesting watching that capital punishment doesn't only extend to political revolutionaries. Just recently, Shaka Sankofa, victim of what many consider to be a lynching in Texas, as a result of one witness changing her testimony—first saying that it wasn't him, then saying that it was him—on that basis having him executed. There is a movement now to have a moratorium on the death penalty, not abolition, but a moratorium, and I was wondering what you thought of that?

Well, a moratorium is good, but we need to abolish the death penalty. We need to join the rest of the industrialized world, which has abolished capital punishment altogether. This country has the dubious reputation of having the highest incarceration rate of any industrialized nation in the world, five times higher than the South Africa regime under apartheid. So, I think that most people recognize that capital punishment is cruel and unusual punishment in the sense that it is irreversible, it's capricious, it's racist, it's classist, and it doesn't do anything to deter crime in society. So, it doesn't work and it is inhumane and cruel.

‹ 81

There is something I would like to throw out to my right-wing buddies out there, who are very nationalistic and proud of the United States. In 1997, the governments that killed the most of their own people per capita in this world were, I mixed up the order of the first four, but the last two are correct: the top four were Iran, Iraq, North Korea, Nigeria; number five was Texas and number six was Florida. Our states are killing more people than most other governments in this world—I think that is quite a statement. Looking at the way the death penalty is applied, it is usually against poor people ...

Poor, uneducated people.

Yes, because their generally white lawyers are usually public defenders and the prosecutors are more likely to bring those charges against someone who is poor and not white. But moving on, I would like to talk about the role of culture, arts, and music in the movement. It is something you are very involved in. Your music is not distributed by Sony or any of the big labels; I was wondering how you get it out there and how we can get hold of it?

I primarily record for small, alternative, however prestigious labels. I guess I have been successful as a composer, bandleader, and musician, in the sense that I am one of the few people who can make a living from what he does and not have to compromise my political positions. I feel very fortunate in that respect. Currently I have bought up all my own back stock from as many labels as I used to record for, and I probably have about fifteen recordings now as a leader under my own name. I would encourage everyone to check out my Web site, www.bigredmedia.com. You can order my music online or come to my shows and buy them directly. I have just entered into a partnership with a local label called Innova Recordings, part of a non-profit group called the American Composers Forum here in St. Paul. I would encourage independent artists to check out what is going on with Innova Recordings in the sense that it allows for complete artistic freedom and control over what you are doing. The trade-off with all of that is that we have to pay for it ourselves, but I would rather do that and have the control over it. So, my production company, Big Red Media, is entering into a partnership with Innova Recordings. Their Web site is www.innovarecordings.org. And a project I did called "The Way of the Saxophone," featuring a group that I co-lead, called The Brooklyn Sax Quartet, has just come out, and a new CD of mine will come out very soon, a musical soundtrack of a martial arts ballet called *Once upon a Time in Chinese America,* which we may even have copies of this evening for the show.

I think the main issue that faces artists is: how do you resist being commodified and commercialized by the mainstream music business? The only answer to that is, for every Rage against the Machine, which we know has dissolved, there are hundreds of other artists who can't get signed. The whole filtering-out process of artists who do make it in the mainstream is so intense that it is almost a fairy tale to become signed on a mainstream label. Most of us should wake up from that fairy-tale dream and realize that we have to be independent organizers, cultural organizers, and activists and learn how to self-produce and be self-reliant. That is the critical thing. We can welcome a diversity of expressions and have camaraderie. We should be trying to improve the production quality of what we are doing, develop our aesthetic concepts further, expand the forms of our music, push the boundaries, educate audiences and listeners, not play down to them or perform down to them, not ape and imitate mainstream popular trends, to really truly be the original transgressor—unique, radical, fresh, genre-busting, cross-cultural, and visionary in what we do. That is how we are going to help people in the movement in the sense that the movement should not be locked into stereotyped, homogeneous, imitative kinds of forms. Oftentimes, whereas I might like the lyrics of a performer, but find their music to be very tired or repetitive, or not challenging enough. I think we need to have both aspects of it, otherwise we fall into the realm of simply becoming propagandists and cheerleaders for certain kinds of causes and we don't push the form itself, the craft itself. When we think of what it is going to take to build a new society from the ground up in terms of figuring out how to design things like buildings, furniture, to meet the needs of people in terms of food production, all these kinds of things, yet not get into hierarchy, exploitation, artificialness, reliance upon marketing and subterfuge advertising, deceptive advertising. All these questions require complex and sophisticated efforts to address them and not simple-mindedness. I think that having a sophisticated, complex, and rich cultural life is part of developing a creative and sophisticated political movement.

‹ 83

The revolution will be improvised, right?

Improvised and composed, both.

OK, I was wondering if briefly we could talk about the role of jazz in the movement, as giving people energy as a musical form.

Well, one of the things I have to correct is that I don't use the word "jazz," because in my understanding of its etymology, it is a racial slur. There are many interpretations of where the word comes from, but basically it is associated with prostitution, from the word "jizz" or "jism," which means semen, the slang term for semen, or from the French word "jaser," which means to chatter nonsensically or gibberish. In any case, it is like the words "Oriental," "Hispanic," "Negro." These are terms that people did not give to themselves but were labeled. Our language continues to be filled with these terms that we did not create or define. It took the Asian movement to discard the term "Oriental" or the Black Liberation struggle to discard the word "Negro." It is going to take a similar kind of cultural revolution to come up with a new term for twentieth-century African American music or revolutionize that term itself so that it doesn't become the kind of stereotyped concept that is promoted these days.

So, for me, this music of the twentieth-century African American tradition has been a vanguard cultural expression in the sense that it has been very sophisticated, complex, and, at the same time, highly improvised. It is what I call a "perpetually vernacular avant-garde." I don't want to seem too pedantic about this, but basically it's avant-garde in the sense that it is about innovation and experimentation as it reflects the needs of the people, of the African American oppressed nation for liberation. It is the musical vanguard of the black nation. It epitomizes that in the sense of being internationalist and incorporating influences from Asia, Latin America, from the whole world, and at the same time never allowing itself to be assimilationist, always being firm in its projection of African American identity and consciousness.

So, I know last night we spoke about the whole thing, race versus nation. I think again one of the damages that your generation has faced from only getting its Left politics from academia is that race has become the main thing, and the national questions have been eliminated. The problem with race is that it doesn't acknowledge the fundamental struggle for land and territory. The oppression of an entire people comes from the conquest of their territory, land, and resources that have come from the wealth of their labor and their work in a particular national territory. So, for example, I am of the opinion that enslaved Africans who were brought to the United States and concentrated in what is referred to as the Black Belt South, basically their blood, sweat, and tears and labor provided the wealth for the development of American capitalism, but they were never allowed to get their 40 acres and a mule once Reconstruction happened. Therefore, they were denied control of the means of production, so they became an oppressed nation. That is still a debated question in the Left, whether black people constitute an oppressed nation in the South. Even more clear is the Chicanos, since that territory in the Southwest, from San Francisco to Denver, actually belonged to Mexico and was seized by the United States through the war with Mexico in the mid-nineteenth century and the rights that were supposed to be granted to the indigenous people of that territory, both of Mexican and native descent, were never honored through the Treaty of Guadalupe Hidalgo, so the national rights of these people were discarded. So there are many oppressed nations here, including indigenous people, African Americans, Chicanos, Hawaiians. Puerto Rico is a colony, clearly. The fifty-first state in America may be Puerto Rico; this just represents the adding on of territory seized through conquest. The problem of race is that it primarily juxtaposes the political question as one of integration, as one of learning how to get along with one another, and not dealing with the question of returning land and territory and national equality. So it is about how to get rid of our racist ideas or how do we deal with white privilege. White privilege is only one phenomenon of national oppression. The privileges happen because of the inequality between peoples, of which the first basis was depriving people of their national territory, their right to the resources and control over land and territory and the absorption or assimilation of that territory and those people into this mythical white-supremacist thing called America. African Americans become black Yankees. In other words, they identify through assimilation with the imperialist history and values of the United States, as opposed to seeing themselves as an oppressed nation or oppressed nationalities. As Malcolm X says, "We are not Americans, we are victims of America." When people say "south," it means south of the Canadian border. So, it is these kinds of concepts that unfortunately the Left has been derailed by, largely because the revolutionary movements of the 1960s and 1970s were crushed and were co-opted and academia came to fill in the vacuum with stupid notions such as postmodernism, and so forth. The white Left was obviously not attacked as heavily as the movements of oppressed nationalities, so you have intellectuals who are basically liberal integrationists who did not want to accept these more revolutionary concepts of return of land, return of wealth, reparations, for instance.

In Africa, the culture is very much based around music, social criticism comes through music, and a lot of the struggles were really put out well by a lot of musicians. Fela Anikulapo Kuti had a lot of problems with the state in Nigeria and Ghana, and I know that his music, which is Afro beat, the style that he developed and a lot of the ideas that he developed were influenced when he came to the United States in 1969 and met some of the Panthers. He got this idea that there was this link combining black people throughout the world and he based a lot off of that. I also really like that there is a lot of social criticism and a lot of honesty in African music. Do you have anything to say about Fela or about African music?

Fela was definitely ahead of his time; he was a Pan-Africanist. He believed in some kind of—he was not, like most of us artists, we don't have all the details worked out, because we are not social theorists or social policy makers, but he believed in a United States of Africa concept, something that Kwame Nkrumah put forward in the late 1950s. I was very fortunate to be in Nigeria and to visit Fela's shrine and to meet members of his family. Again, Fela had many contradictions: I am not sure if you would have wanted to have been one of his forty wives, though I don't put any value judgment on that per se. Fela's main contribution, if we are to properly contextualize people, is that he was a great artist, a radical artist, a voice of Pan-Africanism, certainly an anti-imperialist who scathingly condemned both the sellout of the Nigerian government to Exxon and to Shell Oil and also to U.S. and British imperialism. He paid a heavy price for it; he was imprisoned, his mother and he were thrown off the second floor of his house, his house was burned to the ground, and he was certainly hated by both the local Nigerian ruling class and by the imperialists. Only now are we beginning to get the CD releases of Fela's music. I understand that there is a lot of dispute and legal scrambling over the rights to his music. A number of his CDs have been bootlegged without proper royalty agreements and so forth. To me Fela has been an inspiration; I have all of his recordings, the ones that I can find. I think more people need to hook into Fela. I think Fela stands in a category by himself. I am more critical of some of the other Afro beat musicians, who I feel have succumbed to commercialism, but I feel like Fela falls into a category and class by himself, and I think we need to honor artists like Fela.

We would like to thank Fred Ho for being here.

What Makes "Jazz" the Revolutionary Music of the Twentieth Century, and Will It Be Revolutionary for the Twenty-first Century?

I DO NOT USE the term "jazz,"[1] as I do not use such terms as *Negro, Oriental,* or *Hispanic.* Oppressed peoples suffer when their history, identity, and culture are defined, (mis)represented, and explicated by our oppressors. The struggle to redefine and reimage our existence involves the struggle to reject the stereotyping, distortions, and devaluation embodied in the classifications of conquerors and racists. The struggle over how to describe past and present reality is the struggle to change reality, and the continued usage of the term "jazz" persists in marginalizing, obfuscating, and denying the fact that this music is quintessentially American music. However, it is the music of an American oppressed nationality and not the music of the dominant, American, white, European heritage. It is white-supremacist racism that will not properly and justly accept both the music and its creators in a position of equality.

As a result of the movement of oppressed peoples that exploded in the 1960s, we have replaced terms such as *Negro* with *black* or *African American,* and *Oriental* with *Asian* or *Asian American.* More problematical are *Hispanic* (literally, of or belonging to Spain) and *Latino* (emphasizing, again, the Latin or European). I personally use "Spanish-speaking oppressed nationalities" when referring to Puerto Ricans, Dominicans, Chicanos, Central and South Americans, and Caribbean peoples in the United States whose only commonal-

Published in *African American Review* 29, no. 2 (1995).

ity is that they speak Spanish (and even that Spanish has national peculiarities). However, a satisfactory replacement for "jazz" has yet to emerge and continues to be part of the ongoing struggle to dismantle white supremacy and Eurocentrism in American culture and society. At times, certain descriptors have gained some currency, such as Rahsaan Roland Kirk's "Great Black Music," or Archie Shepp's "African American Instrumental Music," or Max Roach's preference: "The music of Louis Armstrong, the music of Charles Parker, etc." Billy Taylor simply said "twentieth-century American music." Some might argue that "jazz" should be reclaimed and that its meaning should be transformed from a pejorative term and usage to a statement of celebratory "in-your-face" defiance—as militant gays and lesbians have reappropriated the once-derogatory and insulting *queer* and *fag*. *Black* was once a term loaded with negativity that the Black Liberation Movement transformed to symbolize pride and self-respect.

92 ›

It took a movement of oppressed peoples to adopt new terms and meanings for self-determination and to replace reactionary and oppressive ones. Nineteenth-century racist blood-quantum legislation in the United States had determined anyone with "one drop" of African blood to be "black." Yet African Americans are a hybrid: neither mainly "African" nor "American" (in its dominant, mainstream understanding and context). They have a "kreolized"[2] identity—a revolutionary new cultural and social identity, forged in struggle against an oppressive society that still largely excludes, denies, and denigrates (i.e., "niggerizes" or "chinkifies" or "specifies") entire peoples. Indeed, the struggle of oppressed nationalities in the United States is to transform the very concept of "American" to its multicultural, multinational, multilingual reality. That struggle is inherently revolutionary: More than a proclamation of multiculturalism or integration into the dominant mainstream, it aims to dismantle the entire institutional power of white supremacy and Eurocentrism. Only when that happens will "jazz" become American music.

Yet, as the twentieth century comes to an end, we find a curious phenomenon: "Jazz" has become accepted into the halls of American (white, mainstream) cultural citadels. We find "Classical Jazz at Lincoln Center." We find a black artistic director criticizing other black musicians for not playing "black music." We find the internecine war over what is and what isn't "jazz" and who should define it. I will argue in this essay that, ironically, it is those most bent on defining and essentializing "jazz" that are indeed its greatest enemies, because they contradict the revolutionary essence of the music.

Defining and representing "jazz" is highly and inescapably political, and it seems to me that the politics of music must be understood both sociologically and musicologically—in a dialectical, interdependent, and interactive manner. Yet much of the literature has focused on sociohistory (e.g., LeRoi Jones's *Blues People*, which argues that black music changed as black people changed), ideology (e.g., Frank Kofsky's *Black Nationalism and the Revolution in Music*, which assesses the music's sociopolitical content via the consciousness/attitudes of the musicians), or political economy (a lot of writing on the profiteering and exploitation of black music and artists). Only the work of Christopher Small (*Music of the Common Tongue* [London: River Run Press, 1987]), a British musicologist, systematically attempts to examine "jazz" or African American music primarily from a musical/aesthetical perspective.

‹ 93

As a young Chinese (Asian) American growing up in the 1970s I was profoundly drawn to and inspired by African American music as the expression of an oppressed nationality, because of its social role as protest and resistance to national oppression, and for its musical energy and revolutionary aesthetic qualities. I identified with its pro-oppressed, anti-oppressor character: with the militancy the musicians displayed, with its social history of rebellion and revolt, and with its musical defiance to not kow-tow to, but challenge and contest, Western European "classical" music and co-opted, diluted, eviscerated commercialized forms that became American pop music.

"Jazz" or African American music is the revolutionary music of the twentieth century—not just for America, but for the planet as well. It is the music that embodies and expresses the contradiction of the century, fundamentally rooted to the world's division between oppressor, imperialist nations and the struggle of the oppressed nationals and nationalities. Its historical emergence and development parallel the rise and development of imperialism—the globalization of finance capital—at the turn of the century. Its musical and stylistic innovations reflect the changes in the twentieth-century life of the African American oppressed nationality.

"Jazz" is the music of the emerging African American proletariat or urban, industrial working class. Its predecessor, blues, was the music of post-Reconstruction. Just as old socioeconomic formations persist while new ones supplant them, so also do musical forms overlap. One exception is the persistence of pre-twentieth-century Western European "classical" music today—a result of the continual institutional/cultural expression of white settler-colonialism in North America.

"Jazz" emerged as formerly rural African American laborers traveled north to urban industrial and commercial centers of Chicago, Kansas City, Detroit, St. Louis, New York, and Philadelphia. A new music arose with a new class of urban workers, grafting the rich and unique African American music of formerly enslaved plantation laborers, rural tenant farmers, and migratory workers onto a sophisticated, cosmopolitan, industrial, and multiethnic urban culture of growing capitalist America.

No longer Southern, blues, or field songs, the music draws on all these cultural precedents and transforms them. All of the characteristics of African American music that are distinctive and transformative of Western European concert music are retained but intensified. The Western European concert tradition of a metronomic sense of time and general singularity of rhythm vis-à-vis the grafting of West African multiple and layered rhythms produces the polyrhythmicality of African American twentieth-century music; the fixed pitch and fixed diatonic temperament of Western European concert music vis-à-vis West and Central African oral tradition produces a revolutionary unity of composition and improvisation for twentieth-century African American music; and the primacy of the conductor and composer for Western European concert music vis-à-vis call and response/soloist-leader and group leads to the player-as-leader-as-soloist-as-virtuoso improviser/performer/composer.

The music develops a high degree of sophistication and complexity, utilizing and combining features of both the compositional/notational and improvisational/oral traditions. Yet, due to national oppression, "jazz" was, ironically, spared the canonization and institutionalization that the concert music of Western Europe underwent as part of the establishment of white-supremacist settler-colonialism in U.S. society. Thus, the music became *both* folk/popular music and an art/classical music that could be performed and enjoyed in not only the "lowest" of venues but also the "highest" concert halls. Until recently, the music, by virtue of its very position as the creative expression of an oppressed nationality excluded from most of American mainstream society (except when acceptably "covered" by white artists), resisted the calcification and ossification that "classical" music had undergone. For the most part, "jazz" has never looked back to the past as "classical" music has—fixated upon finer and finer degrees of perfection in the interpretation of past, "classic" treasures. Rather, "jazz" has been about the present ("Now Is the Time") and the future ("Space Is the Place").

Its entire history has been the freeing of time, pitch, and harmony from fixed, regulated, predictable standards. Every major innovation in the history of the music has been from the struggle of musicians to attain greater and greater levels of expressive freedom through liberating the two basic fundamentals of music: time (meter) and sound (pitch/temperament/harmony). I shall briefly discuss the basic changes that have resulted from this process of music making.

New and Reconfigured Instrumentation

A new instrument was introduced to the world of music during the 1890s and early 1900s in the United States: the drum kit.[3] The multiple, layered rhythms of both West African and New Orleans drum ensembles merged into a kit played by one person instead of several players. For the first time, one individual using all four limbs played several percussion parts simultaneously.

European instruments such as the piano and bass violin (strong bass) were transformed both in their role and in their manner of playing. In the Western European orchestra, their roles were primarily melodic. But in the African American music ensemble, both instruments became part of the "rhythm section." The piano's role is both rhythmic and harmonic. The string bass, now rarely played in its traditionally Western European arco, or bowed, manner, is played primarily pizzicato, or plucked, supplying rhythm, keeping time, and providing a harmonic foundation. Piano playing (especially in "comping"–from the word "ac*comp*animent") now involves a rhythmic approach to harmony, supplying chordal/harmonic percussion-like rhythms. By the 1960s, as musicians sought more boldly to escape from fixed, Western temperament, the piano was either left out entirely or played without regard to conventional harmony. Pulse and some establishment of tonality were left to the bass. Even the drum kit was no longer confined to keeping time or to meter. Certainly Max Roach since the 1940s has demonstrated the melodic artistry of the drum kit.

Probably the most characteristically "jazz" instrument is still the saxophone. Created by a Belgian, Adolphe Sax, in the mid-nineteenth century,[4] the saxophone would have become an obsolete, novelty instrument, archived in some works by French and Belgian composers, if it were not for its role in twentieth-century African American music. Replacing the clarinet, the saxophone became the "voice" of the "jazz band." Heretofore, popular music had been predominantly a vocal music. But with the saxophone, an instrumental popular music had emerged. Much has been made of the saxophone's vocal qualities. In the clearest of examples of the dialectical nature of African American twentieth-century music, horns perform like voices (from the cries, shouts, screams, hollers, and talkin' to its yakety-yak, burlesquey humor, and caricature) and voices perform like horns (from the inflection and phrasing of the human voice to "scat" soloing, etc.).

Indeed, every feature of the music is an expression of revolutionary dialectics. Demarcations are dissolved between soloist and ensemble; among the elements of melody, time, and harmony; between composition and improvisation; between "traditional" and "avant-garde"; between "artist" and "audience"; between "art" and "politics"; between "Western" and "Eastern," etc. If there is any "tradition," it is the continual exploding of time and pitch in quest of greater human expressiveness and a deeper spiritualizing of the music that is fundamentally rooted in the struggle to end all forms of exploitation and oppression and to seek a basic "oneness" with life and nature.[5]

Much ballyhoo has been made about essentializing "jazz" as basically blues, swing, and improvisation: If these are lacking, then the music ain't "jazz." Interestingly, the proponents of this dogma can range across the ideological and political spectrum from black cultural nationalists to black and white neoconservatives. Let's look more closely at what is meant by *blues* and *swing*.

Blues

In my view, blues is not simply a "style," or a 12-bar AAB form, or a certain chordal progression. Musically, blues is first and foremost a unique expression of temperament—African American temperament! It is not, as Eurocentric musicology may attempt to codify, flatted or lowered thirds, sevenths, and fifths (notated in Western musical theory as sharp or raised seconds, dominant sevenths, or sharp or raised elevenths). Blues notes can be played on Western instruments without fingering minor thirds, dominant (flatted) sevenths, and flatted fifths if the player has the African American conception of temperament. The African American system of blues temperament is the synthesis of the Western European fixed, diatonic temperament with an amalgam of West and Central African pitch and modal systems. With this new temperament system, the distinction between major and minor is lost.[6]

‹ 97

Many authentic blues performers will actually retune their instruments to be more "in tune" with being bluesy. Conversely, inauthentic players who attempt to perform the mechanics of the blues notes by fingering minor thirds, etc., may sound unblue. The key aspect is not a fixed style (Jones/Baraka's "noun") but a process or approach to music making (Jones/Baraka's "verb"): the highly African blurring of pitch to reach an emotive and spiritual catharsis—in West Africa, literally, to "allow the gods to descend"—and thereby affirm both personal and communal humanity in the face of inhumanity.[7]

Secondarily, blues is a "form." The 12-bar, AAB form has become, in the analogy made by Jones/Baraka, another case of the verb-to-noun syndrome. It has been so thoroughly appropriated by (white, mainstream) "American" music in rock, country and western, disco, etc., that the "standard" blues form has practically ceased to be the blues! Historically, blues "form" has been expressed in 12 bars, 10 bars, 8 bars, 11½ bars, 12½ bars, 13 bars, 16 bars, etc. There have been blues based on three or more chords, blues based on one chord, and blues based on no chords!

Although a discussion of the "blues sensibility and aesthetic" significantly and meaningfully aids an understanding of the blues both socially and culturally, in my view, the blues musical form is best understood as a musical representation of African American poetry. Blues pre-dates "jazz" as a sung, vocal genre—a griot tradition that has become secularized and existentialized (through individual self-expressionism). In "jazz," blues is metamorphosed: once sung, now instrumental; once performed by an individual, now by an ensemble; once literal, now nonliteral. The blues form cannot be reduced simply to a number of bars and type of chord progression or phrase structure. To do so would be to oppress and suffocate the music's essence and creative, dynamic being as an expression of an African American oppressed nationality.

The music, thus, has no wrong notes, no wrong progression or fixed number of bars, so long as it has the feel, the expressiveness of African American life and culture. Once it has been thoroughly codified and appropriated by the mainstream, dominant oppressor culture, then it ceases to be.

Swing

African American "swing" is not, as some Eurocentric musicologists would try to characterize in Western musical paradigms, syncopation,[8] nor does it have a "tripleted feel." Rather, it is a hybrid concept of time/pulse and rhythm: the result of the miscegenation between West African triple meter and multiple rhythmic layering with Western European duple meter and singular rhythm. This "3 inside 2" is fundamentally a West African-descended phenomenon, found in all African diasporic musics where more than one time and more than one rhythm coexist. Enslaved Africans in the diaspora developed unique types of "swing"—in Cuba, Haiti, Puerto Rico, Brazil, etc.

In African America, where drums were banned by the oppressors, a unique type of "swing" developed: time and rhythm were conveyed through singing, instrument playing, and a collective, internal "feel" expressed in body movement, dance, "pattin' juba," language, and vocal inflections. Since drums and drumming were illegal, West African percussion and rhythmic traditions came through in everything else—musical and extramusical. Some have characterized African

American swing as a rhythmic energy and life force—a far greater influence than the simple role meter and rhythm play in Western European music—indeed, a form of African-based kinetics, a multiple rhythm perspective, a shared communal bond of time, motion and energy. It is simultaneously both exciting and relaxing (what Archie Shepp has characterized as the tension and beauty of being both on the front and back edge of the beat—its forward and laid-back quality). The beat can swing whether it be in units of three or two, in metrical patterns of 2, 3, the common 4, or 7, 7½, 11, 15, 9, 13, etc. Swing can be in time, in different time, and in no time! From Baby Dodds and Sid Catlett swinging in 4/4, to odd meters done by Max Roach, to polyrhythms of Elvin Jones, to the free, no time of Sunny Murray.

Improvisation

Finally, let me address the issue of composition/notation and improvisation. Some have argued that once the composition is heavily notated and improvisation is necessarily diminished, the music becomes more "European" and less "African American." Initially, Western European music also relied on improvisation; player/composers under economic pressure were required to come up quickly with new works to entertain and satisfy their aristocratic employers. Though these musicians were "literate," improvisation satisfied both economic expediency and their own creative desire to avoid the repetitive boredom of performing the same hits the same way all the time. As solo and small-group works expanded to large ensembles and extended compositions, and as paying audiences began to demand faithful replication of their favorites, notation assumed increasingly greater dominance.

African American music has never, until recently, had to face the prospect of institutionalization, canonization, standardization, and codification by a ruling class (presently, bourgeois). Paradoxically, the music of an oppressed nationality was free to be free. Duke Ellington's orchestra could play the same show every night for years and still retain spontaneity and freshness, no matter how much notation, choreography, and staging was set. As "jazz" became more of an "art" music (i.e., primarily listened to and not danced to), and the "jazz" composer (who could still be a player/leader) began to pen extended works such as suites, ballets, theater and film scores, etc., the best and strongest writing always allowed for an enhanced spontaneity and for improvised contributions from the players. Ideally these written compositions are memorized and internalized until the written page is no longer looked at and the players play from understanding and interaction. The essence of African American music is a whole, which is greater than the sum of its inseparable and mutually dependent parts—player and composer, notation and performance, composition and improvisation.

Notation is not the enslaver, the oppressor of spontaneity and improvisation. Calcification, de-African Americanization, co-optation is not caused by musical deviations and practices, but, in my view, by ethical violations. Clearly, in Ellington's large-scale works, the essence of African American spontaneity is reflected in a highly composed music. And there are players who play "correct jazz" which is sterile and reactionary.

As a non-African American, but a person of color (oppressed nationality in the United States), I was drawn to and inspired and revolutionized by the music's musical and—possibly more profoundly—extramusical qualities. Many years later, after becoming a professional musician, I came across a statement by V. I. Lenin, which crystallizes this confluence: "Ethics will be the aesthetics of the future." Twentieth-century African American music is part of an extramusical ethical/spiritual/sociopolitical revolution—the commitment, attitude, resistance, perseverance, celebration, love, and joy opposing oppression, brutality, poverty, persecution, and exclusion. Archie Shepp expressed it in poetic language: "Jazz is the lily in spite of the swamp." It is the triumph of the human spirit, of spirituality and ethicality in the midst of cannibalistic and corrupting capitalism.

The carrier of the music (the musician) must not violate the ethical bond between the music and the people (i.e., a bond of merit, of excellence, of meaning, of purpose, of significance in the people's aspirations and efforts to be free). The musician bears a responsibility that transcends careers, critical praise, conservatory training, and cash to affirm the music's fundamental celebration of humanity, and to remain committed to the liberation of an oppressed nationality—African Americans—in an age of internationalized commodity production and exchange.

"Jazz" was born amidst the contradictions of our epoch. The music changes just as the people, the society, and the world change. African Americans in the twentieth century have been the largest and leading oppressed nationality of U.S. society. Their political, social, and cultural impact has been revolutionary. By the twenty-first century, Spanish-speaking oppressed nationalities will become numerically the largest group of oppressed nationalities. Asian/Pacific Islanders are proportionally the fastest-growing oppressed nationalities. And indigenous peoples facing the most extreme and desperate conditions are resorting increasingly to armed struggle (cf. Chiapas, Mexico) to defend their land and way of life. In the years to come—it has already begun—a new music will arise, rooted in all that has come before, yet moving with greater volatility, altering and exploding time and sound, and thereby changing music itself.

‹ 101

The petty machinations that attempt to "institutionalize jazz," the reactionary "back to the tradition" (tradition is not something one can or should go back to, but move from), the business-suited corporate and government recognition that legitimizes "jazz" and makes it acceptable—all of these violate the spirit, the sacred bond between culture and people, the ethics of the aesthetics. The appropriation of oppressed peoples' culture and history for the service of Yankee imperialism is antithetical and inimical to creative development. Whether "jazz" comes to be the vital, transformative, revolutionary music of the twenty-first century that it has been in the twentieth century depends on how this struggle plays out. A new "jazz"—maybe something that won't use this term because it has become so co-opted and reactionary—will affirm and attest to the revolutionary heritage that began in the twentieth century: that the music of all oppressed peoples fighting imperialism is indeed *Jazz*.

An Ethical Mandate among the Music, the Musician, and the People

1. Speak to the People. The music has to and will embody messages, either explicitly (in the form of lyrics and/or song titles) or implicitly (in the sound and in its spirit). Some examples have been, but are certainly not limited to, "Strange Fruit" (composed by Lewis Allen and popularized by Billie Holiday), "A Tone Parallel to Harlem" (Duke Ellington), "A Love Supreme" (John Coltrane), "Things Have Got to Change" (composed by Calvin Massey and performed by Archie Shepp), "Remember Rockefeller at Attica" (Charles Mingus), etc.

2. Go to the People. The music must be performed where people can enjoy it. Rather than expect the people to come to the music (an approach that depends more on marketing hype and advertisement dollars than on artistry or quality), bring the music to the people. Often, artists have very little control over how their music is distributed, promoted, and presented. In many ways, the musician and the music have both left the community in which both were spawned. The parallel to "underdevelopment" is striking: A people's cultural and natural resources are drained off for the benefit of corporate plunderers and not the people. Activists, managers, cultural presenters and producers, and artists need to work together to build a community base to support the music.

3. Involve the People. Just as we need environmentally sustainable development for natural resources, we need culturally sustainable development for the arts. We need to bridge the separation between artist and audience, between professional and amateur. The essence of cultural democracy is true popular culture—culture and the arts created by and for the common people and not by and for an elite. The rationalization of corporate entertainment is to "give the people what they want." Unfortunately, the truth is really "give the people what the corporations want them to want."

4. Change the People. Ultimately, the music and culture of oppressed peoples, if it is to have value and meaning, must revolutionize the consciousness, values, aesthetics, and actions of the people. This is the music's "spiritualizing" quality: to fortify and prepare us to continue the struggle until liberation.

NOTES

1 Several etymologies have been asserted for the word "jazz." The less credible ones assert an African derivation, but these words are from languages not spoken south of the Sahara and therefore were not commonly used among the West and Central African, sub-Saharan peoples enslaved and brought to the Americas. More likely, "jazz" comes from either *jass* or *jizz*, which means "semen" (the original piano music was common to houses of prostitution). Another explanation is that "jazz" comes from the French verb—New Orleans, the birthplace of the music, was a French colonial territory—*jaser*, meaning "to chatter nonsensically." In either case, "jazz" has a pejorative context, as do many terms from the legacy of colonialism and exploitation.

2 Spelled with a *k*, "kreolization" is a concept advanced by Dorothy Desir-Davis, to be distinguished from "creolization" of M. Herskovits et al., pertaining to the intermixing in the Caribbean. Kreolization refers to cultural and social cross-fertilization as a process that leads to the formation of entirely new identities and cultures, often—in the case of oppressed-oppressor relations—selectively appropriated by dominant social groups into the dominant identity and culture, but de-politicized and deracinated.

3 See Royal Hartigan, "The Heritage of the Drumset," *African American Review* 29, no. 2 (1995): 234-236.

4 See Al Rose, "The Saxophone: Its Strange Origins," *African American Review* 29, no. 2 (1995): 233.

5 Musicians' various ideological/spiritual pronouncements reflect this quest and struggle.

6 The percussionist Royal Hartigan has described this phenomenon as African Americans trying to get the Western seven-note scale back to the five notes common to many West African pentatonic systems (although he also recognizes that there are seven-note African scales).

7 I am interpreting LeRoi Jones/Amiri Baraka here.

8 Extensive syncopation (the emphasis on "off" or "weak" beats) is very prevalent in the musical cultures of the Pacific Islands, Southeast Asia, and other parts of the world. But none of these musics "swing" in the African American sense, even though it can be asserted that they are their own forms of "swing."

Musical Borrowings, Exchanges, and Fusions: New/Experimental Genres

104 >

SINCE THE MIDDLE of the twentieth century, the human community has become, as Marshall McLuhan phrased it, "a global village." Cartographers have mapped every proverbial corner of the earth; technology—expanding at a phenomenal rate—through mass communication and mass transportation, has shortened distances to literally the push of a button and made physical travel possible within hours; achievements in the aerospace field have made it possible to even photograph the planet from space; two world wars have occurred; international political, economic, legal and cultural bodies have emerged; and every facet of human existence has become increasingly interconnected and interdependent in a global, planetary context.

The end of World War II marked two major shifts in geopolitical power. Former Western European colonial powers had lost significantly to the rising economic and military dominance of the United States of America as a superpower. As part of the decline of European colonialism, the former colonies of Africa, Asia, Central and South America, and the Pacific Islands had gained independence and emerged as significant forces in international affairs. These develop-

Published in *Garland Encyclopedia of World Music, Volume 3: The United States and Canada*, edited by Ellen Koskoff (New York: Routledge, 2000).

ments would have impact upon the American musical processes and practices for the latter half of the twentieth century.

The United States has a peculiar historical development. Founded by European settler colonization, the United States grew to its present borders through military force and by a concerted campaign to repopulate the continent of North America. Military force was used in genocidal wars against the Native peoples for seizure of their land. Further land and territories were acquired through economic purchase (e.g., the Louisiana Purchase from France) and military annexation of other territories, including what is now the Southwest via war with Mexico, the occupation and overthrow of the constitutional monarchy of Hawaii, the seizure of Spain's former colonies during the Spanish-American War (including Puerto Rico, Cuba, the Dominican Republic, and the Philippines), and imperialist control over Haiti, Jamaica, Panama, Grenada, and many others.

The repopulation of the North American continent in the construction of the United States included both voluntary and involuntary/coerced forms of labor immigration. The voluntary immigration—welcomed and encouraged—consisted of populations from Europe, though primarily accorded to peoples from Western European extraction. The involuntary or coerced labor consisted of the transportation of millions of enslaved Africans to this land; the forms of indentured servitude and contract or coolie labor for Asians; the oppressive and coercive labor programs such as Operation Bootstrap carried out in the Caribbean and the bracero labor programs for Mexican immigrants. While indentured servitude did apply to Europeans in the early stages, their immigration was never subject to racist restrictive and exclusionary laws and "white" Europeans were not subjected to a perpetual oppressed status as were "minority" people of color nationalities (which included laws that forbade such groups to become citizens and to enjoy basic civil rights granted to the "white" populations until the 1960s, when de jure discrimination was finally eliminated). Because of this unique and peculiar development of the United States as a "white" settler-colonial state, and the massive importation of labor from many parts of the globe, the United States is today a very multicultural society, yet one with a long-standing history of institutional white racism that continues to permeate and pervade much of the society. Demographically, it is projected that the so-called "minorities" will become the numerical majority of the U.S. population by the middle of the twenty-first century, and are already the majority of most major U.S. cities. However, political, economic, military, and social-cultural power continues to be predominantly "white." These contradictory and conflicted social realities contextualize the new forms of music that have emerged in the latter half of the twentieth century in the United States.

Since the 1950s, various forms of experimentation have occurred between existing styles/genres/idioms, such as Western European concert ("classical") music and African American traditions (primarily "jazz")—both between "classical" music and "jazz" and between one or the other of these musical traditions with world or "ethnic" musics. Despite what artists and others may claim, musical and cultural borrowings and mixing cannot be divorced from the sociopolitical power relations between cultural and social groups, and hence aren't value-neutral. The debate around what constitutes respectful borrowing/mixing/blending and what constitutes rip-off (or cultural imperialism) is at its core an issue less about artistic motives and integrity and much more about oppressor-oppressed relations mirrored in the economic and political struggle between North-South/developed-developing countries and societies.

Experimentation in "Classical" Music

In the realm of American concert music—i.e., "classical" music (the music that draws primarily from Western European traditions, requiring formal training usually in academic institutions or conservatories, primarily notated, and performed in concert venues)—the experimentation with "jazz" in the 1950s occurred in the work of "Third Stream" composers and ensembles fusing "classical" and "jazz," including Gunther Schuller, the Modern Jazz Quartet, Gerry Mulligan, Gil Evans, Stan Kenton, Samuel Barber, and others. In the case of "Third Stream," it has always been easier for the "jazz" composer and player to go to "classical" music than the reverse—I would hypothesize an explanation for this situation simply being a case analogous to where it is much harder for the master to identify with the slave than it is for the slave to identify with the master, to speak the master's language, to absorb and adopt the master's idioms because the humanity of the master is inculcated in the slave but the slave's humanity is never accepted by the master.

"Third Stream" was for the most part an effort by "jazz" composers and players to adopt the acceptability of "classical" music—from its heavy reliance upon notation and minimalizing of improvisation, to its formal presentation performed in concert halls with performers wearing tuxedos, to its "cool" style devoid of "hot" guttural blues-based playing.

Other "classical" composers and performers sought to revitalize and transform the ossification of canonized "classical" music in U.S. society. John Cage, deemed an iconoclast, led the way. In the 1950s, Cage studied Zen Buddhism and used the principles of the Chinese *I Ching* (Book of Changes) in developing a compositional and performance approach based upon indetermination or chance. As increasing international contact introduced world music into American society, particularly to higher education institutions, more and more white American composers and musicians began to explore "non-Western" musical approaches, instrumentation, and principles. These included Steve Reich, who in the 1970s studied and incorporated Indonesian gamelan, Ghanaian drumming, Hebrew cantillation, and "classical" music to develop a popular and influential minimalist/systems/process/repetitive (pick your label) trend; and Lou Harrison, whose interest and study in Asian/Pacific musics has been incorporated in his highly composed works that call for Asian/Pacific traditional instruments in combination with Western ones. Other composers, based on the West Coast with its proximity and access to the Pacific Rim, who have experimented in combining "Eastern" and "Western" idioms include Terry Riley and Colin McPhee. The influence of "Eastern" music, particularly in the area of invariable temperament and fractional or microtonal pitch, is evident in the work of Harry Partch, who created his own instruments to supersede diatonicism.

While the generation of American "classical" trained composers and performers of the 1950s and 1960s was to look to world music for inspiration in experimentation upon the concert music canon, the trend since the 1980s seems to be to incorporate American "popular" idioms (which are African American rooted forms). Since the 1970s, this has been taken up by a younger generation of "classical" trained composers, including Meredith Monk, Philip Glass, Robert Telson, Laurie Anderson, and the success of such trendy, fashion-oriented groups as the Kronos Quartet—a "classical" string quartet spiced up with punk haircuts and high-fashion designer clothing instead of the staid tuxedo, performing an eclectic repertoire of commissioned work and covers of Jimi Hendrix and Thelonious Monk in a quest to be "hip."

The "Third World" Revolution as Inspiration

The 1950s and 1960s were a period of rising African independence and national liberation movements. On March 6, 1957, in winning its independence from British colonial rule, Ghana became the first independent sub-Saharan African nation-state. The movement's leader and first president was Kwame Nkrumah, who espoused Pan-Africanism: the unity of the peoples of African descent both on the mother continent and throughout the diaspora. In the United States, African American "jazz" artists were inspired by the vision of Pan-Africanism to explore musical collaborations with African musicians, including pianist/composer Randy Weston with North African Moroccan musicians, saxophonist Johnny Griffin with an oud master musician in a late 1950s recording, John Coltrane with Nigerian drummer Babatunde Olatunji, and others. U.S. drummer Max Roach traveled to Ghana to study traditional West African drumming. The "jazz" avant-garde of the late 1960s was in part looking to world music sources in its search for the "new" and to liberate pitch and meter from Western European conventions.

In American rock and popular music, as part of the 1960s counter-cultural and anti-establishment thrust, world music—especially from the "third world"—was embraced and explored. Beatles member George Harrison collaborated with Indian sitarist Ravi Shankar—which subsequently helped to popularize South Asian music in the United States; the late Brian Jones, a member of the Rolling Stones, collaborated and recorded with the Jajouka musicians from the Atlas Mountains of Morocco during the late 1960s; years later, saxophonist/composer Ornette Coleman and the New York City contemporary klezmer group The Klezmatics would also concertize with the musicians from Jajouka.

Multicultural Hybrid Forms

Emerging in the early 1960s in New York City's Latino (primarily Puerto Rican) community was a new form of dance music, salsa, that blended earlier popular Cuban dance forms with "jazz" and rock. This uniquely North American urban music, while a song-based form, developed increasingly complex horn arrangements and virtuosic solo artistry as it drew from "jazz" influences. By the 1970s, salsa was undergoing a profound renaissance, paralleling the social, political, and cultural upsurge among Latinos in the United States and throughout the Caribbean and Central and South America for liberation and equality. Composer/bandleader/performers such as Eddie Palmieri and the late Bobby Paunetto were among the leading innovators. In the case of Palmieri, he recorded entire album-length extended suites. Along with the blues, salsa has become an indigenous American musical form with international popularity and influence.

‹ 109

In the mid-1970s, primarily in the San Francisco Bay Area, Asian/Pacific American musicians and composers—many from an avant-garde "jazz" orientation—were experimenting with traditional and folk musics from their ancestral Pacific Rim cultures. A loose community of "Asian American jazz" musicians, including Bay Area exponents such as Russel Baba, Paul Yamazaki, and Jeanne Aiko Mercer, would pioneer the combining of traditional Japanese instrumentation and idioms with improvisational "free jazz." By the mid-1980s, a number of Asian/Pacific American musicians scattered across the United States would experiment in developing an "Asian American sound" that wedded African American traditions with Asian/Pacific concepts, including baritone saxophonist/composer Fred Ho of New York City, bassist Mark Izu, pianist Jon Jang, kotoist Miya Masaoka of the Bay Area, pianist Glenn Horiuchi of Southern California, taiko drummer Kenny Endo of Hawaii, and others. A more commercial "pop" fusion of Japanese and American rock/soul styles was spearheaded by the predominantly Japanese American band Hiroshima of Los Angeles.

During the course of his studies at Wesleyan University's World

Music and Jazz Studies Program, Iranian American tenor saxophonist Hafez Modirzadeh innovated a major new theoretical and performance approach—what he terms "chromodal discourse." Modirzadeh, as a tenor saxophonist, has developed a way of playing the instrument to utilize Persian temperament via a system of alternative fingerings and applied it to "jazz" improvisation, including improvisation based on "chord changes" as vertically based as, for example, John Coltrane's "Giant Steps." "Chromodal discourse" is a cross-cultural theoretical and practical application and may possibly be the first significant theoretical development in American "jazz."

Similarly, Royal Hartigan, a drum set player and another former longtime Wesleyan University student, has a highly developed application of West African (Ghanaian) and other world and ethnic rhythms to the Western trap drum set. The multiple rhythms and meters of various world music rhythmic forms are fluently incorporated into his playing of the drum set. His book *West African Rhythms for the Drum Set* (Warner Brothers) is a detailed exposition of cross-cultural performance and a breakthrough method to a new way of playing the drum set in the incorporation of traditional Ghanaian rhythmic forms.

Creolization and Resistance

As rap/hip-hop has emerged from its underground, New York City/ south Bronx-based origins to become a major U.S. pop cultural influence, cross-cultural fusions with ethnic/world music sources have been part of the multicultural mix of American youth-based music making, including fusions with South Asian (*bangra*), Native American (e.g., W.O.R.–WithOut Reservation), and Caribbean idioms. The Caribbean has a particular fecundity for cultural mixing given its colonial/plantation sociohistorical development, including forms such as Jamaican ska, reggae, calypso, Dominican meringue, Puerto Rican bomba/plena, Cuban mambo, etc. In a similar colonial/plantation sociohistorical development, Hawaii has also generated hybrid musical/cultural forms—from the Japanese American *hole hole bushi* (immigrant women plantation workers' songs) to today's popular/ commercial style Jawaiiam (from the words "Jah," representing the influence of Rastafarian reggae and the mellifluous Hawaiian *hula ku'i*). In the early twentieth century, Hawaiian guitar virtuoso Sol Hoopii had pioneered a hula blues style, and the Hawaiian 12-string slack key guitar has introduced an interesting and unique regional, multicultural American form of temperament.

World Beat Pop

Since the 1980s, world music forms have become increasingly utilized in Western pop music, in the examples of such pop stars as Paul Simon, David Byrne, Malcolm McLaren, and others. "World Beat" has become a pop category that includes both First and Third World artists, of whom the latter are those on the cusp of international commercial success and superstardom, such as Youssou N'Dour of Senegal, Ladysmith Black Mambazo, and others. The irony of the success of "Afro-Pop"—as more and more units are purchased by Westerners—has been the stark contrast with devastating and obscene poverty, grisly internecine wars, brutal tyrannical repression by African governments (many of which are military dictatorships), and the ongoing neocolonial exploitation by multinational corporations of the African people and their resources. The successes of an elite are often never transferred to the masses.

‹ 111

The question of cultural borrowing or appropriation is at the core of a debate about cultural imperialism, or the relationship between members of dominant and powerful groups and members of colonized, oppressed, and marginalized groups. Who has the right to use another's music? Is the use exploitative/disrespectful/inauthentic, or is it subversive/transformative/innovative? Who benefits and gains? Who is harmed or ripped off? Is it an ongoing case of "Third World roots/First World enjoying the fruits"? Is it the generally typical case of a First World superstar or producer "discovering" the native and thereby introducing the native's music/culture to the West and internationally via commercialization? Musical hybridizing and mixing also occurs between members of marginalized and oppressed groups, as cited in the case of "creolizing" in plantation societies among a multiethnic oppressed labor force or U.S. urban inner-city communities. Usually in such cases, the music/culture of the dominant, white, Eurocentric mainstream—be it commercial pop or "classical" forms—are not looked to for inspiration as they tend to be identified as part of the oppressor culture. The identification with African American forms in American musical experimentation of the twentieth century has generally proceeded, at some level, as rebellion, resistance, and opposition to the dominant white racist and Eurocentric paradigms and canons.

Kreolization and the Hybridity of Resistance vs. Cultural Imperialism

NOTIONS OF CULTURAL PURITY are as spurious and odious as notions of "racial" purity. The ideological and social construct of "race" arose with the colonization of the "dark" peoples of Africa, Asia, the Pacific Islands and the Americas by the "white" people of Western Europe as a pseudoscientific rationalization for the domination by a small portion of the world over the rest. Conquest, invasion, genocide, and exploitation undoubtedly did not begin with European colonial expansion and capitalism. Nor was Western Europe a sociopolitical-cultural monolith. Aggressive competition and rivalry between nation-states led to the reconfiguration of colonial power and extension, replacing Spanish-Portuguese dominance with Italian and German, later Dutch, and, in the last two centuries, by French, British, and American. Rising capitalism also generated fierce class struggle within the European and North American nation-states. While European national cultural and artistic forms did take hold, inevitably they were the result of the suppression, domination, and appropriation by the national bourgeoisie over folk and popular expressions of the peasantry and working class. The high-art and classical traditions are Eurocentric because they are bourgeois, that is, embraced and supported by the various European ruling classes.

The rise of Eurocentrism and capitalism in the last five centuries

Presented as a speech at the College Art Association conference in January 1994, on a panel led by Dorothy Desir-Davis.

marks for the first time in history the complete subordination on a planetary level of all social formations and modes of production to a singular world-system, which is both capitalist and Eurocentric.

Why does capitalism—not particularly or intrinsically original to Europe—assume the dominant mode of production in Western Europe? Or, to ask the question another way: if the Chinese, for example, invented gunpowder, why did the Europeans apply it to firearms? Essentialist arguments include a range and mixture of explanations that are cultural and socio-environmental: "European-ness" inevitably is aggression, competition, and domination over everything (nature, people, knowledge, etc.), and curiously, accepting of the European drive for superiority. However, challenging perspectives analyze a complexity of factors that account for European specificity vis-à-vis the rest of the world. In not accepting European superiority or its specialness, explanations can be found in Europe's relative backwardness. One thing is clear: capitalism and Eurocentrism have become structurally and culturally interdependent and inseparable.

Global relations of commerce, and its attendant social, intellectual, and cultural infrastructures, are structured for the primary profit of the capitalist centers, though these relationships are never simple one-way flows. The material and cultural resources of Asia, the Pacific Islands, Africa, and Central and South America are appropriated for the wealth and consumption of the ruling classes of the West, while the rest of the world has served as new markets for Western goods, ideas, and lifestyles, whether they want these or not. Today, Western capitalism has penetrated every site on the planet. As it oppresses and subjugates entire nations, peoples, and cultures, it breeds its own negation. Contrary to both its apologists and its cynical dissenters, capitalism, while it absorbs, co-opts, and appropriates, simultaneously generates new contradictions and intensifies its own internal ones. One clear example is the United States of America.

Billed as the "New World" despite the presence of indigenous populations for at least 12,000 years, the Americas and the United States especially were a significant and unique site for the massive transfer of human labor. The Transatlantic Slave Trade and the Asian coolie trade, along with the white-European settler colonization, repopulated the entire hemisphere, a process predicated upon the forced removal, annexation, and genocide against the native peoples. (For

North America, in 1491, native peoples were 100 percent of the population. By 1992, they were less than 1 percent.)

Since the European invasion of this continent, for more than five hundred years, entire peoples have been repopulated, wiped out, and new nationalities and cultural identities have been forged. The prevailing racist, mythological notion of "American" is equated as "white" or European-originated. The reality of "American" is precisely the opposite: the great bulk of the food, music, language, symbology, and way of life are byproducts of miscegenation, the cross-influencing/cross-fertilization of many traditions and forms. The movement for multicultural education continues to dismantle Eurocentric and white supremacist lies and mistruths and to reveal the indigenous, African, Asian, as well as European, recombinations into our daily lives. What is less revealed is the political character of these recombinations.

As in genetics, variety and recombination of the gene pool ensure greater probability of survival and development. Just as the Pilgrims had to adopt Native ways of food cultivation and storage to ensure their survival, Native peoples had to adopt the technology of the whites (from horseback riding to the use of the gun) for their resistance. In relations between oppressor and oppressed, the oppressor seizes a disproportionate amount of the material and informational resources for their gain at the expense of the oppressed. On the other hand, the oppressed, by any means necessary, must take whatever they can and fashion new and more effective forms of resistance and struggle.

Most of what we take for granted in our multicultural discourse is the kreolization among the oppressed as resistance to oppression. We need only to look at American national music, which is quintessentially African American. The slave songs or spirituals in lyric employed the double entendre of coded, two-level meaning. Singing in English, the language of the slave master, and using Christian Biblical references (the slave master's religion), the songs were a form of underground communication and a celebration of the spirit and act of rebellion. Musically, African American music has been characterized as a synthesis of Western European tonal harmony and West African modal melodicism. African American music has been the revolutionary music of the twentieth century, not just for the United

States, but for the planet as well. It has revolutionized the world of music: by introducing new instrumentation (e.g., the drum kit) or refiguring others (e.g., the saxophone, the piano more as a rhythm and less as a harmonic instrument, the string bass played primarily pizzicato and in a role as time keeper and less played arco as a melodic line, and many other examples); its aesthetical transformation of the very components of melody (e.g., the primacy of improvisation), rhythm (e.g., the concept of swing), and harmony (e.g., parallel voicings, "blue notes," altered chord changes, etc.).

Art-for-art's-sake ideologues may argue with me: Were the singers and musicians politically conscious or were they simply making music from their cultural milieu? Since much of the music, art, and culture of an oppressed people is not deemed worthy of scholarly attention, we lack the honest and in-depth interviews and historiography to clearly assert a conscious political design. But even if the performers were simple "creating" from their experiences, clearly these experiences are contextualized by their social, political, and economic conditions. As Marx stated, conditions shape humans; that's why we must struggle to make them more human. Part of that struggle for humanity is music making—its particular forms and expressive character are shaped by the material, social, and cultural conditions.

African American music is sociohistorically, and not racially, "black." Similarly, the African American people, as an oppressed nationality, are sociohistorically "black" according to racist blood quantum legislation established in the late nineteenth century; that is, no matter how minuscule the blood quantum from an African ancestor, that person is not "white." If we have understood the concept of nationality and discard the falsity of "race," then obviously so-called white people can play "jazz" and have made important contributions. Indeed, the music continues to incorporate influences from many cultures and experiences, yet remains African American. So-called whites can embrace and identify with African American culture, but as long as the system of white supremacy exists, they will always be "whites," whether or not they consciously desire this. Whites become race traitors (like John Brown) only when they commit themselves to unremitting struggle against the system of white privilege and to overthrowing the system of white-racist national oppression. Thus, "whites" can never be innovators or be cultural/artistic leaders in the cultural forms of oppressed nationalities, only skilled imitators and followers. That is because the arts and cultures of oppressed nationalities are inevitably and intrinsically bound up with the oppression and struggle of our peoples; that is, our survival and development is a refusal to identify with, or submit and capitulate to the oppressor. Just as non-whites in a racist, white supremacist society are oppressed nationalities, then whites are the oppressor nationality as long as they accept that system. There is no individual neutrality, or nonracist white people, but it is possible for there to be anti-racist "whites."

To be a white liberal, or an apologist for white assimilation, and try to legitimate and give respect to the arts and culture of oppressed nationalities by boosting up the European influences or arguing for its similarity or proximity to European standards, is still to be racist. The culture and arts of the oppressed owe nothing, need not be thankful to, the culture and arts of the oppressor. What oppressor cultural aspects there are have been refashioned and transformed, and, dare we say, violated and miscegenated. This has been the way of the oppressed masses: the field slave, the coolie, the savage, the bandit, the heathen, the guerrilla.

For mixed or hybrid nationalities, especially those who have been incorrectly termed Hispanic or Latino, identification with the Spanish or the Latin is internalized oppression. This is tantamount to saying that the man who raped your mother is your father, and not part of the rapist/racist, oppressor/colonizing class. In reality, the great bulk of the ancestry of the Spanish-speaking oppressed nationalities is derived from the heritage of enslaved Africans and the indigenous peoples.

Kreolization and cross-fertilization must be understood in a sociopolitical context. Too often, as part of colonial design, the Creole has been used and manipulated as a buffer between the ruling elites and the oppressed and exploited masses. Most of the commingling between oppressed and oppressor has been forced rape. This is a false and objectionable kreolization, that is, assimilation and acculturation with the dominant oppressor culture and society. True kreolization, the free and voluntary intermingling, cultural synthesis, and cross-fertilization, occurs at the bottom of society, among the varying oppressed peoples. We see this today. Chicano, Dominican, Puerto Rican, Asian and Pacific Islander youth, who, even lacking much identity with their own nationality, will tend to identify with African American culture and radical politics. To choose "black" over "white" reflects and strengthens a potential anti-imperialist bond. However, real kreolization is synthesis and not imitation or simple identification with another.

Cultural imperialism, while masking as cultural blending/borrowing/mixing, enforces dominant privilege, power, and profit. So much for "free-market art"! Here are several ways it manifests in contemporary music relations:

1. The Christopher Columbus Syndrome à la Paul Simon, David Byrne, Malcolm McLaren, the World Beat trend, et al., in which "other" cultures are "discovered" by a white artist.
2. The Exotic Syndrome, in which "other" cultures are frivolous, superficial, exotic flavoring for an otherwise tired and formulated music.
3. The Elvis Syndrome, in which white artists cover Third World artists, as in the example of Buster Poindexter's "Hot Hot Hot" covering of Montserrat musician Arrow's original recording.
4. The Great White Father or Bawana Syndrome, in which the luminaries are white, albeit surrounded by all non-white bands, as in the case of a white star like Sting who has the budget to hire the best artists from "other" cultures.

As I stated before, "jazz," rock, and most popular music in the United States are basically African American. However, through white cultural imperialism, these forms have been assimilated, and therefore become acceptably American. The exportation of American pop music around the world represents American cultural imperialism: not the culture of oppressed African American people, but the Americanization of African American culture. We can see Americanized African American political counterparts, from Pearl Bailey to Andrew Young (as U.N. ambassadors) to Colin Powell. They are, as one Caribbean person stated, condemned to be "black Yankees," tools of U.S. imperialism. In the 1960s, when the movements of African Americans and other oppressed peoples were high, African American representatives abroad were such revolutionary and militant figures as Malcolm X, Robert F. Williams, Huey P. Newton and the Black Panther Party, Muhammad Ali, Paul Robeson, Angela Davis, Abbey Lincoln (a.k.a. Aminata Moseka), and so on. Today, since the movement is low, we have Michael Jackson, Oprah Winfrey, Whitney Houston, and Michael Jordan.

Better to have Fela Kuti identify and draw from the music of the I'm-Black-and-Proud James Brown, than, say, a white derivative or cover like Barry Manilow, Elvis Presley, or Vanilla Ice.

The oppressed nationalities in the United States are fast becoming the majority of the population. This demographic phenomenon alone is a massive threat to white supremacy and Eurocentrism in U.S. society. The U.S. ruling class will continue to try to divide, co-opt, and contain our peoples. As oppressed nationalities begin to unite and create new cultural and political forms, new ploys and buy-offs will be devised. This includes the "mainstreaming" of multiculturalism, the token integration of the middle classes, the depoliticizing of kreolization, the co-optation of cultural diversity, and so on.

I am a Chinese American musician who plays the baritone saxophone and who composes what I call Afro-Asian New American Multicultural Music. I am *not* a musician of Chinese descent in America who happens to play and compose "jazz." For most of my life, African American and Asian American culture and politics have been both synonymous and sonorous. I am self-taught, so I was spared the Eurocentric cultural indoctrination and training that occurs in conservatory training, in the process of getting an MFA. When I became a revolutionary, I understood that ethnicity is not sufficient, unless it proceeds from a consciousness and identification with all oppressed peoples. The Asian American Movement gave me a Pan-Asian sensibility, and since I reject white supremacy, my American heritage meant the predominant musical tradition of African Americans.

It is not easy for the oppressed to unite within each group, not to speak of between groups. Both white assimilation and narrow nationalism are major obstacles and flow from the same systemic condition: we fight each other over crumbs and for integration into the system rather than to overturn that system and to construct a new one based on the revolutionary socialist principle of "the last shall be first, the first last."

The linking of our common struggles, the mutually shared identity as oppressed nationalities, rather than subscribing to nationalism or ethnicity, is the beginning basis of genuine cultural synthesis. Artistic cross-fertilization proceeds from a deep respect and consciousness of the richness and complexity of the varying oppressed nationality heritages. A revolutionary kreolization is the interdependent, interconnected struggle to forge a common identification as oppressed peoples. New cultural forms will inevitably flow from this unity.

NOTE

For an example of the synthesis of Chinese folk music and African American music, see Fred Ho and The Afro Asian Music Ensemble, *The Underground Railroad to My Heart*, Soul Note Records, 121267-2, 1994.

Highlights in the History of "Jazz" *Not* Covered by Ken Burns: A Request from Ishmael Reed

IN THE SPRING OF 2001, I met Ishmael Reed in Oakland, California, for lunch to discuss his writing an article for the anthology *Afro Asia: Revolutionary Political and Cultural Connections between African Americans and Asian Americans,* which I was working on with Professor Bill Mullen, then of the University of Texas–San Antonio. Ishmael agreed to write something, but in return asked that I send to him "ten important dates left out by Ken Burns in his documentary, *Jazz.*" I agreed, eager to cite what I believe to be significant dates to the confluence of music and liberation politics in the United States. The following is what I sent, with some revisions for this collection.

September 29, 1947

Premiere trumpeter "Dizzy" Gillespie introduces to the American "jazz" world Cuban *congero* Chano Pozo, and the "Latin-Jazz" or "Afro-Latin" sound is "born" at the historic concert at Carnegie Hall that featured the composition "Cubana Be, Cubana Bop." This concert also marks Gillespie's leading his first big band, which quickly establishes itself as one of the greatest big bands of all time. However, the development of "Latin-jazz," as in all artistic fermentations, began much earlier. Cuban composer/band leader Mario Bauza recalls

....

Originally a personal exchange between Fred Ho and Ishmael Reed; later published in *Shuffle Boil* 5/6 (2006).

introducing Chano Pozo as a possible percussionist for Gillespie as early as 1939, and Gillespie's own composition "A Night in Tunisia" (composed in 1942) reflects "Afro-Latin" rhythms. Besides "Cubana Be, Cubana Bop," another popular "Afro-Latin-jazz" composition is "Manteca."

1950s

Charles Mingus records "Fables of Faubus" as a sarcastic, pungent condemnation of segregationist-racist Arkansas Governor Orval Faubus.

1959

Composer George Russell publishes his book *Lydian Chromatic Concept of Tonal Organization,* the first systematized revolutionary "jazz" music theory, which he first began to develop as early as 1953. Russell's theory contributed to the growth of "modal" jazz. In his theory, improvisation could apply "horizontal" scales to "vertical" chords in varying degrees of consonance and dissonance. His system expanded the possibilities for soloists and composers to develop melodic lines beyond conventional harmony. Pianist Bill Evans and trumpeter/ musical avatar Miles Davis were familiar with Russell's theory and were leading artists in the "modal" jazz of that time.

Early 1960s

Charles Mingus in alliance with Max Roach, fed up with the exploitation of the Newport Jazz Festival, organized and self-produced the Breakaway Festival, an alternative festival occurring simultaneously with the Newport Festival. Mingus also started his own small labels during this time as an effort by musicians to control the means of their cultural production, a politically advanced cultural activist effort.

August 31 and September 6, 1960

In two recording sessions led by drummer/composer Max Roach, the *Freedom Now Suite* is recorded, supporting the struggle against both U.S. segregation and South African apartheid, a significant Pan-African statement made by a musician. Roach's stature across generations of musicians brought the tenor saxophonist Coleman Hawkins with younger artists such as singer Abbey Lincoln and saxophonist Booker Ervin together for this historic recording. Decades later, Roach continues to be a vanguard leader in his collaborations with younger, radical musicians, as shown in such works as his phenomenal duets with Anthony Braxton, Archie Shepp, Abdullah Ibrahim (Dollar Brand), Fab 5 Freddy, Cecil Taylor, and many others.

December 9 and 10, 1964

Tenor saxophonist/composer John Coltrane records *A Love Supreme* for Impulse! Records, an entire album-length suite that is considered by many as one of the most influential recordings of all time, with a musical impact that extended far beyond "jazz" into many other musical styles, as well as a signature recording for the generation of the 1960s.

July 17, 1967

John Coltrane dies in Huntington, New York, at the age of forty-one. By the time of his death, Coltrane had come to be regarded as the veritable musical shaman and avatar of the 1960s cultural revolution in Western society from his constant cross-cultural explorations and excursions beyond established musical parameters and norms. He was embraced by a whole generation of cultural radicals among blacks, whites, and many others as symbolizing the inexhaustible pursuer of truth, spiritual peace, and higher consciousness.

January 24, 1971

For 15 minutes on a national television broadcast, the *Ed Sullivan Show* is stormed by radical, militant black "jazz" musicians, including Archie Shepp, Rahsaan Roland Kirk, and others, who seize the airtime before a national television audience to perform "free" music both to protest of the exclusion of "jazz" on network TV as well as to herald the revolutionary assertions of the new music.

September 10, 1976

Upon the death of Chinese revolutionary leader Mao Zedong and the uprisings by Azanian (black South African) youth in Soweto in South Africa, Max Roach calls upon radical tenor saxophonist Archie Shepp and longtime friend bassist Charles Mingus (who, interestingly, did not like or respect Shepp) to perform two extended works, "Sweet Mao" and "South Africa '76" while touring Italy at the behest of the Italian Communist Party. Mingus, as Roach tells it, was on contract signed to Atlantic Records, which wouldn't allow him to do this, so the recording was made as a duet between Roach on drums and Shepp on tenor sax. This double album recording, simply entitled *Force*, won the Grand Prix du Disque, France's highest recording award.

April 1981

The First Asian American Jazz Festival, organized by the Kearny Street Workshop in San Francisco, featured two evenings of concerts at Fort Mason Center, produced by George Leong. The featured artists were Stockton Filipino American pianist Rudy Tenio; the Afro-Asian band United Front (with Japanese American bassist Mark Izu, African American alto saxophonist Lewis Jordan, African American trumpeter George Sams, and mixed-heritage Japanese-Black American drummer Anthony Brown); a band led by Japanese American saxophonist and *shakuhachi* (traditional Japanese vertical bamboo flute) player Russel Baba (with African American violinist Michael White and drummer Eddie Moore, who also played the saw); a trio led by Mark Izu with Paul Yamazaki on bass clarinet and Ray Collins on tenor and soprano saxes; and a young band with leader/drummer Guapo Lee (the stepson of Japanese American woodwindist Gerald Oshita), featuring the young tenor saxophonist Joshua Sherdoff (later known as Joshua Redman). The Asian American Jazz Festival has been an annual event and has the distinction of being founded a year before the more mainstream and larger-budget San Francisco Jazz Festival (formerly called Jazz in the City).

October 12, 1991

Persian American tenor saxophonist and composer Hafez Modirzadeh publically introduces "chromodal discourse" theory at the Palmer House Hotel in Chicago during the 36th annual conference of the Society for Ethnomusicology. "Chromodal discourse" theory may be the latest revolutionary musical theoretical system since George Russell's "Lydian concept" (Modirzadeh was a student of Russell's at the New England Conservatory, where he first developed the "chromodal discourse" theory and documented it in his personal diary on September 20, 1983). Through a systematic application of alternative saxophone fingerings, Modirzadeh has applied a Persian "quarter tone" temperament system to Western diatonic harmony, skillfully maneuvering complex vertical chord changes such as those in Coltrane's "Giant Steps" with a modal horizontality. His "chromodal discourse" theory was formally published in a copyrighted dissertation submitted April 15, 1992, and defended May 20, 1992, at Wesleyan University, a campus once known for its stellar World Music and African American Music programs. Modirzadeh's dissertation committee was chaired by Jon Barlow and included Anthony Braxton and Javanese gamelan Indonesian specialist Sumarsam. Modirzadeh began to teach this theory in the fall semester of 1990 at San Jose State University. Through a National Endowment for the Arts Jazz Composition fellowship, he performed and recorded various compositions demonstrating this theory on May 30, 1989, in San Francisco which were released in 1993.

The following is Modirzadeh's more detailed chronology of his chromodal discourse theory:

1. The concept was first articulated in late September of 1983, while [I was] attending the New England Conservatory, in Boston. George Russell's course on Lydian Chromaticism encouraged the development of the theory. I entered in a

journal, at that time, some of the following: "Can modality and tonality be brought together somehow?"; "To keep the essence of the mode . . . with chords that are colored themselves (with extensions)"; "The final goal should be to strive for a way to play over conventional jazz changes, but with new melodic material to draw from"; ". . . to expand the dastgah (Persian modal) system, and its tuning, into harmonic regions, giving it vertical sound as well as horizontal, while keeping it intact modally"; "and the tuning system should be kept intact, even when a western-tuned instrument is accompanying." The theory continued to develop through stints in Los Angeles, at UCLA (1984–86), and while living in New York City (1987–89).

2. Due to [an] NEA Jazz Fellowship, on May 30th, 1989, three original compositions based on the theory were recorded in San Francisco, California. These were idiomatic transformations of "Stella By Starlight," "Autumn Leaves," and Monk's "Round Midnight."

3. During the Fall of 1990, the first formal teachings on "chromodal discourse" were integrated into the Jazz Studies program at San Jose State University. The introduction of "tetramodes," "metricodes," and "idiomatic transformation" were initialized into a practical cross-cultural approach.

4. "Chromodal Discourse," as a then-new cross-cultural approach, was given its first professional introduction as a paper read at the 36th Annual Conference [of] the Society for Ethnomusicology, on October 10–13, 1991, at the Palmer House Hotel, in Chicago, Il.

    The reaction was not a memorable one.

5. On April 15, 1992, "Chromodality and the Cross-Cultural Exchange of Musical Structure" was submitted in dissertation form for the PhD at Wesleyan University, in Middletown, CT.

On May 20, 1992, Modirzadeh's defense of the dissertation was held with committee members Sumarsam, Anthony Braxton, and Jon Barlow (chair). The dissertation represented an interdisciplinary philosophy in both music theory and practice through story-telling.

For a listing of chromodal projects since then, refer to http://userwww.sfsu.edu/~fezmo, or simply type "Hafez Modirzadeh" into a search engine.

. . . .

Many criticisms have been levied against the highly touted and super-marketed *Jazz* by Ken Burns, including the fact that while only a recent lover of the "music," Burns has virtually no expertise on the subject matter and relied heavily upon the perspectives and contacts of the Wynton Marsalis/Jazz at Lincoln Center cabal. While many valid criticisms regarding omissions and ideological biases were made by critics of the PBS series, I believe the main problem stemmed from its heavily propagandistic tone in support of Marsalis/Crouch/Albert Murray/Ralph Ellison's integrationist view of "jazz" as "American music." The documentary seemed to denounce any black nationalist or Pan-Africanist ideologies or expressions, particularly the avant-garde of the 1960s. Branford Marsalis is featured denouncing Cecil Taylor as promoting "self-indulgent bullshit," but Taylor is never afforded a response. No leading artists of the 1960s movement, many of whom are still alive (and some are quite articulate, such as Bill Dixon and Archie Shepp, among others), were interviewed. Furthermore, Wynton himself is called upon to pronounce the nexus between "race in America" and "jazz" in his stumbling, canned statement that "jazz" is the challenge to America to live up to its ideals and promises of democracy, freedom, ad nauseam.

‹ 127

This is the mainstream, pro-Yankee integrationist/imperialist political position regarding "jazz" as America's "classical music," which legitimates the music according to bourgeois, Eurocentric standards of American art. Rather than characterize the music as resistance to oppression (e.g., Archie Shepp's lyrical metaphor, "Jazz is the lily in spite of the swamp"), or as a music that sounds the aspirations for freedom (implying that the struggle for freedom is both historical and ongoing), the integrationist-imperialist position proclaims "we are all Americans" and that the "music" is consistent with, rather than in contradiction with, the values espoused and practiced by this social system. It was Malcolm X who so clearly and sharply stated, "I'm not an American. I'm a victim of America," and that "Democracy is disguised hypocrisy."

The class struggle within the music of the African American ("New Afrikan") nation is reflected in these two fundamental differing positions: music that stands with the oppressed nations and nationalities of the settler-colonialist multinational United States, or music that identifies with the oppressor United States, used by its State Department when sent on tours to Africa and the Third World to promote integrationism and the façade of democracy. Among the artists, this struggle is reflected in positions of artistic integrity and defiance versus accommodation to minstrelsy (watered-down commercial "jazz") or bourgeois artistic pretensions (canonized classical music à la Marsalis).

The Damned Don't Cry:
The Life and Music of Calvin Massey

AFRICAN AMERICAN MUSIC was Cal Massey's life. He gave so much
of his life to the music of his people—a music filled with their cries of
suffering and irrepressible spirit of struggle for freedom.

I never met Cal Massey, never heard him perform live, but I was
introduced to Mr. Massey's music through his compositions performed and recorded primarily by Archie Shepp. Titles such as "Hey,
Goddamn It, Things Have Got to Change!," "The Damned Don't Cry,"
and "The Cry of My People" spoke directly to a consciousness of oppression and a politics of liberation. These pieces were instrumental
works, evoking soulful and searing melodies, which soared over rich,
sophisticated, and glorious harmonies. As a young composer with an
interest in radical and revolutionary music, Cal Massey seemed to be
the embodiment of the composer/band leader I needed and wanted
to know about, but who had died just before I started into music (Cal
Massey died at the age of forty-four on October 25, 1972, while I started
playing the baritone saxophone and began my composing interests at
age fourteen, around 1971-72). My first encounter with Mr. Massey's
music was at age sixteen, playing baritone saxophone in a chamber
orchestra led by Archie Shepp for a faculty-student performance of
the radical music/theater work *Lady Day: A Musical Tragedy,* written by Aishah Rahman, at the University of Massachusetts-Amherst

Published in another form in *Unity* newspaper (the political organ of the League of
Revolutionary Struggle), February 15, 1985.

on April 19, 1975. The music was a collaboration of compositions by Archie Shepp along with Cal Massey and Stanley Cowell.

I wanted to learn more about this composer, who paid some "hard dues," who wrote epic, large-scale, extended suites dedicated to the revolutionary Black Liberation struggle, and who was regarded as a folk-hero/mentor by many of the leading "jazz" musicians of the day. After I moved to New York City in late 1981 to embark on a "jazz" career, I quickly met many of these musicians whom I had admired and who were associated with Cal Massey. In my spare time in the early 1980s, I researched Cal Massey's life and music, which culminated in this full-length article. The more I researched and learned about the music of Cal Massey, the more I was compelled to perform it, to keep it alive through a series of Tribute Concerts for which I was the principal organizer during the 1980s.

....

Calvin ("Cal") Massey was born January 11, 1928. His mother, Edna, and his father, Calvin, Sr., had separated by the time Cal was one year old. His father was a cook and his mother was a domestic worker. Raised by his mother in Pittsburgh, the young Calvin was told by her that his father had died. But by his teens, his mother revealed that his father was not dead, just that she did not know where he was. The teenage Cal began to search for his father, whom he finally found when he was eighteen.

According to his widow, Charlotte Massey, at around Cal's tenth or eleventh birthday, his mother's boyfriend, who was considered his "stepfather," gave the young boy a pawn shop-bought trumpet for a gift. Cal would sneak out of the house to go listen to the bands that were playing in town, such as at the Lodge Hall near his home, where he heard Erroll Garner for the first time. Cal's musical instruction came by hanging around the musicians, asking them questions, and absorbing the knowledge and information around him. "He applied his street smarts," is how Charlotte Massey described Cal's learning process. At age fifteen, Cal left home to go on the road with a band and thus began his musical career.

This first professional outing would repeat the pattern of so many struggling musicians: Cal was eventually stranded in Kansas City with no money and had to wire his mother for enough funds to return home.

In searching for his father during his teens, Cal went to Philadelphia. There he met a young saxophonist named John Coltrane. As Charlotte tells the story, Cal was walking the streets and heard an alto player of immense strength of sound wailing from a basement. "At first, Cal thought it was Bird (Charlie Parker)." But it turned out to be Coltrane, also in his teens. Drawn to Coltrane's mesmeric sound, Cal began a lifelong friendship and close musical association with Coltrane, just at the formative time of Coltrane's genius and titanic abilities. As Charlotte Massey described the relationship between the two young musicians:

> Cal would follow Trane around like a puppy. Coltrane and Cal lived together in Coltrane's mother's house. Cal used to call Coltrane "country" because of Trane's quiet personality; Coltrane never had much to say verbally. They constantly talked about music. Coltrane eventually bought a house for his mother in West Philly. Coltrane and Cal would commute between Philly and New York City for gigs.

‹ 131

At a party in the East Harlem apartment of Cal's cousin Bill Massey, a prominent musician who had performed with Gene Ammons, Cal met his soon-to-be-wife, Charlotte. Harlem-born, of West Indian descent, she was nineteen when they met. She remembered Cal as a "foul talker, loud at parties." He would call her "bitch." "But as soon as he set eyes on me, I knew he was attracted to me." While fascinated by her, Cal called her a "conceited bitch." Charlotte explained: "Cal was very straightforward about his opinions. He used a curse word in every sentence. People would later, after we were married, ask Cal, 'Where did you get such a nice wife and kids?' since first encounters with Cal often did not give the best impression of his manners."

Charlotte and Cal would go to the Apollo Theater to hear Dizzy Gillespie, or to the Red Rooster and hear Thelonious Monk. In the black community, musicians were admired as "community rebel-heroes," and Charlotte admitted her attraction to musicians. At the time that she and Cal began dating, she was attending Hunter College and had to sneak out on dates because she couldn't tell her parents she was seeing a musician. "That would be like marrying the devil" as far as her parents were concerned. They finally eloped, she at age twenty-one, and he at twenty-four, and were married in City Hall. Charlotte moved in with Cal into Coltrane's Philadelphia house.

Charlotte Massey recounted to me how bored she was being around Coltrane and Cal. "From morning to evening, the two would talk about music, chord progressions. Coltrane's mother saw this, and she would bake a cake to get these two young guys to stop their conversations about music. Coltrane's mother would tell Cal to leave me with her since Cal was 'always under Coltrane's ass.'"

Though the dates were unclear in Charlotte Massey's mind when I interviewed her, it appears that in the late 1940s, Cal and his family moved to New York City. She recalled that the young pianist Walter Bishop, Jr., was staying in their apartment, and that many musicians would drop by and hang out. This would continue for the rest of Cal's life; his home was always open to fellow musicians. Charlotte recalled, "Miles Davis would drop by and hang out for long periods of time. Others, too, like Eddie 'Lockjaw' Davis. Cal was becoming known on the New York scene through the many combos and big bands he was working in."

During this time Cal Massey began to compose. He had studied arranging with a teenage idol of his, Freddie Webster, along with his cousin, Bill Massey. An early Cal Massey composition, "Fiesta," was recorded by Charlie Parker, and it was the first time that Bird used congas played by Chano Pozo, as opined by Charlotte Massey.

By the late 1940s, Cal Massey had begun to distinguish himself as a composer and band leader. Since his teenage years, Massey had been working with a number of rising musicians, including Jay McShan, Eddie "Cleanhead" Vinson, the George Shearing big band, the Jimmy Heath big band, and Philly Joe Jones; he toured briefly with Billie Holiday. When Cal Massey started his own band, it included a sterling group of musicians, including Albert "Tootie" Heath (drums), Jimmy Garrison (bass), "C" Clarence Sharpe (alto sax), and a seventeen-year-old pianist named McCoy Tyner.

By the late 1950s, Massey had settled his growing family in Brooklyn's Crown Heights neighborhood. He had bought a house at 235 Brooklyn Avenue, where he raised his five children (India, Taru, Zane, Singh, and Waheeda). The house while Massey was alive would become a virtual cultural center for Brooklyn musicians. Massey was respectfully known as "The Teacher" for the openness he exhibited to younger musicians and for his generous sharing of musical information. He was also affectionately nicknamed "Folks." Archie Shepp described Cal Massey as "a beacon to the growing community of musicians in Brooklyn."

Cal Massey paid many dues. He was very frustrated for being recognized more for his writing and composing than for his trumpet playing, which hurt him deeply. "He so very much wanted to be recognized for his trumpet playing," according to Charlotte Massey. She recalled that when they first started living in their Brooklyn house that he would bring his trumpet to bed with him. The two slept with the trumpet between them, "but I quickly put an end to that," said Charlotte. The life of a musician is economically precarious. They made enough to get by, but often they lived at the edge of poverty. Massey earned most of his money not through performing but from the many arrangements he wrote for local bands and singers. Most of his income, according to Charlotte, was earned from orchestrations and recordings. When Coltrane needed large-scale orchestrations for his Africa Brass sessions, he called upon Massey. The legendary Africa Brass recording sessions included Cal Massey's "The Damned Don't Cry," recorded with a large ensemble on May 25, 1961, and conducted by Romulus Franceschini.

Indeed, Massey is best remembered for the magnificent and beautiful compositions he wrote, some of which have become near-classics. Cal Massey's compositions possess a brass-like quality, the majestic resonance and brilliant colors of a trumpet. His music evokes the breadth and depth of the African American musical continuum, entrenched in the blues. The Massey melodies are easily recognized for their soulful, singing quality. His harmonies are complex and richly vibrant, and convey a sophisticated, urban-intellectual sound. Charlie Parker, as noted earlier, recorded Massey's "Fiesta" in the late 1940s. When Coltrane recorded his first album as a leader, the title piece was a Massey composition, "Bakai." Coltrane recorded other Massey works, including the well-known "Nakatini Serenade" and the posthumously released "The Damned Don't Cry." Other great musicians have recorded Massey compositions, including McCoy Tyner ("Love Song")—the young Tyner getting his professional debut in the Massey band; Woody Shaw ("Message from Trane," originally entitled "Sunday Morning," recorded on Shaw's *Moontrane*); Herbie Mann

("Trinidad" on the *Just Wailin'* recording); Jackie McLean ("Message from Trane," "Toyland," and "Demon's Dance"); Freddie Hubbard ("Assunta" and "Father and Son"). Trumpeter Lee Morgan recorded several Massey pieces, including "These Are Soulful Days" and the poignant "The Cry of My People." But the greatest number of Massey compositions have been recorded by Archie Shepp on albums such as *Things Have Got to Change*, *Attica Blues*, *The Cry of My People*, and others. "Things Have Got to Change" has become an often-recorded and performed piece in the Shepp repertoire since the 1970s. The much younger Shepp began a close collaboration with Massey only in the later years of Massey's life. A comprehensive list of Cal Massey compositions and the artists and recordings on which they were featured was compiled by Bertrand Uberall and Michael Fitzgerald and is online at http://perso.wanadoo.fr/hardbop/Massey/Massey.html.

Tenor saxophonist Roland Alexander met Cal in 1959. As Alexander described it, the late 1950s were "the tail-end of the jazz club scene in New York." Cal had formed his own quintet in New York that worked around the Brooklyn circuit with himself on trumpet, Sadik Hakim on piano, Alexander on tenor sax, Scoby Stroman on drums, and Roy Standard on bass. The band worked such Brooklyn clubs as the Moulin Rouge, the Turbo Village, and the Coronet. The band never worked outside of Brooklyn, according to Alexander, and never performed in known Manhattan venues such as Birdland, the Half Note, or the Five Spot. As Alexander recalled, "musicians would come listen, hang out, and play." The list of luminaries included Freddie Hubbard, Junior Cook, Wayne Shorter, and Coltrane. Massey in this period would occasionally do concerts with Sonny Stitt and Coltrane in Philadelphia. Roland Alexander noted that Cal's gift for arranging included pop tunes such as the Italian hit "Volari." Roland Alexander believed that the Brooklyn quintet worked for two to three years.

Cal Massey's life was devoted to music, with the only exception being his devotion to his family. Everyone recalls Massey as a family man who loved his children very deeply. Charlotte recalled how Cal would stay and work in his house, rehearse in the living room, or, if the weather was nice, in their backyard. Whenever he had a concert, he'd bring his whole family. She said, "He always insisted that his children, from the oldest to the newest baby, had to be there."

Being a musician's wife wasn't easy for Charlotte Massey. "Being married to a musician, other wives were jealous of their husbands' music. There'd never be a steady income. And musicians like Cal would give so much of their time and attention to music. It was like they were married to both a wife and to their music." While Cal deeply loved his wife and his family, it was clear that they had to share that love with his love for music, too. The stresses of making a living in the precarious music business fanned jealousies and rivalries between the wives of the musicians depending on how much money their husbands were making, or how famous they were becoming. Charlotte Massey recounted how a certain group of musicians' wives, the "Just Us Club," as she called them, would go out on the town, play cards, go to bars and clubs, and have a ball. They'd hold affairs, "cook food like chili and fried chicken . . . these were the 'hip women.'" Charlotte was never asked to join them. She simply stayed at home. "I was left in the background," she stated.

‹ 135

In 1958, Cal began a close musical friendship and partnership with a soft-spoken, quiet, Italian American composer/arranger based in Philadelphia named Romulus Franceschini. Archie Shepp recalled how Cal was of the opinion that Romulus was one of the best string orchestrators around. Franceschini was about a decade Massey's senior. They would remain close friends and partners until Massey's death. Together, the partnership of Romulus and Massey (expressed as "RoMas" in their co-led RoMas Orchestra) would be a formidable creative team, much in the tradition of Ellington-Strayhorn, Basie-Nestico, and so on. In meeting and exchanging musical ideas with Franceschini, a dynamic and cutting-edge musical force in his own right, but almost exclusively in the European new music concert world, Massey found a mutually brilliant musical thinker and fellow radical (Franceschini was an avowed socialist). As Franceschini stated in a 1986 tribute to Massey, "It is hard to describe exactly how Cal and I worked together. In general, Cal composed the tunes and I did the arrangements and orchestrations. But it was far more intricate than that—we were constantly feeding each other ideas." Including singing back and forth over the telephone, noted Charlotte Massey.

Cal Massey's life was a constant struggle against the vicious exploitation of the music business. Charlotte Massey recounted to me a story of her husband's veritable blacklisting by the then Blue Note

THE DAMNED DON'T CRY

records, considered one of the preeminent "jazz" labels of its time. As she told it, one day Cal met Blue Note records co-owner Francis Wolff in an elevator and tried to talk to him. Wolff just ignored Massey. As Massey exited the elevator, he kicked Wolff. From that time on, according to Charlotte Massey, all publishing and recording companies effectively blacklisted her husband. I personally know only of two recordings that featured Massey himself and his band. One was an album called *The Jazz Life*, an anthology that was headlined by Massey on the short-lived but creatively important Candid label, which included other "breakaway" independent-minded musicians such as Charles Mingus, Booker Little, and Max Roach. On this recording, Cal Massey had a quintet that performed Massey's composition "Father and Son." Massey takes a trumpet solo in which he quotes the old slave song/spiritual "Nobody Knows the Trouble I've Seen." *The Jazz Life* was released in 1961.

The sole recording that featured Massey as a leader, *Blues to Coltrane* for the Candid label, was recorded on January 13, 1961, and was released in 1963. It featured Massey on trumpet, Julius Watkins on French horn, Hugh Brodie Foster on tenor sax, Patti Brown on piano, Jimmy Garrison on bass, and G. T. Hogan on drums.

In his short life of forty-four years, Massey had three nervous breakdowns and was hospitalized. He lost one kidney from tuberculosis and bloated up to 300 pounds. At 5 feet 7 inches tall, he had to wear robes to cover his girth of a 54-inch waistline. Constantly in poor health, he often mistreated his own body as a heavy drinker and chain smoker. His body would be on a constant rollercoaster between pills and alcohol. He would stay up without sleep for nights and days working on music and producing his own concerts. During the 1960s, while Cal had established his reputation among the elite circle of New York City black musicians, he remained a relatively unknown artist to the greater public. Only near the end of his life did he finally stop drinking heavily, feeling that his hard luck was beginning to change for the better as a growing portion of the "jazz" public was starting to recognize him.

In the mid-1960s, Cal Massey became associated with a younger, more militant-minded circle of musicians, including the tenor saxophonist and outspoken radical Archie Shepp. This new wave of artists spearheaded the revolutionary musical upsurge of the burgeoning

Black Liberation Movement and its attendant cultural wing, the Black Arts Movement. It was trombonist-arranger Charles Majeed Green-lee, a contemporary of Massey, who introduced the younger Shepp to "The Teacher." In Shepp's words, "I was attracted to the legend of Cal Massey, the Coltrane collaborator. Cal wrote songs out of the same theory as Coltrane composed solos, with angular melodies . . . intricate turnbacks . . . Cal Massey was a consummate composer."

Not to be deterred by the lack of gigs, Cal Massey began to produce his own concerts during this time. He organized benefit concerts at St. Gregory's Church across the street from his house (on St. John between Brooklyn and New York Avenues) to raise money for a new community playground. One such benefit concert was a two-day marathon that featured the Coltrane quartet with the incredible Rahsaan Roland Kirk as guest artist. The concert featured Coltrane's *Love Supreme* suite, with Trane reading the Prayer. The marathon also included Thelonious Monk. Charlotte Massey recalled how powerful the music was, even with drummer Elvin Jones wearing a cast on his foot. While Zane Massey, Cal's son and today a professional musician in his own right, was only age six at the time, he recalls the power of the music at that concert: "Trane played so much horn." Zane recounted that after the concert, Trane went over to the Massey house to have some food, but his horn was always out of his case, lying on the bed, ready to be played. This event occurred about a year before Coltrane died. The high regard that musicians held for Cal Massey enabled him to call upon their services to perform at these benefits. Given his status among both his own and the younger generation of musicians, Cal single-handedly brought together musicians who were in different cliques and circles. According to trombonist Charles Stephens, Cal was "the musical presence and center in Brooklyn."

‹ 137

Cal Massey's self-produced concerts were also part of the thrust for artistic self-control and the Black Liberation Movement's goal for self-determination through creating alternative cultural institutions and forms of cultural production for the benefit of the black community. Massey's benefit concerts were historically important as artistic events and were economic successes as well. These highly successful concerts, including three benefits he organized for the Black Panther Party, demonstrated the mass support for the concept of community-based cultural production as thousands of community people turned out to attend cutting-edge concerts in the heart of black Brooklyn. Massey was able to convince black businessmen and entrepreneurs to invest in the music as he produced concerts on ocean cruises that were financially and artistically successful.

These benefit concerts became projects for the entire Massey family. Because the music industry was not interested in his music, Cal took his music directly to the people. These self-produced benefit concerts reflected Massey's strong community orientation and commitment to get the music to the people, to raise consciousness within the community, to get his music performed *by any means necessary*, and, at the same time, to create more employment for other musicians. With close help from his wife, Charlotte, Massey organized these concerts in every detail. Charlotte was especially important as the accountant who budgeted expenses. Cal's eldest daughter, India, was secretary. Through organizing one of these benefit concerts, India met her husband, Eric Chambers, the son of bassist Paul Chambers. After the musicians were paid and the expenses reimbursed, Cal and Charlotte almost never collected a salary for themselves. Usually, the family got their phone bills covered (which ran as high as $500 a month during the 1960s).

Cal Massey was a living legend, a sort of community celebrity, well-loved and respected by musicians and his Brooklyn community. Charlotte Massey told how teenagers especially loved her husband. He was respected by the Five Percenters, a local street gang. Local kids would come over to the Massey home, which was always crowded, and offer to run errands to help Mr. Massey. They'd also run to Cal for help with their problems. Cal was accessible to young people. Several of these benefit concerts featured youth bands, including his son Zane, a tenor saxophonist, who practiced with his father after school from evening to dawn.

The Massey home was a haven for many musicians, especially those going through marital problems, thrown out of their homes by their wives. These temporarily homeless musicians would sleep on the Massey sofa. One time Charlotte was so fed up with so many people staying at their home that she demanded her husband get rid of the sofa bed or tell them to "go back to your wife." Cal was very fortunate to have such an understanding wife who sympathized with the struggle of creative musicians. Because Cal never could stand to leave his children, he was never thrown out by Charlotte; he would finally have to consent to his wife's protestations and demands to let out their many house guests.

At home, according to Charlotte Massey, Cal was a very disorganized person. "His music would be lying all over the house. If he needed a part, it'd be missing. He'd get everyone in the house to look for it. The kids would put peanut butter and jelly on his albums. But when it came to the music business, he handled that very carefully. There never were any problems with his musicians being paid. This was something else considering how moody musicians are."

"Cal Massey had a lot of energy, man!" exclaimed Roland Alexander when I interviewed him. Cal Massey's work habits included practicing from 7 P.M. to 3 A.M., and then writing music. According to Charlotte, her husband would often watch the sunrise. He wrote one of his most beautiful works, "Quiet Dawn" (recorded by Shepp on *Attica Blues*), while inspired by a magnificent sunrise in Paris in the summer of 1969. He was with Archie Shepp, who had brought Massey with his band on an extended tour that included the First Pan-African Arts Festival in Algiers, Algeria. It was in Paris during this tour that Cal was invited by Duke Ellington to contribute arrangements to two of his compositions, "Quiet Dawn" and "Father and Son," to the Ellington Orchestra. For Cal, as for any musician, this was an extreme honor to be asked by the maestro.

‹ 139

Cal Massey would sleep during the day, and practice with his mute in his horn while his family slept. Massey was never really into teaching music formally and had at most three students at any one time, according to his wife. A very rough-mannered man, he'd be very warm once people got to know him. As Charles Stephens described, "Cal had the foulest mouth around, but he loved you. One minute he'd be cursing you out, the next he'd hug you."

The tour to Europe with Archie Shepp was a big moment for Cal. The Shepp band worked in Europe for a month and then spent two weeks in northern Africa at the historic FESTAC, which served as a convocation for radical black nationalist artists and activists. His wife felt the tour did wonders for him, "made him calmer, more diplomatic, not so frustrated." While in Paris, Massey lived in a sublet apartment with Don Byas and Shepp.

In Algeria, Massey met Eldridge Cleaver, former minister of information of the Black Panther Party, who was living in exile. Cleaver asked Massey to compose *The Black Liberation Movement Suite* for the Panthers. Massey would embark upon this project with full force upon his return to the United States, phoning Romulus Franceschini to collaborate. As Romulus described, "Cal called me and told me he wanted to compose a long suite which would represent the consummation of his life work. He knew, I believe, he would die soon." The suite would consist of much new material with some older material like 'The Damned Don't Cry,' which Cal had composed some dozen years earlier, and which, in fact, we had already recorded with John Coltrane back in 1960. The suite was called *The Black Liberation Movement Suite* and it was virtually completed by 1970. It consisted, at that time, of eight movements, some of which were dedicated to black leaders."

The tour turned Cal's life around. His wife told of how Cal slept in the desert in Africa beside the Sphinx. Cal Massey had taken all of the family's money to go on this tour, but he came back refreshed and reinvigorated, and had even saved some money.

The unique and special relationship between Massey and Shepp was not so much between older teacher and younger student, as both inspired and influenced each other. It wasn't the same kind of peer relationship that Massey had shared with the now-deceased John Coltrane, in which the two grew up together as musicians and as men. Shepp was unique among the "young avant-garde lions." He highly respected and revered the old "jazz" masters, oftentimes referring to them as "Mr. Coltrane," "Mr. Ellington," and so on. Shepp was also intellectually very radical: he had been in Marxist study groups, lived in the same Cooper Square apartment with writer/radical intellectual LeRoi Jones (now Amiri Baraka), and he understood the continuity in African American culture and its connection to political struggle. In many ways, Shepp was more politically and intellectually advanced and connected easily with someone like the older Massey. According to Charlotte Massey, Archie Shepp in many ways learned to play "inside" chord changes from Cal Massey. And Cal Massey, in her words, "loved Archie Shepp. Cal felt Archie's music was revolutionary." The two were a potent combination, bridging generations and styles of the most advanced of African American music and radical intellectualism.

Many consider Shepp's recordings of this era to be an eclectic exploration of more expanded black musical forms, including rhythm and blues and big band writing, choral works, and so on. Saxophonist Roland Alexander recounted how Cal Massey contracted the musicians for one of Shepp's greatest recordings, *Attica Blues*, recorded over two days from January 24 to 26, 1972. *Attica Blues* stands out, not only for winning the highest rating from *Down Beat* magazine (five stars)—a magazine that wasn't too friendly to Shepp and fairly unsympathetic to the 1960s avant-garde black nationalist musicians—but also, and more importantly, for its political support of the Attica prison rebellion and the particularly interesting and novel artistic choices made on the album, which included featuring William "Beaver" Harris's poetry intoned by radical attorney William Kunstler on two tracks and singing by Cal Massey's then six-year-old daughter, Waheeda, on the beautifully orchestrated Massey ballad, "Quiet Dawn." With the innocence of a child's voice, "Quiet Dawn" evokes the serene magnificence of an African sunrise and expressed Cal Massey's celebration of life and spiritual beauty.

‹ 141

Returning to the United States, Massey plunged into organizing a series of historic benefit concerts for the Black Panther Party. The first benefit Panther concert proved tremendously historic and successful, and was held on February 22, 1972 at 1310 Atlantic Avenue, Brooklyn. It premiered Massey's opus, *The Black Liberation Movement Suite*. No alcohol was permitted at the concert, and childcare was provided on the premises. The concert featured such great artists as Alice Coltrane, Freddie Hubbard, Lee Morgan, Archie Shepp, Leon Thomas, Pharoah Sanders, and Joe Lee Wilson, among many others. The concert raised funds for the Black Panther Party's legal defense fund and its political prisoners.

A second major benefit was held in Harlem, and a third was organized in Philadelphia. While the first successful benefit was solely organized by the Massey family, the latter two major benefits were solely organized by the Panthers, who lacked the experience and connections to do concert promotion. The failure of the last two major benefits·was clearly the fault of the Panthers, who wouldn't allow Massey to organize the business aspects. The Harlem concert was especially disastrous. No flyers were done, and the stage had no piano; people had to rush at the last minute to Massey's house to bring his piano there. While doing these benefits, the Massey home received many threatening phone calls warning Cal not to go on with these concerts. In my interview with Zane Massey in 1985, it was his opinion that some of the Harlem concert organizers turned out to be informers, who were partly responsible for the concert's problems.

This was a very beleaguered time in the Black Panther Party, which was disorganized and under siege by the police and FBI, with harassment, jailings, or killings of their cadre an almost daily occurrence. From paranoia and an ultra-control mentality, the Panthers didn't want Massey to handle any part of the concert organizing except for the music. Cal warned them, "You've got to know what you're doing."

The tremendous success of the first concert on February 22, 1972, was reflected in its tight organization: there were cots for people to lie down, there was plenty of food available for sale, and the Panthers had mobilized people from many districts on the East Coast to attend. The concert was well-guarded. In an opening act, a youth group performed with a notable young guitarist still in high school named Noel Pointer. The concert drew tens of thousands of people from all over the world and was a huge success artistically, financially, and politically.

The writing of *The Black Liberation Movement Suite* led to the formation of an ensemble that was needed to perform the music. As Franceschini described it,

> In order to play the suite, Cal and I organized and co-led a sixteen-piece ensemble which we named the RoMas Orchestra (from Romulus and Massey). This ensemble included such fine artists as Leroy Jenkins, James Spaulding, Carlos Ward, Roland Alexander, Dan Jones, Charles McGhee, Michael Ridley, Curtis Fuller, Charles Stephens, Kiane Zawadi, Lonnie Liston Smith, Reggie Workman, and Rashied Ali. Cal then proceeded to organize and produce some two dozen concerts—benefits for the Black Panther Party—in the New York area and elsewhere. The RoMas Orchestra played at all these concerts alongside such artists as—and these are just a few off the top of my head—Thelonious Monk, Betty Carter, Archie Shepp, Carmen McRae, Frank Foster, Pharoah Sanders, Sunny Murray, Jackie McLean, Freddie Hubbard, Lee Morgan, Junior Cook, and many others. During this time—1970 to 1972—Cal and I continued to make changes in the suite. Before Cal died, we jointly composed a piece

entitled "Back to Africa," dedicated to Marcus Garvey. This became the ninth movement. The RoMas Orchestra played it just once—at Amherst, Massachusetts. Cal died shortly after.

The suite would undergo another revision in 1986 by Franceschini for a series of Cal Massey tribute concerts organized initially by Fred Houn and Zane Massey, which featured all nine movements.

The original performance of the suite consisted of a modified big band with strings. The RoMas Orchestra had an unusual instrumentation that included three bassists (Larry Ridley, Hakim Jami, and Reggie Workman) and a bassoonist (Dan Jones) along with the conventional saxes/winds, brass, and rhythm sections. When the RoMas Orchestra was formed in 1970, it had twenty-one players. Franceschini lived in Philadelphia and regularly commuted to New York for rehearsals and performances. Romulus had the uncanny ability to transcribe anything, "like taking steno," as described by Charlotte ‹ 143 Massey. Romulus and Cal would exchange musical ideas over long-distance phone calls. "Romulus would write down what Cal would sing to him over the phone." There are stories about this unusual pair, with a white man co-leading an all-black band, and some of the musicians being pretty nationalist in their sentiments. Some of these black musicians would complain to Cal about the fact that Romulus, a white man, was conducting. As Charlotte Massey told it, "Cal never paid much mind [to these complaints], but when it got excessive, he told them off: 'If you want the gig, it's my decision.'" According to Charlotte, Romulus was the best person to understand Cal's music in Cal's view. Charles Stephens, at the time a young trombonist in the Sun Ra Arkestra when that band was based in New York's Lower East Side, commented: "Cal said he couldn't tell where he stopped and where Romulus began. They were really partners." Stephens also remarked how "Cal could draw the most accomplished musicians. Cal took care of business. You could believe in him. People were eager to be there. Cats were excited to work with Cal."

The original eight movements of *The Black Liberation Movement Suite* consisted of:

1. "Prayer" (recorded on Archie Shepp's *The Cry of My People*)
2. "Things Have Got to Change" (recorded on several Archie Shepp albums)

3. "Man at Peace in Algiers (for Eldridge Cleaver)"
4. "The Black Saint (for Malcolm X)"
5. "The Peaceful Warrior (for Martin Luther King, Jr.)"
6. "The Damned Don't Cry (for Huey P. Newton)"
7. "Reminiscing about Dear John (for John Coltrane)"
8. "Babylon (to the U.S.A.)"

A ninth movement, "Back to Africa," was added just before Massey died, and was played only once, at the University of Massachusetts-Amherst in 1972. Movement 5 had lyrics written by Cal Massey, which he would occasionally sing in performances.

One of the highlights in Cal's career occurred during this time, when he was invited to appear on ABC-TV's *Like It Is* show hosted by Gil Noble. Massey was featured along with another veteran freedom-fighter musician, Max Roach.

The genius of Cal Massey, besides being a prolific composer, also included writing some of the most beautiful and poignant lyrics to songs such as "Looking For Someone to Love," "What Would It Be without You," a song for his wife entitled "Lady Charlotte" (recorded by Cedar Walton), and words for a Carmen McRae song, "I Thought I'd Let You Know." And Cal would sometimes sing. He was "a real charmer," described Charles Stephens. Even though Cal Massey never finished high school, the poetic quality of these lyrics was amazing. His wife recounted how Cal would borrow all kinds of books from the public library, "though sometimes he wouldn't return them." He studied East Indian music and Asian music. He would tell his children about the giants of black American history. He organized children's choirs for his benefits and even for recordings, such as Archie Shepp's 1971 release, *Things Have Got to Change.*

According to Zane Massey, his father knew he was going to die soon and expressed his desire to write a black revolutionary opera before he died. Massey conceived of this epic work as spanning time from slavery to the future, "drawing from slave chants up to jazz and beyond; that would have been my father's next project," recounted Zane Massey. Cal Massey died on October 25, 1972, at the age of forty-four, from a heart attack. The day of his death was to be the opening of a new musical play, *Lady Day: A Musical Tragedy,* written by Aishah Rahman, directed by Paul Carter Harrison, with music and co-musical direction by Archie Shepp with Cal Massey and Stanley Cowell. Two Massey songs were featured in this experimental musical: "Looking for Someone to Love" and "What Would It Be without You." The musical play ran at the Brooklyn Academy of Music, and was produced by the Chelsea Theater Center of Brooklyn (then Executive Director Michael David is now president of the Broadway production company The Dodgers). This musical play was very innovative, not at all following the Broadway formula of using the music to underline the drama. Rather, the music was the core driving force. The songs were glorious examples of soulful and sophisticated black music, and not simple crowd-pleasing gospel or soul-pop tunes. Replete with great songs, one highlight was a masterful ballad called "The Lady" written by saxophonist/pianist/arranger Bob Ford. It can be heard sung by Joe Lee Wilson on Shepp's recording *The Cry of My People*. Ford was, like Cal Massey, part of a group of brilliant but underrecognized Brooklyn black artists. When I was researching Cal Massey's life and music during the mid-1980s, Bob Ford was virtually a homeless person on the streets of Brooklyn. I have no idea of what has happened to him.

White critics excoriated the show for not rendering a nostalgic and sentimental portrayal of Billie Holiday, and for choosing to feature original music with only two Holiday-identified standard songs. Writer Aishah Rahman defended her artistic approach in one review: "According to Aishah Rahman, the critics came to see a tragic black lady singing these sentimental songs. She emphasized the fact that Billie Holiday was 'just like you or me, or like any other black artist out here trying to make it, and capitalism killed her. I hand them the real life story and they were enraged. The play was very controversial and people either loved it or they hated it.'" I was one of those who absolutely loved it, having had a chance to play the music while a teenager sitting in with Professor Shepp's ensemble. "Lady Day" became a template in many ways for the kind of music/theater I'm composing and creating today.

On the morning of the musical's opening, Zane Massey recounted how his father from their living room called to him to bring him a glass of juice. "My father would drink juice by the quarts. Whatever he did, he did it to extremes. He didn't want a doctor." By the afternoon, Cal Massey had departed.

In my interviews of Charlotte and Zane Massey in the mid-1980s, neither expressed any bitterness for the lack of support shown to them by the musical community after Cal had passed. Roland Alexander recalled that at the funeral, violinist Ray Nance played "My Buddy" to the departed Cal Massey. No benefits were organized to raise money for the impoverished Massey family. Charlotte did recount how bassist Reggie Workman "was the only one" who helped to raise some money, about $800. Workman and Massey, as some tell it, were both very closely aligned but also competitors. During the time of the RoMas Orchestra, Workman was starting his own large ensemble, Collective Black Artists, with overlapping musician members and music. Charles Stephens and Archie Shepp both attested to how Cal Massey was a dedicated community man to musicians. Massey was part of the Collective Black Artists and even served as a board member in the 1960s. The group received a grant from the New York State Council on the Arts. Massey would later apply for grants for the RoMas Orchestra, to help sustain the four or five concerts a year it would do. Charles Stephens, a regular member of the RoMas Orchestra, remembers how Cal "believed in keeping musicians working; we'd perform in churches, halls, wherever Cal could set up a concert."

In the 1960s, it was the opinion of many that the major new composers and arrangers in "the Music" who wrote for large ensembles were Mingus, Sun Ra and Cal Massey. Charles Stephens, in an interview I did with him in the late 1980s, I think best assessed the role of Cal Massey for the era of the late 1960s:

> Until I got into Cal's music, I was convinced that Sun Ra was the best composer. But Cal was equally, if not more, beautiful, in the same musical stream of consciousness—so high and beautiful. [Cal Massey] made political statements through his music. The politically conscious would come to hear [his music]. He was one of the musicians known at that time to be at the forefront of the political thing. . . . Cal was a beautiful cat—he'd talk about Black Arts, Black Power, but his partner was Romulus . . . that's because he lived what he believed. He believed in the sincerity of people regardless of race. He was forward thinking, he'd work with anyone. People would approach him, he'd never turn them down. He spoke through his music; he was very outspoken, like "Things Have Got to Change, God

THE DAMNED DON'T CRY

Damn It!" Cal really wanted to make a difference in people's hearts and minds. He wanted to connect with the good in all of us, yet recognize injustices in this land through his music. [He] really made an impact. Everything came together in him—the music, social consciousness, camaraderie; it gave you a feeling that there was hope, that things could get better, that music could make a difference. Since his death, there's a real gap concerning all aspects of music reflecting social, political things on the whole American scene. Cal put everything on the level people could immediately understand. Sun Ra gets rather deep, talking about space, putting things on a different plane. Other guys put it on the level of funky types of computer sounds. But Cal made direct statements. No doubt he was very political. . . . Both Sun Ra and Cal were politically conscious but expressed this in different ways. Sun Ra was into the space age; he believes this planet has been visited by higher beings in prehistorical times, that higher beings have influenced man's development. For example, Egyptian mythology and other ancient unexplained wonders. Cal dealt with what was happening at that minute from his perspective. Sun Ra is looking at the whole thing, Cal was talking about what was happening that day.

I came to New York City in the fall of 1981 to embark upon a career as a professional musician. Being in New York, I met many of the artists I had only known about from their recordings and press write-ups, many through drummer Charlie Persip's big band, called Superband, for which I was the regular baritone sax player from 1982 to 1987. I met Taru Massey, Cal's oldest son, while he was working for Cobi Narita's Jazz Center of New York, one of the last of the jazz loft performance spaces. Working with Zane Massey, I organized the first of three Cal Massey Tribute Concerts at the Jazz Center of New York on June 1, 1985, which featured Archie Shepp as guest soloist and Charles Majeed Greenlee as conductor. The evening featured both small group performances of Massey compositions and a large group performing the original arrangement of *The Black Liberation Movement Suite* and new arrangements I had done of "Quiet Dawn," "The Cry of My People," and "Goodbye Sweet Pops (for Louis Armstrong)." I wanted to involve Romulus Franceschini, but no one knew how to contact Cal's long-time colleague and friend.

The second Tribute Concert was performed on July 6, 1986, in

Brooklyn's Prospect Park as part of the annual summer Celebrate Brooklyn outdoor festival produced by Burl Hash, who knew Cal Massey from working on *Lady Day* fourteen years before. By this concert, I had contacted Franceschini, who ironically was connected to the Relâche ensemble in Philadelphia, a new music group he helped to found and often did orchestrations for, and for whom I would be commissioned in 1991 to compose "Contraction, Please! The Revenge of Charlie Chan." Archie Shepp wasn't able to do this concert, and so Junior Cook became the guest soloist for this and the subsequent Tribute Concert.

The third and final Tribute Concert for which I was a part of organizing was given on June 19, 1988, in Philadelphia. The concert was presented at the Painted Bride Art Center as part of the Mellon Jazz Festival. While Romulus was to conduct that evening, a few days earlier, after the last rehearsal in New York City, he had collapsed on the streets of New York from chest pains and shortness of breath. For the concert, Zane Massey and I shared conducting duties from our respective saxophone chairs.

I could tell the writing was on the wall. While Shepp, Greenlee, and a number of the musicians who were formerly closely associated with Cal Massey gave generously with their involvement in the initial concert, it was clear that by the second Tribute Concert, interest was waning. Zane Massey himself had decided to forego the Tribute Concert for a tour with Ronald Shannon Jackson, much to the disappointment of his mother and family, though ironically, the tour was delayed and Zane joined his family in the audience for that event. The musicians were less committed to my goal of celebrating the music and ideas of Cal Massey and more for just doing a gig. After the third Tribute Concert was finished, I decided to completely hand over the project to Zane. I hope someday he'll do a recording of the full suite and a collection of his father's works.

Another interesting change happened in the creative black "jazz" scene in New York City from the 1970s to the 1980s with the arrival of a number of "avant-garde" or "free jazz" players from other cities, particularly the West Coast (David Murray, Stanley Crouch, Lawrence "Butch" Morris, etc.) and the Midwest (the former AACM musicians, Julius Hemphill from St. Louis, etc.). Basing themselves primarily in the Lower East Side/East Village, they supplanted the earlier generation of Sun Ra, Shepp, and others. This new wave quickly tapped into the then-fecundity of funding for new performance art venues, such as The Kitchen, and by the 1980s these younger new arrivals had eclipsed the earlier generation of New York creative black musicians of the 1960s and early 1970s. The former group, as I picked up on their vibe, had a low regard for this new wave, believing that they were avant-garde posturers and scammers. The former group were very skilled players, who could read music, play "inside" chord changes as well as "outside" in a free jazz idiom, and considered these younger, newer players to be less musically grounded. The former group came to be based around the Harlem nonprofit organization of Jazzmobile, which sponsored weekend music classes and free summer outdoor concerts, and included many of the musicians who were connected to the Cal Massey era.

These two camps rarely intersected, but one rare occasion was a project for a live on-air concert for WHYY Radio in Philadelphia in 1987, organized by drummer Sunny Murray and vibraphonist Khan Jamal. The project was a John Coltrane Tribute orchestra that performed the music of Coltrane and Cal Massey, for which the arrangements and conducting were done by Romulus Franceschini. The large aggregation included such veterans as Sunny Fortune and John Stubblefield, Odean Pope, Ed Blackwell, Dave Burrell, and Reggie Workman, with newer players like David Murray, Joseph Jarman, Henry Threadgill, Frank Lacy, myself, and others. The music was in complete disarray as egotistical soloists elbowed one another and the charts were dismissed. An even poorer musical performance by this project was done at the 1987 Berlin Jazz Festival with its theme of celebrating the twentieth anniversary of Coltrane's passing. By the late 1980s, any sense of musical community or collective musical/cultural movement had dissipated and all but disappeared, supplanted by the leader-as-star syndrome. As the Reagan era was in full swing, the black community was suffering from a void of militant, progressive, and visionary African American political and cultural leadership and fractured into divided political and musical camps.

‹ 149

The near-forgotten memory of Cal Massey is an indictment of the national oppression of the African American people and its truth-bearing artists. The fact that stacks of Cal Massey's music are gathering dust for the most part, except for the recordings and performances done by his son Zane, points to the need for African American institutions to preserve and promote these artistic contributions. The movement needs to support such committed cultural workers, to work closely with them to organize concerts and a sustained full cultural program to raise people's ideological level and to strengthen their struggles. Cal Massey was not simply a "political" artist, but a people's artist in the truest sense, inspired from his people's history and heritage. His work contributed to the creating of a revolutionary working-class aesthetic rooted to the African American musical tradition: not the ruling-class aesthetics of alienation, obfuscation, ambiguity, fear, domination, submission, passivity, mimicry, and sycophancy, but the aesthetics of collective survival and struggle, pride, dignity, love, beauty, intelligence, and commitment to freedom. Music in tune with reality to compose a new reality.

NOTE

The research for this article was done from 1984 to 1988 and included interviews with the now-deceased Charlotte Massey, Cal's wife, who passed on December 25, 1995; with musicians Archie Shepp, Charles Stephens, and Roland Alexander; with two of Cal Massey's children, Zane and Taru; and, of course, with long-time collaborator Romulus Franceschini, who passed away in 1994 and who became a close friend and comrade to me up to the last days of his life.

Though my records are sketchy, there was an obituary for Cal Massey in *Down Beat* magazine in 1972. Other sources of information are "Tribute to Cal Massey: Jazz Center of New York," by Howard Mandel, a review of the first Tribute Concert organized by Fred Houn with Zane Massey, *Down Beat* (September 1985): 55; "A Saxophone and a Legacy of Suffering," by Norman Riley, a review and feature on the second Tribute Concert organized by Fred Houn in Prospect Park, Brooklyn, on July 6, 1986, as part of the annual Celebrate Brooklyn summer festival series, *The Prospect Press,* July 31, 1986; "Mellon Jazz Shows Begin with Two Original Works," by Francis Davis, a review of the third Tribute Concert organized by Fred Houn at the Painted Bride, Philadelphia, on June 19, 1988, as part of the Mellon Jazz Festival, *The Philadelphia Inquirer,* June 20, 1988; and "Obituaries: R. A. Franceschini, Eclectic Composer," by S. Joseph Hagenmayer, *The Philadelphia Inquirer,* 1994 (exact date uncertain); and "Black Singer's Life Theme of 'Lady Day,'" a review by Lavinia Brookfield for Black News Service.

How to Sell but Not Sell Out: Personal Lessons from Making a Career as a Subversive and Radical Performing Artist

WHEN PEOPLE ASK ME, How long have you been playing the saxophone? I tell them, As long as I've been in the struggle. When activists ask me, How long have you been in the movement? I tell them, As long as I've been playing the saxophone. Music is not just my service or contribution, it is not just my profession, it is not just my art: it is my revolutionary life work.

As performing artists, we need to learn more than the craft and tradition of our particular disciplines. We need to learn the business of thriving as professional subversive radical artists. Politically, we should be antiprofit! I approach this, first of all, by rejecting the non-profit approach as a nonsolution. Since we can't all "escape to the hills" and become completely extricated from the capitalist system, we have to learn to function within it, gainfully, and at the same time never compromise or diminish the politics of our artistic expression or our political practice.

Under capitalism, everything can be turned into a commodity, therefore anything that can be sold as art is art. Until we can replace the capitalist system with either socialism or something in which the needs of people and the planet are placed above the pursuit of profit/accumulation, we have to not only survive, but also politically and economically thrive, make victories, and gain greater ground overall. Individual success does not necessarily have to be counterposed to

Published in *Movement Research Performance Journal*, no. 12 (1996).

collective gains and progress; indeed, it should be concomitant and mutual. "Success" can be evaluated by how much an artist and his or her work has attained greater force: the broadening of one's base of support, the gathering of greater resources, and the extent to which one has become a threat to the status quo.

The very concept of "art" arises with class division. Eliminating the specialized artist is what a revolutionary culture is about. As Marx put it, "Instead of the working artist, we'll have workers who do art." Artists need to be socially and politically connected to movements for social change. The term "cultural worker" used by movement activists working in the arts rejects both the bourgeois and Eurocentric concept of "art" and "artist" as the privileged, highly specialized, elite. "Culture" pertains to "a way of life of a people," including language, customs and rituals, clothing, cuisine, furniture, artifacts, architecture, and so on, and "cultural worker" identifies us with ordinary craftspeople, artisans, the "arts" of the lower classes, performed and created for, by, and about the people.

I hope more guerrilla artists will enter dialogue and collaborate. Here is my brief offering:

1. Don't Be Desperate. Refuse to Be Used and Abused! As a professional musician, I stopped performing in nightclubs in the United States for three reasons: Clubs exploit artists; clubs exploit audiences and patrons; clubs are carcinogenic environments. By rejecting clubs, I was forced to seek out other venues. I now primarily work in colleges, concert halls, festivals, community and cultural centers, and I record, receive composition commissions, as well as lecture, write, and do an occasional guest teaching position.

2. Adopt Trade Unionist Principles! Someday I hope we can organize a performing artists' union that minimally can set fee scales, demand benefits and better conditions, and so on. One of the reasons musicians, as a group, earn more money than, say, dancers, is because of the established pay standards (prevailing rate) determined by the presence of a musicians' union—in New York City, Local 802, American Federation of Musicians/AFL-CIO. Dancers, via the National Performance Network, an organization that works for presenters, has set a $450 a week out-of-town pay scale. I refuse to submit to the NPN pay quota. The musicians in my band make that in one out-of-town performance.

As artists we should demand that the government and foundation funders reverse the current arrangement in which 501(c)3 organizations get the lion's share of the monies. Individual artists should be directly funded. So-called arts service organizations, I find, don't even serve artists by providing any basic health coverage. Rather, they tend more to service funders than artists by hosting "studies," or "symposiums," hosting "seminars" for individuals for which individual artists can apply for grants—which individual artists generally aren't eligible for anyway.

A noteworthy funder, however, is Meet the Composer (MTC), for having published its *Commissioning Music* handbook, which gives guidelines for composer fees. The MTC, like so many funders, still requires funding applications for composers to come from or through 501(c)3s. Only in their basic MTC Fund Program are checks made out to individual artists. I advocate that all the checks should be made out to individual artists, from the smallest to the largest grant. Funders retort: What about accountability? Well, what about it? The history of corruption, abuse, and scamming has been committed overwhelmingly by organizations, not by individual artists.

‹ 153

The problem with relying or depending upon the "nonprofit" grant-chasing scene is the inherent tendency of government/corporate funding to increasingly contain and make more conservative the artists and their work. This is the Golden Handcuffs or On-Leash Syndrome. The Piper Plays the Tunes Paid for by the Payer. Artists must indeed be prepared to bite the hand that feeds you!

3. Go on Strike! Refuse to "work the door." When you work the door, presenters are let off the hook, since most of the audience who comes, will do so only by your efforts. Remember: Don't be desperate to perform. We should understand that we have a labor-management relationship with presenters/producers/venues, unless these are artist-cooperative-run spaces. By allowing ourselves to "work the door" or for "exposure," especially for big and mainstream institutions, we perpetuate our exploitation and disrespect, and leave those institutions/presenters off the hook.

I'd rather perform in benefit concerts/performances for activist groups, thereby building and strengthening a mutually supportive base, than work the door for a club or presenter. By performing at an activist benefit, a whole new audience will be exposed to you and appreciate your offering. Two basic commendable things about a place like Dance Theater Workshop are, one, they pay artists a guarantee; and, two, the place is kept clean and well organized and the bathrooms are well maintained. This is a credit to the entire organization from its top leadership down to its daily maintenance staff.

4. Adopt a Guerrilla Ethic! To be a guerrilla, one has to be prepared for a protracted struggle. It is important to study, and to confiscate the technology, skills, and resources of the ruling class, which is what you should be doing with your college education. However, the purpose is not to use these to climb up in the capitalist system, but to turn these over to the movements of oppressed and exploited peoples. To confirm "the personal is political" is to accept Audre Lorde's statement, "You can't use the master's tools to dismantle the master's house." As new music necessitates new forms, new instruments, and new musicians, a new society necessitates new people. Resist personally getting bitter, frustrated, jealous, and self-destructive. Decolonize your mind, your diet, and your values. It is important to stay spiritually and physically healthy. In recent years, I have been swimming/exercising regularly, reducing animal intake in my diet, and trying to make love as often as possible. What I lack in terms of money, I more than make up for in creativity, physical and spiritual strength, and passion.

Among guerrilla comrades, supporters, and sympathizers, we need networks, collaborations, and community. We should be honest, direct, and generous. Toward those bullshitters (who want us to work for little or nothing), we should be bold and fierce in our condemnation.

Big Red Media, Inc., a Composer/Musician-Driven Production Company: Doing It Yourself

THE MISSION OF MY newly formed production company, Big Red Media Inc., is "to create and produce new radical and revolutionary expressions in all media: audio, performance, print, visual, cyber." I formed the company after recognizing two serious realities both for myself specifically and also for independent-minded artists in general.

First, recent New York State laws now require that I legally become an employer and that all artists who work for me are employees. Henceforth, I am required to make statutory deductions, pay workers' compensation, unemployment insurance, file quarterly taxes, and so on. Since I am a composer/bandleader/producer, I needed to create a legal entity to fulfill these legal requirements—many of which are extremely burdensome and crushingly onerous for the individual artist who employs performers. A hard financial reality is that just to break even I need to earn 40 percent above the total artist salaries just to cover the cost of doing business (for example: workers' compensation insurance for a project that involves dancers onstage is taxed at a rate of 25.22 percent. Add on the other taxes, insurance, payroll processing, etc., it's close to 40 percent). So if the artists get a payment of $1,000, I need an additional $400 just to cover my costs as an employer.

Second, my music/performance and other media projects are both

Published in the newsletter of the American Composers Forum, Summer 1998.

aesthetically and politically too "radical," too "transgressive," not the sort of work that a standard opera company, musical theater producing organization, or commercial recording company or publisher will go for. I am well aware of this, accept it, and have developed a strategy of independent guerrilla entrepreneurship—created my own alternative.

My production company can create and produce work at a very high level of quality and enter into agreements with presenters/venues, major distributors (both recording and small press). Rather than be frustrated about getting a record or book "deal," praying/hoping/prostituting myself to be "discovered," I decided I would learn how to and do a better job at producing my own work, from the first-idea stages to final "product" (I use quotes because I resist the dehumanized commodity conceptions of capitalism—we're in business, creating and doing what we do not to be capitalists, i.e., profiteering, but to make revolutionary art).

Over the years I have found collaborators who share my vision and are extremely committed and professional. They have become the nucleus for what the hip-hop artists call "your team." I am the President/Chief Executive Artist; I have a Creative/Design Director (who works a day job at an educational institution with all the latest design technology at his disposal); an Outreach/Marketing and Publishing Director (she has years of experience being the editor/publisher of a leading women-of-color small press publisher), a Company Manager (while young, she is being trained to handle the operations of the business), and others who work with us on a project basis (including a web designer, regional and international booking agents who line up performance engagements, etc.).

No one officially works for a salary. Everyone is on a commission basis—they earn what they bring in. Of course, at this time, the great bulk of the earnings come from me, so I get the majority of the commissions. However, the others earn something on the order of the following: when the Creative Director designs a new recording cover, Koch International (the label that presses and distributes my recordings) pays him a design fee. When the Marketing/Outreach person sells our books and recordings, she earns 10 percent of the sales. The Company Manager earns 10 percent of all grants she writes which are funded, and 10 percent on all bookings she engages.

I find that I am better off being self-managed and having this production company than when I was "signed" with a manager, who had a roster of artists and could not give the fullest attention to the broad scope of my work (beyond bookings as a performer and obtaining composer commissions, but not seeing projects through to completion). With a manager representing me, the reality was that I still brought in the vast majority of the work and earnings, of which the manager then took 20 percent.

I run the production company, meaning that I am the sole owner and final decision maker, yet we reach consensus on virtually everything since it is a team that has built trust, respect, and a common outlook from years of collaborations with one another. Eventually we will consider other artists, but everyone will have to be equally excited and committed. We are a combination of a small business corporation and old-time Leftist collective. We want everything we produce to be uniquely and provocatively radical and revolutionary, yet very professional and competitive with what we see as a marketplace of mediocrity, fashion, hype, and superficiality. Clearly, we have our own political and artistic identity and now we're building the mechanism for dissemination.

We're guerrillas and have been and can continue to run on a shoestring budget. We can do major operas at the BAM Next Wave Festival for $60,000 and still turn a profit. We raise monies through a mixed strategy (including grants, individual donor solicitation, fundraisers) but rely on EARNED INCOME—through each engagement fee, through the sale of each unit. I realized that simply through the sales of my own books and recordings at events and mail-order, I could pay for my living expenses (i.e., food and shelter). I did better than the record companies, since they weren't going to put much effort into one artist (me) among many bigger, more commercial artists. I also studied how social change movements distributed their publications and other propaganda (I've been an activist for more than two decades). I knew I could organize for something I really believe in. After the Leftist movement that I was a part of collapsed in 1989, I knew I was still committed, still believing, so I turned to generating my own "propaganda"—what I do best, making music, performance works, and writing and editing publications. I applied my vision, aesthetic, and organizing abilities and found allies, comrades, colleagues, fellow travelers, and supporters (including patrons/donors who may not agree with me politically but who respect and enjoy some of what I do artistically and have the honesty and sincerity to be candid with me about what they can and cannot support).

I believe that I will wear the "producer's hat" for only a couple of years, until the company functions more on its own. So I work 70 hours a week, though I set my own schedule and am fulfilled every minute because I have total control of and confidence in every aspect. My own personal earnings are often plowed back into the company. Long ago I made the decision not to subscribe to the patriarchal nuclear family, so I don't have dependents. My "children" are my projects; they take as much time and effort to develop and grow, and just as much heartache, too. I could go on and on about the personal choices and decisions, but suffice it to say that I know this is the direction in life for me: to sell but not to sell out, to be a self-reliant revolutionary artist. Like Ani DeFranco's "do-it-yourself" approach, starting my own production company has been both a realization of philosophical/political principles and economic practicality to living those principles. Thank you to the American Composers Forum for giving me this forum.

had entered my teens and my "identity" awakening began. As I have discussed in many previo
es, the black experience catalyzed my own self-awareness as a Chinese/Asian American. I came
ify with the black struggle in drawing parallels with my personal struggle for self-awareness a
ity and for the struggle of Asian/yellow peoples as a whole in U.S. society to end racism, injust
nequality and to achieve self-respect, dignity, and liberation. ¶ Even as a teenager, I intuitiv
nized that black American culture and the arts are inseparable from the dynamic of the Bla
ation struggle. In my youth, I sought to find a comparable connection between the culture a
of Asian Pacific Americans (APAs) with our liberation struggle for full equality and justice. I
d of forms, including political organization, cultural activism, artistic expression, and cultu
ction, I have sought to promote the unity of African Americans and Asian Americans, includi
ng my core band, the Afro Asian Music Ensemble, in 1982, when I first moved to New York City
e becoming a professional artist. In this essay, I want to reflect on how the Black Arts Movem
cted my personal development as well as what I believe to be its impact on the APA movement a
¶ Many conscious APAs—meaning those of us who are proud to be APA, who are politically c
s of our collective history of oppression and struggle in the United States, and who recognize
ing, systematic white racism we continue to endure and resist—have admired the black Americ
gle and especially what we perceive to be the strength, rootedness, and communality of the bla
ican cultural experience. Much of the Asian Movement that emerged in the late 1960s and ea

{ III }

ASIAN PACIFIC AMERICAN
CULTURAL THEORY AND CRITICISM

took inspiration politically from the Civil Rights Movement and the Black Liberation Movem
he anthology *Legacy to Liberation: Politics and Culture of Revolutionary Asian Pacific America
nually he from APA acti and intelle I've expressed the subject which is paraphrased a
we Asians were more [fill in the blank] like the blacks." The "fill in the blank" are generally ch
istics or attributes the more conscious APAs feel we as a "people" lack: militant, radical, unit
oken, assertive, etc. Sometimes this is expressed as "Where is our Asian Malcolm X? Or Langs
es? Or John Coltrane? Or [fill in the name of a leading great black figure]?" ¶ Certainly the bl
gle has had a longer and considerably more developed history, and consequently a broader a
recognized impact than that of APAs upon American history and society. Much of mainstre
ica has still to even recognize our presence in American history and society, with the exceptio
model minority" stereotype that has the effect of negating our struggle and portraying us col
as ethnic successes. However, in a serious study of APA history and political/cultural strug
is much to be proud of, to recognize, uphold, and celebrate. While we may not have produ
rical "giants," we have our inspirational, leading militants and radicals, including Carlos Bulos
Vera Cruz, Yuri Kochiyama, Richard Aoki, Karl Yoneda, Yun Gee, Mitsuye Yamada, Merle W
Wong, Janice Mirikitani, and numerous others. Many of these figures, both deceased and livi
have published biographies or autobiographies. While more biographical profiles and even so
s have recently been published, they have little circulation and receive limited attention beyo
all group of conscious APAs. None of our APA giants are "household names." ¶ Until Spike Le
, *The Autobiography of Malcolm X* had withered into relative obscurity during the 1980s. Lee's f
everely criticized and condemned by many conscious black activists and radical intellectu
accused Lee and his film of blatant historical distortion and for diluting Malcolm's revolution
cs, arguments with which I am in agreement. Even among the greater black American populati
amiliarity, recognition, and celebration of radical and militant leaders and movements, which v
common in the 1960s and 1970s due to the heightened level of the Black Liberation Movement
less today as black "firsts" and celebrities who are often accomodationists, integrationists, a
cally less-than-militant are given much more attention by the U.S. mainstream media and e
nal system. Today's black youth may only have a very superficial and cursory awareness of t

An Asian American Tribute
to the Black Arts Movement

Mao and Cabral

Mingus and Coltrane

Variations on the same tune.

—poem inspired by Felix Torres

I CAME OF AGE in the early 1970s, at the tail end of what Amiri Baraka calls "the Roaring Sixties." By 1970, I had entered my teens and my "identity" awakening began. As I have discussed in many previous articles, the black experience catalyzed my own self-awareness as a Chinese/Asian American. I came to identify with the black struggle in drawing parallels with my personal struggle for self-awareness and identity and for the struggle of Asian/yellow peoples as a whole in U.S. society to end racism, injustice, and inequality and to achieve self-respect, dignity, and liberation.

Even as a teenager, I intuitively recognized that black American culture and the arts are inseparable from the dynamic of the Black Liberation struggle. In my youth, I sought to find a comparable connection between the culture and arts of Asian Pacific Americans (APAs) with our liberation struggle for full equality and justice. In a myriad of forms, including political organization, cultural activism,

Published in *Critical Studies in Improvisation* 1, no. 3 (2006), and in *CR: The New Centennial Review* 6, no. 2 (Fall 2006).

artistic expression, and cultural production, I have sought to pro-mote the unity of African Americans and Asian Americans, including forming my core band, the Afro Asian Music Ensemble, in 1982, when I first moved to New York City to pursue becoming a professional art-ist. In this essay, I want to reflect on how the Black Arts Movement impacted my personal development as well as what I believe to be its impact on the APA movement and arts.

Many conscious APAs—meaning those of us who are proud to be APA, who are politically conscious of our collective history of oppres-sion and struggle in the United States, and who recognize the ongo-ing, systematic white racism we continue to endure and resist—have admired the black American struggle and especially what we perceive to be the strength, rootedness, and communality of the black Ameri-can cultural experience. Much of the Asian Movement that emerged in the late 1960s and early 1970s took inspiration politically from the Civil Rights Movement and the Black Liberation Movement (see the anthology *Legacy to Liberation: Politics and Culture of Revolution-ary Asian Pacific America*). I continually hear from APAs envy and ad-miration expressed through a wishfulness paraphrased as "I wish we Asians were more [fill in the blank] like the blacks." The "fill in the blank" are generally characteristics or attributes the more conscious APAs feel we as a "people" lack: militant, radical, united, outspoken, assertive, etc. Sometimes this is expressed as "Where is our Asian Malcolm X? Or Langston Hughes? Or John Coltrane? Or [fill in the name of a leading great black figure]?"

Certainly the black struggle has had a longer and considerably more developed history, and consequently a broader and more rec-ognized impact than that of APAs upon American history and so-ciety. Much of mainstream America has still to even recognize our presence in American history and society, with the exception of the "model minority" stereotype that has the effect of negating our strug-gle and portraying us collectively as ethnic successes. However, in a serious study of APA history and political/cultural struggle, there is much to be proud of, to recognize, uphold, and celebrate. While we may not have produced historical "giants," we have our inspirational, leading militants and radicals, including Carlos Bulosan, Philip Vera Cruz, Yuri Kochiyama, Richard Aoki, Karl Yoneda, Yun Gee, Mitsuye

Yamada, Merle Woo, Nellie Wong, Janice Mirikitani, and numerous others. Many of these figures, both deceased and living, don't have published biographies or autobiographies. While more biographical profiles and even some books have recently been published, they have little circulation and receive limited attention beyond a small group of conscious APAs. None of our APA giants are "household names."

Until Spike Lee's film *X*, *The Autobiography of Malcolm X* had withered into relative obscurity during the 1980s. Lee's film was severely criticized and condemned by many conscious black activists and radical intellectuals. They accused Lee and his film of blatant historical distortion and for diluting Malcolm's revolutionary politics, arguments with which I am in agreement. Even among the greater black American population, the familiarity, recognition, and celebration of radical and militant leaders and movements, which was more common in the 1960s and 1970s due to the heightened level of the Black Liberation Movement, is a lot less today as black "firsts" and celebrities who are often accomodationists, integrationists, and politically less-than-militant are given much more attention by the U.S. mainstream media and educational system. Today's black youth may only have a very superficial and cursory awareness of Harriet Tubman (who organized and led the first black underground militia against the system of white supremacy in the United States), the revolutionary views of Malcolm X (such as "capitalism is a bloodsucker," etc.), the Black Panther Party, Assata Shakur, Mumia Abu-Jamal, among others. Indeed, Oprah, Magic Johnson, and P. Diddy are far better known. Even worse, the only mass-media image of yellow-black unity today for both APAs and African Americans is probably the Jackie Chan–Chris Tucker collaboration in the *Rush Hour* movie series.

But back "in the day" (i.e., Baraka's "Roaring Sixties" and early 1970s) as a teenager growing up during this period of accelerated political, intellectual, and cultural growth, black-yellow connections and unity were much more real, substantial, meaningful, and politically anti-imperialist.

One of the most significant aspects of this period of the late 1960s and early 1970s was the broad popularization of "Third World" unity and anti-imperialist consciousness and politics. There was much more "mass" popular identification between yellow and black peoples in the United States than what exists today. A lot of this is documented in the anthology that Bill Mullen and I are co-editing: *Afro Asia: Revolutionary Political and Cultural Connections between African Americans and Asian Americans.* In 1964, Malcolm X, in arguing for black American identification with, support for, and even repatriation back to Africa, cited the example of China's growing strength in world politics upon U.S. racist attitudes by stating:

> The Chinese used to be disrespected. They used to use that expression in this country: "You don't have a Chinaman's chance." You remember that? You don't hear it lately. Because a Chinaman's got more chance than they have now. Why? Because China is strong. Since China became strong and independent, she's respected, she's recognized. So that wherever a Chinese person goes, he is respected and he is recognized. He's not respected and recognized because of what he as an individual has done; he is respected and recognized because he has a country behind him. They don't respect him, they respect what's behind him.
>
> By the same token, when the African continent in its independence is able to create the unity that's necessary to increase its strength and its position on this earth, so that Africa too becomes respected as other huge continents are respected, then, wherever people of African origin, African heritage or African blood go, they will be respected—but only when and because they have something much larger that looks like them behind them.[1]

During this same era, world heavyweight champion boxer Muhammad Ali, in stating his opposition to the Vietnam War and his draft induction, echoed the mass antiwar slogan of the Black Liberation Movement: "No Vietcong ever called me nigger." Musician Archie Shepp would compare his tenor saxophone to a Vietcong's AK-47 as a weapon against U.S. imperialism. Shepp audaciously proclaimed "jazz" to be an artistic expression that was pro-Vietcong (i.e., national liberation) and anti–U.S. imperialism, which many less politically conscious music critics and writers disagreed with and objected to such politicization of the music.[2]

What these critics and objectors to Shepp's characterization have failed to understand is the fundamental and quintessential nature of black American culture as a culture of an oppressed people, with its strongest and most vital manifestations as forms of resistance to that oppression by affirming humanity (against inhumanity), beauty (against degradation), and truth (against the lies of racist propaganda and white supremacist ideology).

The Era of Malcolm X and John Coltrane and Third World Political and Cultural Revolution

It was no coincidence or novelty that the radical and revolutionary intellectuals, artists, and activists in black America identified with, looked to, took inspiration from, promoted, and participated in the linking of nationalist and radical politics with "jazz," especially the so-called "new music" or "avant-garde" represented by the musical avatar John Coltrane.

‹ 165

While a self-serving and somewhat contrived connection is made by socialist-Trotskyite cultural commentator Frank Kofsky between Malcolm X and John Coltrane (in *Black Nationalism and the Revolution in Music*), as symbolic statement and as a cultural metaphor, there is much credibility and cogency to the comparison. Malcolm X represented the vanguard "cutting-edge" of revolutionary black nationalist politics. John Coltrane represented the musical and cultural "cutting-edge" vanguard. While no overt connections existed between the two giants, it is clear that they both enormously affected and were effected by the *weltanschauung* of the era and considerably contributed to and were shaped by the zeitgeist of the 1960s. Malcolm X fired the political vision and upsurge in the Black Liberation struggle in the North American "belly of the beast" to join the worldwide anti-imperialist national liberation struggles being waged in Africa, Asia, Central and South America, and the Pacific Islands. Coltrane fired the music and culture with volcanic energy and irrepressible innovation. Both personified and embodied the apex of black American political and artistic creativity and commitment: gloriously un-co-optable and unquenchable. In many ways, a dynamic dialectical interplay existed between both political and artistic energies. Political manifestos and position papers by black radical activists often looked to, sought inspiration from, and united with the dynamic energy of the music:

> The task of the Revolutionary Action Movement [one of the early Black Liberation Movement underground organizations] is to express via political action the dynamism embodied in Afro-American music.[3]

I remember meeting the militant Robert F. Williams after his return from exile in the People's Republic of China, where he had spent many years with his family. Williams used the term "New African Music" instead of "jazz."[4]

During this time, I wore dashikis along with other black-inspired and -influenced urban accoutrements such as platform shoes and bell-bottom pants; I carried big leather book bags and emulated my immediate "role models/mentors" such as musician/composer Archie Shepp, who had a particularly loping-like gait to his walk, who wore second-hand sheepskin coats during the winter, and who held a cigarette in his right hand as he was playing the keys to his saxophone. Even though I never really was a smoker, my brief attempt to try smoking was motivated to posture like Shepp.

There were other Asians who also closely identified with black culture, though of varying degrees of political sincerity and commitment. I remember one was Robbie from New York City, who then attended Amherst College as an undergrad, who dressed and danced urban black, lived in a black dorm, who had connections to New York Chinatown through kung-fu and lion dance clubs, who took black studies courses, who played basketball with the black brothers, who spouted the rhetoric of anti-white black cultural nationalism. Robbie was very good-looking, closer in facial appearance to icon Bruce Lee than I (as he was of southern Chinese extraction, and I'm much more northern Chinese in appearance). I remember he had a gorgeous West Indian girlfriend. Years later, I would run into him again on the streets of New York Chinatown, now a corporate lawyer in expensive suits, whose only interest in Chinatown was going out to lunch with his white corporate lawyer buddies.

Higher education was the boom industry for the predominantly white community of Amherst, Massachusetts, where I grew up. Amherst was known as both the Pioneer Valley for its colonial-era roots and as the Five College Area for the growing presence of area campuses such as the University of Massachusetts (the largest) and four smaller private institutions: Amherst College and Hampshire College, Smith College in neighboring Northampton, and Mount Holyoke College in South Hadley. During the Cold War 1960s, public education was a high growth area as the United States sought to contend with its then-rival superpower, the Soviet Union, by investing in the scientific, technical, and professional expertise of its population. The expansion of these five colleges attracted a steadily increasing faculty, staff, and student population, dwarfing the town's population then of about ten thousand by seven-fold during the academic season. A growing "minority" (i.e., oppressed nationality) community, the vast majority of whom migrated to Amherst, was also making an impact on the area.

‹ 167

The children of grad students, staff, and faculty of the colleges were diversifying the public school district as well. My two younger sisters and I were among these "minority" students from about two hundred Asian Pacific American families in the area, virtually all of whom were affiliated with the colleges. Growing up in this predominantly white community, we faced a combination of white liberal academia "benign" racism along with the racism of the parochial local white rural "red-neck" farming community. Along with the general politicization and heightened social consciousness of the times, the Third World junior and senior high school students (which included me) identified with the Third World college students and attended the activities of these area campuses. As high school students, we would go to parties, social events, cultural performances, lectures, and mobilizations at the various "Third World" spaces, especially the New Africa House (a former dorm building at the University of Massachusetts that had been converted to include the offices of the Afro-American Studies Department and Third World student activist offices, a Nation of Islam–run cafeteria, and a hub of cultural and political activities).

The Five Colleges drew a number of illustrious radical Third World faculty, including artists such as the poet Sonia Sanchez (Amherst

College's first chair of Africana Studies); musician/composers Max Roach, Archie Shepp, Reggie Workman, Roland Wiggins, Vishnu Wood, and many others; writers Michael Thelwell, Chinua Achebe; and visual artist Nelson Stevens, just to name a few while I was there. I especially took advantage of their presence by regularly attending speaking events, performances, and workshops, and sitting in (auditing) classes. The two classes that impacted me the most were Professor Sonia Sanchez's "Creative Writing and Poetry" and Professor Archie Shepp's "African American Music" ensemble performance class. Since I still was in high school, evening classes were easier for me. I was very interested in Shepp's other lecture class with its bold title "Revolutionary Concepts in African American Music" but it was given only during the day.

I came to New York City in the early fall of 1981 to begin a professional life in "jazz." In the summer of 1982, at the invitation of Norman Riley, who was then directing a Ron Milner play, *Jazz Set,* at the Henry Street Settlement Playhouse in the Lower East Side, with music by Max Roach, I was asked to provide after-play music. This was my first professional opportunity as a band leader. Previously, in Boston, I had organized and led small bands to fundraise for community causes, the main one being to pay the rent for the Asian American Resource Workshop, a cultural and curriculum-development center I had organized and led while living in that city. I formed a sextet featuring three saxophones (because I played sax and most readily knew other sax players) and a standard rhythm section of piano, drums, and bass and called the band the Afro-Asian Music Ensemble (AAME). In the early 1990s, at the suggestion of my then-manager, I dropped the hyphen as I politically always found hyphenated identities to be problematic. I took the name from the historic Afro-Asian Unity conference held in Bandung, Indonesia, in April 1955, which created the Non-Aligned Movement of newly independent countries and national liberation movements, and which came to be symbolically known as the "Third World" of Africa, Asia, and Central and South America and the Caribbean ("Latin America")—independent and self-reliant, not part of the "First World" U.S.A.-Western European capitalist bloc, nor the "Iron Curtain" Soviet Union-Eastern European socialist bloc. As my core band for more than twenty years, it has been my main vehicle as a composer, baritone saxophonist performer, and leader. My large-scale operas, martial arts ballets, and music/theater epics have as an instrumental nucleus the AAME.

Black and Yellow Cultural Nationalism

While it is still highly debated both in general Leftist circles and among black radicals whether a "black nation" exists and/or the political implications for "nationhood" (from cultural autonomy to independence), except for a small, self-identified "yellow" nationalist current in the Asian Movement, most don't dispute that Asian Pacific Island peoples in the United States are not an "oppressed" nation (with the clear-cut exception of Hawaii). Black studies scholar Bill McAdoo has documented the development of the ideology of black nationalism since its inception during the pre–Civil War 1800s.[5] Black cultural nationalism, especially in the late 1960s and early 1970s, probably most projected and practiced in the Black Arts Movement, with leading practitioners and ideologues such as Imamu Amiri Baraka and Maulana Ron Karenga, adopted an eclectic array of African signifiers and symbolism from assuming new names, taking up new rituals (such as Karenga's Kwanzaa), donning African styles of apparel, and incorporating African interpretations in artistic forms. Black cultural nationalism has been perhaps unduly criticized for being "narrow nationalism" for its concentration on lifestyle and cultural practice and tendency to deprioritize political struggle (what today would be termed its preoccupation with "identity politics"). The Black Panther Party particularly waged a vigorous struggle with cultural nationalism, equating it with counter-revolutionary "pork chop nationalism." However, mass organizations such as the Congress of African Peoples, one of the largest black cultural nationalist groups, were actively and consistently anti-imperialist and involved in struggles to fight police brutality, political and economic empowerment campaigns, and building support for national liberation struggles, especially on the African mother continent. What critics of black cultural nationalism have tended to not credit is the role cultural nationalism has played as a counter to white Eurocentric cultural aggression with the promotion of African pride and historical awareness.[6]

Today, academic Asian American literary critics have applied the

‹ 169

term "cultural nationalism" to Chinese American writer Frank Chin and others who vigorously espouse views tending to both promote and argue for an "Asian American aesthetic."[7] The implication is that this view is "narrow" and "essentialist." While Chin and others were part of the broad and eclectic rise of the Asian Movement during the late 60s and early 1970s, they were not as politically affiliated to the Asian Movement as the Black Arts Movement was consciously the "cultural wing" of the Black Liberation Movement. An APA political counterpart to the black cultural nationalist movement was a very small bicoastal activist circle that espoused the view of an Asian (cultural) nation. According to veteran activist Mo Nishida, it was primarily based in Los Angeles around people close to the East Wind Collective and New York Asian Americans who had close ties to these people. Poet Lawson Inada wrote an ode-like manifesto entitled "You Know How It Was: An Historical Treatise on the Founding of the New Asian Nation."[8]

During the early 1970s, my initial political identity was as a "revolutionary yellow nationalist." My primary ideological framework, while anti-imperialist, viewed the source of Third World peoples' oppression and exploitation as a white people and a white culturally created system called capitalism. I energetically sought to divest myself of European/white influences and acculturation, with a primary emphasis directed toward extirpating myself from white social life. I especially oriented myself to African American social life and culture as there was only a very small Asian American community in Amherst, Massachusetts, where I grew up. I maintained a balance of my activism and energies toward both a group of Asian American activists and the bigger African American political and cultural activity in the area. Since my youth, I have fairly evenly shared my focus and involvement between both the Asian Movement and the Black Liberation Movement.

For a brief time, I was attracted to the Nation of Islam (NOI) and joined it as part of my intent to completely divest myself from white society. Two women members of the NOI were especially influential upon me. One was an English teacher in my public school, Marilyn Lewis, who was the first black teacher hired by the Amherst public school systems. She was very conscious and introduced the first Black Experience classes, which catalyzed my awakening. She became a very close mentor, from whom I sought guidance and direction. She was very warm, accessible, and generously gave her time to the Third World students. She particularly took a close interest in myself and my Chinese American buddy Todd Lee. We constantly sought her out for political discussions as our identity was awakened and energized.

Another influential figure for me, and a towering figure in her own right in the Black Arts Movement, was Sonia Sanchez. I remember Sonia Sanchez for her warmth and accessibility to students. A very short woman, less than 5 feet tall, thin, and at that time dressed in Islamic clothing (she had briefly joined the Nation of Islam during the mid-1970s), she commanded respect and attention from a crowded room of students. Her own poetry reflected both the vernacular language of urban black America and the poetical avant-garde. Written words would be spelled differently, almost phonetically, and have a musical quality when she read them. She'd rarely ever use her own works as examples and preferred to have students read their own writings in class. For her creative writing class, her assignments were all about constantly writing poems and short stories. While she upheld what she termed "didactic poetry or writing" (i.e., "political" poetry and writing), Sonia was never didactic in class, and set a tone that encouraged student discussion and ease to read in front of the class. She'd encourage feedback and commentary from students, and gave her own criticisms, which never seemed harsh or critical. This contrasted immensely with another writer, Michael Thelwell, who I remember came to one of Sonia's classes as a guest. He sat on a table in the middle of the room and lectured the whole time with his eyes closed as in a "stream of consciousness." There was barely time at the end for discussion. He was an example of a didactic lecturer, unconcerned with the students around him, self-absorbed. Sonia was the opposite; she used what I now appreciate and recognize as a "dialectical" method of teaching. I and my friends would call on Sonia at home, simply drop by, since her house was only a couple of short blocks from the center of town where Amherst College was situated. She didn't seem to mind this, and even received us when she was sick. I remember she drove a Mercedes-Benz, parked in front of her house. Since I was young, I thought to myself that this seemed like a contradiction, for a radical to own such luxury things. While even today, I personally am anti-consumerist and live modestly, I realize that certain "celebrity" artists, and people in general, will have their peccadilloes. However, her revolutionary poetry, respectful and open personality, and genuine humanism far outweighed her owning a Benz.

Archie Shepp, as I came to experience him, was an even more intensely contradictory character. More than any artist, his work and persona has had the biggest impact upon mine. Even before meeting him, he was larger than life to me. I voraciously read everything about him and interviews of him. I bought all of his recordings I could, sought out imports when I traveled down to New York City (which had better record stores), and regularly scouted the bins for new releases. What fascinated me about Archie was the combination of his outspoken militant political views, fused with Marxist influences (I later learned he participated in Marxist study circles when he lived in New York City), and his soulful and incendiary tenor saxophone playing. Shepp had moved his family to Amherst when he joined the University of Massachusetts faculty in the early 1970s. His eldest son, Pavel (a Russian name, possibly from Shepp's wife, now divorced, who is of Russian descent), attended junior high and I came to know him. Pavel played drums (not so proficiently) in some of my ensembles.

Shepp's charisma comes from his reserved personality and the "bad boy" reputation the press has given him for being such an *enfant terrible* in "jazz." Shepp irked these music critics, beginning with his rejection of the term "jazz," which he regarded as "pejorative." He explained at a forum at Sweet Basil's during the Greenwich Jazz Festival in the 1980s that the word "jazz" came from the French verb *jaser,* which means "to chatter nonsensically," or gibberish. Then and today, "jazz" pundits and commentaries, most of whom continue to be white males, denounce and object to Shepp's views, especially the ones given the most publicity from the 1960s.

When I was around Archie Shepp in the early 1970s at the University of Massachusetts-Amherst, he was notorious for his tardiness, often coming to class at least an hour late, but staying at least an hour longer. A few times I smelled wine on his breath, possibly from just leaving dinner, as my class with him was at night. His classes often seemed unprepared and improvised. He'd bring in handwritten arrangements of his own and other composers' works and we'd rehearse them over and over again. As drummer Royal Hartigan has often pointed out to me, since we were at UMass at the same time (Hartigan was an undergrad and I was a high school student "auditing"), Shepp allowed anyone to play in his classes, from the most proficient players to the least experienced. Shepp would give everyone a chance to solo, and never say anything about how people played. Mistakes would simply be dealt with by repeating over again the difficult passages. While one could complain about the lack of formal rigor in Shepp's classes, his method of teaching was extremely democratic and "proletarian" since it was totally inclusive and antihierarchical, welcoming everyone's participation and contributions regardless of formal training and expertise.

One of the many strange aspects of Shepp was that the tempo of the piece he counted off was not what he performed it at. But we'd catch on and adjust.

‹ 173

Shepp had many harsh critics. A former saxophone teacher of mine, a music department colleague to Shepp, would vent that Shepp was anti-music, since it seemed he didn't care if things were done correctly or were well-prepared. Many years later, I came to realize that Shepp's approach was akin to communal ritual: excellence and quality didn't matter so long as everyone was included and shared in the experience of music making. Shepp's professional bands were for the most part of high standard. These same critics of Shepp explain this as the result of Shepp being able to hire the top players, a mixture of veterans well-versed in "straight ahead jazz" with the more free music players, ranging from drummers Beaver Harris and Charlie Persip (formerly of the Dizzy Gillespie big band), trombonists Roswell Rudd and Charles Majeed Greenlee (another Gillespie alumnus), bassists Jimmy Garrison and Cameron Brown and Santi DeBriano, among so many. This might be a reflection of Shepp's commitment to the continuum of African American music and his refusal to abide by stylistic and generational boundaries. The many sidemen to Shepp's recordings have included top shelf studio musicians such as bassist Ron Carter to free players such as trombonist Grachan Moncur III.

While I knew Shepp, he wasn't much of a conversationalist. He'd talk in short, one-sentence phrases. But I knew if he wanted to "talk," he was a master of conversational charm and the schmooze. I remember when he called me, needing a baritone sax player to perform (for free) in the musical *Lady Day* when it was being staged at UMass in 1974. My mother answered the phone and recounted to me how Shepp asked, "Is Mr. Fred Houn available?"[9] My mother was amused that anyone would ask for me as "Mr." Fred Houn. I spoke to Shepp at length on the phone. He was very loquacious. He even brought up how people have griped about his lateness (and I thought to myself, did he know I was one of these people?). He was very pleasant, well spoken, and convincing. Shepp is also a writer and very well read. He can use multisyllabic words that have the effect of intellectual intimidation (and I believe this is part of cultivating his persona). Sometimes Shepp's classes became open rehearsals for his own projects or tryouts for his new works, with unexpectedly invited heavyweight name musicians from New York sitting in. Occasionally, utter chaos would reign, as Shepp wouldn't have parts copied or arrangements fully completed. I remember at one evening class/rehearsal how one of the singers from the male vocal group Reconstruction opened a bottle of wine, which was quickly passed around the room. Since I was then entering the Nation of Islam, I passed on the alcohol. But I remember Shepp was very happy to partake. But as the class got more disorganized, Shepp raised his voice and said, "Let's not get carried away by the convivialities." Of course, the whole room quieted, both from Shepp's commanding figure and from his use of such an erudite vocabulary.

Amiri Baraka, years later as I was driving with him, remarked about how "schizo" Archie was. There's the Shepp who identifies with the urban streets and "jazz" subculture and there's the erudite-projecting, petit-bourgeois Shepp who sends his children to private schools, enjoys the finer European luxuries, and who speaks in big words. The raw brilliance and emotive power of Shepp's art flows from who he is. The late baritone saxophonist Kenny Rogers, whom I had a chance to meet and briefly talk to when I saw him with the late Rahsaan Roland Kirk in Boston, remarked that "Archie's a genius."

In what today we would call "playing the race card," Shepp was a master. My first experience with him doing this was one of my first classes with him. The class was supposed to take place in a trailer classroom, but it was locked (or Shepp had forgotten the key). Shepp called Fred Tillis, a black music faculty colleague, and asked Tillis if he could come by and unlock the room. I believe Tillis asked Shepp to call campus security to do this, since Tillis probably had finished the day and was at home. Shepp then replied in a tone of well-acted sarcasm, "Now Fred, why would they do that for a nigger?" In a short while, Dr. Tillis came by, not too happy, but he did unlock the door.

Another time, Shepp's class was performing at a local Northampton music club. Shepp had picked me up at home, arriving almost two hours late. We arrived at the club quite late and Shepp double-parked his car to unload the music stands and the string bass. All during the first set, Shepp was drinking from the bar. During the second break, I noticed a commotion outside. Apparently, Shepp's station wagon was being towed by the local police for being parked in the middle of the street. The angry and somewhat inebriated Shepp was "wolfing" at the cops, yelling to the effect, "It's because I'm a nigger that you're doing this!" Most of us were very embarrassed by this. At the end of the night, we didn't stick around to see if we'd get paid (from the small admission charged by the club, which I suspect Shepp kept). While I had ridden there with Shepp, I certainly didn't feel like riding home with him, and quickly hitched a ride with others.

‹ 175

Years later in New York, I worked with the League of Revolutionary Struggle to sponsor a benefit concert for the LRS's *Black Nation* magazine, edited by Amiri Baraka. Shepp and Baraka, while once very close cohorts in the early 1960s, even living in the same building in Cooper Square in the Lower East Side, weren't really friends anymore, but occasionally teamed up for gigs. A year before, drummer Max Roach, a senior to both Baraka and Shepp, brought the two together to join him for a trio performance in Philadelphia that had a huge draw and was apparently a great show. Baraka wanted to do the same show at Columbia University's MacMillan Theater to raise funds for the magazine. Roach bowed out at the last minute (claiming he had to go to Los Angeles to receive an award from Mayor Tom Bradley) and was hastily replaced by drummer Philly Joe Jones. I made the arrangements to contract Shepp. My Afro Asian Music Ensemble opened the show and during intermission, as the stage was being reset for the headlining trio, Shepp complimented my band and my music, took a swig from a bottle of whiskey, and took the stage. Since I knew the three of them hadn't rehearsed and had just spent some pre-show time discussing the plan, I could tell that while Baraka was reading, Shepp was guiding the music, performing on saxophone and piano, various standards and free-form excerpts to support Baraka's poetry. While not a great artistic event, the audience was very warm to the three. (However, the event drew about two hundred people, and lost a lot of money as expectations, largely raised by Baraka, of a full house weren't met. Few "new music jazz" concerts in New York City can draw more than two hundred people, as I have come to realize, without tremendous marketing, which is costly and usually subsidized.)

Shepp personified the contradictions of a brilliant and talented black man, imbued with a level of political consciousness about oppression, fired with a spirit of struggle and resistance, but mitigated and distracted by his own petit-bourgeois class aspirations. While anticapitalist, Shepp was never clear or explicit about what he stood for in terms of replacing this system. In many ways, he desired on the one hand to reap the rewards and recognition of the great white counterparts, but, on the other hand, the system would only allow acceptable tokens. He insisted on being called "Mr. Shepp," identifying with the titles of bourgeois acceptability. He justified his wearing of European designer suits because American blue jeans on the European black market were luxury commodities. He wanted the most luxurious hotel suites, the finest European cuisine, and all of the "rewards" and conferred benefits of a celebrity. His personal tastes and consumption were very European and bourgeois. He became very popular in Europe, much more so than he ever has been in the United States, both from his fluency in European refinement and his intellectual Leftism (what black neoconservative critic Stanley Crouch once termed Shepp's "infantile Marxism"). Kalamu ya Salaam remarked that Archie Shepp was the "most inconsistent and erratic" artist of the 1960s. It seemed every other album was either great or garbage. Today, one record reviewer terms Shepp "the Forgotten Man," since he rarely performs in the United States and does so without much attention.

Max Roach was another towering musical giant to whom I was exposed during my teenage years. Unlike the younger Shepp, Roach had already entered the pantheon of "jazz" greats since his youthful days playing drums with the great Charlie "Bird" Parker. Roach's credentials and stature as one of the premiere architects of modern American music were uncontested. He was also considered to be The Best Drummer in the World, or one of the best. The only close competitor was the white drummer Buddy Rich, whom Roach, when I interviewed him in the mid-1970s, called "a friend." And I had read interviews of Buddy Rich, who always recognized Max Roach with great respect. Of course, Buddy Rich would get interviews on network television such as Johnny Carson's *Tonight Show,* while Roach, I don't believe, ever had.

My impression of Max was that he was a very quiet and humble man, but the second he stepped into a room, you felt that godhood had entered. He composed a short exercise tune called "Dorian" (based on the Dorian mode) for his students to practice improvisation in three-quarter (waltz) time, with a bridge in three-quarter "walk" feel. The tune became the rage of every student, including non-jazz ones, and was practiced constantly in campus piano practice rooms. Even Shepp brought an arrangement of it to class.

In performance, there was no ostentation about Roach. He would simply sit at the drum set like a true master, and just start to play incredible, unbelievable music. There was no swagger to his walk, no cool cigarette in his fingers while he played, and little was spoken. Once I did see him on a Sunday late morning, coming out of a luxury Cadillac filled with his family members, apparently leaving Sunday church services somewhere, and he was dressed in a killer all-white leisure suit with bell-bottom pants. His son, Raoul, and I were the same age and knew each other in high school. While I never took a class with Max, we'd encounter each other in rehearsals and at events, and he knew I was his son's peer. Years later, as we'd meet professionally in New York City, he'd fondly compliment me, noting how proud he and Shepp were of how much I'd accomplished and achieved. To this day, I've never personally ever had a disappointing experience with him, though I have known him to lobby for money for his benefit in funding situations. Max introduced me to the concept of black American culture and music as a "continuum," which I adapted to Asian American culture as a diasporic "continuum" that spans the traditional cultural heritage to the American-created "avant-garde."

Bassist Reggie Workman was also an adjunct faculty member at the University of Massachusetts. Workman was less overtly nationalistic and more openly related to the white music students. He also paid more attention to musical pedagogical detail than Shepp. Reggie was always prompt and accessible in imparting musical instruction.

The Amherst area has never since had the renaissance of Third World culture and intellectual activity that it did during this period of the 1970s, brought about by the student and progressive faculty activism that injected radicalism into the "liberal" academic arena. Through the efforts of these activists, the papers of the late great radical and revolutionary scholar-activist W.E.B. Du Bois were housed at UMass. Also, the campus performing arts series brought Max Roach's innovative M'Boom percussion ensemble, the Collective Black Artists big band, the play *Ornette,* and so many other artists, guest speakers, and events to the campus.

I met Amiri Baraka for the first time at Hampshire College on the eve of the African Liberation Day demonstration in 1974. There was some disgruntlement expressed over Baraka's honorarium of $1,000 (which stayed that amount well into the 1980s, as I can attest when I was professionally working with him) and that he had required to be flown out immediately after his talk to go to Washington, D.C., for the demonstration. However, since I was young and relatively inexperienced, such peccadilloes left an impression, but were far outweighed by the content of Baraka's talk, which was a speech he had written repudiating black nationalism for Marxism-Leninism–Mao Zedong thought. Baraka's ideological and political move to the Left was sending shock waves throughout the black movement and was being closely followed and discussed by many, many others, including those of us in the Asian Movement.

The Black Arts Movement and Its Impact:
Multimedia Collaboration as a Third World Thing

The Black Arts Movement was the attendant cultural wing of the Black Liberation Movement that ignited in the mid-1960s after the assassination of Malcolm X. Also known as the Black Power Movement, or Black Liberation Movement, it encompassed an assortment of revolutionary organizations across the United States, including

the Black Panther Party, the Revolutionary Action Movement, the Republic of New Afrika, the Dodge Revolutionary Union Movement (and
the other RUMs), the Congress of African Peoples, and many other
more regional or local collectives and organizations. The Black Arts
Movement included a number of arts and culture-focused groups that
were nonetheless as politically oriented as the political activist organizations, including alternative presses such as Broadside Press,
Third World Press, *Black World* magazine, *Drum* magazine.... In
an excellent yet-to-be-published manuscript by Kalamu ya Salaam
on the Black Arts Movement (*The Magic of JuJu,* the title of which is
taken from the 1967 recording by Archie Shepp on Impulse! Records),
Salaam summarizes the main characteristics and contributions of
BAM:

1. BAM was a national movement, not just centered in
   northeastern cities, and while Amiri Baraka was the most ‹ 179
   prominent spokesperson (credited as "the father of the
   BAM"), the movement had a diversity of organizations
   around the United States, including the South.
2. BAM was a popular grassroots movement, not involving
   just artists and intellectuals, but energized at the mass
   community level.
3. BAM was radical and revolutionary.
4. BAM was multidisciplinary and innovative, and promoted
   a "popular avant-garde."
5. BAM built independent, alternative, self-reliant
   institutions not beholden to white funders for support.

As a movement, many of the artists were actively engaged in cross-
disciplinary expressions. "Jazz" was the central, fundamental, creative gospel: quintessentially African American, an innovative and
sophisticated art form with far-reaching international impact and
influence. I have elsewhere argued that "jazz" is the revolutionary
music of the twentieth century [see "What Makes 'Jazz' the Revolutionary Music of the Twentieth Century?," this volume]. Many "jazz"
artists explicitly rejected the term "jazz," deeming it a racial slur
or pejorative appellation that the makers of the music—the "jazz"

musicians—never really invented, but rather, a label made by white outsiders. Many of the most conscious musicians preferred to call it "the music."[10]

The Black Arts Movement asserted and promoted the concept of a "black aesthetic." Contrary to the criticism of such a notion as "essentialist" and the accusation of being narrow, proscriptive, exclusionary, and dogmatic, the "black aesthetic" embraced a Pan-African scope, asserted and affirmed the presence of African American traditions, forms, and idioms, and, by its very assertion, exposed and countered a "white aesthetic" based upon racist Eurocentrism. If anything, "the music" embodied and exemplified the "black aesthetic" by celebrating African antecedents and interpreting cultural practices, forms, and traditions; by valorizing improvisation, exalting "soul" (or the "blues aesthetic"), as well as innovation and experimentation (signified by a fascination with and appreciation of "hipness"). The "black aesthetic" and "the music" possess formal characteristics such as antiphony (call and response), multiple rhythmic layering, syncopation, soloist-ensemble interplay, and so forth. The "black" or "jazz" aesthetic imbued and embodied much of the dance, film, visual arts, theater, and literature of this period. Probably the closest interaction was between literature (especially poetry as an oral performing art) and "the music."

This generation of black poets could virtually be called "jazz poets" both from their deep and profound appreciation of and usage of "the music" as well as their close collaborations and social connections with the musicians. Many poets would call upon and perform with musicians, even forming poetry bands. Fewer musicians took it upon themselves to invite poets or to utilize poetry in their performances, with the notable exception of Archie Shepp.

Shepp had studied theater and playwriting while an undergraduate student at Goddard College in Vermont during the 1950s. He even had his plays produced in small alternative theaters in Manhattan's Lower East Side during the early 1960s. Known for his articulate outspokenness, Shepp was exceptionally literate, a true "Timbuktu" man, equally at home in the literary arts and music as well as radical political theory. Poetry has been featured throughout his recording oeuvre. A tour-de-force poem by Shepp is "Mama Rose," written in the early 1960s upon the death of his grandmother, but a searing in-

180 ›

dictment of colonialism. Performed and recorded frequently, Shepp's recitation evokes the Baptist preacher and the work hollers of the sharecropper, blues man, and militant orator.

> They say that Malcolm is dead
> and every flower is still
> but I want to tell you Mama Rose
> that we are the victims ...
>
> I want to take this ex-cannibal's kiss
> and turn it into a revolution ...
>
> your corpse turned up to the sky like a
> putrefying Congolese after the Americans
> have come to help ...
>
> your vagina split asymmetrically between
> the east and the west ...

‹ 181

All of Shepp's poetry is performed with evocative theatrical energy. I have yet to find a poet who can perform/read better than Shepp, who is able to draw from a deep reservoir of musical knowledge and great performative talent.

Another of my personal favorites is Shepp's "Blasé," recorded on the French BYG label while a number of expatriate black American "new music" or avant-garde artists were in France after attending the Pan-African Festival in Algiers in 1969. The poem was performed by the late vocalist Jeanne Lee; one music commentator described it as one of the most brilliant poetical works on sexual/racial politics.[11]

> *Blasé*
>
> Ain't you daddy
> You who shot your sperm into me
> But never set me free.
> This ain't a hate thing
> It's a love thing
> If love is ever really loved that way
> The way they say.
>
> I give you a loaf of sugar
> You took my womb 'til it runs.

All of Ethiopia awaits you
My prodigal son.

Blasé
Ain't you big daddy
But mama loves you
She always has.

While a teenager, I did my own "cover" of Shepp's "Blasé." In the mid-1980s, I did my own version of "Poem for Mama Rose" which became part of the libretto to my first opera, "A Chinaman's Chance," a soliloquy called "A Success Story Fable: Poem for Vincent Chin," dedicated to the murdered Chinese American and an homage to all victims of racist violence and murder as well as a poetical diatribe against national oppression ("We will always be foreigners in a land where imported music is called 'classical.' ").

Shepp's stunning and powerful combination of poetry and music would heavily influence my involvement in multimedia performance. Many of my recordings, since my debut "Tomorrow Is Now!" on Soul Note, have featured poetry, text, and even graphics as part of my multimedia creative expression. I have collaborated with many poets, particularly African Americans, including Amiri Baraka (we had a new music/new poetry trio in the early 1980s with the late drummer Steve McCall), Kalamu ya Salaam (we were "The Afro-Asian Arts Dialogue"), Sapphire, Louis Reyes Rivera, Esther Iverem, Puerto Rican writer Alma Villegas, Chinese American writer Genny Lim, and Tony Medina. I have featured the poetry and writing of many others on my recordings and in my performances, including Sonia Sanchez, Andrea Lockett, Ann T. Greene, Janice Mirikitani, Brian Auerbach, Ruth Margraff, and others.

Former Celebrate Brooklyn festival producer Burl Hash said, "Archie wrote some great and beautiful theater music" referring to the *Lady Day* musical theater score that Shepp worked on in the early 1970s. Ntozake Shange's choreopoem-play *For Colored Girls Who Have Considered Suicide When the Rainbow Is Enuf* uses Shepp's music from *The Magic of Ju-Ju* recording. Shepp prefers to call himself a "folk" musician since he eschews the elitism of the highbrow (both concert hall and avant-garde). Indeed, Shepp is both premodern and postmodern simultaneously, drawing upon and juxtaposing elements from the continuum of black culture interspersed with his familiarity with the modernist European avant-garde, inviting performers who played varying African instruments and blues artists such as Julio Finn, straight ahead players such as Hank Mobley, Roland Hanna, Philly Joe Jones, and others, and electronic musicians such as Jasper Von Jost, to collaborate with him, with often mixed results. On "Blasé," Julio Finn takes a harmonica solo a half-step up in key from where the rest of the music is, a very jarring effect, but effective for the tone and content of this dark, disturbing, and ominous work. On other pieces, such as "Pitchin' Can," the results are disorganized, a chaotic mishmash.

I met Shepp when I was a teenager, seeking how to unite radical politics and the arts. The 1970s were a transitional period for Shepp, I believe, both musically and for the man. As a professor in African American music, Shepp would study, practice, and incorporate the broadness of African American musical culture, learning to play chord changes, composing more lyrical and conventional harmony-based songs. The late Romulus Franceschini described this time in Shepp's career as the tenor saxophonist seeking to become more of a pop artist. He was writing and recording vocal songs based on the blues, rhythm and blues, "jazz" ballads, and gospel, including hiring gospel singers. Shepp was himself becoming the bridge in the continuum of black music in America. By the late 1970s, after I had left the Amherst area and had much less contact with him except for attending an occasional performance, Shepp took up bebop and playing "jazz" standards as his main repertoire. Yet, his trickster spirit would continue to stymie the "jazz" critics. He released two duet albums with pianist Horace Parlan—one of spirituals, and the other of blues songs—that were brilliant in their conception and glorious in the beauty of the simplicity of the material performed with Shepp's idiosyncratic stylization. These two albums forced former skeptics in the "jazz" establishment to recognize his stature as he won *Down Beat* magazine's Tenor Saxophone of the Year award from the critics. Coinciding with this recognition, a *Down Beat* magazine article on Shepp had the title "Radical with Tenure" in a politically self-congratulatory way of remarking that the once young 1960s militant had "matured" and discarded the avant-garde for the traditional mainstream. How much of Shepp had ideologically "mellowed" isn't clear, and perhaps may never be, as Shepp himself is mercurial.

The Genius and Ego-Mania of Amiri Baraka

While I was a young teenager voraciously learning about the Black Arts Movement and the Black Liberation Movement, Amiri Baraka's writings were prominent and highly influential. His genius for poetry is widely acknowledged. A particular emphasis in his poetic and polemical onslaughts has been the vacillation of the black petite bourgeoisie, or middle class, its assimilationist-integrationist orientation, and its frequent willingness to sell out and compromise the Black Liberation struggle for token individual gains. It was inevitable that I would study and come to know and work with Baraka as a leading black revolutionary artist-activist.

184 ›

By the late 1970s, many of the former leading Third World nationalists in the United States had come to Marxism-Leninism-Mao Zedong Thought as their ideology. The group I had joined, I Wor Kuen (IWK), merged with a Chicano-based organization, the August Twenty-Ninth Movement (ATM), by mid-1978, becoming the League of Revolutionary Struggle Marxist-Leninist (LRS). A year later, the LRS would merge with Baraka's former Congress of African Peoples (CAP), now the Revolutionary Communist League Marxist-Leninist (RCL). I remember the merger celebration event held in Harlem in the cold winter month of January 1979. At least two hundred people crammed into a small auditorium, the largest gathering of blacks and Asians together I had ever seen and been with. My fledging Afro-Asian music-poetry band, then called Frontline, performed along with the St. Louis–based Infra-Red Funk band, a music group that had formed within the St. Louis chapter of CAP. Two comrades from the former RCL, Kamau and his then-wife, Imarisha, would later tell me that the event was truly historic, not just for the political merger and unity, but because they had seen for the first time former extreme nationalist comrades of theirs dance with Asians, and that blew their mind! Amiri Baraka was supposed to be the keynote speaker, but, after a long delay, he could not show because of an air traffic weather delay that kept him in Chicago. He had phoned in the notes to his speech to Pili Michael Humphrey, a young leader in RCL from Atlanta. Pili's speech was fiery and strong, and I remember to this day one critically important, emphatic point he made in that speech: that the national movements were *independently* revolutionary. The crowd roared its approval as many misconceptions about multinational unity and the national question in the Marxist-Leninist movement tended to be integrationist: that nationality-in-form organizing was "narrow" and inherently "lesser" than multinational formations or forms of organizing. Such a white-integrationist position implicitly and sometimes explicitly took the position that uniting with majority-white Leftists was "more" revolutionary than all-black or all–Third World peoples formations and organizing. Pili's statement, which was the position of the LRS, made it clear in no uncertain terms how we as a Marxist-Leninist group stood on the national question, which was contrary to the predominantly integrationist positions of most of the other groups in the Marxist-Leninist movement.

At the post-event after-party, dancing to the Infra-Red Funk band, my crush began for one of the former-CAP/RCL comrades, Jamala Rogers. She was short, broad shouldered, voluptuous, dark-skinned, with beautiful rounded facial features. It wasn't until the early 1990s, after the split and dissolution of the LRS, that we would begin dating. I was the first non-black man she ever dated. I'd take her to see Chinese films, have meals in Chinatown, take her to Baja and La Jolla to enjoy the ocean beaches. When I visited her in St. Louis, we visited the black rodeo, a black independent free school. She jokingly referred to us as "renegade lovers," since we were both outcasts from the antisocialist majority that had seized control of the LRS by 1989. After several months of a long-distance relationship, I broke us up because I realized that we would never live together, since neither she and nor I was willing to relocate from our beloved home bases of St. Louis and New York City, respectively. I also was interested in dating another black sister living in Brooklyn at that time, and was then subscribing to serial monogamy.

Part of the work of the merger with RCL involved quickly clearing out its former office in Newark, which was condemned to demolition. I was still living in Boston at the time, but traveled down to New York City frequently for meetings and for my own personal enjoyment. The Big Apple was much more exciting than Bean Town. Here were the cultural and political "names," and the amount of activity was staggering. On one of my trips, staying with an LRS comrade in Chinatown, we shared a passion for "the music." One night we attended the debut concert of the World Saxophone Quartet at the Public Theater. A who's who of black artists were there, including Amiri and Amina Baraka, sitting a table away from us. Steve introduced himself and me to them and they politely returned the greeting. The next day, a group of us from New York went to Newark to the CAP office and combed through the boxes of files, record albums, and videos. It was amazing, the amount of Black Liberation Movement history that we had to throw out because we could only take what we could carry. I remember reading some files that had copies of "Chairman" Baraka's articles sent to various periodicals, and the rejection letters. One in particular I remember explained its rejection of Baraka's submission by stating, "We don't publish advocacy."

I moved from Boston/Cambridge, Massachusetts, to New York City in the early fall of 1981 and assumed my work in the New York unit of the LRS, which included going to the many events where Amiri Baraka was featured to leaflet in support of his case against police brutality. Baraka had been beaten by New York City police on the streets of Greenwich Village during a heated argument between him and his wife. The police claimed that they were responding to a call about a wife being beaten by her husband. Amiri had been arrested and charged with "resisting arrest." While many are of the opinion that he indeed had probably assaulted his wife, she would deny this in public rallies and supported her husband's struggle against the police harassment. I attended the court hearing where Amiri Baraka was defended by famed Leftist attorney William Kunstler, who in a last-minute move got the clearly sympathetic young judge to commute Baraka's sentence to serving ninety days on weekends at Riker's Island Penitentiary.

In effect, the sentence allowed Baraka time off to rest and to write more during his weekends for the next year. Toward the end of this sentence, a big fiftieth birthday party bash was thrown for him at his home in Newark. I attended many of his parties and house events, which included long-time activists, neighbors, and luminaries such as Vertamae Grosvenor, Max Roach, Grachan Moncur III, Quincy

Troupe, Ben Cauldwell, Vincent Smith, Louis Reyes Rivera, and many others.

Kalamu ya Salaam assesses Baraka's contribution and role as the BLM's greatest "propagandist," while Modibo (James Baker), a CAP-RCL veteran, believes Baraka was "one of the great organizers in the BLM." Certainly during the peak period of the CAP, more than a dozen chapters nationwide were organized. Baraka played a leading role at the National Black Political Convention in Gary, Indiana; in organizing many benefit cultural events, festivals, alternative theater, presses (e.g., Jihad Publications) and cultural campaigns; in the struggles and organizing work of the African Liberation Support Committee. His history of work and accomplishments is prodigious. As with any great leader, a strong and capable circle of supporters greatly contributed to the successes and accomplishments. But what is noteworthy compared to today is that these organizing efforts were done with virtually no paid staff but by activist volunteers. This is distinct from the nonprofit organizations today that have hired staff and rely upon state and corporate funded budgets. However, when the movement waned, Baraka seemed to lose touch with the new realities and conditions. When I began to work with him in the early 1980s, CAP-RCL had faded to only a handful of chapters nationwide. The organizational base and infrastructure were far weaker than a decade before, yet Baraka seemed to operate on the notion that simply by the sheer force of his will the same level of functioning could happen. People have marveled and wondered about his immense productivity; when I asked his wife Amina about it, she explained that "Amiri has such a strong focus of concentration—he can write even if a party is going on around him." Indeed, Baraka, unlike other more sybaritic artists, is very Spartan and is constantly in motion, intellectually in his constant writing and polemicizing, and physically in his ability to go from event to event. He does relax, as I've run into him at "jazz" clubs and shows from time to time. He does like to "hang out" and converse over a beer or burger.

One of the criticisms of the RCL was its dogmatism and overreliance on quoting the classic Marxist-Leninist-Mao texts. I believe much of our movement of that period was infected by Stalin's interpretation of dialectical materialism. Indeed, Stalin's short book

‹ 187

Dialectical and Historical Materialism was a movement primer and classic text used in study groups. Stalin tended to view most contradictions at a level of being antagonistic, which was a battle with the enemy. He also tended to politically characterize most contradictions as "either/or," in which one true, correct proletarian position fought with the enemy, bourgeois line. There was very little synthesis or view of reality as a complex interpenetration of opposites, but, rather, two stark and diametrical opposites for which the one correct line had to vanquish the incorrect one. Baraka possesses much of this influence. On the positive side, Baraka is one of the few Marxist intellectuals and theorists to give sharp, analytic political assessments of artists and cultural trends. However, his views about the "class struggle" in African American literature and in "the music" reflect draconian hard-line positions that place artists in either the camp of the people's tradition of struggle or in the camp of "tail Europe," i.e., white assimilation and capitulation to Western imperialism. To read that one has been categorized by Baraka as "tail Europe" doesn't do much to persuade anyone to rethink their musical and political direction.[12]

Baraka can be a scathing critic, but he is also able to offer programmatic proposals. I've often looked to his manifestos for ideas about *how* to create alternatives. For example, his calls for a cabinet position on the arts for the U.S. government have merit. His call for certain American films and important cultural icons to be certified as national treasures of art so that they won't be sold to Sony or foreign multinational corporations are also valid reforms. With this, I've learned that every critique should come with a proposal for an alternative. Yet today, Baraka, possibly suffering from delusions about his own role as an agitator-propagandist, is either incapable of or won't do much ground-up organizing. Exhortations can't substitute or replace the crucially necessary day-to-day, grassroots work that is so lacking in today's U.S. Left. The cadre of people who will do this work in a disciplined, professional (but inevitably unpaid) collective mode is what we lack.

For all of Baraka's great accomplishments and impact, his greatest weakness is his inability for true, honest, soul-baring self-reflection. While much ado has been made about his changes in identity and politics from LeRoi Jones (Bohemian beat poet) to Imamu

Amiri Baraka (cultural nationalist) to Amiri Baraka (Marxist Left-ist), in all of his poetry and writings there is very little personal feeling and self-criticism beyond the coldly ideological and political. He unfortunately is caught up in his own cult of personality. Often his ideological and political battles take on personality wars and are dismissed by many as such, harming the political message and position. His use of ad hominem attacks through his frequent use of "the dozens" as a form of "dissing" his ideological opponents often leaves a bad taste. A recent example was his ferocious condemnation of Ralph Nader supporters in the 2000 presidential elections, when he accused those who voted for and backed Nader against Gore of having delivered the presidency to rightwing fascism represented by Bush. In some ways, his continual fascination with electoral politics since the days of "black electoral empowerment" strikes me as so-cial-democratic: socialism in words but supporting the Democratic Party in deeds. He is less able to persuade than to attack. I believe he is incapable of ascertaining his own impact, especially negatively, upon people when he gets into one of his frothing rants. In recent years, his temper has become testier. Except for his poetry, his writing has become sloppy and sometimes even incoherent.[13] His role continues to be primarily as a propagandist-agitator, though his effectiveness as an organizer and as a leader has significantly diminished with his inability to unite and train new circles of cadres and organizers. He continues to be a scrappy warrior-artist: bold, brazen, and brilliant in his rapier-like attacks and critiques of the U.S. white racist ruling class. Without showing any signs of "mellowing" (i.e., increasing ideological and political conservatism), Amiri Baraka as poet-warrior continues to fight when many others have capitulated to career self-aggrandizement.

Unity and Struggle with Kalamu ya Salaam

I met writer, poet, producer, and cultural activist Kalamu ya Salaam (a Swahili name for "Pen for Peace," formerly Vallery Ferdinand III) in the spring of 1989 while my Afro Asian Music Ensemble was at the Houston International Festival, invited by then-curator Baraka Sele. Baraka had told both Kalamu and me that we had to meet each other, so a dinner between us, along with others who were traveling with each of us, took place in an upscale black restaurant. Ya Salaam and I had both known of each other for a while but had never personally met. I knew him originally from the *Black Scholar* debates[14] in the early to mid-1970s between black nationalism and Marxism, a historic transition period in the Black Liberation struggle, with tremendous ideological and political debates occurring in the then-African Liberation Support Committee (ALSC). The ALSC was a broad black-activist united front to build support for the African liberation struggles in then-still decolonizing countries such as then Rhodesia (now Zimbabwe), Guinea-Bissau, Mozambique, then South West Africa (now Namibia), Angola, and South Africa; it had the leading exponents of black nationalism and the emerging Marxist current in the Black Liberation Movement. Ya Salaam at that time was anti-Marxist and pro-Pan-African cultural nationalism, joining with Haki Madhubuti (poet-activist, formerly Don L. Lee) and others against Amiri Baraka (who had been a leading cultural nationalist and had just turned to Marxism), Mark Smith, and a group of North Carolina-based black Leftists, including then-Revolutionary Workers League leader Owusu Sadaukai (then Howard Fuller), Abdul Alkalimat (then Gerald McWorter), and others. During this time (by late spring 1976), I, too, had moved from my revolutionary yellow nationalism to Marxism in my second semester at Harvard; I was highly influenced by the young Marxist organizers on campus (particularly those from a small Boston-New York collective called the Proletarian Unity League), but I eventually joined I Wor Kuen, having more unity with them on the "national question" during the winter of my sophomore year (late 1976-early 1977).

Ya Salaam and I were cautious with each other in our first meeting, but each of us asked the other about our views on a number of topics. He attended our performance at the festival the next day. I left our initial encounter with a positive impression about him. Soon after this initial meeting, I took the initiative to telephone him at his home base in New Orleans. We talked further about politics and the arts. I was very positive about his accessibility and openness to me, not at all the narrow nationalist impression I had gotten of him through the published debates. I directly asked him if he were a socialist and he replied that he supported socialism as a system to replace capitalism, but didn't subscribe to or identify as a socialist/Marxist because he believed the ethics of socialism were far more important to him than the theory or ideology. He continues to self-identify as a Pan-Africanist, but has formally renounced black nationalism.[15] I proposed we work together in a poetry/music duo, and he agreed.

I had just joined a progressive speakers/performers agency called Speak Out: Artists and Writers, which had received its initial start-up from *Z Magazine,* a progressive political periodical headed by Left-ist Michael Alpert, but, as I would soon learn, decidedly anti-Marxist, especially Marxist-Leninist (the magazine and its attendant small press, South End Press, would propel the publishing careers of bell hooks, Cornel West, and Manning Marable—now three of the most well-known and well-paid integrationist democratic-socialist writers/pundits/intellectuals of "color"). Speak Out had found me a gig to perform at the University of Michigan–Ann Arbor and I suggested that it become a duo with Kalamu, to promote African–Asian American unity. The sponsors liked the idea, and I immediately called Kalamu, and he agreed to join me. Kalamu also took the initiative to call his contacts in the Michigan area, professor and writer Melba Joyce Boyd and white militant poet-activist John Sinclair, and he found an extra gig for us at the campus at which Melba was then teaching. Kalamu's initiative impressed me. Our performances together went off very well.

Kalamu ya Salaam is truly a "jazz" poet, adaptable, flexible, not fixed to a set way of reading/performing his poetry: the very qualities of creative interaction that true "jazz" musicians have. A number of other "jazz" poets I've had the experience of performing with were fixed, stiff, and couldn't read any other way but how they'd been doing their poems. I was supposed to just simply follow them in their set way of reading. There was no interplay between the poetry reading and my baritone sax musical performance. Kalamu can actually interact and interplay with my improvisations. While he, too, like many of the other "jazz poets," called for "jazz" standard tunes to be the framework of many of his poems, he wasn't stuck on just following these melodies and he could hear my transitions and departures and new directions and join with me.

As good friends, comrades, and artistic collaborators, Kalamu and I have enjoyed much in-depth discussion, debate, and ideological struggle on a wide range of issues. He has shared much of his thought processes, experiences, and opinions, including his book manuscript analyzing the Black Arts Movement, *The Magic of JuJu* which is to be published by Haki Madhubuti's Third World Press. For the most part, I believe, Kalamu "walks his talk." When he let me have a copy of this manuscript to read, I thought it was a major work of great importance to understanding the BAM from a participant's point of view and with valuable insights, information, and analysis, and I offered to help him find a publisher. But true to his Pan-African nationalist convictions, he wanted the manuscript to only be considered by a black publisher and for it to be targeted to black bookstores and to a black audience, though perhaps a white Left small press might have more quickly published it or offered better distribution. He has often said that his audience is primarily a black one first and foremost. He hasn't sought to "cross over" to a white poetry or arts audience or institutions. He is a cultural producer, having produced radio programs, festivals, and publications of black poetry and music through black organizations, even though some have been less than professional in their business dealings. He explains his interest in the music and poetry, as well as his interest in China, as having been sparked by the work of Langston Hughes. Hughes had made recordings of his poetry with "jazz" and had written poems, especially during the 1920s and 1930s, that expressed internationalist solidarity with the peoples' struggles around the world, including the poem, "Roar, China, Roar!" for the Chinese Revolution. Ya Salaam shared with me the costs and work of organizing our duo, the Afro-Asian Arts Dialogue (I believe he proposed the name from a small conference by that same title and theme organized by dancer/choreographer Peggy Choy during the time of the Los Angeles rebellion in 1992).

Ya Salaam is an ardent cultural activist who is firmly committed to black independent cultural production and has self-published many anthologies as well as his own poetry chapbooks. He criticized an edition of the *African American Review*[16] devoted to the topic of "the music" when it didn't include even one black writer. The *Review* offered him the opportunity to edit another volume on the same topic, for which he included predominantly black writers, but others as well, including myself and Irish American drummer Royal Hartigan. Ya Salaam also introduced me to Christopher Small's book on "the music," *Music of a Common Tongue* (River Run Press), which, at the time of the early 1990s, he considered the best analysis and understanding of "jazz." His own insights into "the music," his analytic writings about music and African American culture in general, have been for the most part very insightful. I remember during the time of our first Afro-Asian Arts Dialogue, when we were performing at the University of Wisconsin–Madison with Peggy Choy, we had lunch with a "jazz" professor who seemed to believe the black "free music" avant-garde had been halted and replaced by the rise of commercial "fusion jazz" in the 1970s. Kalamu took exception and cited another current, the rise of the CTI label and other black fusion-funk music, such as artists as Donald Byrd (who was a hard bop trumpeter-composer–band leader) and the Blackbyrds (a band of his Howard University students who played much more commercial black urban dance music). Ya Salaam also asserts that "jazz" is a "world music," as the black jazz musicians were among the black community's first "internationalists," touring and traveling overseas and returning to their communities with a broader internationalist understanding. Kalamu has always asserted the social importance and impact of "the music" and black culture. His was the only voice of criticism of Clint Eastwood's film *Bird,* about saxophonist-composer-titan Charlie Parker, in a review entitled " 'Bird' is a Turkey!" published in Canada's *Coda* magazine. More than anyone, Salaam has, I believe, best understood the impact and importance of John Coltrane upon black music and culture, which has shaped my views in this article. In an interview with ya Salaam, Bill Mullen asked what he felt about my opinion about the "enormous" impact of Coltrane. Ya Salaam replied that Coltrane's impact was "beyond enormous." Which I concede is indeed the truth.

‹ 193

Kalamu ya Salaam and I have worked well together as artists, shared many hours of debate and struggle over ideological and political questions, and are close friends. Our unity has its limitations, consistent with ya Salaam's nationalism. As a nationalist, ya Salaam obviously hasn't taken as strong an interest in learning about the APA history and struggle and experience as I have taken toward African Americans and Africa. But my greatest disappointment with Kalamu comes from his deliberate silence in criticizing the leading reactionary in "jazz" today, Wynton Marsalis, and Marsalis's right-wing ideological advisor, Stanley Crouch. Even though Marsalis is

Kalamu's cousin, in private to me, ya Salaam has expressed his problems with Marsalis's ideological adherence to Crouch. In our many debates and discussions about Wynton, Kalamu would come up with weak defenses for Wynton, such as Marsalis's emphasis on going to public schools to "promote" jazz to black children while the most noted avant-garde musicians, such as David Murray in particular, don't. Kalamu knows Marsalis's opinions that the avant-garde musicians can't read music or that they lack technical rigor in the traditional aspects of "jazz" are misdirected and remiss, just as thirty years ago the very same charges were leveled at the 1960s avant-garde. The avant-garde chooses to make music differently, and its merits or faults should be judged not on "straight-ahead mainstream jazz" criteria, but by its own.

To my knowledge, the two most explicitly critical opinions voiced about Marsalis by leading black artists were from the now-deceased musicians Lester Bowie and Julius Hemphill (the latter charged Marsalis with being an "Uncle Tom" in the pages of *The Nation* and other national publications). I have discussed my own criticisms of Marsalis elsewhere[17] but, suffice it to say, I'm of the position that Wynton Marsalis is to Lincoln Center what Clarence Thomas is to the U.S. Supreme Court, a black neoconservative, right-wing, second-rater.

My admiration and friendship for Kalamu continues despite our disagreements and differences. His commitment to cultural organizing, to independent black cultural production, education, and training within the black community, based in the South, is exemplary and an affirmation of Cabral's fundamental principle of national liberation movement building for artists and activists to "return to the source."

Creating a Popular Avant-Garde: How the Black "New Music" Inspired Asian American Creative "New Music"

Unlike the "avant-garde" of a colonialist Western Europe or white North American culture, which isn't necessarily politically progressive or transgressive, and may indeed reinforce privilege, promote solipsism and self-indulgence, oppose social responsibility and consciousness, and elevate "art for art's sake," the "avant-garde" of oppressed peoples' cultures generally tends to fuel liberation, challenge cultural dominance and hegemony (usually of the oppressor, colonial traditions and forms), and promote rebellion, struggle, dissidence, disturbance, militancy, and opposition to the mainstream and the status quo. The African American "avant-garde" of the 1960s and early 1970s was such a force. The "new music" and "new poetry" and "new theater," and so on were part of a cultural and social movement for a "new society." In a broad sense, the artists sought to "deconstruct" and support the destruction of the "old" society of white supremacist, Eurocentric patriarchal capitalism for a "new" society based on full equality, social justice, and "power to the people." The terrain of struggle for these "avant-garde" transgressors and radicals was as cultural and artistic activists, though many also contributed through their social activism. Of course, the "new" jazz, with Coltrane as avatar, was the most potent and compelling wave of artistic experimentation and expressive force. As the late trumpeter Lester Bowie explained, in a retort to neoconservative "back to the tradition" exponents à la Wynton Marsalis, who dismiss the "avant-garde" as musically invalid and illegitimate: "The tradition of jazz is innovation."

‹ 195

I assert that the members of the early black avant-garde, beginning with Sun Ra in the 1950s, and extending to the Art Ensemble of Chicago in the 1960s and 1970s, were precursors and leading examples of a "black postmodernism." The Art Ensemble of Chicago's mantra, "Black Music from Ancient to Future," best signifies the self-conscious reworking, borrowing, reinterpretations, and musical juxtaposing and collaging in their collective performance rites. Sun Ra's cosmic theory, Julius Hemphill's fascination with the Dogon, are just examples of this Afrocentric "postmodernism" that seeks to understand the past with an avant-garde sensibility. Sun Ra was the preeminent forerunner to today's fascination with extraterrestrial contact/visitation and interspecies communication joined with hopes for world peace and unity through man's connection to the extraterrestrial. I disagree with people who try to explain Sun Ra as a manifestation of Space Age modernity. Rather, Sun Ra's interest in extraterrestriality is much more about spirituality than a fixation upon high technology, though certainly Sun Ra was interested in the latest electronic musical instruments. For Sun Ra, music and space exploration would point the way for humanity to develop a higher consciousness for the need for a changed orientation beyond the limitations of earthly material accumulation and acquisitiveness.

The late 1970s and early 1980s avant-garde in New York's loft scene, however, was, in my opinion, weaker as an example of vulgar postmodernism that promotes obfuscation, obscurantism, and empiricism. These black avant-garde musicians and artists of the 1980s New York Soho loft scene retreated into self-indulgence (hiding or jettisoning the former socially conscious work) and jumping onto the white performance art bandwagon of Meredith Monk, Philip Glass, Robert Wilson, Richard Foreman, and others. The fire of the 1960s and early 1970s had dissipated into esotericism, ambiguity, and shallow postmodern pastiche by African American artists such as Bill T. Jones, choreographer Donald Byrd, Bebe Miller, and Carl Hancock Rux, among others, who questioned even "blackness" as essentialist.

Just as African American popular culture has a leading influence upon American popular culture in general, so too does African American avant-garde music and artistic expression have a similar impact upon the overall avant-garde. A small but important group of APA musicians embraced "the music" and its philosophical, political, and cultural radicalism. My other essays discuss the who, what, where, when, and why of the so-called Asian American "jazz" scene on both coasts, so I won't repeat any of that discussion. Multi-woodwindist Gerald Oshita, bassist Mark Izu, woodwindist Russel Baba, clarinetist Paul Yamazaki, and East Coast violinist Jason Kao Hwang were "free jazz" players exploring Asian musical and performance concepts. I met Gerald Oshita before he died in his San Francisco Japantown studio in the early 1980s. He had a large collection of woodwinds, including a number of unconventional and uncommon ones, which reminded me of Rahsaan Roland Kirk, who performed on the manzello and the stritch. In the opinion of Asian American "jazz" impresario Paul Yamazaki (who helped to found and organize the first annual Asian American Jazz Festival in the Bay Area), Gerald warranted props as the first Asian American to be on a Soul Note/Black Saint recording (as a sideman/colleague of Roscoe Mitchell). The Italian-based Soul Note/Black Saint label was considered by many to be the "creative new music" label of the 1980s. In 1984 I would become the first Asian American to record as a leader for that label, eventually releasing three recordings and having one of my pieces recorded on a fourth, a recording by the Rova Saxophone Quartet. My first Soul Note album earned much notice both from the circle of Asian American "jazz" artists as well as from the larger "creative new music" circle, both for the significance of my outing as an Asian American band leader but also for my explicitly radical politics and "Afro-Asian" concept.

One very overlooked Asian American composer/musician/band leader of the late 1970s and early 1980s was the Chinese American Los Angeles–based Benny Yee, who, with singer Nobuko Miyamoto, had a band called Warriors of the Rainbow. Yee had the musical skills to play chord changes and to go between "free jazz" improvisations and structured/notated arrangements, whereas most of the others mentioned above were primarily "free" improvisers. Warriors of the Rainbow enlisted highly skilled African American sidemen, including trombonist Julian Priester and saxophonist Bennie Maupin, both of whom had played with such greats as Herbie Hancock, among many others. As the name of their band denoted, the assemblage was both multicultural (Asian and African) and politically militant ("warrior" or "warriors" was commonly an African American conception of someone engaged in the struggle for liberation).

As a young Asian American musician, I sought out other Asians playing in primarily black bands, though many turned out not to be very politically conscious. Many were Japanese nationals in the United States who embraced and identified with "jazz" and black music for its cultural iconoclasm, hipness, and alternative lifestyle and cultural norms. I haven't met a Japanese national who played excellent "jazz" who was motivated and inspired by, and identified with, black nationalist or explicit anti-imperialist politics.

Indeed, "jazz" is a cultural commodity of exotic fascination in Japan, where, along with Europe, lucrative touring possibilities have existed for black American artists. However, in accounts told to me by Japanese American drummer Akira Tana and other Asians (even Japanese nationals), the tour promoters have at times explicitly told American band leaders not to bring Asian musicians on their tours. White or black artists are viewed as more "authentic" or exotic, while Asians are viewed as "inauthentic" and less interesting for marketing purposes.

The Asian American "jazz" scene was much more active on the West Coast, with the most radical and "free" music centered in the Bay Area. The "scene" could be grouped into three loosely connected styles: a "jazz fusion" scene with its most prominent group the Los Angeles–based band Hiroshima, along with Deems Tsutakawa in Seattle, and others; a mainstream straight-ahead "jazz" group, mostly older generation players such as Filipino pianist Bobby Enriquez, pianist Toshiko Akiyoshi, alto saxophonist Gabe Baltazar (of the Stan Kenton big band fame), and the younger drummer Akira Tana (whose professional career started from touring with the Heath Brothers); and the "free" creative music players. To George Leong and Paul Yamazaki's credit, when they first organized the Asian American Jazz Festival in the Bay Area, all three scenes or styles were featured, even if some of the artists didn't particularly care to be or were interested in identifying with Asian America. Another scene that claimed the term "Asian American music" was a pop folk-music style of Asian American performers, including the East Coast trio A Grain of Sand and West Coast groups such as Yokohama, California, the subsequent projects by Robert Kikuchi-Yngojo, a loose gathering of musicians based around San Francisco's Japantown Art and Media Workshop, among others. The Japanese American taiko groups were another subset of self-consciously organized Asian American musical activity. Except for the "straight-ahead jazz" players, most of the artists and organizers of all these "scenes" identified with the Asian Movement and community.

The bands Commitment on the East Coast (three black musicians and Jason Kao Hwang) and United Front in the Bay Area (Mark Izu with the half Japanese–half black drummer Anthony Brown, and two black horn players), were primarily "new music" jazz-focused, though they did perform occasionally at Asian community events.

Rarely have musicians developed any sustained and coherent collaborations across these scenes, possibly due to stylistic differences and the lack of artistic leadership and skills to bridge such differences. However, pioneering efforts between the creative new music "jazz" artists such as Izu, Baba, and myself and late-comers such as Jon Jang, Miya Masaoka, Glenn Horiuchi, Francis Wong, and others would incorporate traditional instruments and players in cross-stylistic collaborations.

One other major scene that has never really embraced, much less identified with, the Asian American Movement or community is the world of individual "new music classical" composers, who have incorporated traditional Asian instruments and elements into highbrow concert music, such as Chou Wen-chung, Chinary Ung, Chen Yee, Chou Long, Bright Sheng, Tan Dun, Yoshiko Torikai, Toru Takematsu, and others. These composers more typically subscribe to the "art for art's sake" position and seek legitimation from the musical academy and Eurocentric establishment.

Alternative Cultural Production: The Rise and Fall of Black Artist Collectives

The Black Arts Movement spawned numerous alternative, community-based collectives and guerrilla-style organizations in all disciplines. For music, the most well-known and influential groups were the Association for the Advancement for Creative Musicians (AACM) in Chicago and the Black Arts Group (BAG) in St. Louis. I named my first multimedia "performance art" group, the now-defunct Asian American Art Ensemble, after the famed Art Ensemble of Chicago, a collective music group that emerged from the AACM that presented ritual-style performances with the musicians in African-mythological-inspired make-up and costumes combining indigenous "primitive" instruments with modern saxophones, drum set, and bass. The late 1960s and early 1970s black alternative music organizations promoted Afrocentrism, multimedia, and experimental performances with a strong grassroots community orientation and collective musical sharing and organizational decision making. They were attempts to create alternatives to the bandleader-as-star syndrome, to foster creative dialogue, to promote unity over stylistic differences, and to collectively build a cultural movement closely aligned with the Black Liberation struggle.

The Art Ensemble of Chicago promoted their music as "Great Black Music: From Ancient to Future" as a direct expression of their Pan-African avant-garde consciousness. By the late 1980s, Bay Area-based Chinese American pianist Jon Jang had started his own record label, AsianImprov Records (AIR) to release his own music. By early 1988, Francis Wong and I joined Jang to expand the concept in the effort to become a leading center of "Asian American jazz" or "Asian American improvised and creative music" as part of exerting cultural leadership to the Asian Movement, since we were then all cadres in the League of Revolutionary Struggle (Marxist-Leninist).

Our record label and production company was modeled on the early black creative music collectives. The first non-Jang recording was my "A Song for Manong" (AIR 003), a collector's edition LP that featured my Asian American Art Ensemble in collaboration with the Filipino American Kulintang Arts that performed primarily traditional southern Philippines kulintang music but was open to and seeking to create contemporary work as well. The score I composed was to a large music/theater production by that same name as the third part in my performance art trilogy, "Bamboo That Snaps Back!," which celebrates the resistance struggles of Asian Pacific Americans. This third installment, "A Song for Manong," celebrated the epic struggles of the Filipinos, beginning with the arrival of Magellan in 1522 to the fall of the International Hotel in San Francisco Manilatown in 1977.

By the late 1980s, many of the black alternative cultural collectives had either collapsed or gone the route of becoming a social service arts-in-education provider. None maintained the radical, experimental, avant-garde performance thrust. A newer "movement" was Mbase, centered around alto saxophonist Steve Coleman, with Brooklyn and New York City black musicians. However, it quickly faded as many became disgruntled and disillusioned with it as simply promoting and serving the career interests of Coleman. Elsewhere in Brooklyn, the Musicians of Brooklyn Initiative (MOBI) had been started by Lester Bowie and others, and had incorporated as a nonprofit arts organization. But musicians quickly left MOBI, believing that it only served the bigger-name artists as a conduit to get grants.

In forming my own production company, Big Red Media, Inc., in 1998, I recognized that the collective "movement" was dead because the political sensibilities and leadership that were a direct result of the Black Liberation Movement had disappeared. Former collective-functioning artists were more interested in pursuing solo careers. This was the same experience that undermined the early 1960s October Revolution movement started by trumpeter Bill Dixon for the purpose of being a black creative music collective that would break from the recording industry. However, as Dixon tells it, October Revolution member Archie Shepp was secretly negotiating his own record deal with Impulse! during this time. Shepp's position was that he needed the money to pay for the costs of his growing family. Other members quickly became disenchanted and the group fell apart.

Collective artistic and financial/business decision-making can only be viable if the artist members totally submit to the governing mission and principles and are truly able to function collectively, putting self-interest secondary to the goals of the movement. This is especially challenging for artists, who necessarily have very big egos and strong personal visions. In the 1930s, similar types of alternative and artist-led "unions" attained a certain level of impact and collective functioning because they were secretly led by Communist cadres. Such collectives require a strong political core that will resist co-optation and careerism.

In the 1970s, black nationalist recording labels also developed, including Strata-East in New York City and Black Jazz in Chicago. While I am not knowledgeable about the history and final outcome of Black Jazz, I was around the music scene in New York to hear gossip about the demise of Strata-East, with a gamut of accusations ranging from one of the leading musicians absconding with the money to the label simply failing as a viable business. An alternative distribution company, the nonprofit New Music Distribution Service, also collapsed by the early 1980s. Certain lessons can be learned from all of these experiences about alternative cultural organizing:

‹ 201

1. Grant monies are fickle and unreliable; a strong political core leadership must exist to maintain the collective context.
2. Artists must share in the business work and expect their returns to be contingent upon their shared input.
3. The collective must be a guerrilla enterprise and rely upon its own earnings.

My production company isn't a collective, but my own private company in which the profits and losses are solely borne by myself. Therefore all final decisions are mine. I believe in this era, without strong political leadership from movement organizations or a revolutionary party, we can enter into mutually beneficial alliances that are primarily or strictly for business interests. Simply sharing the same political ideas and values doesn't make for a good or viable business alliance. Indeed, the primary consideration, if we are to function with gain, and not from altruism, must be serious business principles. We should and must continue to work with community-based and movement organizations, however, but not hold professional expectations. Indeed, I still believe in building movement benefit concerts and cultural events, but no one should expect to be paid, though these events should sell artist merchandise, which can be very successful.

Since the 1990s, a new wave of younger APA "spoken word" and hip-hop–identified artists have organized their own performance opportunities, self-produced recordings, self-published chapbooks, and organized APA student tours and even national conferences. Like the earlier Asian American music scenes, these younger artists continue to struggle with questions about Asian American aesthetics and cultural production, including: What makes for a unique and distinctive Asian American artistic expression? How do we make professional careers being APA artists doing APA art when no infrastructure exists within our communities to support this? What are our standards? How does our art-making and work relate to the broader APA communities, including campuses, immigrants, and to APA activism? Who is our audience? What kind of institutions/businesses do we need to build?

While many of these APA hip-hop/spoken word artists recognize the major influence and inspiration of blacks and Latinos in the development of hip-hop culture, there is much variegated opinion about whether APA interpretations and expressions range from the imitative to the innovative.

By the 1990s, interest in "Asian American music" and "Asian American jazz" had begun to grow among a few cultural studies and Asian American studies professors, including a survey course taught on this topic at the University of California–Berkeley by pianist Jon Jang. A few articles by Susan Asai, Su Zheng, Weihua Zhang, Yoshitaka Terada, Joseph Lam, and others have begun to appear in ethnomusicology journals.[18] A few conferences have included topics on Asian Americans in music. The Asian American Jazz Festival in the Bay Area continues annually and a short-lived East Coast festival was organized in the mid-1980s by the Jazz Center of New York (led by Cobi Narita) with curatorial support from artists including myself, Jason Kao Hwang, Akira Tana, and others. Other small community festivals of Asian American creative music have occurred in Boston and Chicago. Ethnomusicology conferences have occasionally hosted performers as well. Taiko, kulintang, and more traditional "ethnic" concerts occur more frequently as part of folkloric celebrations and ethnic heritage festivals.

Phony Afro-Asianisms and the Way Forward

During the mid-1990s, the Asia Society of New York City sponsored two consecutive annual Asian American jazz festivals, both of which occurred virtually unnoticed and had low audience attendance. The Asia Society also tried to host an event of African American and Asian American artists that was also a dismal failure, and for which this artist took an adversarial position by demanding my usual performance fee, which the Asia Society declined to meet, thus precluding my involvement. They had asked my collaborator Kalamu ya Salaam in the Afro-Asian Arts Dialogue to come, to which he agreed, trying to leverage me to appear with him at a very reduced fee. I later spoke to another invited participant, poet Sonia Sanchez, who confirmed that the event was a sham, since she never received her honorarium. For almost a half century, since its founding, the Asia Society has ignored Asian Pacific Americans, as well as controversial topics on Asia and the Pacific Rim, such as the Vietnam War, socialist China and Korea, the revolutionary and national democratic struggles in the Philippines, Nepal, Burma, and so on. Rather, their focus has been on teaching exotic Eastern culture to, as someone described it, "the wives of upper East Side businessmen who have business dealings and clients in the East."[19] The topic of APAs would inevitably broach such controversial topics as racism, discrimination, and inequality. The New York Asian Movement since its inception in the late 1960s and early 1970s always regarded the uptown, arrogant, and elitist Asia Society as a legacy of U.S. colonialism in Asia, part of the problem of exoticizing and otherizing the "East." The organization hired white executives until the 1990s, when the first Asian directors were finally hired. One of the biggest insults and travesties of their Asian American Jazz Festival was failing to invite me, a leading Asian American "jazz" artist who has had an impact on both coasts and who lives in New York City! When repeatedly asked by some press writers and curious individuals familiar with my work as to why I wasn't invited, the Asia Society has never given a public explanation.

Another new, emerging topic is African American and Asian American relations. A couple of conferences, one at Columbia University in 2000 and another at Boston University in 2001, have occurred, both organized by African Americans at these institutions. Smaller forums and panels have also been organized in different cities, mostly by academics. Most of these events have only minimally included the arts or artists. All have ignored the long-standing work that I have done in this field. The fascination with the topic of "black-Asian conflict," sensationalized by the mainstream media during confrontations between Asian (usually Korean) merchants in predominantly African American communities, wrongly presumes that there is a special "conflict" of importance other than a "black-white conflict," or a "black-Latino conflict." With the waning of Third World consciousness and unity from the late 1960s and early 1970s, which I described earlier in this essay, it is not surprising that division and conflict have risen. Certainly examples of Third World unity and collaboration have never received media attention, except for the crassly commercialized neo-minstrelsy of the Jackie Chan–Chris Tucker *Rush Hour* movies of today. The *Rush Hour* movies don't have even a fraction of the politics of, say, the 1973 blockbuster *Enter the Dragon* with the late famed Chinese martial artist Bruce Lee and black American Jim Kelly (playing a black militant character on the run from the police), who remarks about the poverty and oppression he sees in Asia: "Ghettos are the same around the world. They stink." The martial arts have been a site of much black–Asian–Latino–poor white inner-city interaction and intersection between popular culture (movies and kung-fu Saturday afternoon movies on local television stations) and individual and collective uplifting (as training for self-discipline, personal and community security, building self-esteem and confidence) among the most highly at-risk youth populations.

While scholarly investigation, analysis, and study of the systemic roots of Third World division are important to an anti-imperialist consciousness, many of these academic conferences and forums are mired in self-referential language and topics and don't attract or reach out to community participants. It would be better if we had Third World film and cultural festivals, activist workshops, and community forums. But the key to building Third World unity has been coalitions and alliances forged in common struggles, both on local issues and for international solidarity.

The building of our respective movements requires ideological development through the course of building grassroots struggles and organizations. A radical, anti-imperialist and revolutionary thrust to our organizing and propaganda must be central. The anthology *Legacy to Liberation: Politics and Culture of Revolutionary Asian Pacific America* (AK Press) has attempted to summarize, analyze, and share the lessons of the revolutionary and radical formations and struggles of the late 1960s and early 1970s and connect this legacy to today's organizing for the Asian Pacific American Movement. Such projects need to be developed for the Black Liberation Movement, the Chicano Movement, the Puerto Rican Movement, the Native Movement, and others. At the same time, collaborative anthologies, be they artistic-cultural and/or political, across oppressed nationality movements, need to be developed as well. To get beyond the multikulti "racial" unity reformism that proceeds from the premise that unity is mostly attitudinal, we must reaffirm the importance of the oppressed nationality struggles in the United States as "national questions" based upon the struggle to control land, resources, and economic and political power with a common enemy: the system of U.S. imperialism. Afro-Asian unity isn't simply learning to appreciate one another's cultures and experiences, but a historical outgrowth of the need for alternative political paradigms that are independent from U.S. white-settler colonial integration and Western European hegemony. Oppressed nationalities can share the lessons of their common struggles and build solidarity, inspire one another, and construct a new paradigm that doesn't subscribe to the racialized welfare line and participate in the divide-and-conquer competition over crumbs constructed by the white power structure and its token compradors. Once we've "de-Europeanized" our orientation—looking to the Third World (both domestically in the United States and internationally) as our main allies and grounding ourselves in an internationalist, global, world "anti-imperialist" orientation—we can begin the task of true decolonialization and disentanglement from the tentacles of imperialist cultural and economic domination and begin the forward march to liberation and world unity.

NOTES

1   Malcolm X, *Malcolm X Speaks: Selected Speeches and Statements* (New York: Pathfinder Press, 1965), 211.

2   Frank Kofsky, *Black Nationalism and the Revolution in Music* (New York: Pathfinder Press, 1970), 64 (Archie Shepp quoted from *Downbeat* magazine, 1966, 20).

3   Revolutionary Action Movement (RAM), "The Relationship of Revolutionary Afro-American Movement to the Bandung Revolution," *Black Power* (Summer–Fall 1965), from the Robert F. Williams Collection, Box 2, Bentley Historical Library, University of Michigan, Ann Arbor.

4   I met and conversed with Robert F. Williams while he was on a speaking tour sponsored by the U.S.-China People's Friendship Association when he visited the then-Chinatown People's Progressive Association during the winter of 1977 or 1978 in Boston.

5   Bill McAdoo, *Pre-Civil War Black Nationalism* (New York: D. Walker Press, 1983).

6   For a comprehensive history of the Congress of African Peoples (CAP), see the very hard to find *Forward* no. 3, the journal of the then–League of Revolutionary Struggle (Marxist-Leninist), Getting Together Publications (now defunct), published in 1979.

7   A number of Asian American literary critics/scholars/academics have used the descriptor "cultural nationalist" when applied to Asian American writers such as The Four Horsemen of Asian American Literature (viz., Frank Chin, Lawson Inada, Shawn Wong and Jeffrey Paul Chan), including leftist-feminist critic-scholar Cheryl Higashida in her essay, "Not Just a 'Special Issue': Gender, Sexuality, and Post-1965 Afro-Asian Coalition Building in the *Yardbird Reader* and *This Bridge Called My Back*," in *Afro Asia: Revolutionary Political and Cultural Connections between African Americans and Asian Americans,* edited by Fred Ho and Bill V. Mullen (Durham, N.C.: Duke University Press, 2008). In my role as editor for this anthology, I gave Cheryl the following critique of her (and others') usage of "cultural nationalism" when applied to Asian/Pacific American writers and artists in my March 27, 2004 email to her: "be careful with characterizations as 'cultural nationalist' as Chin,

et al., never adopted this description, nor did the Asian Movement of that day do that either (whereas the Panthers did characterize Baraka and Karenga as 'cultural nationalists'). The similarities between the black cultural nationalists and the Asian ascribed ones needs elaboration as the Asians rejected any romanticism of their ancestral Asian heritage. Therefore, I think you need to do an analysis of what from the Black Arts Movement was taken and what was originated by the Asians."

8   Circa early 1970s, in personal files of Fred Ho. Poet Lawson Inada inscribed "Written to commemorate the first New Asian Nation Poetry Reading." The full text of the poem follows:

> Course you know how it was.
> But I couldn't think of anything more fitting to
>   Commemorate this occasion.
> So I thought I'd just run it down to you.
>
> That was way, WAY back,
> You know those famous dates,
> But those first ships knew exactly what was happenin'
> The heaviest minds in all of Asia had seen to that
> But they didn't quite plan on meetin' up again with
>   Their long lost brothers,
> Those who had cut out when things were bad
>
> Now, those brothers have their own culture going
>   And a beautiful way of being and seeing
> Not too different from our own,
> Naturally, we got together, grooved on things together
> And naturally, left the land and animals as they were
> We knew better,
> Remembering how some of the "old folks" tried to
>   Mess our homeland up
> We knew better
>
> But also, knew about the ghosts across the oceans
> So decided to set up defensive measures in small
>   Parts of our lands just to keep the ghosts
>   Off our backs
>
> Then things REALLY got nice
> That was the start of this New Nation as we know it
> People—yellow, brown, black and red—going back and forth,
>   Or settling, exchanging wisdom and gifts,
> We joined our lands together
> We had so much to share with each other

So when the ghosts came crawling with their crosses to our shore
We sent 'em south
Burdened down with their monstrosities of war
Figurin' to let 'em take out their primitive aggressions in the jungles

You know their funny books
About how some Washington drowned in the Amazon crossing there
    With a cannon on a canoe
While how some dude named Boone got chewed up by piranhas
While wrestling a python.
Those ghosts were CRAZY!
SHIT!
They tried to carve their faces on a mountain and then they fell flat
On their collective ass

And about that time we got hip that some of our best brothers were
Settled there anyway, really doing beautiful in the jungle
So we got together and tossed the ghosts back to their land we call
    OKLAHOMA
You KNOW what that means in our language

So if you still see some of those ghosts around,
TAKE PITY
HELP 'EM OUT
It's our duty
They knew they were foolish and called us in to give them color and
    Culture,
So they too could flourish
TAKE PITY
Couple of more generations and they'll be colored, and together,
    And beautiful like the rest of us
And you KNOW that's how it's supposed to be!

    —Lawson Inada

9   I was known as Fred Houn until the fall of 1988 when I legally changed it to Ho, phoneticizing a problematic spelling of Houn, which was always pronounced Ho.

10 For more discussion of the etymology of the word "jazz," cf. Lewis Porter, "Where Did the Word 'Jazz' Come From?," in *Jazz: A Century of Change* (New York: Schirmer Books, 1997), 1–12; and Alan P. Merriam and Fradley H. Garner, "Jazz—the Word," in *The Jazz Cadence of American Culture,* edited by Robert G. O'Meally (New York: Columbia University Press, 1998), 7–31. I still maintain that Archie Shepp's explanation is the most plausible and convincing.

11 Cf. John O. Calmore, "Critical Race Theory, Archie Shepp, and Fire Music: Securing an Authentic Intellectual Life in a Multicultural World," *Southern California Law Review* 65 (1992): 2129.

12 Amiri Baraka's draconically polemical and categorical judgments are well known. My beginning reading of his either-or and binary categorizations of "gut bucket" vs. "tail Europe" (in evaluating musicians and their music) as well as "in the tradition" vs. "comprador" or "confused" (meaning NOT "in the tradition") are from articles such as "Afro-American Literature and Class Struggle," *Black American Literature Forum* 14 (1980): 5–14; and "Afro-American Music and Class Struggle," *Black Nation* magazine, a publication of the League of Revolutionary Struggle Marxist-Leninist, ca. 1986.

13 Re Baraka's sloppiness, this criticism encompasses both his literary professionalism and his often outlandish and near-if-not-outright paranoiac profferings. The accusations of irresponsible hyperbole contained in his controversial poem "Somebody Blew Up America" were supported by his own admission that he simply obtained his information from the Internet and failed to do any serious factual investigation. In "Why I Believe Betty Shabazz and Diana Spencer [the late Princess Diana] Were Assassinated," *Unity & Struggle,* (October/November 1997): 4–5, 14, his commentary about a possible conspiratorial link between the deaths of Betty Shabazz (killed by her grandson) and the automobile collision that killed Princess Diana disturbingly reads much more as a rant and tabloid conjecture than any serious investigative journalism or political argument. Lastly, anyone who peruses his political journal *Unity & Struggle* since its republication in May 1999 will find a mess of run-on sentences, sloppy grammar, and misspellings.

‹ 209

14 The debate between advocates of Black Nationalism and Marxism ran during the early to mid-1970s with the September 1974 issue being the classic *Black Scholar* issue for this historic and important ideological struggle.

15 Kalamu ya Salaam unequivocally renounces Black Nationalism in the essay "Why Do We Lie about Telling the Truth?" in Ho and Mullen, eds., *Afro Asia.*

16 A double issue of the *African American Review*, 29, no. 2 (1995), was edited by ya Salaam on the theme of "The Music."

17 While not named per se, Wynton Marsalis is clearly implicated in Fred Ho's essay "What Makes 'Jazz' the Revolutionary Music of the Twentieth Century, and Will It Be Revolutionary for the Twenty-first Century?," in this volume.

18 Two recent, if not the first, books devoted entirely to the music by and music-making of Asian Pacific Americans are Deborah Wong's *Speak It*

Louder: Asian Americans Making Music (New York: Routledge, 2004) and Su Zheng's *Claiming Diaspora: Music, Transnationalism, and Cultural Politics in Asian/Chinese America* (London: Oxford University Press, 2005).

19 The description of the Asia Society is paraphrased from conversations with Bill J. Gee and Peter Chow, former directors of Asian CineVision and *Bridge* magazine (an important, though now defunct, national Asian American periodical). Both projects operated as Asian American grassroots media organizations based in New York's Chinatown.

Asian American Music and Empowerment: Is There Such a Thing as "Asian American Jazz"?

UNTIL RECENTLY, THE MUSIC of Asian Americans has been two virtually divergent streams: a primarily traditional, immigrant musical
culture on the one hand and, on the other, a primarily Western music
played by musicians who happen to be Asian American.

The musicians involved with either stream have had little or no
contact with each other and often a divisive attitude has existed between the two—similar in many ways to the division within the Asian
American communities between the American-born and the immigrant (the *jook sing* vs. *jook kok* syndrome).

The immigrant musical culture is a rich one for the early Asian
American communities, consisting of Cantonese opera, folk songs,
and ballads (e.g., the *seisapluk jigo*, or the forty-six-syllable Cantonese folk song form), and the wood-fish chants of the Chinese
immigrant laborers; the Japanese in America have the *hole hole
bushis*—traditional *bushis* or Japanese peasant work songs imbued
with a distinctly Japanese American workers' sensibility in lyrics
that express their struggle and predicament in the United States;
the Filipino have *rondallas*—serenades heavily influenced by Spanish colonialism, popular folk ballad forms that the *manongs* (the first
wave of Filipino bachelor male workers in the United States) sang
and played in migrant labor camps to the accompaniment of a banjo

Presented as a speech at the Seventeenth Annual Black Musicians Conference and Festival, University of Massachusetts–Amherst, 1989.

or guitar. And, for more recent Asian/Pacific immigrant communities such as the Koreans, Vietnamese, Southeast Asians, East Indians, and others, the traditional music and songs predominate. For the native Hawaiian peoples, the ancient *meles* (poetic song/chants accompanied by rhythm instruments and the *hula* dances) are barely surviving, just as the native peoples are struggling tooth and nail to preserve their way of life and land.

Emerging research and scholarship by Him Mark Lai, Marlon Hom, Franklin Odo, Ron Riddle, and myself historically affirm an actively thriving music scene in the Chinatowns, Japantowns, and Asian labor camps and settlements of both professional and amateur musicians. Invariably, the music and songs were traditional forms carried over virtually without change from their Asian homelands; however, some influences and transformations did occur as a result of the American experience. In the textual content of the Cantonese opera, the *hole hole bushis*, the chants and other songs, the lyrics came to speak of the hardships, struggle, and contradictions of an experience as oppressed nationalities in America. (Indeed, a more significant transformation and emergence of a distinct cultural tradition can be found in the literature of Asians in America, but the musical forms, by and large, remain traditional.)

Beginning in the 1930s, Asian American musicians were also involved in very Western, often commercial music; Chinese American performers were active in the Chinatown nightclub scenes in both New York and San Francisco; Japanese American big bands were quite popular and continued so, even during their incarceration during World War II in concentration camps; and Filipino musicians formed dance bands and combos, as taxi-dance halls flourished both in urban and rural areas of Filipino concentration. A sprinkling of Asian American musicians could be found working professionally outside of their own communities and circuits. Tak Shindo, Jack Shirai, the Manzanar Jive Bombers, Rudy Tenio, Flip Nunez, impresario Harry Lim, and vocalist Pat Suzuki are just some of the Asian Americans professionally involved in swing, bebop, and big band groups.

But, in all cases, these Asian American players and groups were imitations of the commercially popular jazz and dance bands, making no distinctive or unique artistic contribution. In some cases, as with Asian female performers or singers, in order to have a career, they had to comply with some of the most insulting stereotypic show business practices, dressed up in cheongsams or kimonos, doing Flower Drum Song types of acts.

Interestingly enough, some of the more artistic uses of Asian influences in Western music were made in the 1950s by European classical composers such as Chou Wen Chung, who experimented with Chinese folk musical influences in post-impressionist-composed music. Later, white composers, such as Philip Glass and Steve Reich, would incorporate Asian instruments and influences in the minimalist European white musical avant-garde, though again they are simply expropriators using gamelan and other "Far East" orientalisms to exoticize their music.

Both streams—the immigrant traditional music and the imitative Western music—continue simultaneously today with practically no overlap of significance.

But, in the late 1960s and early 1970s, the emergence of the Asian American Movement, influenced by the Black Power Movement and its accompanying Black Arts Movement, manifested a new consciousness and activism. During this period, Asian American art and culture exploded. The concept or term "Asian American" came to express a higher level of consciousness and unity; that Japanese, Chinese, Filipino, and other Asian Pacific nationalities in America face a common, collective experience as peoples of color: an Asian American experience. But most of the musicians, singers, and groups that now refer to their music as "Asian American music" were mostly Western in form and source. The New York City-based group A Grain of Sand, the first Asian American group to record, was part of the folk music trend of the sixties. Heavily influenced by the antiwar movement and its major performers, such as Joan Baez, Bob Dylan, Pete Seeger, and Joni Mitchell, other Asian American singers and music groups, such as Yokohama, California (from San Jose, California), Patricia Shih, Phil Gotanda, Terri Watada, Siu Wai Anderson, and others, followed this style.

Subsequent bands and musicians followed other popular American forms of music: rock and roll, soul, and "fusion." The latter—what most "Asian American jazz" has become, labeled with such examples as Dan Kuramoto and Hiroshima, Deems Tsutakawa, Visions, Mothra—are primarily Japanese American and from the West

Coast. In my opinion, the most musically sophisticated and politically progressive endeavor was Benny Yee's Warriors of the Rainbow band, again based in Los Angeles, with some musicians in the Bay Area. Benny is a forerunner to many of us: composer, arranger, band leader, singer/pianist, and lyricist. I remember meeting him and his co-leader/singer, Nobuko Miyamoto, in Los Angeles in 1980, and playing with them as a benefit program for *Unity* newspaper that summer. Benny impressed me as the number-one Asian American piano man.

In the 1980s, we find a large number of Asian Americans and Asian nationals in the United States playing professional music. They range from Yo Yo Ma in European concert music to Lucia Hwang to Toshiko Akiyoshi and Makoto Ozone. Yet only a handful of artists are endeavoring to create a new Asian American music, often called Asian American jazz. Artists such as Jon Jang and Mark Izu and the San Jose Taiko Ensemble possess a conscious understanding of Asian American music as a continuum that combines traditional and folk forms and the influences of contemporary American forms to create a definitively unique Asian American musical expression. These artists are distinctive in their contributions both to a new Asian American musical form and to extending the scope and conception of American "jazz."

Why have these Asian and Asian American musicians taken to this originally and essentially African American art music? "Jazz" has always been expansive and inclusionary, incorporating other cultures as a truly internationalist art form, to which its international greatness is an attestation. Notes Amiri Baraka, "Jazz has been perhaps the most impressive thrust of a multinational American culture. . . . The best-kept secret in the U.S. is that American culture is not white."

Original ideas and expression, experimentation with different instruments and their combinations, multimedia—all are part of the creative vitality inherent in the music. For the music is fundamentally about freedom: freedom of expression (the individual and collective *simultaneously* and *dialectically*) in its insistence on the expansion of real democracy, historically embodied in the struggle of the African American people, the music's primary originators and innovators.

The important and significant contributions by Asian American musicians to this American classical music will pay high respect to the dynamic traditions and aesthetic foundations of the music: improvisation impelled by an irrepressible striving for freedom. The music and the people want to be free. The maxim says it all: "It don't mean a thing if it ain't got that swing."

The least important and meaningful Asian American effort is the chop suey "fusion" music—those Oriental ornamental dilutions prevalent in trite East-meets-West endeavors akin to grade B movies and television shows about white ninjas and half-white kung-fu wandering cowboys, or about the exotic East, or the slick high-tech/New Age deceptions; stereotyped music with stereotypes generally abounding; cute koto fills, ceremonious Chinese gongs, and parallel fifths thrown in for spice, like MSG.

Striving for the highest artistic excellence and fresh creative expression, and understanding the historical passions that have animated this music, Asian American musicians will make important contributions to America's art music, "jazz." At the same time, these artists will bring new developments to the heritage of Asian American music that began more than 140 years ago with Cantonese opera brought by the first contract laborers to the United States. This is the striking dialectic: the deeper and more honest the Asian American inspiration, the more American will be its significance.

But new Asian American music or art faces obstacles to support, growth, recognition, and development; that is, Asian Pacific Americans are subject to the condition of economic and political powerlessness as oppressed peoples in the U.S. social structure. The fact that the music or art can be consciousness-provoking, inspiring, and visionary is important, but it will be continually limited, threatened, and circumscribed without Asian Americans possessing the economic and political control of their own communities and institutions.

Asian Americans don't control major cultural institutions, or own recording companies, concert halls, publishing houses, media production companies or networks, film studios, or theaters. There are only a handful of nonprofit festivals, small theaters (many don't even own their own space), independent film companies, galleries, and performance spaces, and a majority of these nonprofit Asian American cultural organizations are primarily service and education/training-oriented.

The bottom-line question is: Is Asian American art and culture profitable? Does it have a market? It can be argued that millions have been made from exploiting aspects of black culture (music being the chief example), which justifies the demand and struggle that blacks should control the returns from their own creations. However, besides cuisine, Asian American culture and art has not yielded profit-making products. But the Asian American market is growing. By the twenty-first century, Asian Americans will number over 10 million, or 4 percent of the U.S. population, though in certain regions of the mainland United States, such as parts of the West Coast, our numbers will be much greater.

The movement for Asian American political and economic power is part of building and developing our own cultural institutions—that is, expanding consciousness and organization on the part of the masses of Asian Americans. To build our own major cultural institutions requires trained professional administrators, technicians, fundraisers, producers, and so on. While a few such people do exist and work scattered in the ranks of commercial and established art institutions, our own Asian American cultural organizations are weak and underdeveloped and therefore unable to pay comparable salaries to have these skills working for the benefit of the Asian American communities. The same situation exists for artists: they'll go where the money flows.

In the "jazz" business, Asian American music and musicians aren't taken seriously. While some musicians from Japan have gotten recognition and support, the American-born Japanese or Chinese or Filipino continues to face the racism, discrimination, exclusion, and neglect that is our experience in America. Even though "jazz" has a diminishing percentage of the total U.S. recording sales, and it is said to be not economically viable, it is still an industry with a network of festivals that pay professional wages, university programs, clubs, recording companies, and magazines, albeit quite small relative to the other commercial forms of music, and to the private and public support for bourgeois European classical music.

So the situation for the Asian American musician is that, while it's hard enough being simply "a jazz musician," you still might possibly make a living. But it is impossible to make a living playing Asian American music or jazz.

Our struggle must be organized into a dual strategy, conducted simultaneously. We must be unrelenting in the struggle to expand democracy overall, to assert multiculturalism in policies and for support at all levels in all American cultural institutions: local, state, and national arts agencies, foundations, universities, and the commercial recording, arts, and entertainment industries.

At the same time, we need to build our own alternative, independent institutions that don't rely on outside funding, but instead develop a funding and organizational strategy of self-reliance. Beyond creating music is a struggle to change society, to empower our communities and ourselves; to educate both Asian American and general American consumers; and to train our artists in the administration of our own business and organizational affairs.

Interview with Amy Ling

AMY LING: *What are the origins/genesis of your work?*

FRED HO: My music is a synthesis of African American musical influences with Asian folk musical elements, first explored when I was an activist in Boston's Chinatown in the late 1970s–early 1980s. I wanted to pursue artistic/aesthetic forms that were *not* Eurocentric.

As a teenager, the Black Revolution of the late 1960s, early 1970s inspired my own awakening in terms of cultural identity and political and cultural consciousness. I immediately plunged into the most radical politics and music/literature of the day: Malcolm X, the Black Panthers, Archie Shepp, Amiri Baraka and the Black Arts Movement, Sonia Sanchez, and so on. Writing and playing music, writing poetry became an outlet for the explosion of ideas and emotions I was going through as an Asian American, realizing that my pain and troubles with white racism were not my fault (the blaming-myself-as-the-victim syndrome) but the result of a racist society that profited from slavery, contract labor, a divided working class—a whole system of inequality and injustice. The Black Liberation struggle gave a framework and reference to understanding my own oppression and struggles. Later, as I got involved in Asian American activism, I began a

Conducted via questionnaire with a written reply from Fred Ho, circa 1994. Published in *Yellow Light: The Flowering of Asian American Arts,* edited by Amy Ling (Philadelphia: Temple University Press, 1999).

process of learning about the histories and cultures of the Asian/Pacific peoples in the United States. As one of the founding organizers of the Asian American Resource Workshop in Boston's Chinatown, I learned the folk songs and music of the immigrant workers. This is how I began to forge both African American and Asian musics. My music is simply a reflection of my own development, as well as a larger socio-cultural-political vision of dismantling Eurocentrism and white supremacy and implementing a new, genuine, revolutionary Afro-Asian multicultural musical expression. It is neither American nor Asian, but quintessentially Asian American.

For whom do you create?

I create for all open-minded, justice-loving people. My validation and legitimation is oriented not toward the (white) mainstream, but among oppressed nationalities (primarily African and Asian Americans).

‹ 219

My work is revolutionary, therefore "experimental" and not mainstream, conventional, or easily digestible because it is immediately familiar. I don't expect everyone to understand or embrace it. If that were the case, then it wouldn't be provocative and challenging the status quo—the existing state of things, ideas, and sounds. Therefore, mass acceptance is not my goal. I, however, seek to inspire oppressed peoples, particular Asian American and African American people who want to struggle against our common oppression. Those who don't want to struggle, or who may not yet have come to that position, will have a difficult time with my stand and views, but they might respect and/or appreciate my artistic craft. If they continue to connect with the music, they may begin to change and realize that my politics can't be divorced from my musical ability, because both will continue to be very, very strong!

Which artists do you most admire and why?

I do not subscribe to "admiration." My sources of individual artistic inspiration include, but are not limited to, John Coltrane, Charles Mingus, Archie Shepp, Ngũgĩ wa Thiong'o, and Aretha Franklin, among others. I am moved by profound cultural rootedness (ground-

ing) and soulful expression and originality as well as attendant social consciousness.

Conversely, I do not admire or have much tolerance for insincere
opportunists trying to cash in on fads, who exploit and steal the
cultural resources of others, aiming for mainstream success, lusting after white critical anointment, who lack serious talent and
creativity. I am most impressed by sincerity and depth (which are
not measured necessarily by technique, production values, that is,
quantitative measurements, but rather by qualitative efforts and results—the soulfulness and emotional and intellectual profundity of
a good story, a down-to-earth fullness about life, ideas and human
experiences).

*Do you see yourself in a tradition of Americans, Asian Americans, or peo-
ple of color? Are these distinctions meaningful or even separable?*

My traditions are African and Asian American in artistic forms. My
philosophy is internationalist and revolutionary socialist.

What is "a tradition of Americans" if it isn't multicultural and hybrid? "American" is not mostly white or European except in terms
of power and control of institutions and resources and wealth. I am
in the tradition of rebels, guerrillas, agitators, heathens, that is, all
those rejected, despised, hated, and opposed by the white patriarchal
bourgeoisie.

The cultural distinctions simply illustrate the breadth and diversity of all those who have been oppressed by this system. This diversity is our source of strength and most important weapon of struggle.
Just as in genetics, our survival comes from our ability to recombine
and to transform everything and make it useful to our struggle. Once
the ruling class co-opts one form, the oppressed go on and meta-
morphose something else to hurl against our enemies. For example,
once Asian American studies gets co-opted by the academy (and all
the professors are academy certified and on-leash), rather than de-
lude ourselves that we can change it from the inside, those of us on
the outside will create something new, more creative, more vital and
relevant, while the previous form gets more staid, more academic,
more irrelevant, more inimical, more impotent.

Is there an "authentic" Asian American sensibility? If so, how would you define it?

No singular Asian American sensibility exists because Asian Americans are a plurality of nationalities and national heritages, cultures, and languages.

What makes Asian American art/culture Asian American? Is it simply the ethnicity of the artist? Or, is it the cultural forms and traditions contained either explicitly or implicitly in the works? I reject the notion that anything by an artist who happens to be Asian American makes it Asian American art. "Asian American authenticity" is both the content (explicit) and the form of today's modern Asian American artists, who, while trying to express Asian American themes and experiences, don't know the first thing about Asian cultural traditions and forms as carried to the United States by the immigrants. They merely ape or imitate Western (mostly white/European) forms and traditions. That's because they are mostly middle class and not from working-class and immigrant communities; they learned their craft in college and desire a career in the mainstream. However, there are also a number of Asian American artists who have embraced Asian American cultural forms and traditions, either practicing it close to tradition or seeking to synthesize new forms. Some of these artists are Peggy Choy, Music from China, H. T. Chen, Genny Lim, Mark Izu, Brenda Wong-Aoki, Dan Kwong, the various taiko groups, Frank Chin, Mu Theater, Kulintang Arts, Silkroad Theater, among others.

What are the most pressing burdens/urgencies/responsibilities facing Asian American artists today?

First, creating our own standards of excellence and aesthetic criteria. Asian American scholars and intellectuals can contribute greatly to revealing our rich and varied national cultural forms and traditions, to developing *independent* criteria and standards of cultural excellence that are based upon commitment to community, and to struggle and liberation from Eurocentric and white-supremacist standards and values. Asian American cultural and arts journalism needs to be more than ethnic cheerleading, to critically examine the content and forms of our artistic works and not simply hype on the favorite flavor of the month. As we truly develop independent and unique forms and standards, our work will become more profound and powerful, rather than second-rate imitations, and penetrate into the overall transformation of American culture and society. As long as we are docile, passive, albeit hardworking but kowtowing to the mainstream and status quo, our work will be shallow and superficial and token.

Second, institution building and cultural empowerment to produce and disseminate our work. The "nonprofit" grant hustling has created a sector of cultural pimps, of arts brokers and accommodationists who are literally dependent upon mostly government and (some) corporate "benevolence." This dependency has gutted our cultural movement and weakened our artistic efforts. Even the word "empowerment" has been co-opted by these hustlers (cf. several Bay Area Asian American arts groups) who espouse the rhetoric that funding "is our share of tax dollars." As they get more grants, their work gets weaker and weaker, their politics less militant and critical —especially of the system (except to cry discrimination re: funding dollars). *Real* empowerment is not more elected officials, more funding dollars, or more colored faces in high media places, for some Asian Americans who are ideologically and politically acceptable to the system; rather, it is the strength of our own independent forms of struggle, the alliances forged with other oppressed peoples, and the overall threat to the status quo/system via redistribution of the wealth, a fundamental change in property relations, and a dismantling of the repressive state apparatus. Grants qua grants are not wrong or pernicious, but the ideological and political dependency upon them is simply tokenism and co-optation. Our own independent institutions and forms can be a mixture of grants as well as community support. More and bigger isn't better; indeed, as any administrator will attest, mainstream-style institutional expansion is an albatross of bureaucracy, corruption, and ineptitude. We need more grassroots, militant, bold, and daring organizations, collectives, and enterprises.

Third, uniting activists, artists, and intellectuals toward a movement for our collective liberation from white racist national oppression. Without a movement, we are simply individuals struggling and trying to do our work up against tremendous obstacles and booby-traps. A movement collectivizes points 1 and 2 above and provides the base of support, direction, clarity, and vision for us to succeed both artistically and financially (i.e., more of us rather than a few superstars). This movement can only be built by the most conscious and committed core rather than by a diluted democracy that starts at the lowest common denominator and goes nowhere.

Do you think there are risks and challenges peculiar to Asian American artists? What are they and how do you attempt to resolve them?

The challenge is to avoid the trap of seeking white critical and financial acceptance and dependency. Too often, if the white media certifies one of us as legitimate or "good," our communities finally recognize us. This is simply internalized oppression: we wait until our oppressors say it's okay, then it's okay. We will be trapped in this syndrome until we become more independent and liberated, and develop our own arts and cultural journalism and media grounded upon militant struggle. Otherwise, we'll just be another Asian American so-and-so (insert any white standard of reference).

How do I, individually, resolve this? First, I'll never become a non-profit entity! (I don't believe in nonprofit since the money is based upon the state and the super-profits of imperialism, and nonprofit success is increasingly replicating the for-profit models, e.g., board of directors, slickness, marketing, etc., etc. I guess I'm anti-profit!) I earn my money the honest way: First, I work and sell my creative labor power and I occasionally get aid from sympathizers inside institutions. Second, I don't read or care about what the mainstream arts media says. Third, I accept that I am a revolutionary artist, that my path will be one of tremendous hardship and sacrifice and that I will fight by any means necessary for victory and progress. My goal is clear, my commitment and spirit are strong, my integrity uncompromising.

A common belief is that the dominant society has emasculated the Asian male, commodified the Asian female, and exoticized Asian culture in general. Do you agree? Please explain, and, if you agree, how do you confront this in your work?

As part of our systemic oppression, we cannot define our own identity or control our representation. To confront this oppression, we need not only to oppose stereotyping but also to more actively generate our own cultural production *independently* from white mainstream legitimation and support, whether it be funding (NEA, PBS, Rockefeller, etc.), critics (the *New York Times*, white academia, etc.), or careers.

"Emasculation" vis-à-vis what values of "manhood"? "Manhood" equated as The Big White Man! As part of the destruction of patriarchy, much of social life and meaning has to be de-genderized, especially since gender intersects with power. In a sexist society, there is very little chance of being nonsexist. Both men and womyn have to be antisexist. Violence against womyn will only end when womyn defend themselves. Male monopolization of the means of violence is the primary pillar of womyn's oppression: people don't accept their oppression if that oppression isn't backed up by force.

With more revolutionary Asian American men and womyn who transform both their personal and political lives, we will reject our oppressor's sexual commodification, internalized oppression, and feelings of inferiority.

I am one of the few Asian American male artists who has created such a vast, explicit body of work about the struggles of Asian and Asian American womyn: *Bound Feet,* "What's a Girl to Do?," "(The Earth Is) Rockin' in Revolution/Drowning in the Yellow River" (poems by Janice Mirikitani), "Song of the Slave Girl," "Lan Hua Hua" (an anti-arranged marriage Chinese folk song), the opera *Warrior Sisters: The New Adventures of African and Asian Womyn Warriors,* the suite *Yes Means Yes, No Means No, Whatever She Wears, Wherever She Goes!* (commissioned by the Brooklyn Women's Anti-Rape Exchange and Women's Health Action and Mobilization), and many others. I have collaborated with Genny Lim, Janice Mirikitani, Marina Feleo-Gonzalez, Alleluia Panis, Peggy Choy, Cindy Zuoxin Wang, Sonia Sanchez, Alma Villegas, Esther Iverem, Didi Dubelyew, and many others.

Regarding my brothers, I take the position put forward by Pearl Cleage in *Mad at Miles* (i.e., Miles Davis, the jazz icon): Those who beat us (womyn) cannot be our cultural heroes! In my "jazz" profession, objectification and exploitation of womyn is so rampant; for example, there's a big-name jazz flute player who keeps score of his more than two hundred sexual conquests and here's an Asian American pianist who secretly admires this and confers his respect and friendship toward such men. These men are not my heroes, nor are they my friends, nor my professional colleagues anymore. How many men break off their professional and/or personal relations with men who disrespect and/or abuse womyn? I have, and will do so. More of us must. The whining cries of the "emasculated Asian man" need to be silenced, with even a fist to the mouth if it comes to that. We haven't the energy to waste on such patriarchal rubbish because we should be fighting the patriarchal, white racist capitalist system!

Do you think this is a particularly receptive moment for Asian American artists?

No, only for those who are "safe" and "polite" to the white gatekeepers. The small "gains" (really token) like the *Vanishing Son* movies, Margaret Cho, the writers (tell me, who really makes $40,000 a year off their creative writing?), one or two filmmakers (most are still in "nonprofit"), among others, don't amount to anything significant: we still don't own or control or have decision-making power in any corporate communications companies, entertainment conglomerates, much less anything except for some tepid and "safe" nonprofits. Anti-Asian violence hasn't diminished; on the contrary, it has skyrocketed! Instead of Bruce Lee, we now have the revival of an aging and potbellied David Carradine, a Russell Wong who can't fight, John Lone as a pulp-era Yellow Peril baddy, a whole bunch of Asian actresses who can't act and are always the love object of white men (on screen and in real life), the continual peddling of Asian-as-exotic by Asian Americans, and so on. This is a particularly receptive moment for co-optation of Asian Americans.

What circumstances (historical, political, social, or other) have shaped this moment?

Our status is shaped by institutional racism and our collective and individual struggle against it, not by stupidly naïve notions of ethnic trendiness and marketing, "quality," and crossover appeal.

*How would you characterize the reception of your work? What do you
feel is most lacking? For what are you most grateful?*

Reception by whom? I *hope* the white bourgeoisie doesn't like it. I
hope oppressed and justice-loving people find it provocative, interesting, and possibly inspiring and catalytic.

What is most "lacking" is the disappointing level of Asian American arts journalism and cultural criticism/studies.

Because I don't expect justice and fairness from the system, whatever I've achieved has been a victory. I am able to live off my music,
which even for whites in my profession is rare! I have paid the mortgage on my home. Despite a personal injury I've been able to exceed
my personal best and can now swim 500 meters of the butterfly, do
300 sit-ups, 300 push-ups, 60 chin-ups. I design my own clothes,
cook wonderful meals, enjoy both monogamous and open relationships, and only a handful of baritones in the world can do what I do
technically on the instrument. I have won numerous highly competitive awards and, not the least: I am still a revolutionary socialist. I
am very grateful for the revolutionary movement of the late 1960s
and early 1970s for changing my life forever, giving me a profound
life purpose and challenging me with the questions: Who am I? Am I
who I am? Am I all that I ought to be?

*How do African American influences contribute to an Asian American
musician's work?*

African Americans have been the largest and most significant oppressed nationality group in the United States. I am an Asian American artist who desires to resist Eurocentrism and white supremacy.
In terms of my cultural references and standards, I have looked to
the leading and principal oppressed nationality in this society: the
struggles and culture of African Americans. Despite persisting institutional racism, American music is quintessentially African American. So-called classical music is really Western European concert or
"classical" music. American "classical" music is "jazz," American
"popular" music is blues, rhythm 'n' blues, soul, funk, rap/hip-hop,
and so forth. So the American aspect of being Asian American in the

context of music must connect with all the African American musical traditions and forms.

Furthermore, the themes and ethos of African American music and culture are more readily resonant and relevant to us as oppressed nationalities: themes such as hope, struggle, redemption, celebration of resistance and perseverance, and the triumph of the spirit and soul despite persecution, oppression, and injustice. As a young Asian American, black music spoke to my pain, suffering, and struggle and gave me joy, hope, the spirit of struggle, and the moral fortitude that made me affirm that the oppressors are not our superiors, but, indeed, morally inferior and repugnant.

Too many artists and intellectuals trained by the academy have internalized European values, standards, methodology, aesthetics, and paradigms, including those who claim to be "critics," but tail Foucault, French philosophy, and European art history.

‹ 227

Does it even make sense to identify music by ethnic labels?

Of course, since music is part of a culture, it has a tradition shaped by a sociohistorical context. Cultural imperialism and exploitation by white racist-oppressors seeks to deny, obscure, and hide the actual sources of much of American culture, which, contrary to white-supremacist thinking, is *not* mostly white! Much of what is American culture is a cultural amalgamation of indigenous, European, African, mestizo, and Asian influences. Musical standards and techniques are products of aesthetical values and not *universal*, but culturally specific and grounded. For example, playing "in tune" has meaning if you specify which tuning system, such as the Western European diatonic system versus variable or different or "not-tempered" systems.

How can music contribute to political agendas such as making known little-known histories of the oppressed and the forgotten, or internationalist and revolutionary socialism?

Music, like art, does not exist or stand above society, but is a part of society, part of a culture of a group of people. Music alone cannot make a new society or produce a social revolution. But music has been used and been a part of social movements that when organized have created social change. Music expresses the spirit, emotions, and ideas of change, struggle, of rebellion and discontent with the established social order and cultural status quo. Music evokes a cultural, aesthetical, spiritual, and intellectual challenge from both its forms and its content. Music becomes a material force when it interconnects with movements, activists, and organizers: when it becomes the sound of social unrest and revolutionary vision. Musicians and artists assist and become part of a revolutionary process in several ways: from the works they create, from their own political practice, from how their works are embraced by social movements irrespective of their intention or conscious activity.

Have you any words of advice for individuals of the next generation who might want a career like yours?

I don't give advice, since I'm self-taught and stumbled into a music career. I still don't put much thought or energy into a "career." I just do what I do. For those who can pay, they pay what I should get. For those who can't, but can connect with my political vision (i.e., I don't do charity, so they have to support my politics), I do it for free. Just keep struggling and never be complacent as long as people are oppressed and exploited.

> Fred Ho and a "No More Genocide: Abolish Columbus Day" poster by the Colorado American Indian Movement, summer 1997. Photograph by Linda Jenkins.

∨ Fred Ho and a Cuban poster of Ho Chi Minh by Raul Medeiros, summer 1997. Photograph by Linda Jenkins.

^ Publicity photo for *Warrior Sisters: The New Adventures of African and Asian Womyn Warriors,* December 2000. Clockwise from top: Hai-ting Chinn as Fa Mu Lan, Jacqueline Patricia Howell as Assata Shakur, Alison Easter as Nana Yaa Asantewa, and Miki Yamashita as Sieh King King. Photograph by Rainer Fehringer.

> Fred Ho with his baritone saxophone, Djerassi Resident Artists Program, Woodside, California, 2003. Photograph by Brook Tankle.

^ Fred Ho, summer 2001. Photograph by Peggy Kaplan; used with kind permission.

˅ Publicity headshot photograph of Fred Ho by Rainer Fehringer, 1999–2000.

^ Afro Asian Music Ensemble, 1989. From front to back: Fred Ho, Hafez
 Modirzadeh (tenor saxophone), Sam Furnace (alto saxophone), Carleen
 Robinson (vocals), Jon Jang (piano), Kiyoto Fujiwara (bass), Royal Hartigan
 (drums). Photograph by Ken Shung.

^^ The touring group for the anti-quincentennial performance project "Turn Pain into Power," 1992. From left to right: Allen Won (tenor saxophone), Peter Madsen (keyboard), Esther Iverem (poet), Royal Hartigan (drums), Fred Ho (baritone saxophone/leader), Kiyoto Fujiwara (bass), Alma Villegas (poet), Juan Sanchez (visual artist), and Sam Furnace (alto and soprano saxophones). In the background is mural art by Juan Sanchez.

^ Afro-Asian Arts Dialogue, featuring Kalamu ya Salaam and Fred Ho, 1992. Photograph by Andrew Rawson.

‹ Fred Ho in 1993.
Photograph by Jack
Mitchell, a retired arts
photographer for *The
New York Times*, 1995.
As a board member for
the Atlantic Center for the
Arts, Mitchell undertook
a project to document all
of the "master artists" in
residence there, Fred Ho
among them.

⌄ Fred Ho with a mohawk,
which would eventually
evolve into the triangular
tuft he calls a "vulva
vector," early to mid-1990s.
Publicity photograph by
Jason Jem.

^ First nude publicity photo of Fred Ho, at 11:00 A.M., on a sunny-hot Saturday, around the Brooklyn Naval Yard, summer 1997. Photograph by Jason Jem.

A Voice Is a Voice, but What Is It Saying?

PROFESSOR ELAINE KIM'S *Asian American Literature: An Introduction to the Writings and Their Social Context* is an important pioneering volume of Asian American literary criticism and analysis. Written in a flowing and highly readable style, it is the first and only major study of its kind and offers much detail, including an extensive bibliography and very useful footnotes. There is an abundance of documentation with ample usage of a good selection of quotations and excerpts from many examples of Asian American poetry, short stories, and novels (although theater is not dealt with).

The wealth of detail and documentation in the chapter on stereotypes of Asians further confirms the pervasiveness of white racism in American letters. Kim does a thorough job of cataloging the range of noxious stereotypes, including the heathen hordes who don't value human life, the image of the inscrutable, unfeeling purveyors of an ancient formaldehyde-preserved exotic tradition, as well as the "good" Asians—the obsequious Uncle Tom servant-types and the happy-go-lucky, childish sidekicks (à la Indiana Jones's Short Round).

Yet, Kim avoids analyzing the *function* of racist stereotyping, that is, *why* these stereotypes continually abound. She soft-pedals the vital questions as she states:

....

Unpublished review of Elaine Kim's *Asian American Literature* (Philadelphia: Temple University Press, 1982), written by Fred Ho and Arthur Song in New York City, 1984.

> It is indeed ironic that the stylized depictions of quaint, exotic
> lifestyles or lurid fantasies about Chinese sin and vice created by
> Anglo-American writers about Chinatown were the ones that gained
> relative prominence. (120)

To explain racist stereotyping as a function of white racism—that is, white racist ideas and attitudes—is circular and tautological, explaining nothing. Rather, racist stereotyping functions as an ideological component of the systematic national oppression of Asians in America: to justify and legitimize oppression in every aspect of the lives of the Asian nationalities in America, to keep the oppressed believing that they should continue to be oppressed (for their own good, because they deserve it).

Why certain stereotypes are projected during specific historical periods also needs to be analyzed: for example, the heathen image propagated during the anti-Chinese Yellow Peril movement of the nineteenth century as part of the intensifying attacks upon the Chinese laborers, first to super-exploit them and then to completely lock them out of this society.

Without such an analysis, Kim offers no clarity on how to attack the roots of white racist stereotyping so that even academicians and liberals can agree with the fact of racism against Asians, and even find this objectionable. However, there is a struggle about the question of the sources and the material bases of white racism—is it a tradition of xenophobic ideas and attitudes, or a system of monopoly capitalism and U.S. imperialism? The former position only requires reforms and to change wrong thinking. The latter necessitates revolutionary struggle.

To Kim's credit, she explains the literature in its historical and social context, which correctly affirms Asian American writing as a living, dynamic reflection of the experiences of the various Asian nationalities in America, and furthers its understanding and appreciation as well. Kim has elected to limit her scope to the writings in English by Chinese, Japanese, Filipino, and Korean Americans. By examining the literature in its social context, Kim has, albeit unevenly, addressed some very important issues of language, the oral folk traditions, the writer's attitudes and stance toward the Asian communities, images of women, consciousness, and social background, and, most important, audience—about, to, and for whom does the Asian American writer write? Kim's study is, overall, an impressive overview of English-language Asian American literary work.

But that is also its major limitation. The definition and scope of Asian American literature *cannot* be restricted to just literature written in English. Indeed, a great part of the literature of Asians in America includes writings in the native Asian languages and these emanate from predominantly working-class and immigrant communities. Kim correctly points out that most of the published literature in English by Asian Americans is small in number and the writers themselves most invariably have not been representative of the vast majority of Asian laborers in America. Rather, they have been for the most part highly educated and from privileged backgrounds. Thus they were the ones who wrote in English, for publications by white publishers, to a white audience, for white acceptance.

Kim does give some discussion to the early roots of Asian American literature, such as the talk story oral tradition, as well as the poetry carved in the Angel Island Detention Station in the early 1900s. However, she overlooks the output of community literature written in native Asian languages, especially the Chinatown literary movements of the 1930s and 1940s, which is only now beginning to be studied and researched.[1] Nor is the poetry and writing produced in community newspapers, journals, and writing clubs given much attention.

Unlike the English writings of the privileged Asian Americans, the focus of Kim's examination of early Asian American writing, the content of this great body of community-generated writings in the native Asian languages evokes a wider range of emotions and experiences of struggle, anger, bitterness, sadness, militancy, suffering, compassion, and earthy vibrancy of the Asian working masses in the United States.

To posit that Asian American literature is writings in English is a pivotal conceptual error in the definition of Asian American literature itself. Kim's book does not grasp the critical significance of Asian American literature (and culture and art for that matter) as a *continuum,* based on the early oral and folk forms and community writings—the basis of the Asian American literary tradition. By dealing only with the English-writing, white-published authors, one is left with Kim's mistaken notion that "Asian immigrant workers vanished without leaving behind much written account of their individual lives in America" (23). Furthermore, Kim's explanation for the paucity of early Asian American writing—that oppression "must have dampened the desire to communicate"—is also in error. Such a view smacks of the odious "cultural deprivation" perspective of liberal white racism. On the contrary, oppressed people have continually generated cultural expression as a dynamic extension of our continuous resistance to oppression. Rather, it is the bourgeois definition of literature that must be criticized for its emphasis on published works in English and recognition from the Anglo American literary circles.

Kim proceeds to organize her discussion of Asian American writing into a "generational" framework, beginning with the early twentieth-century accommodationist writers, such as Lin Yutang (*My Country, My People*, 1935) and Etsu Sugimoto (*A Daughter of the Samurai*, 1925), among others. These Western-educated, upper-class writers saw themselves as "ambassadors of goodwill" (Kim's description), their role as interpreters of Asian culture, or glorified tourist guides for whites into the ways of classical Asia. Of course these writers were not part of the Asian ghetto communities and regarded themselves as above the masses. They sought white acceptance mainly for themselves as bearers of elitist classical Asian culture. Kim has characterized this tendency as typifying the "first generation" of Asian American writers.

The "second generation" of Asian American writers, according to Kim, is characterized by the "sacrifices for success" syndrome, that is, advocating white assimilation, passivity, bootstrap-pulling and 200 percent Americanization. Such writers include Pardee Lowe (*Father and Glorious Descendent*, 1950), Chin Yang Lee (*Flower Drum Song*, 1957), Jade Snow Wong (*Fifth Chinese Daughter*, 1945 and 1950, the "most financially successful book by a Chinese American"), Jeanne Wakatsuki Houston (*Farewell to Manzanar*, 1973), and Daniel Okimoto (*American in Disguise*, 1971), among others. These writers sought to make themselves a "credit to their race," striving to be "model minorities." They apologized for their Asian heritage. Their writing contained exoticized or negative portrayals of the community. They also catered to white fascination with exotic orientalia; Jade Snow Wong even included recipes for Chinese dishes in her self-glorifying autobiography. (Just as *After Maꞁh* star Rosalind Chao gave Johnny Carson lessons in eating Chinese food and using chopsticks on national television, and we puked.) These writers epitomized, and their writings reflected, the depth of the self-hatred and self-negation of the small, upwardly mobile, Asian American petite bourgeoisie.

These tendencies are not simply generational-bound characteristics, but rather are cross-generational—class tendencies found among all generations. Just as today we find assimilated petit-bourgeois writers who think of themselves as just "happening to be Asian American," clearly whited-out, as well as elitist cultural nationalists who view the great glory of two thousand years of Chinese culture as the only meaning to being Chinese.

‹ 233

That is why Carlos Bulosan cannot be correctly categorized with the "first generation" of "ambassadors of goodwill." It is a meaningless academic discussion of Bulosan's writings to abstract them as either "personal history" or "social document." His powerfully militant *America Iꞁ in the Heart* (1946 and 1973) is both! It is one of the strongest examples of Asian American social realist literature. Bulosan was conscious of his personal struggle as part of the collective struggle of all immigrants, minorities, and workers to transform America, to end exploitation and oppression. Bulosan embraced a vision of America with equality among all nationalities, a society controlled by and serving the common working person. Bulosan cherished his Filipino heritage and homeland, but realized his destiny was to stay and fight in America. Bulosan's militant, revolutionary working-class stand is entirely different from Lowe, Jade Snow Wong, Sugimoto, and other token sell-outs who never advocated for Asian Americans to struggle for equality, justice, and freedom, but sought to ingratiate themselves individually with the system. Bulosan did not want to win American acceptance for himself, but dedicated his life and writings to winning America for the masses of workers of all nationalities!

Throughout her "explaining" the social context of the varying responses and approaches by Asian American writers to American society, Kim avoids *taking a stand* herself. Her academic neutrality is based on a cop-out concept of Asian American literature that accepts everything by an Asian writer as "a voice among voices" about our experiences, thereby avoiding evaluating the writings according to a continuum of literature based in the Asian communities.

A voice is a voice, but what is it *saying*? Is the political path proposed by the accommodationists and assimilationists viable for the masses of Asian Americans? Does what the author projects about the condition of our lives (i.e., their view of reality) reflect the truth of our shared, collective experiences? What is it to be condemned or condoned? Does the understanding of our reality offer insight and inspiration toward our personal and collective struggle? What is the writer's commitment: to stand with the people or to gain personal favor by white acceptance? These are the critical questions that Asian American literary and cultural criticism must address.

234 ›

The chapter "Portraits of Chinatown" is one of the strongest. Especially important and noteworthy is Kim's highly perceptive treatment of Louis Chu's classic *Eat a Bowl of Tea* (1961). Kim devotes some excellent, much-deserved discussion of Chu's wonderfully realistic and insightful portraits of Chinatown life. Indeed, it must be said that Chu is our only Chinese American literary innovator! Chu's writing captures the very rich feelings and multilayered meanings of everyday Chinatown communication simply, but in all of its complex profundities. No English-writing Chinese American writer has been able to match Chu's literary innovations with Chinese American speech.

"Japanese American Portraits" contains important examinations of two major Asian American writers who only in recent years have been rescued from obscurity and literary oblivion: John Okada (1923–71) and Toshio Mori (1910–80). Okada's *No-No Boy* (1957) reveals the psychological torment produced by the concentration camp experience for Japanese Americans through a poignant and painful story. Kim has done a fine analysis.

Kim's compelling insights also highlight Toshio Mori's fundamental compassion and celebration of the everyday lives of the common people in the Japanese American community. Kim correctly assesses Mori's contributions:

> A sensitive observer of the people and events of his community,
> Mori searches for significance and beauty in the ordinary, for the
> general and universal within the particular . . . (169)

For Mori, as Kim puts forth, the community "emerges as the strongest, sustaining force for its individual members" (172). Mori celebrates the human spirit, though not without its failings, yet always
tenacious and possessed by his beloved Japanese American community folk. Kim has contributed a beautiful and rich portrait of Mori
and his endearing writing.

Another major contribution by Kim is the attention given to the
generally overlooked, lesser-known, earlier generation of Asian
American women writers, especially the many short stories of Hi-
saye Yamamoto. Kim clearly delineates the uniqueness of the wom-
en's experiences as embodied in their writings. But more discussion
than a lengthy footnote should have been given to the Eurasian
woman writer Sui Sin Far/Edith Eaton (1865-1914). Her many stories during the late nineteenth and early twentieth century period
"remained fiercely proud of her Chinese heritage and unwilling to
attempt to 'pass' for white or to let an insult to the Chinese go un-
challenged . . . [and] her refusal to accommodate exoticization of her
Chinese heritage for the sake of white acceptance . . ." (284). Clearly,
Siu Sin Far warrants fuller attention.

‹ 235

Two Chinese American writers who have received greater attention, controversy, and publicity, Frank Chin and Maxine Hong Kingston, are discussed in a separate chapter, "Chinatown Cowboys and
Woman Warriors." The major problem with Kim's Cowboy/Warrior
comparison is the presentation of Chin and Kingston as the Chinese
American male and female literary archetypes, respectively. Neither
is our best model. Furthermore, Kim has dropped her previous academic neutrality for a one-sided, all-critical view of Frank Chin and
a completely uncritical look at Kingston, acting as Kingston's de-
fender.

Kim correctly criticizes Chin for the individualism, male chauvinism, cynicism, and pessimistic view of the Chinatown community,
which consistently mark his works. Yet, contrary to Kim's assessment, Chin's contributions are based less on raising the issue of

Chinese American manhood, than the defiant stance of his earlier period toward white assimilation, imitation, and paternalistic white racist evaluations of Asian American writing. Chin boldly condemned the use of Asian Americans as model minorities. Chin and his partners (Shawn Wong, Lawson Inada, et al.) also worked to republish the core classics of Asian American writing, such as Okada's *No-No Boy* and Chu's *Eat a Bowl of Tea*, among others. Most of Frank Chin's contributions to Asian American art have been more for the calls he has put out than what he has himself actually created artistically.

Though Chin has taken an "angry" posture toward white racist critics, and has been outspoken against racist stereotypes, white racist definitions and standards of art, and white imitation and assimilation by Asian Americans, he fails to offer any real alternative. Chin's writings preclude any positive image of our lives or any vision of the possibility for change. Chin's one-sided, one-dimensional portrayal of Chinatown is one of impotence and decay, cadaverous and suffocating. Any struggle for change is absent. Alienation abounds. For Chin's characters, the solution is to leave Chinatown to pursue an existentialist individuality.

For all of Chin's diatribes against white racism, not one of his characters actually strikes back, except by fantasizing about raping white women. But raping and fucking white women is not revolutionary, though killing them as part of the oppressor class in acts of revolutionary struggle (as did Nat Turner, for example) is. Indeed, Chin is more preoccupied with casting Asian Americans as pathological victims of racism with little effort or capacity to fight back. Chin's errors are rooted in his narrow view of our tradition—ignoring the great swing of our history, our resistance. Chin's rabid male chauvinism is the logical extension of his Chinese American male emasculation perspective: castration has been ultimate, there has been no resistance; Chinese American women contribute to this emasculation. For Chin, the victims are their own victimizers. The Chinatown community offers no support, but suffocates him. As the song goes, for Chin, "home is where the hatred is."

Chin's petit-bourgeois bohemianism (Let-Me-Be-Who-I-Want-to-Be) cannot possess a view toward liberation, the struggle to change oneself through changing the social world. Rather, Chin actually wants to be accepted into the current social configuration, to be the rugged, ballsy male in the image of his white counterparts, fashioning himself as a cowboy. Chin doesn't want to bring down this system for a new one, just to get in on it for himself. He's a typical, aging bohemian: Me-against-the-world, cynical and undesirous of collective change. His own people are regarded as drags and Asian women are never equal partners in struggle and in love.

But, contrary to Kim's evaluation, Kingston, too, offers little inspiration and vision. Kim seems so overly preoccupied with responding to Kingston's anti-female critics that she accepts Kingston uncritically as the finest representative of the Asian American literary voice.

In the late 1970s, Maxine Hong Kingston skyrocketed into the national literary eye with her critically acclaimed, best-selling book, *Woman Warrior*. She scored again a year later with *China Men*. Unlike Chin, Kingston doesn't see herself as a spokesperson for Chinese Americans. Nor does she argue that her stories are representative of that experience. But her prominence and promotion by the white cultural establishment has that effect. It's the familiar case of art used by profiteers to further their own ends. The stories of Asian women have suffered from suppression by the white male ruling powers, as well as from feudal and male chauvinist practices within the Asian communities. So that the appearance of Kingston's stories about and by a Chinese American woman have been greeted by Asian Americans as a welcome contribution. Kingston is strongest when she actually deals with real history and weakest when she fills in with her own interpretations, which is most of the time.

Kingston views the Chinese community as static, backward and stifling to the individual. Indeed, Frank Chin and Maxine Hong Kingston share more in common than they differ, though certainly neither would ever like to think so. For Kingston, women are regarded as burdens; the mother figure is portrayed as the main oppressor holding back the individual-striving daughter. The images of community life and mannerisms tend to be exoticized, as if Kingston was trying to explain and describe them to outsiders, to really make them seem strange and weird.

Both Chin and Kingston identify with two mythic Cantonese figures. For Chin, it is Kwan Kung, the God of War and Literature. For Kingston, it is Fa Mu Lan, the Woman Warrior. This celebration of lone warrior types underscores their basic lack of faith in the masses of Chinese Americans, whom they see as superstitious, primitive, petty, and real drags. The Chinese working-class community people are never looked to as the backbone of the Chinese struggle in America, then, now, and for the future. Chin and Kingston deal in effects (racist suppression of manhood, the limitations of self-growth), but not in *causes*. Both catalog the effects of oppression only at the surface level, describing but not bringing out *why*. Thus neither Chin nor Kingston offers anything that would liberate us, to inspire us to unite and struggle.

Kim's final chapter, "New Directions," takes account of a great deal of the writings from the contemporary Asian Movement from the late 1960s to the late 1970s. This chapter could benefit from greater examination of the alternative, community-based presses and publications generated by the movement, such as *Gidra, Getting Together, Bridge,* and others. Clearly, as we see from the examples that Kim cites, the literature of the Asian Movement has had an anti-imperialist orientation, reflecting the issue of a racist, genocidal, U.S. imperialist war of aggression against Asian peoples and national oppression of Asians in the United States.

In such a chapter, Kim also needs to discuss the important influence and inspiration of the Black Arts Movement of the 1960s, a cultural extension of the revolutionary outburst of the Black Liberation Movement, upon Asian American artists/cultural workers and their fiery art.

It is a disappointment that "New Directions" provides no direction! It is indicative of the whole book that Kim does not take a stand to offer her own views as to the direction for Asian American literature, besides her overly general comment that the literature is challenging stereotypes by presenting Asian voices or perspectives on their own identity.

Overall, *Asian American Literature* is a recommended and welcome contribution as a comprehensive survey of English-writing Asian American literature. There are some excellent discussions about the writings, though the approach is an eclectic mixture of academic sociology and English comparative literature. The book is significant as a first work of broad detail, but lacks a guiding cohesive and cogent theoretical framework. Furthermore, it is a weakness that the author avoids taking a stand on the function and direction of Asian American literature as a continuum of cultural and artistic expression of *oppressed nationality peoples*. With the exception of African writer Chinua Achebe, cited in the bibliography, Kim makes no use of the theoretical essays on the function of Third World literature and art by the major critical and artistic exponents, such as Amilcar Cabral, Mao Zedong, Luxun, Ngũgĩ wa Thiong'o, Amiri Baraka, and Jose Marti, among others. The task of analyzing Asian American literature as a continuum, reflecting the struggles of Asian American peoples, remains.

NOTE

1 See the research by Professor Marlon Hom and Him Mark Lai, especially "Chinatown Literature during the Last Ten Years (1939-1949) by Wenquan," translated by Marlon K. Hom, *Amerasia Journal* 9, no. 1 (1982): 75-100.

Where Is the Asian American Love?

ROMANCE. Falling in love—the joys and ecstasies. Falling out of love—the hurt of broken hearts. Love is an essential feature of the human experience. Daryl Chin, a writer who often does articles for Asian CineVision, decries what he views as Asian American filmmakers and festivals preoccupied with Asian American themes and subjects (i.e., "immigration . . . laundries, piecework at factories, restaurants . . .") to the exclusion of ostensibly broader subjects such as "voyeurism . . . auto-eroticism," to cite examples he raises. I would go beyond Daryl's critique and argue that Asian American filmmakers, along with Asian American artists in all the other disciplines, haven't begun to scratch the surface of Asian American life. Except for Phil Gotanda's "The Wash," a love story between two elderly Japanese Americans, there is a glaring absence of contemporary artistic work on Asian American love, that is, simply, Asian Americans who fall in love with other Asian Americans.

Just check out the contemporary plays, poetry, novels, short stories, music and songs, visual art, photography, and dance by Asian Americans. A highly sexual and political book of poetry, Janice Mirikitani's *Awake in the River,* published in the 1970s, has one singular love poem, but it's for her husband, Cecil Williams, an African American, and it is his blackness that inspires her passionate imag-

Presented as a speech at the Association of Asian American Studies Conference, Honolulu, Hawaii, 1992.

ery. The male Asian American writers who came of age in the Asian American Movement of the late 1960s and early 1970s, such as Frank Chin, Lawson Inada, Garrett Hongo, among others, never approached the subject. One writer/poet, Ronald Tanaka, wrote a poem called "I hate my yellow wife." One quick explanation might be that they were married to or related to whites. As Charlie Parker stated, "If you haven't lived it, it won't come out of your horn."

This same quick explanation might be applied to Maxine Hong Kingston. Though neither Chin (and his posse) nor Kingston might like to admit it, their shared imagery of Chinese American/Chinatown family and community life is cold, suffocating, and cadaverous, as parents and the weight of tradition seem to stifle and oppress the young, individualistic Chinese Americans. In Chin's early works, cadaverous images abound of the dying father as a metaphor for a decaying and dying Chinatown society. Nowhere is there rejuvenating, exhilarating, liberating love with its attendant metaphor of a community that is a source for selfhood and liberation. One also wonders about the strong anti-female tones of Chin and his posse's harangue against Kingston (both her work and her success) and notions of "Asian American emasculation" akin to Ishmael Reed and his posse among African American male writers in decrying the "feminization" of African American literature vis-à-vis the successes of Alice Walker, Ntozake Shange, and Gloria Naylor, among others. It seems that among oppressed peoples of color in a white racist/supremacist society, men and women are not united in political and cultural struggle or in their intimate relations.

The "quick explanation" might also apply to the younger writers. In Cathy Song Davenport's *Picture Bride* or Amy Tan's *The Joy Luck Club,* the Chinese men who married Chinese women die. Ruthann Lum McCunn's story of Chinese heroine Lalu Nathoy in *The Thousand Pieces of Gold* is again an interracial love story (between Chinese and white).

And films, music, and songs and all the other art forms don't have any consummated love stories. But the tradition of Asian American culture offers more expressions of Asian American love than most of us are aware of or would think likely.

From the mid-nineteenth century, when the first wave of young, male Asian laborers came to America, to the mid-1960s, with the liberalization of the immigration quotas, Asian American social history was a period of exclusion and severe oppression. Asian labor was to be used and then discarded. Except for the self-contained plantation system of Hawaii, in the mainland United States, Asians were a bachelor society, without the possibility of raising families. For example, among Chinese on the West Coast, men outnumbered women twenty to one. The majority of these few Chinese women were prostitutes. Many of the Japanese women in America were picture brides—marriages based not on love, but on commerce. (Because of the stronger position of Japan as an emerging industrializing, capitalist power, immigration laws with the United States tended to be less harsh, though eventually Japanese immigration to the United States was halted, too.) The Chinese American population in the mainland United States was declining until the 1960s, unable to procreate, a lonely bachelor society in the Chinatowns; with the immigration flow cut off, it was like genocide.

Antimiscegenation laws also contributed to this genocidal-like condition for Asian Americans. The Filipino manongs, with a reputation as flashy and flamboyant dressers and dancers (and "lady killers"), frequented taxi-dance halls. With virtually no Filipino women, for "a dime a dance," these young Filipino male workers found companionship with white American women working these dancehalls. Filipino American poets and the musical theater work *A Song for Manong* depict this period—desperate loneliness and the illusion of romance as a continuing part of their exploitation (as their entire wages were spent in a night out).

Taxi-dance halls and prostitutes provided ways for these Asian bachelor workers to get their rocks off, but true love was almost an impossibility.

But research into early Asian American cultural forms reveals poignant expressions of love in the context of the pain, suffering, and struggle under oppression.

The most significant but little-known example is the Japanese American immigrant sugarcane worker songs from Hawaii, the *hole hole bushi*. The *hole hole bushi* is one of the first truly Asian American musical forms (a transformation of traditional Japanese folk songs, or *bushi*, but suffused with a Japanese American working-class sensibility both in lyrical content and in musical aesthetic). Even more significant is that the *hole hole bushi* was sung exclusively by women (this aspect is an essential and important example to any feminist analysis of Asian American culture), who had the division of labor of stripping sugar-cane (hence the term *hole hole*—referring to the act of cane stripping). Expressing the lives and emotions of the Japanese American immigrant working women, many of the songs spoke of disappointing arranged marriages and served as double-entendre coded communication between these women and younger men with whom they had extramarital sexual relations.

Asu wa sande jya yo	Tomorrow is Sunday, right?
Asobi ni iode	Come over and visit
Kane ga hanawai	My husband will be out watering cane
Washa uchi ni	And I'll be home alone.[1]

The various Chinatown immigrant ballads and wood-fish chants expressed feelings of longing for lovers left behind in China, the hardship of separation, sexual frustration, and fantasy. Similar expressions of love struggling against oppression are found in the Japanese American tanka poetry during the concentration-camp period.

‹ 243

Han-nen buri	After a long half year
tsuma to akushu shi	I take my wife's hand into mine
sono te o ba	And for at least half a day
arawazu ni ori	I do not wash away her touch.[2]

Contrary to expectations, the early Asian American immigrant cultural expression was sensual, affectionate, passionate, militant, tender, sarcastic; the breadth and range of human emotional expression through the experiences and struggles of Asian American life. During a period of bitter exclusion, antimiscegenation, and frustrated sexual relations, the hope and experience of love endured through the writings, songs, and drama of Asian America. One reason why little is recognized about this experience is that many Asian American studies scholars have a limited concept of Asian American literature and culture that only encompasses works in English and made available by white publishers or impresarios—the narrow notion that Asian American literature's "firsts" are Louis Chu's *Eat a Bowl of Tea,* John Okada's *No-No Boy,* and Carlos Bulosan's *America Is in the Heart.*

The Asian American Movement of the late 1960s and 1970s produced cultural work that was highly charged politically, tended to oppose white racism in its struggle for "identity," but did not emphasize the affirmation of what made for "Asian American life" in its most intimate and essential experiences, for example, being in love. Singer/songwriter "Charlie" Chin, described as a romanticist, did not marry an Asian American woman until he was well past the age of forty. I have yet to hear a love song from him. And you would think that the band Hiroshima, in their drive to be "Top 40," would have at least one pop love song about Asian Americans? Even my own love ballads, such as "Pretty as a Morning Sunrise" and "We'll Make Tomorrow!" on my debut album, while dedicated to Asian American women with whom I've been in love, are not apparently Asian American in their lyrics.

Betty Lee Sung's new study, *Chinese American Intermarriage* (Center for Migration Studies, 1990), suggests a correlation between higher education and incomes (i.e., class) with higher rates of intermarriage (mostly Chinese and white). And much to-do has been made out of the astronomical percentage of Japanese Americans who outmarry to the point of concern about their extinction as a people. I would submit that today's Asian American artists are reflective of these social trends—an educated, film department or English MFA, middle class, career-aspiring group, but increasingly distanced from the concentrated social life of a Chinatown, Little Tokyo, or, for that matter, an affinity with the Asian American Movement and its cultural struggle.

Except for Genny Lim (a Chinese American woman writer with a Japanese American boyfriend), I can't think of one prominent Asian American woman writer, artist, or filmmaker who is with an Asian American husband or lover. While there are some Asian American artistic couples of prominence (Tisa Chang and Ernest Abuda, Phil Gotanda and Diane Takei, Bob Lee and Eleanor Yung, H. T. Chen and Dian Dong, etc.), does their love inform their artistic creation? Has it inspired any work that we could say expresses an Asian American experience or sensibility on the matter of loving? Do Asian Americans experience love ethnically? It can be found in African American cultural expression, a unique sensibility with reference to black love as both an affirmation of group pride and personal choice (the notion that the personal is political): Zora Neal Hurston, Sonia Sanchez, Kalamu ya Salaam, Amiri and Amina Baraka, to name a few writers. But the most incontrovertible expression has been in music and popular song.

Are we culturally/ethnically self-effacing by subscribing to the notion that love is "color blind," "universal," "transcendent"? Or are we victims of white assimilation: that interracial love has been mostly with whites, usually the upscale Asian American with a white lover or spouse. Media racism in the white man's erotic-exotic fascination and possession of Asian women can't be denied. Since when have Asian men been in commercials selling beer, cars, cologne, and all the other trappings of success and the good life in bourgeois society? I have never seen an Asian American man make love to a white woman onstage, in film,[3] in literature, in music, in dance. The racial taboos have indeed permeated our consciousness, symptomatic of our social oppression.

‹ 245

The case has been made that racist stereotypes of Asian men are images of him as sexless, servile, comic-relief, undesirable, the epitome of evil with Fu Manchu lusting after the white virgin, who is always rescued by the white hero. With Charlie Chan, you never get a clue about Mrs. Chan—how did Charlie ever get so many sons? (Even Mrs. Columbo eventually appeared, and even got her own TV series!) Whites adopt children of color—be they refugees from the ghetto (the TV series *Different Strokes*) or from Southeast Asia (the movie *Welcome Home*).[4]

In *Karate Kid II,* Mr. Miyagi is reunited with an old flame from Japan, and Ralph Maccio gets the pretty young Tamlyn Tomita. (As in Gotanda's "The Wash," it's okay for older folks; post-menopausal love poses no threat of reproducing a generation of Asian Americans. But in bourgeois American society, the primacy is placed on the young and virile, the attractive and sexual. And Asian American love is excluded from this.) At the end of *Karate Kid II,* like Batman and Robin, lasting girlfriends aren't meant for the martial arts adventuring duo of Miyagi and the Kid. Alan Parker's new film about a love story between a young (of course, pretty) Japanese American girl interned in a concentration camp during World War II with a white American soldier is just another slap in our collective faces for both its implausibility as fact, but also for its reprehensible contribution to the tradition of racist insult to Asian American men. (Alan Parker, if you recall, was the target of protests and boycotts by African American civil rights organizations for distorting history and making the FBI heroes in the struggle against the KKK in *Mississippi Burning*, when in actual history the FBI worked to undermine Dr. Martin Luther King and many civil rights and Black Liberation groups.)

Obviously, we cannot expect whites to tell our love stories, sing our love songs, to show us in love. While it has been noted that Asian American cultural expressions with new films, books, and music has never been greater in quantity, the diversity and depth of treatment of the fundamental, most essential features of our experiences has been disappointingly narrow and limited. An Asian American love story hasn't been done in contemporary times. Without love, and its inspiration as reflected and offered in art, it is not possible for Asian Americans to sustain a full, spiritual resistance and challenge to the forces of white assimilation and racism.

NOTES

1 Karleen Chinen, "Hole Hole Bushi: Voices of the Canefields, Songs of the Heart," *The Hawaii Herald*, May 4, 1984.

2 Keiho Soga et al., *Poets Behind Barbed Wire* (Honolulu: Bamboo Ridge Press, 1983).

3 The one time was James Shigeta, but the price for an Asian man to love a white woman was his death.

4 Starring Kris Kristofferson and Jo Beth Williams.

Bamboo That Snaps Back! Resistance and Revolution in Asian Pacific American Working-Class and Left-Wing Expressive Culture

ASIAN PACIFIC AMERICANS (APAs) have been metaphorically compared to bamboo, a social metaphor for a U.S. minority group that pliantly bends to adversity. The bamboo metaphor is meant to praise APAs (a so-called positive stereotype) for having the qualities of being quiet and hardworking, putting up with hardship and oppression with stoicism and patience. As an example, among Japanese Americans there is an expression of resignation, of fatalistic acceptance of adversity and suffering, "*shikata ga nai*" (in Japanese, literally, "it can't be helped" or "it must be done"). Japanese Americans are also cited as having "*gamen*" (to put up, or tolerate, in silence). This is alleged to be a cultural trait that is promoted as tolerating and putting up with the hardships and injustices of racism in America, especially the experience of being interned in detention camps during World War II by the U.S. government as a potential enemy alien threat or fifth column even though two-thirds of the Japanese in the United States were American citizens.

Such stereotypes function to dehumanize and depoliticize a people. In the case of the bamboo metaphor, APAs are deemed apolitical, accepting of their oppression, with the effect of promoting accommodationism: of collective passivity, nonresistance, and reliance on

Published in *Left of the Color Line: Race, Radicalism, and Twentieth-Century Literature of the United States*, edited by Bill V. Mullen and James Smethurst (Chapel Hill: University of North Carolina Press, 2003).

hard work as the chief means of social mobility. However, an alternative understanding of the "bamboo" metaphor might ask: If bamboo is bent back too far, it will either break or snap back and hit an opponent in the face. Contrary to "positive" stereotypes as hardworking, silent, passive "model minorities," APAs have "snapped back" in a continuous history of resistance to oppression and struggle for full equality, dignity, and liberation.

APAs have a long history and tradition of struggle, resisting oppression by any and all means, including social rebellion and protest, and building revolutionary movement. The scope of this article presumes a familiarity with APA history, well documented in many sources, especially from the growth of Asian American studies. Less familiar and written about are the forms of APA cultural expression. While APA literature has in recent years received growing attention, this interest by Asian American literary critics and scholars has overwhelmingly emphasized texts written in the English language and not the ancestral languages of the immigrant groups. The performing arts (music, theater, dance, etc.) remain an area of relatively little attention even within Asian American studies, albeit now slowly developing with more critical and scholarly writing, including by artists themselves. Asian American media studies have generally emphasized the litany of stereotyped images of APAs from mainstream works. APA visual arts, while still not widely examined in academia, have received growing attention in exhibitions and catalog essays. The focus of this article is the immigrant working-class forms of APA expressive culture (literature, visual, film, and the performing arts) and the left-wing, radical, and revolutionary expressions by APA writers, visual artists, filmmakers, and performing artists. Space limitations allow for only a general survey of this discussion. It is hoped that this preliminary discussion will spur further historical research and analytical interest.

. . . .

Asian and Pacific Islanders came to the United States primarily as laborers during the first century of APA immigration, beginning in the mid-nineteenth century. They arrived on the West Coast of the mainland United States and on the islands of Hawaii to work in the mines,

agricultural fields, sugar plantations, fisheries, canneries, and growing industries of textiles and manufacturing. The Chinese were the
first, followed by the Japanese, then the Filipino, and by the second
half of the twentieth century, virtually every Asian Pacific group,
making APAs the fastest-growing population of any American group,
doubling in size every decade since the 1960s. The current U.S. census has well over two dozen APA ethnic nationalities, speaking more
than one hundred different languages and dialects.[1]

For over a century and a half, APAs have reclaimed thousands of
acres of land, mined coal, canned salmon, pioneered the fruit and
vegetable industries, cut and stripped sugarcane, sewn shirts, pants,
and overalls, invented the Bing cherry and the navel-less orange,
fished the ocean, completed the western leg of the Transcontinental Railroad, made cigars and shoes, discovered beta endorphins and
superconductors, established dynamic community businesses and
revitalized inner cities, fought discrimination, segregation, racism,
and national oppression, and have advanced the cause of social justice and the struggle for full equality throughout American society.
APAs have not been marginal to American history, but have been
marginalized *by* American history. As oppressed nationalities who
have faced a systematic oppression that includes superexploitation
(lower wages and worse conditions than their European American
counterparts), legalized segregation, myriad restrictions, discrimination, racist violence, scapegoating, stereotyping, lynchings, and
inequality throughout American society, APAs have a long and proud
history of struggle, resistance, and even revolutionary activism to
end oppression, exploitation, racist injustice, and inequality and to
transform U.S. society overall.

‹ 249

This historical struggle has generated an attendant culture of resistance, including an expressive culture with uniquely APA forms
of syllabic verse chants, poetry, literature, songs, Chinese opera, the
talk-story tradition of oral storytelling, and other forms of artistic
expression. During the Great Depression and in the late 1960s and
1970s, influenced by left-wing activism and upsurges, APA revolutionary artists have emerged expressing militant, radical, and revolutionary political perspectives, sometimes with transgressive new
forms.

All immigrant groups bring with them folk and classical traditions from their ancestral cultures. The term "folk" in this essay is used to describe traditional expressions that: (1) usually have no known author; (2) are transmitted largely orally and through repeated community practices; (3) are performed as part of a community, usually by both professionals (i.e., artists who primarily are seeking payment) and nonprofessionals who are usually ordinary common people (who may or may not have formal training, but who don't seek to earn a living as artists). "Classical" refers to: (1) work that requires special training and is considered more refined and sophisticated; (2) is usually performed by professionals; (3) is usually performed for the upper classes and in court settings; (4) is often the "official" culture promoted, supported by and for the consumption of the upper classes. Classical forms are often drawn from folk traditions.

Early Chinese American Immigrant Working-Class Expressive Culture

The first Asian laborers to be recruited and shipped in large numbers to the United States were the Chinese, especially in the 1860s to complete the western leg of the Transcontinental Railroad. After the railroad was completed, the Chinese laborers dispersed to the new western cities such as San Francisco. They formed small "Chinatown" communities, often in the worst sections of cities, forcibly segregated by both legal restrictions and the constant threat of racist violence. Although it is conjectured that while in the rural terrains of the western United States working on the railroad, the Chinese workers practiced storytelling and sang folk songs, there is no documentation of this cultural activity.[2] The Chinese presence was regarded as temporary, workers who would leave once the railroad was completed. Given the harsh conditions of the frontier and racist attitudes toward the Chinese by whites, and their perceived status as temporary workers who were unassimilable and undesirable, no accounts of their lives and experiences were deemed worthy of documentation. Only a few early photographs of Chinese labor in the mid-nineteenth century were taken. The writings by whites about the Chinese exuded racist hostility and opposition.

However, as the Chinese established their own communities, unable to return to China since most workers were not able to save much money, a thriving cultural life took root. The most popular form of entertainment, besides gambling, opium smoking, and prostitution, was the Chinese opera, specifically Cantonese opera, since most of these workers originated from the southern province of Kwantung (Canton). Jack Chen, the late Chinese American historian and cultural impresario, cited that in a typical Chinatown such as San Francisco's, performances of Chinese opera would go on every night. According to Chen, as many as six theaters existed within the half-dozen square blocks of San Francisco Chinatown—a theater on every block. Chen documented the "Pear Garden in the West" (the English transliteration for Chinese opera in America) through a traveling exhibition of Chinese opera posters and old photographs, which reveal a circuit of Chinese opera touring that extended from Vancouver to Central and South America, to Cuba's Chinatown, and to New York City.

The spread of Chinese opera to the many overseas Chinese communities that had begun to emerge and take root throughout the Americas was in large part spurred on by the Taiping Rebellion and social upheaval in China during the mid-nineteenth century. The Taiping Rebellion in China had erupted in the 1840s and would go through a series of upheavals for two decades. Many of the Taiping Rebellion leaders were well-known opera artists. The Manchu Ch'ing government, China's last dynasty and a foreign, invading one, banned all open performances of Chinese opera. Chinese opera was thus forced to be performed overseas, and a sophisticated touring circuit was established. Various Chinese opera troupes would tour regularly and visit the growing number of small Chinatowns in the Americas. A well-known opera performer, Mei Lan Fang, came several times to the United States from China during the first half of the twentieth century and was greeted by Chinese American audiences as a superstar celebrity.

For the most part, these operas were traditional works. However, small changes to the form had begun by the early twentieth century, which reflect the emergence of a Chinese American culture. Western instruments such as the saxophone, twelve-string guitar, and violin joined the traditional instruments. Cantonese opera was written about the experiences of Angel Island, the Ellis Island of the West Coast, where for decades Chinese, in their attempt to gain entry to the United States, were detained from weeks to years in prison-like barracks, interrogated and persecuted by U.S. government authorities. Since the initial passage of the Chinese Exclusion Act of 1882, persecution and harassment against the Chinese and other Asians was part of the mounting anti-Asian immigration restrictions and quotas and a growing racist "Yellow Peril" xenophobic hysteria nationwide. When cheap labor is needed, Asians (along with other immigrants, now primarily from the "Third World") have been recruited and brought to the United States in large numbers, but when economic decline occurs, these immigrants are excluded and persecuted. This experience contributed to the feeling of dislocation and alienation so commonly expressed in much of the early Chinese immigrant "sojourner" cultural expressions.

The exclusion laws created a bachelor society—a community of overwhelmingly single, male workers in the city ghettos where Chinese resided. Chinese women were not allowed entry to the United States, except for those few who were smuggled in as prostitutes or those who were part of the exempt classes, such as wives of merchants and officials. The impact of these racist exclusion laws was tantamount to genocide, preventing wives and lovers from joining the male workers, preventing the Chinese in the United States from procreating. The Angel Island opera expresses the pain, suffering, and anger felt at the mistreatment of the Chinese.

According to Jack Chen, the popularity of Chinese opera, which lasted until the 1940s, served three very vital functions to the Chinese American community:

1. It preserved the Chinese cultural heritage in the face of severe racist persecution and hostility by the dominant Euro-American society.
2. It gave the Chinese in the United States a sense of history through the various myths, legends, and historical dramas portrayed in the operas.
3. It gave the Chinese self-esteem with heroes, warriors, great leaders—figures who fought hardship and triumphed against oppression, giving the oppressed Chinese a sense of pride and succor when their existence seemed hopeless and miserable.

According to Chen, Chinese opera "was an educational experience re-telling the ancient legends and history; a school for social ethics in-culcating the ancient lessons of right living and honorable behavior. It was a living course in literature and aesthetics with its grace and colorful costumes, a school for music, singing, martial and acrobatic skills. Chinese opera is still all of these."[3]

Probably the most popular character in Chinese opera for the im-migrants was Kwan Kung, the god of war and literature. Kwan Kung originally appeared in the classic Chinese epic novel, *The Three King-doms,* and personified loyalty and heroism as a warrior-scholar. The Chinese male in the west identified readily with Kwan Kung. Kwan Kung rode a horse (like the American cowboy), he was the protector of those who traveled for a living (the immigrants, the merchants, and touring performers), he fought injustice, he was loyal to his com-rades (important for community identity and solidarity), and he was a bachelor who upheld principle and honor (important values in a lawless and frontier place).

‹ 253

Chinese opera reached its height of popularity during the early twentieth century as other forms of American entertainment (such as going to theaters and movie houses and any public events) were not allowed to the Chinese, enforced by both segregation laws and the threat of racist violence and hostility. The Chinese were deemed pariahs and venal by mainstream America. Chinese opera declined by the 1940s as motion pictures and television successfully com-peted and replaced most live performing arts in the United States, as suburbanization and assimilation increased, and as U.S. foreign pol-icy severed relations with the new Communist Peoples Republic of China. Only recently has Chinese opera started to make a comeback in the U.S. Chinatowns, with the lifting of the century-long racist im-migration restrictions and quotas, which has resulted in the current dramatic increase in Chinese immigration to U.S. cities.[4]

Unlike bourgeois European opera in the United States, Chinese opera in the Chinatowns is a mass popular cultural form consumed by workers, now mostly in the restaurant and garment industries. A typical Chinese opera show is typically in a makeshift theater where patrons would go to eat and have tea, chatter loudly until their fa-vorite scenes came on stage, and shout their approval or loudly vent criticisms of the performances. All of the age-old stories are known to the entire audience, so story details are never important. Audiences come to the opera to be thrilled by new, virtuosic singing and martial arts–like acrobatics. Most non-Chinese Americans would be horrified at the behavior of Chinatown opera audiences, who eat, smoke, drink, and are rancorous in their approval or disapproval of the shows.

Other significant early Chinese American immigrant working-class expressive cultural forms included the *muk-yu go* (Cantonese wood-fish head chants or songs), a thirty-six-syllable verse poetic chant accompanied by the metrical beating of a fishhead-carved woodblock. Thousands of these songs (really chants) were compiled in a two-volume collection entitled *Songs of Gold Mountain*. Two hundred forty-six of them were translated into English by Professor Marlon K. Hom in 1992. Many of these chants expressed indignation, anger, outrage, protest, frustration, depression, and sorrow for the isolation, persecution, suffering, hardships, and oppression that marked the lives of the Chinese immigrants in the United States.[5]

In the Angel Island barracks in San Francisco Bay, thousands of Chinese poems were carved by the detained immigrants. The loneliness, anxiety, confusion, despondency, and anger at their persecution and detention by the U.S. government are all evident in these poems. After the Angel Island detention center was closed in the 1940s, many of these poems were forgotten until a later generation of Asian American cultural activists and scholars rediscovered them when the holding center was reopened as a historical museum. Some of these poems, with English translations and excellent historiographical annotations, are contained in the book *Island: Poetry and History of Chinese Immigrants on Angel Island, 1910-1940*. One example of these poems follows:

> I have ten thousand hopes that the
>   revolutionary armies will complete their
>   victory,
> And help make the mining enterprises
>   successful in the ancestral land.
> They will build many battleships and come to
>   the U.S. territory,
> Vowing never to stop till the white men are
>   completely annihilated.[6]

Simultaneous with these immigrant working-class Chinese language forms were more assimilated expressions of Chinese American novels, short stories, and musical theater nightclub cabaret
performers, all basically imitative of white American cultural forms.
For example, the nightclub performers, many of them very talented
and hardworking, shown in the Arthur Dong documentary film *Forbidden City,* named after the nightclub of that name, performed to
white-only audiences, and pandered to this audience's desire and interest in the exotic. While it may be argued that the Duke Ellington
Orchestra did so similarly in its jungle musical revues at the white-
patronized Cotton Club during the Harlem Renaissance, the fact is
that the Forbidden City performers did not innovate any new forms
or anything uniquely Chinese American, while Ellington, of course,
extended and elaborated radically upon "jazz" and made for a deeper
and more significant African American expressive musical culture.
In the case of the Chinese American performers in such venues as
the Forbidden City nightclub in San Francisco, they were imitating
mainstream white entertainers and the most commercial styles of
their day, such as white big band swing jazz, vaudeville comedy, and
trendy popular dances.[7]

‹ 255

Early Japanese American Immigrant Working-Class Expressive Cultural Forms

The Japanese first arrived in large numbers on the islands of Hawaii
in the late nineteenth century to work on the sugar plantations. They
brought with them many of their peasant folk traditions, including
their work songs, called *bushi.* The Japanese male workers worked
in the sugarcane fields cutting the long, tough stalks of cane while
the women workers worked outside of the fields in groups doing *hole
hole* (the Hawaiian term for the work of stripping cane leaves off the
cut stalks). Unlike the Chinese, who were precluded from bringing
women to the United States, the Japanese women were permitted to
enter the United States under the Gentlemen's Agreement of 1907 between the governments of Japan and the United States.

The women workers, many of them very young of age as teenagers,
came to the islands through an arranged marriage system as "picture brides." As the term denotes, they agreed to marry men whom

they had never met simply through the exchange of photographs or pictures. These men in return agreed to pay for their transportation from Japan to Hawaii, which often cost more than a thousand dollars, a huge sum considering that these men made about 69 cents a day for back-breaking labor from sunup to sundown. As one can imagine, when these women arrived on the docks of Hawaii and met their husbands in person for the first time, they were sorely disappointed. The men often looked nothing like their pictures. They were much older than depicted in the pictures, sunburned and haggard from years of stoop labor. These women were in miserable and disappointing marriages. They sang of their sorrows, suffering, hopes, and dreams through a cappella songs as they worked, based upon their familiar peasant folk tune melodies, but with new words that expressed these new, often bitter, experiences in the United States. Hence, a unique Japanese (Asian) American working-class folk song form developed called the *hole hole bushi,* a hybrid term combining the Japanese *bushi* song form with the new experiences of *hole hole* work in Hawaii, no longer as rice farmers or fishing people, but now belonging to a mass of plantation workers in a burgeoning capitalist agribusiness.[8]

Some *hole hole bushi* utilized the double entendre as a form of coded message-making by these women to arrange trysts with men with whom they had extramarital affairs:

> Tomorrow is Sunday, right?
> Come over and visit.
> My husband will be out
> Watering cane
> And I'll be alone.

Such usage of the *hole hole bushi* could be construed as a form of protest against patriarchal monogamy.

The *hole hole bushi* were sung by the Issei, or first-generation Japanese women workers in the sugar plantations of Hawaii. The tradition did not continue as many of these women left the fields and went to the cities. However, today, with a resurgence of Japanese American pride and identity, younger people are learning the *hole hole bushi,* albeit not as field workers.

On the U.S. mainland, Japanese worked both as workers in industry and as small farmers who, despite anti-Asian oppression, managed to excel in agriculture, often turning deserts into arable farmland. This success through hard struggle earned the jealousy and envy of greedy white racist agribusiness, bent on dispossessing the Japanese Americans of their farmlands. One of the most traumatic and singular historical episodes for Japanese Americans was the World War II internment, or U.S. concentration camp experience. One of the economic consequences of the Japanese American internment was the seizure of Japanese farmlands and the confiscation of Japanese-owned property. More than 120,000 Japanese Americans, two-thirds U.S. citizens, on the mainland were rounded up and herded into twelve detention camps in deserts, surrounded with armed gun towers and barbed wire, housed in makeshift barracks from 1942 to the end of World War II. This intense oppression produced many forms of resistance, including riots, dissent, protest, and legal challenges that eventually culminated in a presidential apology and token reparations to survivors of the camps and their families signed into law by President Reagan after years of organizing by the Japanese American community for redress and reparations. However, the $20,000 in reparations to each individual was a paltry amount compared to the wealth that had been made from the farmlands taken away from the Japanese, not to mention the loss of lives, mental illness, suicide, and psychological devastation.

‹ 257

During the internment years, as part of affirming their humanity in the midst of inhumane conditions, Japanese Americans created paintings, wrote poems and stories, made sculpture and gardens, and a myriad of other forms of expressive culture to fend off boredom, to maintain their spirit, and to express their feelings about their condition. Japanese Americans have come to call this collective body of expressive culture "Camp Art"—art that was produced during the years they were in the internment camps. Some visual artists came to national prominence, including Yasuo Kuniyoshi and Mine Okubo. A stunning collection of transliterations (in *romaji*, or Anglicized Japanese) is *Poets Behind Barbed Wire,* which contains the poignant poetry of four writers during the Camp experience.[9]

The Japanese American community has a vibrant tradition of tanka syllabic verse poetry circles, with more than one thousand such poetry clubs at its height before World War II. Tomoe Tana was the first Japanese American to receive the highest award for poetry from the emperor of Japan. These tanka poems were written both in Japanese and later in English, conforming to the 5-7-5-7-7 five-line syllable verse, and the poems had to include an image from nature, as Tomoe Tana explained to me.[10] Japanese festival dances, songs, and other performances continued after the Camps, and in the contemporary Asian Movement, the tradition of taiko drumming was taken up by younger Japanese Americans as they formed numerous *taiko dojos* (Japanese drum corps) in many cities across the United States.

Early Filipino American Immigrant Working-Class Expressive Cultural Forms

Filipinos followed the Japanese in large numbers to both Hawaii's sugar plantations and to the agricultural fields and industries of the West Coast. Many worked as seasonal workers, part of the year working in the salmon canneries of the Northwest and Alaska, and part of the year doing stoop agricultural labor in California's "factories of the fields."

The Filipinos who came to the United States were primarily from the northern regions of the Ilocano and Visayan speaking peoples. The Philippines had been colonized by Spain for three centuries and then by the United States as part of the transfer of spoils from the Spanish-American War of 1898. Consequently, Filipino culture had been heavily "hispanicized" and, since 1898, Filipinos shared the contradictory status of being "Americans" and "foreign aliens" as immigrants to the United States. The American colonial rule lasted three decades with an intensive Anglo American cultural indoctrination campaign.

Thus, many Filipinos who came to the United States were multilingual in their native Filipino dialects, in Spanish, and in English. However, one region of the Philippines was never colonized either by the Spaniards or the Americans: the southernmost Maranao and Maguindanao areas retained their Muslim and Polynesian cultural heritage, including unique musical and dance forms based on the kulintang traditions. Because of "Hispanicization" throughout the majority of the Philippines, these Muslim peoples and their culture have been regarded as "inferior" and "primitive." Not until the advent of the modern Asian Movement did the kulintang traditions become of interest and influence among younger Filipino Americans. Several kulintang groups are active in Filipino American communities on both coasts.

One of the "giants" of Asian Pacific American literature is Carlos Bulosan, a Filipino writer who possessed a talent for writing in English, a deep familiarity with the folk tales of peasant Filipinos, and a profound sensitivity to the stories of the Filipino American manongs (immigrant bachelor laborers who were the first generation in the United States), and a passionate Marxist-influenced humanism. Bulosan came to the United States in 1931 and worked and lived with the manongs and came to know many of them and their life stories, which he depicted in his epic *America Is in the Heart: A Personal History.* While called "a personal history," in actuality the book is a composite of the lives of different Filipino immigrant men told as Bulosan's own story. Caught up in the struggles of the Great Depression era, Bulosan was heavily influenced by the Left-wing socialist realist writing of the time, which will be further discussed below. Bulosan's writings consciously depict the lives of the Filipino bachelor workers with dignity and poignancy in their experiences with white racism, superexploitation in migratory labor, their yearning for love and female affection in an enforced bachelorhood with anti-Asian immigration and antimiscegenation laws, all the while holding on to naively romantic dreams of acceptance by American society despite constant white racist hostility and rejection. Bulosan was also one of the preeminent "proletarian" writers of the era, a period of socialist-realist literature influenced by the Soviet revolution, the anticolonial struggles—particularly in Asia, Africa, the Pacific Islands, and Latin America—and the rise of Leftist movements in the United States during the Great Depression.[11]

Left-Wing Literature of the Late 1920s and 1930s

Asian Pacific immigrant workers in the United States faced severe oppression during a period of virulent anti–Asian Pacific racist exclusion and persecution, which in part attracted them to the growing Left-wing organizing and ideas, especially as promoted by the Communist Party U.S.A. in leading major campaigns for economic and social justice during the late 1920s and throughout the 1930s. The

CPUSA and communist-influenced organizing gained considerable strength during the Depression era, especially among oppressed nationality workers. Much writing is available on the organizing campaigns initiated and led by the communists: among sharecroppers and tenant farmers in the South, organizing unemployed workers councils, antilynching and racial justice campaigns, and among immigrant workers. A few Asian American historians have documented and discussed the Left-wing organizations in the APA communities, with most research and writing done on the Chinese American Marxists and Leftists by Him Mark Lai.[12]

Another contributing factor to the growth of Marxism and Left-wing radicalism in APA communities was the growing anticolonial, independence, and national liberation struggles in Asia, especially China. But probably the most significant factor was the importance placed upon immigrant and oppressed nationality organizing by the CPUSA, particularly after the Third Communist International, where the party adopted the Negro Nation thesis that mandated special focus and organizing attention to oppressed nationalities. The Negro Nation thesis analyzed African Americans as an oppressed nation with the right to self-determination in the region of the "black-belt South," where blacks were concentrated and were often a numerical majority. Unlike other American Leftists (who were white and white chauvinist), the communists, through the Comintern resolutions on the Negro Nation, recognized the revolutionary character of the black struggle in the United States, which had the effect of extending to other oppressed nationalities, such as APAs and Mexicans in the Southwest. Thus for a period, the CPUSA devoted resources and organizers to these communities. During its heyday in the 1930s, the CPUSA had more than a dozen different daily language newspapers, including Chinese, aimed at spreading Leftist influence among the many immigrant groups it attempted to organize. APA communist organizers were developed and emerged on both coasts. They included immigrant workers who were also writers and poets, including Happy Gim Fu Lim, secretary of the Chinese Workers Mutual Aid Association (CWMAA) in San Francisco; Ben Fee, president of the CWMAA and later the first Chinese field organizer for the International Ladies Garment Workers Union in New York City, who wrote

poetry and short novels in Chinese with Leftist content; Carlos Bulosan; and others.

One maverick writer was H.T. Tsiang, who self-published three
books, including poetry (*Poems of the Chinese Revolution*, 1929), a
novel called *China Red* (1931), and an experimental novel (*The Hanging
on Union Square*, 1933). A lively and humorous novel about the tribu-
lations of a Chinese laundryman in New York Chinatown, *And China
Has Hands,* was published by Robert Speller Books of New York in
1937. Not much biographical detail has been compiled about Tsiang,
but the little gleamed from the files of Chinese American historian
Him Mark Lai from Chinese newspaper clippings seems to indicate
that he immigrated to the United States as a student-intellectual and
based himself initially at Columbia University. He circulated among
the many Left intellectuals and writers of New York City and had his
first publication of a poem in the *New Masses*. Not an organizer, he
attended many rallies and meetings and hovered around the Left
intellectual and activist circles. By the 1940s, from newspaper accounts, he had given up writing and Leftist politics and relocated to
Los Angeles, where he found bit roles in Hollywood movies. It is pre-
sumed that after the Chinese Revolution in 1949 that he may have
returned home.

‹ 261

What is important to note is that in the first century of APA literature, very little was written in English, much less published by
white publishers. After World War II, authors John Okada (his novel
No-No Boy is considered a "first" among Japanese American fiction)
and Louis Chu (his witty novel *Eat a Bowl of Tea* is set in New York's
Chinatown bachelor society and is a funny story of a young, newly
married man who finds himself sexually impotent) were able to be
published by sympathetic small presses (Chu's personal friend was
Lyle Stuart, who owned a publishing company, Lyle Stuart Press).
Both authors and their novels have come to be considered pioneers
and classics in APA literature. Okada's novel captures the anguish
and trauma imposed on Japanese Americans by the camps. Chu's
language is innovative for conveying Chinatown speech. Chu's *Eat a
Bowl of Tea* is praised for its realistic and sympathetic portrayal of
Chinatown bachelor society.

The discussion of English-writing APA writers has been the predominant emphasis of most discourses about APA literature, including the comprehensive *Asian American Literature* by Elaine Kim.[13] This essay will not attempt to survey or repeat any of the discourse except to note that the major flaw in this conceptualization in general and in this otherwise impressive book specifically is that Asian American literature is defined as a literature written in the English language (which excludes the vast body of immigrant and working-class expressions, the focus of this article). Another major conceptual flaw purveyed by Kim in her book is the generation-based model for categorizing APA literature: "first" generation, which Kim characterizes as "accommodationist" (that is, seeking acceptance by and into dominant American society); "second" generation, characterized as having "sacrifice for success" syndrome (striving to be examples to their race as "model minorities"); and the "third" generation, characterized as the assertion of APA pride and sociopolitical identity. The major error in this method of social contextualization is in ascribing social outlook by "generation." APAs evince all forms of sociopolitical characteristics for every generation. Rather, a class analysis would better explain why privileged, English-writing APAs chose to write in English, for white publishers, and for white audiences from whom they sought acceptance, understanding, and approval.

Concurrent with the few publications of APA writers by white American publishers prior to the 1970s and 1980s was a much more substantial output of community literary expressions, often written in the immigrants' ancestral languages, published by community presses for immigrant readership, from the thousands of Japanese tanka poetry clubs throughout Japanese America, to the Chinese language poetry, chants, and musical song forms of U.S. Chinatowns, all of which were published in community journals, newspapers, and self-published forms.

The Asian Movement and Its Arts

The Asian Movement (also known as the Asian American Movement or the APA Movement) emerged during the volatile late 1960s and early 1970s simultaneously on both coasts of the mainland United States and in Hawaii. A comprehensive collection of historical and personal narratives of this period is found in *Legacy to Liberation:*

Politics and Culture of Revolutionary Asian Pacific America.[14] Inspired by the Black Liberation Movement, the mass movement opposing the U.S. war in Southeast Asia, and national liberation struggles in the Third World (especially Asia) and socialist China (especially the Cultural Revolution), the Asian Movement grew both on college campuses and in the APA communities. The identifier "Asian American" was first adopted by the Asian American Political Alliance, a group of militant student and radical community activists at the University of California–Berkeley in 1968–69. Subsequently, many student groups were formed across the United States, which called themselves Asian Student Union, Asian American Students Association, and so on, and several networks were organized in the late 1970s, including the Asian Pacific Student Union (APSU) on the West Coast and the East Coast Asian Student Union (ECASU), which now extends from Florida to Maine. These student activists led the struggles to create APA studies courses, programs, and departments, which generated further interest in APA literature. Many student-formed journals continue to feature poetry, artwork, comics, and creative writing, with varying political perspectives depending on how radicalized the students are. APA literary and cultural criticism has been primarily the domain of APA academic publications, while creative expressions are primarily featured in student-led journals and publications.

‹ 263

The Asian Movement produced a very significant, alternative, and radical cultural movement within the APA communities across the United States, which included new organizations devoted to the arts and to cultural organizing. These included the Kearny Street Workshop and Japantown Art and Media in San Francisco (both were multi-arts), Visual Communications in Los Angeles and Asian Cine-Vision in New York (media groups), taiko dojos in many cities, and groups that focused on literature, such as the Basement Workshop in New York (though it also was multi-arts, particularly in its early years) and the Kearny Street Workshop Press, among others.

In Hawaii, both an APA and native Hawaiian literary and cultural movement have emerged, sometimes in collaboration and sometimes separately. Bamboo Ridge Press and the journal *Seaweeds and Constructions* and other literary projects in Hawaii embraced both a "local" (mostly APA-unique sensibility in Hawaii, which was the focus of Bamboo Ridge) and pan-Pacific, including indigenous Hawaiian, literatures. Writers such as Darrell Lum, Wing Tek Lum, Juliet Kono, Gary Paik, and others are part of a "local" literary movement that addresses the experiences and sensibilities of being APA in Hawaii, the only place in the United States where APAs are the majority and not a small minority. This literature tends to be less preoccupied with identity alienation and reactions to white racism than mainland APA writing, and focuses more on the uniqueness of APA life in the islands. Other writers and cultural activists, such as Japanese American Richard Hamasaki, joined with writers of native Hawaiian and other Pacific Islander ancestry to self-publish, record, and organize community forums advocating and disseminating Hawaiian and Pacific literatures, which were often ignored, excluded, or marginalized (not even regarded as literature but simply as "writings") not only by white-dominated mainstream presses and academia but also, sadly, by APA studies and small press publications. Hamasaki and his cultural activist circle continue to produce recordings and publications that feature traditional as well as contemporary experimental expressions that draw from Hawaiian legends, chants, and other forms. The distinction must be made between the "local" writers, who write about the APA experience in Hawaii, and Hawaiian literature, which is the expression of ancestral Hawaiian writers and writers who identify with the indigenous culture and its struggles.

Japanese American writer Milton Murayama, who grew up in Hawaii, is significant for initially self-publishing an underground bestseller during the 1950s. Murayama's novel *All I Asking for Is My Body* is about the struggles and tensions of a Japanese American plantation worker family and was groundbreaking for its use of pidgin dialect, as evidenced in the very title of the book.

The Asian Movement catalyzed numerous cultural and literary projects, too numerous for this article. Many militant and radical literary voices emerged. Among Filipino American poets and writers, these included the late Serafin Syquia (1943-73), his younger brother Lou Syquia, Al Robles, Virginia Cerrenio, Cyn Zarco, Jessica Hagedorn, and many others featured in the out-of-print anthology *Liwanag* (1976). Among Japanese and Chinese American poets and writers were Lawson Fusao Inada, Frank Chin, Shawn Wong, Janice Mirikitani, Wing Tek Lum, Fay Chiang, Thom Lee, Genny Lim, Richard Hamasaki, and others. A short-lived literary/cultural journal *Aion* featured many West Coast progressive and radical APA writers and artists. An emerging Leftist APA literary criticism could be found in landmark anthologies such as *Roots: An Asian American Reader* (considered a "classic" that featured essays on politics, community, and identity as well as photography, artwork, and creative writing) and its sequel, *Counterpoint,* as well as in progressive and Left movement newspapers such as *The San Francisco Journal, Getting Together* newspaper (the organ of I Wor Kuen, and its antecessor, *Unity* newspaper), *East Wind* magazine (the APA cultural and political journal of the League of Revolutionary Struggle–Marxist-Leninist, the antecessor of I Wor Kuen), and others.

Much of this movement's cultural criticism and views were influenced by Mao Zedong's Yenan talks on art and literature that directed art and artists to "serve the people," to integrate and learn from the working-class masses, and to heighten the national and class struggle. Part of Mao's impact upon these young APA radicals was to search for immigrant, working-class forms, traditions, and influences both in documenting APA cultural history as well as in finding sources for inspiration to create a new progressive and revolutionary APA culture. The Asian Movement produced the greatest outpouring of expressive culture in all media, generated arts-specific organizations with a Pan-Asian and political scope, organized its own presses and publications, and united cultural production with community struggle. Asian American political and cultural activism was greatly influenced by and looked to leadership from the Black Liberation Movement and its cultural wing, the Black Arts Movement, which provided examples of independent, self-reliant institution building and cultural production, asserting its own aesthetic and a commitment to fight oppression and build a revolutionary movement.[15] Combining a commitment to activism and to artistic expression, APA poets and performers joined and did their cultural work as part of rallies, demonstrations, benefit fundraisers, and all types of community programs. Many freely gave of their service, never expecting to make money, much less careers, from their cultural work. Few thought of themselves as professional writers or artists, but rather as professional revolutionaries, some even joining the many new communist organizations that had emerged during this period of political and cultural upsurge.[16]

This tremendous cultural and political upsurge included visual artists such as Tomie Arai, Jim Dong, Zand Gee, Nancy Hom, and many others on both coasts; musicians such as Dan and June Kuramoto, Mark Izu, Russel Baba, Fred Houn, Benny Yee, A Grain of Sand (the trio of Nobuko/Joanne Miyamoto, Chris Iijima, and "Charlie" Chin); and artists of all disciplines. Many of these artists and cultural workers gave their talents to support, educate, organize, and raise needed funds for local community and nationwide campaigns, including the movement to free Korean immigrant prisoner Chol Soo Lee; building support for the redress and reparations movement for Japanese Americans interned during World War II; the struggle to defend the International Hotel in San Francisco's Manilatown-Chinatown; support for Filipino and Mexican/Chicano farmworker organizing; and other issues.

"Third World" literary journals, the precursors to "multicultural literature," also featured APA writers, such as the *Yardbird* readers spearheaded by Ishmael Reed and Al Young, *Time to Greez!*, edited by Janice Mirikitani, and others.[17]

Since the 1970s, increasing numbers of APA writers have been published by mainstream presses, with some notable successes such as Maxine Hong Kingston, Amy Tan, the playwright David Henry Hwang, David Mura, Jessica Hagedorn, Lois Ann Hamanaka, and others. Some have won major literary prizes, such as poet Cathy Song Davenport, Garrett Hongo, and others. Asian American academic literary criticism has given much attention to these writers, whose writings and careers are not the focus of this article.

For every oppressed nationality group in the United States, the struggle for self-definition continues as a necessary part of the struggle for liberation, for the power to know and embrace one's true history and culture. This is reflected in every APA generation with the continuing, often-repeating struggle with ongoing questions of identity (e.g., the relationship between ancestral, traditional culture and American/Western forms and experiences, of resisting racism and stereotyping, of group experience and individual self-expression, of responsibility to community, of audience, of language).

The fundamental question of what is APA literature is rooted in this struggle for self-definition: is APA literature any expressive writing by a person of Asian/Pacific Islander descent in the United States, or does/must it reflect the forms, traditions, sensibilities, and experiences of a people? Are APAs an oppressed group and should APAs and APA artists contribute to the struggle against this oppression and for liberation? How this question is answered and discussed remains political and this political stance informs the APA artist's artistic and literary sensibilities. The political stance and view of each artist toward assimilation and oppression in terms of actual experience, both shared and individual, will shape the ideological and aesthetic direction of their creativity.

The emergence and rise of the Asian Movement promulgated a wide militant, progressive, and even revolutionary consciousness among the APA communities. The cultural expression of this period rejected assimilation and took up the cause of creating its own aesthetic, and organized alternative community-oriented publications and vehicles. However, in the recent decade and a half, the Asian Movement has ebbed as both the Black Liberation struggle and the U.S. Left in general have undergone repression and co-optation, and U.S. society has moved Rightward. Asian American studies, originally formed to support the struggles of the APA communities, have increasingly become self-perpetuating academic islands divorced from the community. In the "mainstreaming" of APA studies, APA success stories are more promulgated, including some of the aforementioned writers now published and lauded by the mainstream. This ascendant assimilationist tendency sycophantically endorses such artists and writers who are anointed by mainstream media and academic circles. For any oppressed nationality in the United States, including APAs, these have been the two paths, coexisting often in dynamic tension and contradiction: assimilation versus resistance/liberation. The path of assimilation has sought acceptance, legitimation, validation, and dependency upon the white mainstream. The path of resistance and liberation has sought to assert its own aesthetics, base its support within its communities, and build its own institutions and means of dissemination. The writers and their writings to differing and varying degrees reflect this contradiction. This essay has focused on the writers and writings, as well as general cultural production and expression, that have consciously resisted white assimilation, stood opposed to APA oppression, and expressed the need for social justice and broader, fundamental social transformation.

> live poems will graze
> on virgin moss growing on
> capitalists' graves.[18]

NOTES

Certain terms may require clarification. "Oppressed nationalities" refers to "minorities" or "people of color" who have faced a history of racism, exclusion, and oppression in U.S. society, who are now generally people of African, Asian/Pacific, Latin American, Caribbean, and indigenous (First Nations, or "Native American" or "American Indian") descent. "Whites" are all those among the oppressor nationality who enjoy white-skin privileges and have become the dominant cultural and social group in the United States, which today is primarily people of European descent who have accepted becoming "white."

1 1990 U.S. Census.

2 Current fictional and dramatic works, such as Maxine Hong Kingston's novel *China Men* and David Henry Hwang's play *The Dance and the Railroad,* among other works, portray vibrant storytelling ("talk-story") and Chinese folk- and opera-singing practices among the Chinese bachelor laborers. I know of no nineteenth-century scholarly or journalistic account of Chinese American cultural activity.

3 Jack Chen, "American Chinese Opera, Chinese American Reality," *East Wind: Politics and Culture of Asians in the U.S.* (Spring/Summer 1986): 14-17.

4 Fuller discussions of early Chinese American music-making can be found in Ron Riddle, *Flowing Streams and Flying Dragons: Music in the Life of San Francisco's Chinese* (Westport, Conn.: Greenwood Press, 1983); Fred Houn, "Asian American Music and Empowerment: Is There Such a Thing as 'Asian American Jazz'?" (this volume).

5 Discussion of the wood-fish head chants can be found in Marlon K. Hom, *Songs of Gold Mountain* (Berkeley: University of California Press, 1992). See also Fred Houn, "Revolutionary Asian American Art: Tradition and Change, Inheritance and Innovation, Not Imitation!,"

East Wind: Politics and Culture of Asians in the U.S. (Spring/Summer 1986): 5-8.

6 *Island: Poetry and History of Chinese Immigrants on Angel Island, 1910-1940,* edited by Him Mark Lai, Genny Lim, and Judy Yung (Seattle and London: University of Washington Press, 1991), 90-91.

7 Houn, "Asian American Music and Empowerment."

8 Fred Ho and Susan Asai, "*Hole Hole Bushi*: Cultural/Musical Resistance by Japanese Women Plantation Workers in Early Twentieth-Century Hawaii," this volume.

9 Jiro Nakano and Kay Nakano, *Poets behind Barbed Wire* (Honolulu: Bamboo Ridge Press, 1984).

10 Fred Ho, "Interview with Tomoe Tana" (this volume).

11 Carlos Bulosan's work and an analysis of it are best found in the following: Carlos Bulosan, *America Is in the Heart: A Personal Story* (Seattle: University of Washington Press, 1991; originally published in 1946); and E. San Juan, *On Being Filipino: Selected Writings of Carlos Bulosan* (Philadelphia: Temple University Press, 1995).

12 Him Mark Lai, "A Survey of the Chinese American Left," *Bulletin of Concerned Asian Scholars* 4, no. 3 (1972).

13 Elaine Kim, *Asian American Literature* (Philadelphia: Temple University Press, 1982).

14 Fred Ho et al., *Legacy to Liberation: Politics and Culture of Revolutionary Asian Pacific America* (San Francisco: AK Press, 2000).

15 Kalamu ya Salaam, *The Magic of JuJu: An Appreciation of the Black Arts Movement,* which the author read as an unpublished manuscript.

16 Fred Ho, "Beyond 'Asian American Jazz': My Musical and Political Changes in the Asian American Movement" (this volume).

17 *Time to Greez!: Incantations from the Third World,* edited by Janice Mirikitani (San Francisco: Glide and Third World Communications, 1975).

18 David Monkawa, untitled poem, *East Wind: Politics and Culture of Asians in the U.S.* (Spring/Summer 1986): 9.

Tomoe Tana: Keeping Alive
Japanese American Tanka

AT AGE SEVENTY-FOUR, Tomoe Tana is an energetic trailblazer in promoting an understanding and practice of tanka poetry in America. Since 1938, a half-century ago when she arrived in the United States, this Issei woman has written numerous tankas; been active in several tanka clubs among various cities in the United States; coauthored the first book featuring English translations of Japanese American tankas (*Sounds from the Unknown*, 1963); earned her master's degree from San Jose State University at the age of seventy-two with a pioneering dissertation, "The History of Japanese Tanka Poetry in America"; and compiled, edited, and self-published another English-translated collection of Japanese American tankas (*Tomoshibi*, 1978).

While many Americans are familiar with haiku, Tana feels that the importance of tanka poetry has largely been unrecognized. She feels her role in life is "to give to the younger generation this special culture of Japan. Haiku is not original to Japan; it's only three hundred years old—a simplified form of tanka, taking just the first three lines. Tanka is three thousand years old. Tanka is really pure Japanese culture, a national treasure. We have to think about giving it to our next generations in the United States."

Tanka (meaning "short song") is a syllabic verse form of Japanese

Published in *Asian Week* newspaper, June 17, 1988.

poetry with an ancient history. Tana stresses that a tanka poem *must* be five lines of 31 syllables separated into an order of 5-7-5-7-7. If it doesn't adhere to this form, then "it is not tanka, but simply a short poem," according to Tana.

It is Tana's adamant contention that English translations of Japanese-written tankas must also follow the 5-7-5-7-7 syllabic form. This, of course, means that a translation that conforms to the syllabic form requirements must be substituted for an exact, word-for-word, literal translation, and retains the essential meaning of the original. "The main idea is what's important; not exact translation. If you understand the meaning, that's key," Tana explains.

She also cautions that conformity to form is not enough. "We have to add [she points to her head] *thought*. That *thought* should never be out of the poem. But we have to make it correct (syllable-wise). Correct syllable means that it will really be tanka."

‹ 271

Other English translations of Japanese American tanka have been done, most notably *Poets behind Barbed Wire* from Hawaii. However, these translations are literal and do not adhere to Tana's precise requirements that even the translations must conform to the 5-7-5-7-7 form.

In 1963, Lucille Nixon and Tomoe Tana published the landmark *Sounds from the Unknown* (Alan Swallow Publishing), the first collection of English-translated tankas of the Japanese in America. For twenty-seven years Tomoe Tana had worked as a housecleaner. Nixon, a white American, was one of her customers. They soon developed a close bond in their love for tanka poetry. In 1957 Nixon became the first tanka poet not of Japanese descent to be selected as the winner of Japan's Imperial Palace Poetry Party—the highest honor for tanka excellence. (Tomoe Tana had received this honor in 1949).

Determined to keep alive Japanese tanka in America, and to encourage its appreciation in the broader American public, in 1978 Tomoe Tana published *Tomoshibi,* a collection of Japanese American tankas translated into English, along with English written selections by two white Americans, the late Lucille Nixon and Joyce Lobner. Tana explains in her thesis that her intention with *Tomoshibi* was to "encourage Americans who want to compose tankas in their own language." Not able to convince any American publisher of the value of this goal, *Tomoshibi* was published from her own savings, with a printing of 1,100 copies. Most of the books have been sold, earning a profit, much to her pleasant surprise.

With these profits, Tana is busily at work translating the three volumes (1,500 pages) of her deceased husband's (Daisho Tana) diaries, written during the Japanese incarceration of World War II. Tana plans to publish those diaries. The diaries are part of the growing array of cultural and historical materials documenting the impact of the camp experience on the lives and consciousness of Japanese Americans. Interned in a separate camp, Daisho Tana's diaries contain correspondence between husband and wife. Tomoe Tana and her children were kept at the Hilo River Camp in Arizona, while her husband Daisho was incarcerated in Santa Fe and then later at Roosevelt, New Mexico. At the end of her letters Tomoe Tana wrote a tanka for her husband. But some of the letters and tankas were censored by the camp authorities, especially when their contents dealt with the actions of the U.S. government.

Probably more than any other literary form, the Japanese American tankas express the hundred-year history of the Nikkei people in the United States. Since the first Japanese arrived in the United States, there have been active tanka clubs in Japanese American communities across the U.S. mainland and Hawaii. Tanka, while an art form enjoyed mainly by the upper classes in Japan, became the cultural expression of an entire oppressed nationality in America. The tanka club members included ministers, small business people, teachers, farmers, gardeners, and service workers, both men and women.

The forced removal of Japanese Americans from their communities had scattered many of the tanka teachers—people who were active in the perpetuation of Japanese culture and language in their communities—who were deemed by war relocation officials as especially threatening in their racist, fifth column doctrine. Many of these community leaders and teachers were incarcerated at Tule Lake, a camp for political dissidents. At Tule Lake, Yoshihiko Tomari, a tanka teacher, was determined to keep tanka an active spiritual and cultural force for his people. Tomari organized a tanka network among the camps, gathered poems, produced mimeographed publications, and circulated them to other camps. Monthly tanka meetings were held in his barracks. Once a year he published by stencil selected poems in a magazine called *Kogen,* which continued many years after the camps.

Since the late 1950s, when a white American writer, Harold Henderson, introduced haiku to the American public, most Americans have come to know haiku as the only form of Japanese poetry. But it is Tomoe Tana's goal to educate Americans about tanka, which predates haiku by more than one thousand years, and has been in America for almost a century, and to foster the writing of tanka in English.

In recent years, Tana has translated a major collection of Japanese American tanka, *Zaibei Dobo Hyakunin Isshu* ("One Poem Each from One Hundred Countrymen in America"), compiled and edited by Dr. Kimura and Mr. Kenzo Ogasawara. These are one hundred poems selected from fifty thousand submissions collected in the early 1950s from Japanese tanka poets throughout North and South America.

‹ 273

Tana strongly feels that second, third, and fourth generations of Japanese Americans need to learn about and to write tanka as part of their cultural heritage. "Many Japanese Americans think tanka is only in Japanese. I want to break that thought. I want to educate Nisei and Sansei about tanka, and how to do it, so they will write." Tana feels that today's Japanese American periodicals can play a critical role in promoting tanka, but have not shown any real interest in doing so. She stresses, "We must pass on our culture to the new generations. They use English. We have to show what kind of tanka can be in English."

But she is optimistic as she meets more and more Americans of all nationalities who are becoming interested in and writing in the tanka form. (A revolutionary black woman poet, Sonia Sanchez, has been especially prolific in haiku and tanka.) Tomoe Tana's dedication, energy, and optimism for Japanese American tanka can be captured in the paraphrased words of Dr. Kimura:

> These poems born in the
> U.S.,
> Like wild flowers that never
> Fade,
> But growing more and more
> Beautiful.

Hole Hole Bushi:
Cultural/Musical Resistance by Japanese Women Plantation Workers in Early Twentieth-Century Hawaii

DURING THE LATE NINETEENTH and early twentieth centuries, large numbers of Japanese immigrant laborers arrived in Hawaii to work on the growing sugar plantations. They came from the poorer, southern regions of Japan to escape crushing poverty, suffocating village life, and to find their dreams for a better life. Many of the laborers were recruited by very active labor contractors seeking to fill the demand for workers.

These Japanese immigrant laborers brought to Hawaii a rich tradition of folk culture and peasant song forms, including the popular *bushi.* However, as the people were transformed from peasant farmers and fishing people in small villages in Japan to becoming plantation workers in a burgeoning capitalist agribusiness of the United States, their identity began to shift from these new experiences. So too did their music change and become a new and unique Japanese (Asian) American folk musical form called the *hole hole bushi.* Later we will discuss the musical changes that reflect the new American experience.

The very name of the music—*hole hole bushi*—is a hybrid term combining the Hawaiian *hole hole* (which referred to the stripping of sugarcane leaves, a task done primarily by the Japanese women cane-

....

Presented with Susan Asai at the Eleventh Annual Conference of the Society for the Study of the Multi-Ethnic Literatures of the United States, Honolulu, Hawaii, April 1997.

field workers) and the Japanese *bushi*, a traditional Japanese folk song genre. In this paper written by Professor Susan Asai, an ethnomusicologist at Northeastern University in Boston, Massachusetts, and Fred Ho, a professional Asian American musician and composer, we will analyze this important but underappreciated song form for its reflection of the emerging identity of Japanese immigrant sugar plantation workers of this period and its special significance as an expression and form of cultural and musical resistance to race, class, and gender oppression experienced specifically by the women plantation workers. In the case of the *hole hole bushi* songs, resistance is primarily viewed in the role of these songs as a "voice" of these women workers in opposition to their systematic oppression. While the songs did not play any conscious role in any organized movement of resistance, such as in strikes or social rebellions, nonetheless, the songs were both personal and collectively shared critiques of plantation society and expressions of personal opposition and rebellion.

Many of the women came to Hawaii through an arranged marriage system as "picture brides." The young women, often teenagers, entered a business contract by agreeing to marry a man who paid for her travel to Hawaii. Neither the men nor the women had ever met and all they knew about each other were the photographs—or "pictures"—they had exchanged. Filled with dreams and hopes for a new life in a new land, upon arrival in Hawaii, many of these women were quickly disappointed. They found themselves working under extremely harsh conditions, from before sunup to sundown, under the intense heat of the tropical sun. One *hole hole bushi* describes:

Kane wa kachiken	My husband cuts cane,
Washa horehore yo	I do the *hole hole*
Ase to namida no	By sweat and tears
Tomokasegi	We get by.

Besides being exploited as plantation workers, they were also oppressed by the racial hierarchy of white supremacy and colonial racism. Within that racial/class hierarchy of the plantation system, the white owners and managers were at the top, enjoying the big profits. This class had minimal contact with the mass of field laborers, virtually living a life apart in a big mansion physically situated above the fields. The go-between for the plantation owners and managers and laborers were the overseers (called *lunas*, a Hawaiian term) who had day-to-day contact with the workers and enforced their exploitation. The *lunas* were drawn from the nationalities of the laboring masses and played an insidious role, pitting ethnic groups against one another, enflaming ethnic and national divisions and competition, and serving as informants to the white bosses. One *hole hole bushi* describes this system both in its understanding of the hierarchy as well as its emotional hatred of it.

Hawaii Hawaii to	Wonderful Hawaii, or so I heard
Kite mirya Jiyoku	One look and it seems like Hell
Boshi ga Emma de	The manager's the Devil and
Runa ga oni	His *lunas* are demons.

While the Japanese men worked cutting the sugarcane, the women primarily worked stripping the leaves from the cut cane stalks. The *hole hole bushi* were sung by the women workers. While we could find no direct interviews that explained this difference as to why songs were sung by the women and not by the men, an explanation can be hypothesized from the different structure between the type and form of work done. On the one hand, the male activity of cutting cane was dispersed and constant, demanding physical involvement: hacking at cane stalks, the men were usually separated and spread apart from one another in the thick foliage. On the other hand, the women workers were situated on the perimeter of the fields, congregated in close-knit groups. Group singing contributed to the women's cohesion and provided a means of coping with the tedium of their particular work. The women were also less under the whip and constant pressure of the *lunas*.

As we can see from the two previous examples of *hole hole bushi*, they sang to relieve the misery of their work and to voice their objection to the system of exploitation and oppression on the plantations. But these women were also miserable and suffered in their arranged marriages. Their hopes for love and passion were quickly dashed upon meeting their husbands, who looked very unlike their pictures. Haggard and sunburned from the years of toil necessary to save their meager earnings to purchase a "picture bride," these men were generally many years older than represented in the pictures. Marriage for these young brides was often devoid of love and sexual passion.

It is our contention that the *hole hole bushi* is most significant as an expression of an oppressed nationality working-class women's sensibility. The *hole hole bushi* gave voice to the fantasies and passions of these picture brides and were used as coded messages to arrange trysts with younger male workers with whom they had extramarital affairs. Here's an example:

Asu wa sande jya yo	Tomorrow is Sunday, right?
Asobi ni iode	Come over and visit
Kane ga hanawai	My husband will be out watering cane
Washa uchi ni	And I'll be home alone.

In any feminist analysis of culture, the *hole hole bushi* must be recognized as a form of protest against patriarchal monogamy. In the next *hole hole bushi* example, with stinging sarcastic humor, the woman fantasizes about being a prostitute, of seducing a Chinaman, and regards prostitution as preferable to the degrading *hole hole* work. The song is revealing for its statement of what few options existed for these women and their perception of sexual commodification as rooted to their systematic oppression:

‹ 277

San jugosen no	Why settle for 35 cents
Hore hore shiyo yori	Doing *hole hole* all day
Pake-santo moi moi surya	When I can make a dollar
Akahi kala	Sleeping with that pake (Chinaman)?

The language of the *hole hole bushi* reflects the pidgin of the emerging creolized plantation culture, blending Japanese words with Hawaiian, Chinese, and Portuguese (the languages found among the multinational/multilingual work force) and English (the language of the plantation owners). For example, Hawaiian expressions such as *moi moi* (to sleep or have sex with), *pake* (Chinaman), *kane* and *wahine* (man and woman), the Portuguese term *luna* (for overseer or field boss), and others.

The *hole hole bushi* are also important and significant as an early Asian American working-class folk musical form. It was natural for Japanese immigrants coming to Hawaii to draw on the melodies of work songs and folk tunes they knew to express with fresh lyrics their new circumstances and environment. For generations, it was often Japanese laborers who disseminated songs from their locales to other regions of Japan in their search for work.

Hawaiian Consul General Robert Walker Irwin heavily recruited Japanese laborers from Hiroshima, Yamaguchi, and Wakayama prefectures located in the southern half of Honshu, the main island of Japan. So it is no surprise that the basic tune to many *hole hole bushi* possibly derives from the Hiroshima rice-threshing melody "To usu hiki uta."[1] Mr. Harry Urata, a musician and second-generation Japanese American living in Honolulu, established the melody of the rice-threshing song to be one probable source for *hole hole bushi,* based on his study of sixty different melodies. He came up with a version that most closely followed the melodies sung by the oldest singer who had sung these songs on the plantation.[2] Despite his findings, Urata warns it may be impossible to directly trace *hole hole bushi* melodies owing to their independent development from original sources over many generations on Hawaiian shores.

Some Issei, however, verify the Hiroshima connection. Hiroshima boatmen evidently sang the melody "To usu hiki uta," but in a slightly faster version. Others heard their parents sing a similar tune while on the ocean shores of Hiroshima prefecture.[3]

From the following examples you will hear, *hole hole bushi* share melodic similarities to work songs associated with rice planting in rural districts around Tokyo. As a rice-growing nation, it is possible that various regions in Japan share similar tunes sung to the different phases of planting, harvesting and hulling rice.

We shall listen and compare them now. The first three short songs (the third song has two verses) are *hole hole bushi* sung by former sugar plantation worker and picture bride Katsue Asakura. The fourth example includes two verses from a *taue uta,* or rice-planting song, from the Itabashi district, now part of metropolitan Tokyo. Listen for the contour or shape of the melodies. In the *hole hole bushi,* the first phrase of the melody arches upward toward higher pitches and gradually returns to the starting pitch. The second phrase dips to lower notes before curving upward with higher notes and descending to the pitch heard at the beginning of the tune. In the rice-planting song from Itabashi, the first phrase similarly arches upward toward higher pitches before descending to the starting pitch. A second phrase also arches upward, but only slightly before descending. And a third phrase dips down to lower pitches before ascending and then descending to the starting pitch again. The *hole hole bushi* melodies consist of two phrases that closely match the first and third phrases of the rice-planting song. There is enough similarity in the melodic contour and tempo to suggest that they may be related.

Teahouse Versions of *Hole Hole Bushi*

The contexts for singing *hole hole bushi* widened as people sang these songs after work in the plantation camps. After 1900, when contract labor of Japanese immigrants ended and the practice of burning leaves off of sugarcane stalks gradually replaced *hole hole* work, these plantation songs made their way to teahouses in Honolulu and Hilo. Teahouses were entertainment centers for men, providing a place to relax, drink *sake,* and be entertained. Teahouse patrons were Japanese immigrant workers who made enough money to set ‹ 279 up their own businesses in Honolulu or Hilo. As part of the teahouse song repertoire, *hole hole bushi* were sung by both men and women. It was mostly women who sang these songs in the fields, since it accompanied *hole hole* work, but in the teahouses men became proficient singers of this repertoire. *Hole hole bushi* were also sung at drinking parties, where this bank of songs acquired nostalgic and mythic qualities.[4]

As teahouse songs, they were called *ozashiki hole hole bushi.* The survival of these songs in new contexts brought about melodic and textural alterations. Originally, the songs were sung at a moderate tempo that matched the rhythm of stripping leaves off of cane stalks and the melodies were relatively simple. The relaxed atmosphere in teahouses slowed the tempo of the songs, and the melodies became more embellished and expressive. Textually, the first lines of the orally transmitted lyrics were usually changed and new ones created, but the remaining three lines of text were usually retained. Another change included the occasional use of a *shamisen*—a three-stringed plucked lute—to accompany the singing of *hole hole bushi.* The use of the *shamisen* is a feature of traditional teahouse songs called *kouta.*

Hole hole bushi continued to be sung in teahouses until the 1960s, when two men made recordings of these songs—Mr. Tagawa and Mr. Nagatoshi. Today, Mr. Urata teaches *hole hole bushi* to third- and fourth-generation Japanese Americans in Hawaii. He also recently produced a CD of the songs sung by one of his students in order to preserve them for future generations.

To conclude, the *hole hole bushi* are akin to the "sorrow songs" or "spirituals" sung by enslaved Africans in the plantations of the American mainland South during the antebellum period. Both musical cultures grow out of the enforced plantation labor exploitation and racial and national oppression, albeit almost half a world apart. The one major exception is that the *hole hole bushi* conveyed a unique female expression of a Japanese American working-class identity shaped by the American plantation system in Hawaii and its exploitation of a unique form of gender oppression, the practice of recruiting Japanese women as picture brides. As such, this musical culture became an expression of both an emerging Japanese American identity as well as of a resistance to class, racial, and gender oppression.

NOTES

1 Franklin S. Odo and Harry Urata, "Hole Hole Bushi: Songs of Hawaii's Japanese Immigrants," *Mana* 6, no. 1 (1981): 69–75, esp. 70.

2 Odo and Urata, "Hole Hole Bushi," 75.

3 Karleen Chinen, "Hole Hole Bushi: Voices of the Canefields, Songs of the Heart," *The Hawaii Herald*, May 4, 1984, 6.

4 Odo and Urata, "Hole Hole Bushi," 70.

ce of inspiration and example to Third World peoples both internationally and within the Un
es. The Chinese Revolution of 1949 established the People's Republic of China (PRC) as a soci
rnment among one-fifth of the world's population, a population that is "nonwhite." ¶ The Chir
lution differed greatly from the Bolshevik Revolution that established the Soviet Union. ¶
d World country, China had a history of colonial penetration and domination at the hands of
ern European, and Japanese imperialism. China was never fully colonized as India, virtually
rica, and much of Latin America and the Caribbean were. China was a semi-colony. Its major
s had come under control of competing foreign powers. These foreign concessions obeyed no
laws and were islands of privilege that humiliated Chinese sovereignty. ¶ Unlike Russia and o
ern countries, China's industrial proletariat was tiny, less than 1 percent of the population.
est of the Third World, most of China's enormous laboring population was peasantry. That's
ese communist historiography has characterized China as a "semi-colonial, semi-feudal" soci
ing oppressed as a Third World country, the Chinese people were subjected to racist stereo
nd deemed inferior, inscrutable, and in need of Western Christian missionary salvation, des
ng history as a highly advanced civilization. China confounded Karl Marx, who, incapable of
ing China's socioeconomic history in the formulation of Western European social history, devi
ranshistorical category of the Asiatic Mode of Production in a circular explanation for Chi
ndia's "Asiatic despotism," i.e., to explain why such societies, with long histories as highly de
civilizations and state bureaucracies, nonetheless were incapable of advancing to capital
eir own. Marx was guilty of the prevailing Orientalist and Eurocentric scholarship. ¶ The Chin
lution could not be explained in a Eurocentric Marxism; communism of its massive peasar
ed by a communist party; a leader, Mao Zedong, advanced the concept of a united front agai
rialism for a national democratic revolution that would lead to socialism. Eurocentric white ch
t Marxists and Trotskyists would criticize and condemn the Chinese Revolution as petit-b
nationalism, and its leader Mao, as a "nationalist." To this day, virtually all Trotskyists and
ut Communist Party U.S.A. and its ideological adherents (like members of the nonrevolution
nittees of Correspondence such as Angela Davis) cannot accept Mao or the Chinese Revolut
e true extension of Marxism-Leninism. ¶ But for most of us, what the white chauvinist soc
ft thinks isn't important. The Chinese Revolution and Mao inspired *most* of the world to s
utionary socialism and Marxist ideology, because *most* of the world was the victim of West
rialist super-exploitation and brutal national oppression. Most Third World workers have t
ime again been sold out by the white socialist and workers movement, whether it be the clas
of the French workers and peasants in the 1950s, to the 1960s with the Communist Party of
calling Malcolm X a police agent and denouncing the Black Panthers and the Trotskyist part
sing the Vietnamese national liberation struggle and only supporting the demand to "Bring
Home," valuing the lives of white boys over Asian peoples. Even today, the term "national lib
is equated with and dismissed as "nationalism" (deemed a dirty word) by these racist sociali
ake-Leftists. ¶ Most of the New Left in the United States emerged and demarcated itself from
eft (primarily the CPUSA and the Trotskyist Socialist Workers Party) by 1969. Several moment
ical factors propelled this emergence: the questions of supporting the Vietnamese national
n struggle against U.S. imperialism; the rise of the Black Panther Party and the reraising of
nto U.S. Left politics or continuing Malcolm X's prophetic question of the Bullet vs. the Bal
he Cultural Revolution in China, in which a tremendous wave of militant radicalism was be
headed by students and youth. ¶ Malcolm X had perceptively remarked, and I'll paraphrase, t
nce-common racist slur, "A Chinaman's Chance"—meaning no chance at all—had gone the way
on since the Chinese now had more chance than most of the dark peoples of the world, hav

{ IV }

WICKED THEORY,
NAKED PRACTICE

The Inspiration of Mao and the Chinese Revolution on the Black Liberation Movement and the Asian Movement on the East Coast

THE CHINESE REVOLUTION led by the Chinese Communist Party and Mao Zedong has been a great source of inspiration and example to Third World peoples both internationally and within the United States. The Chinese Revolution of 1949 established the People's Republic of China (PRC) as a socialist government among one-fifth of the world's population, a population that is "nonwhite."

The Chinese Revolution differed greatly from the Bolshevik Revolution that established the Soviet Union.

As a Third World country, China had a history of colonial penetration and domination at the hands of U.S., Western European, and Japanese imperialism. China was never fully colonized as India, virtually all of Africa, and much of Latin America and the Caribbean were. China was a semi-colony. Its major port cities had come under control of competing foreign powers. These foreign concessions obeyed no Chinese laws and were islands of privilege that humiliated Chinese sovereignty.

Unlike Russia and other Western countries, China's industrial proletariat was tiny, less than 1 percent of the population. Like the rest of the Third World, most of China's enormous laboring population

Presented as a speech on the panel "Mao, the Black Panthers, and the Third World Strike," for the thirtieth anniversary conference on the Third World Strike, University of California at Berkeley, April 8, 1999.

was peasantry. That's why Chinese communist historiography has characterized China as a "semi-colonial, semi-feudal" society.

Being oppressed as a Third World country, the Chinese people were subjected to racist stereotyping, and deemed inferior, inscrutable, and in need of Western Christian missionary salvation, despite its long history as a highly advanced civilization. China confounded Karl Marx, who, incapable of explaining China's socioeconomic history in the formulation of Western European social history, devised the transhistorical category of the Asiatic Mode of Production in a circular explanation for China's and India's "Asiatic despotism," i.e., to explain why such societies, with long histories as highly developed civilizations and state bureaucracies, nonetheless were not capable of advancing to capitalism on their own. Marx was guilty of the prevailing Orientalist and Eurocentric scholarship.

The Chinese Revolution could not be explained in a Eurocentric Marxist formulation. Instead, a massive peasantry was led by a communist party; a leader, Mao Zedong, advanced the concept of a united front against imperialism for a national democratic revolution that would lead to socialism. Eurocentric white chauvinist Marxists and Trotskyists would criticize and condemn the Chinese Revolution as petit-bourgeois nationalism, and its leader Mao, as a "nationalist." To this day, virtually all Trotskyists and the sell-out Communist Party U.S.A. and its ideological adherents (like members of the nonrevolutionary Committees of Correspondence such as Angela Davis) cannot accept Mao or the Chinese Revolution as the true extension of Marxism-Leninism.

But for most of us, what the white chauvinist socialist Left thinks isn't important. The Chinese Revolution and Mao inspired *most* of the world to seek revolutionary socialism and Marxist ideology, because *most* of the world was the victim of Western imperialist super-exploitation and brutal national oppression. Most Third World workers have time and time again been sold out by the white socialist and workers movement, whether it be the classic case of the French workers and peasants in the 1950s, to the 1960s with the Communist Party of the U.S.A. calling Malcolm X a police agent and denouncing the Black Panthers and the Trotskyist parties opposing the Vietnamese national liberation struggle and only supporting the demand to

"Bring the Boys Home," valuing the lives of white boys over Asian peoples. Even today, the term "national liberation" is equated with and dismissed as "nationalism" (deemed a dirty word) by these racist socialists and fake-Leftists.

Most of the New Left in the United States emerged and demarcated itself from the Old Left (primarily the CPUSA and the Trotskyist Socialist Workers Party) by 1969. Several momentous historical factors propelled this emergence: the questions of supporting the Vietnamese national liberation struggle against U.S. imperialism; the rise of the Black Panther Party and the reraising of the gun into U.S. Left politics or continuing Malcolm X's prophetic question of the Bullet vs. the Ballot; and the Cultural Revolution in China, in which a tremendous wave of militant radicalism was being spearheaded by students and youth.

Malcolm X had perceptively remarked, and I'll paraphrase, that the once-common racist slur, "A Chinaman's Chance"—meaning no chance at all—had gone the way of oblivion since the Chinese now had more chance than most of the dark peoples of the world, having made a revolution, kicked out the white imperialist, and created its own nuclear device, joining the up-to-then-all-white boys nuclear club, pushing the question of removing the pipsqueak runt of a country called Taiwan from the United Nations and putting the PRC into its rightful seat as representing the Chinese people.

All of the great twentieth-century radical and revolutionary African American activists and artists have extolled and looked to China. The great radical poet Langston Hughes in the late 1920s, inspired by and supporting the upsurge of Chinese workers' struggles, wrote a magnificent poem, "Roar, China!" Paul Robeson learned to speak Chinese and often sang the revolutionary Chinese anthem "Chi lai!" (which means "Rise Up!"). W.E.B. Du Bois and his family moved to China, where Du Bois died. The fugitive Robert F. Williams, who took up armed self-defense against the Ku Klux Klan in North Carolina and was forced to flee the United States, ended up in China for a very long stay. He raised his two sons there, who speak Chinese fluently. The Williams family were treated as honored political refugees in the PRC. Upon Williams's request, Chairman Mao issued two profound statements in support of the Black American liberation struggle.

The first was in 1963, deploring the rise of racist violence against the U.S. Civil Rights Movement. The final sentence of this historic statement sent profound reverberations through the quickly radicalizing sectors of the Black struggle. Mao said: "The evil system of colonialism and imperialism arose and throve with the enslavement of Negroes and the trade in Negroes, and it will surely come to its end with the complete emancipation of the black people." As I and many others interpreted Mao's statement: the struggle for black liberation, and the liberation of oppressed nations and nationalities in general, is objectively a revolutionary struggle, with or without the support or unity of white oppressor nation workers.

Williams, a few years later, would ask Mao once again for another international statement. On April 6, 1968, after the heinous assassination of Dr. Martin Luther King, Jr., as black ghettos across the United States began to erupt in violent rebellion, Mao made his famous "Statement in Support of the Afro-American Struggle against Violent Repression," calling for total support for black liberation "to end the rule of the U.S. monopoly capitalist class." By the end of the summer of 1968, more than one hundred U.S. cities had gone up in smoke. Robert Williams, exiled in China, was conferred the status of president-in-exile by the Republic of New Afrika, a pro-nationhood radical black activist movement in the United States. Many years later, Robert F. Williams would finally return to the United States and take a job teaching Chinese studies at a small campus in Michigan. He died in 1997.

By the late 1960s in the United States, a New Left had begun to emerge. It rejected several key positions of the Old (white) Left: it supported China as a socialist state and Mao as a genuine Marxist-Leninist and rejected the Soviet Union as having turned into being a social-imperialist power (meaning socialism in words, imperialism in deeds) after its invasion of Hungary, Poland, and Czechoslovakia and its maneuvers to turn Third World liberation organizations and newly independent countries into Soviet puppets. The New Left was fervently revolutionary and rejected the electoral politics and mainstreaming of the CPUSA as it succumbed from the terror of McCarthyism and its own internal rising reformism and liquidationism; the New Left looked seriously toward the Third World, including Third

World peoples inside its own borders (whom I prefer to call oppressed nationalities instead of the depoliticized mainstream term "people of color"). Many in the New Left, by the early 1970s, focused on building a new revolutionary communist party.

I won't discuss the critical importance of China, Mao, and the Black Panthers as my West Coast panelists are in a better position to do so. Let me go into some important examples on the East Coast that reflect this connection and catalyst.

In the early 1970s in New York City, a new revolutionary Asian American organization emerged, composed mostly of college students. They took the name I Wor Kuen, the Cantonese name for the Boxers who were part of an anti-Manchu and anti-imperialist uprising in China at the turn of the century. At first I Wor Kuen described itself as an anti-imperialist revolutionary nationalist organization, though its program, closely modeled after the Black Panther Party Ten-Point Program, did call for socialism. I Wor Kuen started Serve the People programs modeled on the Panthers' Survival Programs. I Wor Kuen soon merged with a Bay Area revolutionary Asian American group, The Red Guard Party, and became the national IWK.

‹ 287

At several college campuses, IWK led the demand for Asian studies as part of the call for ethnic or Third World studies overall. The first Asian studies on the East Coast was at the City College of New York in Harlem, and IWK played a major role. If you simply look at the manifestos of all these early ethnic studies programs you can quickly see how revolutionary they were, and you can see how much of that revolutionary mission has been totally gutted today. Here are some of the main features in the revolutionary vision for Asian and Third World studies:

1. That the curriculum serves the people and promotes revolution. These programs were supposed to be liberated zones to wage the protracted struggle against the mainstream racist, sexist, elitist academy. Instead of producing bureaucrats and yuppies to serve the system, Third World studies would produce revolutionaries with skills and expertise for the movement. The Asian Student Unions, MECHAs, Black Student Unions, and so on, were to be the student wing of

the revolutionary liberation movements. They were to be the incubators for future organizers and warriors. In discrediting and eliminating Marxist and revolutionary theory, postmodernism was promoted in the 1980s and early 1990s as a highfalutin' justification for hyper-individualism and political inactivity by the current crop of antiactivist intellectuals who want to pose as radical. I'm specifically, but not limited to, naming bell hooks, Tricia Rose, Andrew Ross, and the whole bankrupt gamut of what has fashionably become "cultural studies." Studying culture by people who can't create culture.

2. The main way this was to happen was through student-community control over these institutions. The first to be eliminated by the administration and their professorial career-climbing lackeys was the community. So-called "outsiders" were accused of lowering academic standards and wanting political control. Now, I grant you that many horror stories from both sides can be cited, of students being allowed to pass courses simply by political membership, or progressive faculty being denied tenure and fired because of red-baiting, whatever the case—the key questions of What standards and Who decides were clearly decided by the Administration in favor of what we see today. People like myself, who have proven our revolutionary commitment and intellectual/artistic excellence in the real world, without a Ph.D., won't get hired. I have more recordings and establishment honors and awards than most of the professors teaching in this school, and, you know what, not only will they not hire me, I now have no desire to even want a faculty job because I'm having more fun and doing more of what I want on the outside. Not only am I self-taught in my professional career, I paid off my mortgage three years ago at the age of thirty-eight. Now, how many of these professors here can match that? And I'm still a revolutionary!

3. These institutions, we thought, perhaps too naively, could direct resources and talents back to the oppressed communities. Now they've become self-perpetuating and career-aggrandizing vehicles.

The New Left was engaged in many fierce battles, both with the external enemy and within its own. One of the key questions it fought over was what is called The National Question, or the question of how liberation for the oppressed nations and nationalities in the United States would be won. This debate is still being waged. Most of the U.S. oppressed nationality Left started out as anti-imperialist, revolutionary nationalists. But many quickly moved to Marxism, and certainly the prestige and weight of socialist China and Mao had much influence.

I can remember this period in the early 1970s, the great debates between nationalism and Marxism, because I started as a yellow revolutionary nationalist. I strongly identified with the revolutionary thrust of the Black Liberation Movement, Malcolm X, Robert Williams, the Black Panther Party, and the African Liberation Support Committee (ALSC).

‹ 289

Let me now discuss the ALSC, one of the most significant projects in the history of the U.S. twentieth-century Left, but now virtually forgotten, and given almost no attention or recognition by today's social movement scholars or Left historians.

While short-lived, spanning the years 1972 to 1978, the ALSC was possibly the center of anti-imperialist, Pan-Africanist motion in the Black Liberation struggle in the United States. It gathered together a broad ideological range including Maulana Ron Karenga, Haki Madhubuti, Amiri Baraka, Abdul Alkalimat, Mark Smith, and many, many others. In May 1972, as a part of Malcolm X's birthday, the ALSC sponsored a mass demonstration that became African Liberation Day in Washington, D.C. More than forty thousand workers, students, youth, and activists came to support the African Liberation struggles in Guinea-Bissau/Cape Verde Islands, Angola, Mozambique, Zimbabwe (its colonial name was then Rhodesia), Azania (its colonial name, which it still keeps, is South Africa), and Namibia (its former colonial name being South-West Africa). As the Black Liberation struggle moved to the Left, so too did the African American working class assume anti-imperialist positions. African American dockworkers in North and South Carolina boycotted Rhodesian chrome, refusing to unload it from South African ships for U.S. companies. "Ban the Krugerrand" came out of this movement.

In June 1974, the Sixth Pan-African Congress was hosted by

Julius Nyerere in Tanzania, a country that had been friendly to and hosted many an exiled African liberation movement. Black activists from the United States went and were sternly lectured by their African revolutionary brothers and sisters, who were engaged in life-and-death armed struggle, to check their narrow nationalism and to check out scientific socialism. In a few months, former nationalists like Baraka would discard nationalism and turn to Marxism-Leninism–Mao Zedong Thought. One of the most dynamic organizers and theoreticians in this transition from nationalism to Marxism was Owusu Sadaukai, a college activist turned Marxist and factory worker in North Carolina and leader of the Revolutionary Workers League, a black-originated now-Marxist organization. Others were making the move to Marxism, including the Dodge Revolutionary Union Movement (DRUM) in Detroit and other black auto worker-based radical groups, which came together to form the Black Workers Congress. By 1975, the largest cultural nationalist organization with chapters in over thirteen cities, the Congress of Afrikan Peoples under Baraka's leadership, would adopt Marxism-Leninism–Mao Zedong Thought and become the Revolutionary Communist League (RCL). I was then a young teenager, but I attended every meeting in this great debate, vigorously trying to defend nationalism against Marxism as a "white boys'" ideology.

During this time, Stokely Carmichael would become Kwame Ture and take up Pan-African scientific socialism with its strange political orientation of primarily focusing on the mother continent and putting the struggle of U.S. blacks as secondary and only to be supportive of struggles on the mother continent.

But even the most die-hard cultural nationalists still gave props to China. Karenga learned to speak Chinese and has visited China on a number of occasions. Poet Sonia Sanchez, who, when I first studied under her, was into the Nation of Islam, had gone on an American delegation to the PRC in 1972 as one of the trips sponsored by the U.S.-China People's Friendship Association (USCPFA), a mass movement that favored recognition of the PRC and promoted pro-China opinion in the United States. Joining Sonia was another prominent black American writer, Earl Ofari, who wrote *The Myth of Black Capitalism*.

In 1977, with support from the USCPFA, the all-black cultural nationalist Council of Independent Black Institutions brought the first all-black delegation to the PRC after the Black Panthers' historic visit in 1971. These were hard-core cultural nationalists who were building totally independent institutions such as schools, community centers, communal businesses, and presses. The delegation of twenty included Jitu Weusi, founder and leader of The East, an independent community-controlled school and cultural center in black Brooklyn; Kalamu ya Salaam, writer/activist/editor of *The Black Collegian* magazine; members from Haki Madhubuti's Institute for Positive Education in Chicago with its publishing wing, Third World Press, the most successful black-owned independent publishing house.

These were cultural nationalists who disagreed adamantly with Marxism, but who recognized that socialist China had eliminated illiteracy, wiped out drug addiction (when before 1949, one out of four Chinese men were opium addicts), and created miraculous social changes in a Third World country without any white Western help. ‹ 291 Indeed, the Chinese had extended much aid to other Third World countries, including sending its own engineers and workers who ate, worked, and slept alongside Africans in the building of the TanZam railway that connected the inland country of Zambia with the African coast of Tanzania. African guerrillas also secretly trained for armed struggle inside the PRC.

Unlike today, where divisions and mutual stereotypes are held between African Americans and Asian Americans, back in the days of greater "Third World Unity," I can personally attest that much of the Black Nationalist leadership looked at Asians as Third World brothers and sisters. The force of China's example played a major factor in this attitude.

It was Muhammad Ali, refusing the draft, who proclaimed, "No Vietnamese ever called me a Nigger." A proud and glorious tradition of Afro-Asian anti-imperialist solidarity has existed, from Ho Chi Minh spending time in Harlem as a student to a rap group today calling itself the Wu-Tang Clan after a Taoist anti-Manchu and anti-imperialist sect (though one would hope these rappers would be more politically conscious).

Before I close, I want to state that I still maintain that two questions that distinguish revolution from reformism in the United States are:

1. The national question and recognizing the independent revolutionary character of Third World peoples' struggle; the need to reject forced assimilation and the falseness of integration, i.e., the white chauvinist position that our struggles need to be validated by the inclusion of and proximity to white people and traditions.

2. The question of upholding Mao Zedong Thought as Marxism-Leninism applied to the struggle for national liberation against imperialism. By the late 1970s the U.S. antirevisionist communist movement (which all started upholding China over the sell-out Soviet Union and its American shadow, the CPUSA), was unraveling in bitter disagreement over post-Mao China, and, in my opinion, not-so-coincidentally rehabilitating the Soviet Union on international lines and adopting a thoroughly white chauvinist line domestically by totally liquidating The Black Nation, the Chicano Nation, and calling for a repellant socialist integrationism and assimilation. Condemning all nationalism as reactionary, narrow, and totally rejecting national consciousness, national identity, and national pride in the context that our struggles are for liberation and not integration.

Last year I started my own cultural production company, Big Red Media, which produces the Sheroes Calendars and my recordings. The name Big Red comes from two of my most important political icons: Malcolm X, who was known as Big Red for being tall with reddish hair; and for Mao Zedong, who truly was a big Red.

Notes on the National Question:
Oppressed Nations and
Liberation Struggles within the U.S.A.

THIS ESSAY WILL SEEK to address four general topics: What is the National Question(s) and why is it important to the U.S. socialist revolution? What have been incorrect positions and distortions that liquidate the National Question(s) in the United States? What can we propose as a correct understanding of the National Question in theory and in practice? and an analysis and discussion of specific National Questions in the United States.

I have chosen to enumerate the notes or points I will make in order to convey that this essay is a work in progress and to welcome direct debate and discussion on specific points.

What Is the National Question(s) and Why Is It Important to the U.S. Socialist Revolution?

1. National oppression defined is simply the oppression of nations and nationalities. It is the systematic, historical oppression of an entire people—of all the classes of the oppressed nation or nationality. Historically, national oppression includes all of the forms of oppression, including discrimination, racism, ethnocentrism, stereotyping, disenfranchisement, genocide, violence, injustice, and inequality. It is fundamentally a by-product of the division of the world between

Work in progress; not previously published.

oppressed and oppressor nations, accentuated and globalized by the advent and growth of the imperialist stage of capitalist development. This division is marked by intense inequality between the affluent imperialist and developed capitalist "centers" and the impoverished "periphery" of the "third" and "fourth" worlds (a more recently coined term that refers to the indigenous peoples who are oppressed nationalities and nations within third world countries, and, in the case of Australia and the United States, oppressed nationality indigenous peoples within first world nation-states).

....

2. The national question has changed from "an internal question" of rising capitalist Western/Western European nation-states that underwent a bourgeois democratic revolution that consolidated the rule of the capitalist class by replacing the former feudal ruling class, monarchy, and theocracy, to "an external question" of a worldwide imperialist system of finance capital. The national movements in the former period of rising capitalism were bourgeois, dealing with the ascendancy of the new capitalist class to consolidate its territorial market, to construct its infrastructure to administer, facilitate, coordinate, and manage its capital expansion. The struggle of workers in such nation-states was to overthrow their exploiter bourgeoisie. Marxism is the theory and practice of class struggle that arises in the period of rising capitalism. It is "European" because it originated in the heart of the bourgeois revolution, industrialized Western Europe. Under the worldwide system of imperialism, imperialism, and not the local bourgeoisie, is the principal enemy of the national movements. Leninism is Marxism applied to the struggle against imperialism, no longer rising capitalism, but multi- and transnational capitalism. Leninism is revolutionary because it demands real equality (the elimination of national oppression and privileges) and not just judicial or legal national equality (bourgeois democratic rights granted by a nation-state ostensibly to "all" of its citizens). Under imperialism, stronger nations oppress weaker ones and different nations and nationalities are forcibly annexed, even bought (as Alaska was by the United States from Russia), and joined into one nation-state. Entire peoples are dispersed, through forced migration (con-

tract and coolie labor), or split asunder (the United States seizure of the southwest territories from Mexico).

Imperialism, from a Marxist viewpoint, is not simply a nation carrying out a policy of nastiness and aggression toward other nations, but a system of monopoly capitalism in which large corporations (finance capital) extend across the planet and dominate and control vast areas far beyond their home borders. Lenin revealed five essential features of imperialism: (1) Concentration and centralization of production and capital developed to a monopoly stage; (2) The merger of banking and industrial capital to form finance capital or a financial oligarchy; (3) Export of capital, as distinguished from the export of commodities (which of course continues as well in the flood of Western consumer goods and cultural commodities across the globe). The main feature of capital export are the huge loans with vampire interest rates that large banks and monetary organizations such as the IMF make to poor, developing countries; (4) International capitalist monopolies or cartels (the multi- and transnational corporation) that divide the world as their spoils; and (5) Constant redivision of the world (into First World vs. Third World; between regions and countries), which leads to small and world wars as the physical expression of economic conflict, and the intensification of all the world's contradictions, which sets the conditions for socialist revolutions. Competition between economic giants leads to greater and greater monopolies that compete with one another in their quest for cheaper labor, more raw materials, and expanded export markets, which leads to wars of control and domination, and the possibility of revolution, or the opposite of imperialism: wars of national liberation.

‹ 295

In Lenin's analysis, imperialism is a "dying, moribund" system for its parasitism and decay in creating a class of idlers, professional "coupon clippers" who play no role in production, living off of speculation, usury, quicksand credit advancement, ruthless interest rate gouging, cultivation of debt dependency, and a layer of white-collar managers, administrators, ideologues, propagandists, and promoters, who contribute nothing healthy, worthwhile, or useful.

Imperialism (economic domination and indirect rule) has its roots in colonialism (political domination and direct rule), but it is not colonization, though it may be metaphorically described as such. Colonization set the stage for the massive accumulation needed for imperialism. Land, resources, and labor had to be captured and controlled. The super-profits of imperialism fuel opportunism. So great are the trickle-down spoils of these super-profits that entire sections of the working class are bribed and "bought off" (the political meaning of opportunism). They are corrupted with racism, infected with oppressor nation patriotism, trained to identify with the bourgeoisie, and live materially better off than most of the world and thereby have a vested interest and stake in First World supremacy. This "labor aristocracy" began to rise at the end of Marx's life as rising capitalism was transitioning into monopoly capitalism. In today's world, the labor aristocracy is particularly large and potent in the West, being both a stratum of well-paid workers in highly elite trades as well as union bureaucrats with large salaries and company stock options.

While a few colonies still remain in the world, and the United States still has colonial territorial possessions, including Puerto Rico, "American" Samoa, Guam, the Marshall Islands, and the "U.S." Virgin Islands, its largest control extends over "oppressed nations" that have been annexed and geographically incorporated into the American empire nation-state, including Hawaii, the Southwest territory that Chicano liberationists refer to as "Atzlan," and what I and others argue is the oppressed New African (Black Belt) nation, and the ongoing prison house of Native First Nations. At one point, some American radical sociologists (confused by the methodology of bourgeois sociology and not radical enough to study the national question) described the oppressed black nation as an "internal colony," since it seemed to share features of other external colonies such as an external police force, external businesses profiteering from ghetto cheap labor and consumers, and so on.

....

3. Stalin's criteria of a nation overwhelmingly focuses on Western European nations, especially in the period of rising capitalism, and lacks much focus on the rest of the world, especially in the era of imperialism and from the impact of Western European colonization, which drew up many artificial borders to benefit colonial powers. For example, many of the borders known today as nation-states within Africa began by the repartitioning of European colonial powers at the

Berlin Conference of 1885. These borders were artificial and problematic: grouping vastly different cultural, linguistic, and ethnic groups and nationalities into forced unions that exacerbated divisions, conflicts, and hostilities. Stalin never took up the task of investigating the national movements in the "Third World." While his "four criteria" (common territory or land-base; common economic life; common language; and common "psychological make-up" or culture) are a useful guide to understanding the emergence of nations, especially for Western Europe, they are fundamentally flawed for the rest of the world, which had national development disrupted and distorted by colonialism and imperialism. Therefore the oppressed nations and nationalities that have emerged in much of the world will not consistently reflect any or all of the "four criteria." Dialectically, they will reflect unevenness, with partial and inconsistent features. Indeed, for oppressed nations under imperialism, many of their "common" features are a result of coercion and oppression, such as a "common language" from either a former colonial power (such as English or French) or the ruling nationality, all of which makes for intensified national struggle.

‹ 297

Stalin's "evidence" and "research" of the national question ignores the vast majority of the world: Africa, Asia, the Americas, Oceania. Not only is his empirical foundation problematic, but his overall method may also be extremely problematic. A more developed critique of Stalin and "Stalinism" must unfold. It is my position that Stalin's method is fundamentally flawed as being un-dialectical and antimaterialist. Much of the U.S. Marxist-Leninist movement was raised on Stalin's *Dialectical and Historical Materialism* study primer, which even Mao eventually rejected. Stalin elevated all forms of struggle and contradiction to the level of antagonistic contradictions (as evidenced in Stalin's practice of jailings, repression, and killings), an "either/or" proposition. Therefore, to quote Stalin as "truth" or "scientific" is very problematic.

Lenin never advanced criteria or a definition for "nation" but focused on "national movements" and the "right to self-determination," which included at least three options (secession, federation, and some form of autonomy). Lenin vigorously fought the liquidation of any or all of these options as fundamental opposition to the right of self-determination. He repeatedly condemned as "national chauvinist" the preclusion of or preference for any of these options when the national movements themselves haven't made their determination.

Even if Stalin's criteria for "nation" are upheld and used as Harry Haywood did for the Black Nation and as the August Twenty-Ninth Movement did for the Chicano Nation, then the "right to self-determination" should be upheld without qualifications or caveats. The rebuttals to the existence of Black and Chicano Nations primarily are statistical, citing out-migration and integration into the general U.S. population. While Bob Wing, Max Elbaum, and others, particularly around The Line of March Organization almost two decades ago, tried to rebut the Black Nation thesis in favor of the black struggle as antiracism and for integration, they never won over any substantial sector of the Black Liberation Movement. Time and time again, any political position that refuses to respect "the right of self-determination" has been incapable of and ineffective in providing leadership to the national struggles in any revolutionary way as such white chauvinist Leftist positions are taken to be overwhelmingly integrationist and assimilationist.

Why did Lenin not advance any specific criteria for nation? I believe that Lenin knew that new nations would continue to rise under imperialism and that they would take many forms, of which the struggle for land would still be central, along with new demands. New nationalities have definitely emerged out of the cauldron of the multinational United States, and white supremacist settler-colonial national oppression has constantly spawned new national movements. For example, the Asian Movement that emerged in the late 1960s and early 1970s was a movement that combined national movements of the Chinese, Japanese, and Filipinos, along with other Asian and Pacific Islander nationalities. The Chicano Movement seeks to unify Mexican-born, American-born people of Mexican descent and indigenous peoples of the Southwest. The ongoing debate in the U.S. Left is which of these national movements are "nations." Regardless of whether we will be able to determine "oppressed nation status" for a particular national struggle and unite around its having "the right of self-determination," the national movements continue to be a constant source of anti-imperialist struggle. A more focused discussion of what oppressed nations do exist within the United States follows.

The U.S. proletariat is multinational and cuts across the various oppressed nations and nationalities. It is still highly debated as to whether it is even correct to cite a "white proletariat," since some argue that settler-colonialism may have made most "whites" part of the labor aristocracy, or worse, "settlers." Others argue that the white oppressor nation, whose government sits in Washington, D.C. (and refuses to grant statehood to this mostly black district, ruling it like an occupational force purely for its own benefit), has a disproportionately smaller proletariat than the oppressed nations and nationalities. It is my position that, among the U.S. proletariat, there are white, European Americans. However there is no such thing as a distinctive "white proletariat." Indeed, representing and signifying anything to be "white" is racist, such as saying "white American music," which is really the music of appropriation. While there do exist European traditions and forms such as the regional music of Appalachia that are predominantly practiced by white European-descended Americans, to call it "white" is to mean "dominant" and "legitimate." White members of the U.S. proletariat suffer exploitation. They create surplus value that is appropriated by the capitalist. The struggle is to win them away from their historical primary identification with being "white" for a (multinational) class identity and consciousness that consistently rejects national oppression, white privilege, and white supremacist racist exclusion.

< 299

What is the basic problem with the formulation of "racism" and the struggle as "anti-racism"?

National oppression means oppression over nations and nationalities, and is not reducible to racism as the "race/class/gender" non-Marxists would have us think. Racism is a part of the particular historical and social development of U.S. national oppression. The material basis of racism is national oppression. To reduce the national struggles to one of "anti-racism" is both wrong and objectionable for diminishing the extent of national oppression, for narrowing and limiting the political solution to be integration and assimilation as opposed to national liberation and the seizure of state power and control over territory/land.

Race is a myth, a pseudo-science developed by European colonialism to justify the domination of the world's people by the "white" peoples of Europe. There are no pure "races," since humanity is hybrid. Physical features exist along a spectrum of variation and mixture.

Furthermore, physical features don't cause social hierarchy. Race, as a "bio-political" construction, is manipulated. Besides, as one young activist posed the matter, "What race are Puerto Ricans?" They are a mixture of native, African, and European. Why were Japanese legally considered white in South Africa under apartheid, while Chinese and Asian Indians were classified as "colored," even though they are the same "race"? Eastern and southern Europeans, prior to the twentieth century, were deemed inferior races, but were subsequently incorporated into white supremacist-colonist United States when they were sufficiently assimilated as "whites." As Kalamu ya Salaam points out, "The de-ethnicization of Europeans is the process of them becoming white."

The Pan-Africanist Congress of Azania, often accused by then-Soviet supporters as "nationalist," advanced the slogan, "Only one race: the human race!" Therefore, Marxists as "scientific materialists" should reject race as a spurious falsehood. In the sociohistorical development of the United States, the indigenous peoples had to be wiped out or forcibly removed from their lands in order to allow for the expansion and building of white settler-colonial society (the founding thirteen colonies). Whether a white settler-colonial proletariat developed and to what degree continues to be debated and argued. Many of the white settlers were not workers (transplanted proletarians from Europe) but property owners, large and small farmers, craftspeople, merchants and mercantilists, and aspiring industrialists. It remains to be settled in scholarly debates as to when and how a white working class took root in U.S. society. However, in my view, a large influx of white immigrants, beginning with the Irish in the mid-nineteenth century to ongoing waves of southern and eastern Europeans during the late nineteenth and early twentieth centuries, and today's post–Iron Curtain immigrants, came to the United States as workers from Europe and continued to be workers in the burgeoning U.S. steel, automotive, manufacturing, and service industries. The demand for labor by U.S. industry during its surging rise in the late 1800s and early 1900s was so great that European, along with Caribbean, Asian, and Latin American workers had to be recruited in massive numbers, repopulating both the nation-state and dramatically increasing the size of the U.S. proletariat, including workers of European ancestry (who were predominantly Irish, Italian, Greek, Polish, and Eastern European).

The "anti-racism" Leftists virtually ignore the struggle around land rights. They are glaringly silent especially with regard to the struggles of Native peoples, not even attempting to study and to understand how Native peoples in the United States relate to the national question. They tend to see the national question as "race" with a focus not on fighting all forms of national oppression, but only on issues of "racism" and "racial discrimination" with a program anchored on "integration" as the solution. When the national movements or oppressed nationalities don't ally with them (i.e., with these white Left groups) or adopt their positions, they are dismissed and dissed as "nationalist."

Nationalism vs. National Liberation:
Building the National Movements

‹ 301

1. Revolutionary socialists/ Marxists/communists are internationalists and thereby reject nationalism per se. Nationalism is the exclusivity, primacy, and privilege of nations and nationalities over the working class, which is multinational and international. Nationalism, no matter if it is "revolutionary nationalism" and recognizes and fights imperialism, is still "my nation or nationality first." Internationalism is both "the class first over nation or nationality," as well as "my national liberation is supported by and must in turn support the fight against the oppression of all nations." Therefore, the internationalist is the most consistent and leading fighter against his or her particular national oppression, "a patriot" of the oppressed nation, or, as Lenin put it, "internationalism applied" to the national struggle. The international (multinational) working class wants to abolish nation-states, as quickly as possible, in favor of a classless world without boundaries, class divisions, nation-state armies, and governments. However, as active historical materialists, we recognize that the abolition of the nation-state can only happen after the destruction of capitalism (which today is multinational or transnational capitalism, namely imperialism). Capitalism grew upon the construction of the nation-state and the nation-state

dialectically supports capitalism. Colonialism and imperialism constantly redivides and redraws the world map. The phenomenon of nation-states is that they splinter and divide, as well as merge and expand via annexation and merger (both political and economic). The leading role of Mao as theorist and national liberation struggle leader distinguished and demarcated Marxism-Leninism from Trotskyism (Trotsky and his supporters consider Trotskyism to be Marxist-Leninist). Mao rejected the "skipping of stages" advocated by Trotsky and upheld the revolutionary importance of waging the war of national liberation as a necessary stage in the process of socialist revolution. Without removing the external threat of imperialism (in the case of the Chinese Revolution, most immediately Japanese fascist aggression and the penetrating claws of Euro-American imperialism through the foreign concessions exacted upon China), socialism would never be achieved. Unlike Western Europe, the white settler-colonial societies of North America, Australia, New Zealand, and Japan (which was never colonized), the rest of the world had its history "interrupted" by the conquest of colonialism and Western imperialist penetration. Therefore the bourgeois democratic revolution (the coming to power and dominance of capitalist democracies) in the "Third World" would not be possible since the nascent forces of indigenous capital were made to serve the First World. Entire societies and lands were carved up by Western powers, their indigenous leadership replaced by compradors (a class of carpetbaggers and native puppets), and their resources drained for the benefit of foreign profiteers, resulting in "underdevelopment" (the process in which a country is made poor and kept poorer). Only with the removal of both colonialism (direct rule from the outside) by independence and imperialism (native rule but with economic rule from the outside) by national liberation can the conditions be paved for socialist revolution by forgoing the stage of bourgeois democratic capitalist revolution that the West and Japan had undergone.

. . . .

2. The old Revolutionary Union (RU) had the position that "all nationalism is reactionary" and proceeded to condemn all forms of national-in-form organizing and struggle and alienated large sectors of both

nationalists and the national movements. They became easy "straw man" targets for such critics as Native American nationalist ("Indigenist") Ward Churchill in his book *Marxism and Native Americans* (South End Press). Thus, in many unfortunate but understandable ways, the Marxist-Leninist Left became viewed as "the white Left." The various progressive, radical, and revolutionary groups in the national movements are not all nationalists. The national movements are not predominantly nationalist, either. The national movements are a united front consisting of different ideologies and class forces, objectively united against imperialist national oppression, but with very different strategic goals. It would be a serious mistake to equate nationalism with all militants who prioritize national-in-form struggles. Nationalism is not national consciousness, identity, and pride. The former is a consolidated bourgeois worldview that justifies the primacy, exclusivity, and privilege of one nation, nationality, or national struggle over others. National consciousness, identity, and pride, however, is the consciousness that "I am not what my oppressor makes me to be." It is consciousness, identification, and pride in the assertion "I am an African," and not a "Negro"; "I am an Asian," and not an "Oriental"; "I am Latino/a" and not "Hispanic." Many individuals and forces in the national movements aren't nationalist, though their focus is national-in-form struggle. White chauvinism in the U.S. Left has concentrated its attack upon "nationalism" and "nationalist deviations" as the principal error in the debate around the national question. The principal attack and criticism should be on white chauvinism and racist manifestations of the theory and practice of the U.S. Left. Time after time, the most consistent threat to the unity and advancement of the U.S. Left has *not* been nationalism or nationalist errors made by Marxists, but white chauvinism.

....

3. Revolutionary nationalists are anti-imperialists and many do express internationalist sentiments. Malcolm X and the Black Panthers were great revolutionary nationalists, the Panthers even espousing support for socialism; Huey P. Newton expressed a willingness to send Panther cadres to Vietnam to join the fighting forces of the Vietcong. This internationalist proclamation by Newton was both

bold and historic in connecting the Black Liberation struggle with the worldwide struggle against U.S. imperialism and for its expression of Afro-Asian solidarity. However, revolutionary nationalism pulls up short in the revolutionary process of eliminating all classes, for unqualified support for the leadership of the proletariat over all other classes, and for contextualizing the national struggle and its demands and tactical and strategic objectives within the context of the broader international struggle against capitalism. For example, would African American revolutionary nationalists support the struggle of Asian factory workers against black capitalist elites, or even more particularly of Haitian workers against the black American petite bourgeoisie who own wealthy vacation homes and property interests in Haiti and the Caribbean? Internationalists fight within their own nation and nationality to support the freedom of other oppressed nations and nationalities. Huey P. Newton recognized that the Vietnamese were closer to defeating U.S. imperialism than the Black Liberation struggle in the United States, and it was his internationalism (somewhat later bizarrely self-described as "revolutionary inter-communalism") that impelled him to commit the Black Panthers to join the Vietcong should they be asked.

304 ›

. . . .

4. Cultural nationalism and cultural nationalists have earned a particular scorn from many Marxist-Leninist sectors. Such a position of blanket disdain and condemnation for cultural nationalism and cultural nationalists fails to recognize any anti-imperialist aspects to this component of the national movements. In more recent, post-sixties times, Afrocentrism and Afrocentrists have been viewed as cultural nationalism and cultural nationalists, respectively. One unique caveat to the position that cultural nationalism is the most reactionary and narrow form of nationalism is the history of the Congress of African Peoples (CAP), the largest black cultural nationalist formation in the United States during the 1960s and 1970s. CAP would go through much internal struggle and a Marxist-Leninist direction would emerge around its then–General Secretary and Chairman Amiri Baraka, changing its ideology and name to the Revolutionary Communist League (Marxism–Leninism–Mao Zedong

Thought) and, in 1979-80, merging with the League of Revolutionary Struggle (which came out of the Asian and Chicano movements).
By the mid-1980s the LRS would become both the largest Marxist-
Leninist organization in the United States in the New Communist
(anti-revisionist) Movement and have a majority of oppressed nationality membership and leadership. All nationalists and forms of
nationalism—whether labeled "revolutionary" or "cultural"—must be
evaluated by their objective, practical role in the struggle against imperialism. For example, the CAP always supported the national liberation struggles in Africa, the Caribbean, Latin America, and Vietnam.
Maulana Karenga, a renowned and controversial "cultural nationalist" ideologue and leader, has consistently supported socialist China.
He and Kalamu ya Salaam were part of U.S. delegations that visited
the PRC. What probably earned the ire of the "white Left" was the
"anti-white" positions of the cultural nationalists, their seemingly
atavistic promotion of precolonial Africa and their refusal to submit
to white guidance and acceptance (probably very justified, given how
white chauvinist the white Left is). The cultural nationalists emphasized the need to fight imperialist cultural aggression and promote
African identity, pride, and consciousness. They were very capable
on-the-ground organizers, leaders in struggles for political representation, schools, and community control, building housing, cultural
and educational institutions, and alternative presses. When many of
the newly Marxist oppressed nationalities renounced nationalism as
"narrow and backward," and abandoned their former work in such
communities and institution-building projects, the more apolitical
and reformist cultural nationalists took over these "spaces." That is
why their influence is felt so strongly in today's Afrocentricity movement instead of more revolutionary views. Indeed, some of the great
"Afrocentricists," such as Cheikh Anta Diop, were Marxists, as quiet
as it's kept. These more apolitical and reformist cultural nationalists, after the revolutionary cultural nationalists-turned-Marxists
abandoned the national movements, took over and maintained small
community bookstores, organizations, college programs, and publications. The difference was remarkable when in the late 1980s I
visited both Marxist Abdul Alkalimat's (now defunct) 21st Century
Bookstore and cultural nationalist Haki Madhubuti's Center for
Positive Thought bookstore, both in black Chicago. The former was

a barely functioning dustbin, the latter an oasis (albeit Bundist, namely that they refused to carry books of black writers contrary to their political and ideological liking).

. . . .

5. Oppressed nationality Marxists must be both political *and* cultural leaders in the national movements. The mass popularity among poor and ghetto blacks for Garvey or Malcolm X, in contrast to the more white Left support for Du Bois and Robeson, stems from the former two leaders as seen by the masses as symbolic and cultural projections of national pride and militant national consciousness, though Garvey was a criminal and Malcolm's life was cut short before any real alternative institutions were built post–Nation of Islam. When an oppressed nationality militant is seen as tied to whites, be it through marriage, funding, celebrity, or what have you, they are dismissed as dupes or dependents of white society. This is the damage of "integrationism" as the primary goal of seeking closeness, acceptance, and approval by whites, by the oppressor. The oppressed nationality masses seek consistent and militant alternative cultural symbols and representation, counter to the white supremacist, Eurocentric, oppressor nation lifestyles, values, images, and aesthetics. Oppressed nationality culture, or the vast majority of it, creates, defines, and elaborates a tradition and continuum of resistance and struggle. The most vital and significant cultural traditions and forms affirm humanity against inhumanity, freedom against oppression, and beauty against degradation, stereotyped distortions, and minstrelsy. Atavistic and backward cultural nationalist constructs and propositions (such as polygamy, male dominance, romanticized notions of precolonial societies) must be opposed as antihistorical and oppressive. Concurrently, a self-proclaimed "antiessentialist" multiculturalism, which disavows a heritage, continuum, and tradition of resistance and struggle, must also be opposed for being nothing more than a neo-melting pot thesis. Marxists stand for multicultural/multinational unity/voluntary amalgamation *free* of white supremacy, national oppression, and nationalism!

. . . .

6. Oppressed nationality Marxists uphold the best and most progressive aspects of national culture, music, the arts, and literature, and personify and uphold these values as part of being at the forefront of building a revolutionary culture of national liberation. In an interview with Dr. Kenneth Clark, the prominent black social psychologist, who is politically mainstream and integrationist, Malcolm X asserted that those blacks in interracial marriages (that is, with whites) can't be leaders of the black masses. While any person has the right to love, have sex with, and marry anyone they choose, oppressor nationality (white) and oppressed nationality romantic relationships and marriage are especially fraught with problematic issues about the degree of white assimilation and integrationism on the part of the oppressed nationality person. Hypergamy and sociological analyses of out-marriage as forms of social mobility and as indicators of white assimilation are all part of the complicated matrix of national oppression. While it is incorrect to have a policy discouraging "interracial" (i.e., oppressed nationality-white) relationships, it is not incorrect to have a policy encouraging national culture, identity, and pride, including national-in-form romance and relationships. To share a brief anecdote, a member of the Trotskyist Freedom Socialist Party attributed the demise of the LRS to "nationalism." As a former LRS member, I would disagree and attribute it to "integrationism," as almost all of the Asian-majority Central Committee leadership, both men and women, were married to or relating to whites. That part of the revolutionary decline stemmed from the belittlement of national culture except for the more white mainstream–acceptable forms, and the decision to interpret "empowerment" for oppressed nationality communities as becoming integrated into the reformism of the Democratic Party through David Dinkins, Jesse Jackson, and electoral and academic careers.

‹ 307

Building the National Movements, National-In-Form Organizations and "Institution Building"

1. The national struggles inevitably spawn revolutionary national-in-form organizations when there does not exist the leading presence of a genuine multinational communist party in a multinational state as the United States. Such upsurges occurred in the twentieth

century in two periods. The first was in the early 1910s and 1920s with the rise of the African Blood Brotherhood, a collective of black revolutionary socialists and revolutionary nationalists. The second, in the late 1960s and early 1970s, was by far the greatest upsurge, and included the Revolutionary Action Movement, the Black Panther Party, I Wor Kuen/Red Guard Party and other Asian revolutionary groups, Chicano groups such as the Brown Berets, the August Twenty-Ninth Movement and others, Puerto Rican groups such as the Young Lords Party, the League of Puerto Rican Revolutionaries, and others, and the American Indian Movement and the League of First Nations. This will continue to happen as we see today upon the ashes of the Left and nationalist movements, the rise of the New African Peoples Organization and the New African Liberation Front, some new Chicano revolutionary nationalist groups, and other fledgling revolutionary national-in-form organizations, many revolutionary nationalist, with some proclaiming themselves to be a hybrid of nationalists and Marxists.

....

2. "Institution building," "empowerment," "self-reliance," and "community control" are all mass slogans raised by the national struggles against integration, assimilation, and national oppression and for political and economic independence and "self-determination." A great tradition of self-help and independent institutions exists, including the African Free School movement, community cultural centers and social programs, media/cultural/arts projects, the "serve the people" and "survival programs," and so on. However, since the revolutionary upsurges of the late 1960s and early 1970s, many of these efforts have faded out or, worse, been hijacked by reformism. The U.S. ruling class (its government and foundations) initiated the "Great Society" programs in order to undercut and usurp the popularity and mass support for many of these revolutionary-initiated community programs and institutions. The not-for-profit programs and organizations that followed, heavily funded and propped up by the U.S. ruling class, fostered a new strata of "poverty pimps," funding hustlers and Democratic Party brokers. Black studies and other ethnic studies,

the struggle for which was led by revolutionaries, have now become academic ivory towers in striving for legitimacy with the administration and academia as a whole. The departments, once a bastion for radical education and activism, first eliminated student and community activist control and decision-making input, then removed Leftist and committed faculty, and finally replaced both curriculum and personnel with bourgeois acceptable standards and staff.

....

3. When revolutionaries liquidate the national question by abandoning community organizing, in the belief that such a focus is "narrow" and "nationalist," for a multinational industrial workplace focus, they abdicate leadership of the national struggles to the cultural nationalists.

‹ 309

....

4. National-in-form mass organizations must be built as *liberated zones*. They must become beacons to all who want to seriously fight for national liberation by joining the guerrillas. They cannot be 501(c)3 nonprofits that receive the majority of their funds from the government or private foundations; instead they must rely upon membership support and their own entrepreneurial savvy and grit. As liberated zones, they function with discipline and seriousness and thereby earn the respect of the masses. "Serve the people/survival" programs must always include a strong dose of revolutionary propaganda and agitation. People's cultural constructions (such as Kwanzaa) must be clearly anti-imperialist projections. Such community-building (via health clinics, food co-ops, community schools, cultural spaces, and housing) must create *better* alternatives than the mainstream social services. A high standard of red-and-expert must be held for all cadres doing such institution and community building to avoid the co-optation of reformism and reliance upon outside funding. Those revolutionaries working in the universities and nonprofits should devote all of their energies to expanding space and resources for revolutionaries, direct organizing, and channeling

material aid to the liberated zones and to the guerrillas who don't get jobs in the system. Indeed, there is much to learn from the struggles and experiences of immigrant oppressed nationalities who have built underground economies, their own language presses, and schools— the very "institutions" that American-born oppressed nationalities are so lacking.

Building National Culture, Identity and Pride

1. In theorizing and leading the war of national liberation of Guinea-Bissau against Portuguese colonialism and Euro-American imperialism in Africa, Amilcar Cabral proclaimed: "national liberation begins as an act of culture." Cabral, and all who have seriously fought colonialism and imperialist national oppression, recognized that oppressed peoples must decolonize their consciousness first, to no longer worship or fear their oppressors, to discard the image of themselves fostered by the oppressor nationality, as a first step in the process of national liberation. National consciousness, discussed considerably by Frantz Fanon in his brilliant unity of psychological theory and Marxism, is essential to building the national liberation movement. Oppressed people will not fight for their liberation if they are deracinated, cut off from the roots of their history and culture, brainwashed and inculcated by the language, values, cultural practices, and symbols of their oppressor-colonizer. Ngũgĩ wa Thiong'o, the great Kenyan writer and cultural activist, was imprisoned by the Kenyan government for asserting that native African languages (Kikuyu in the case of Kenya) should be promulgated among the people in an attempt to erase the colonial influence of English and European cultural propaganda. The Kenyan government, in homage and in service to European imperialism (a.k.a. "neocolonialism") couldn't accept this affront and challenge to the cultural supremacy of their Western masters.

....

2. Marxists never support nationalism qua nationalism, but are the staunchest progenitors of national culture, pride, and identity. The

nationalism of oppressed nationalities is progressive only so far as it opposes imperialism. However, to lead the national movements in a consistent revolutionary direction, the proletariat must lead. The job of the communists must be to assume the role of being the fiercest upholders and fighters for national culture, community, democracy, inclusion; to oppose narrowness, privilege, and rivalry; and to lead the national movements in a clearly revolutionary direction, heightening the struggle against imperialism in all its forms: cultural, social, political, and economic. To unite the national movements, the communist leadership must show that it will fight for the class interests of the oppressed nationality petite bourgeoisie when they are consistent with opposing imperialism and promoting democracy.

. . . .

3. For those oppressed nationalities in which a large number of the ‹ 311 people are immigrants, such as Asian Pacific Americans or Latinos, uniting the American-born and immigrant is critical, since these peoples are often sharply divided within their communities. White assimilation, with its concomitant loss of language and cultural heritage, is a function of national oppression. Ridiculing and looking down at immigrants is a function of internalized oppression. A unique, distinctive, and revolutionary Asian Pacific American culture expresses a synthesis of traditional cultures and contemporary Western ones, especially "Western" forms originating from other oppressed nationalities in the United States (primarily African American; American national music is essentially African American).

. . . .

4. Much of the Black Arts Movements and its attendant cultural pride movements among other U.S. oppressed nationalities has been criticized by liberal academics as advocating "essentialism," namely a "blacker than thou" proscriptive cultural policing. While some of the forms of nationalism are guilty of being narrow and extreme, the Black Arts Movement was part of a cultural revolution that ushered in a flood of multiethnic and heretofore excluded expressions. Quite the

contrary to "telling people what to write and to think" (Amiri Baraka's succinct paraphrase of the accusation of essentialism), such cultural movements promoted a national culture and identity that included collective experiences with both shared and unique particularities. If one is to affirm the presence and importance of oppressed nationality culture and identity, then a common and shared heritage and history is essential to a people's ability to find unity. The struggle for ethnic studies is simultaneously a struggle for inclusion (an area of scholarship unto itself) and a curriculum of correction/liberation (as part of the struggle to find the truth). The dominant mainstream curriculum is white studies. Perhaps a core curriculum of correction/ liberation in the humanities would include the following:

The Mahabarata and Ramayana epics from India; Chinese novelist Wu Cheng'en's sixteenth-century epic novel, *Journey to the West* and other Chinese literary classics such as *Romance of the Three Kingdoms, Water Margin,* and *Dream of the Red Chamber*; Sufi poet Farid ud-Din Attar's *The Conference of the Birds*; the Arabian *One Thousand and One Nights*; The *Rubaiyat* by Persian poet and mathematician Omar Khayyam (1048-1122); Khalil Gibran's *The Prophet*; certainly Solomon's Song of Songs; the writings of Ibn Battuta, the fourteenth-century Muslim who visited India and China; the Nahuatl poems by Nezahualcoyotl (thirteenth to fourteenth centuries), poet and king of Texcoco (pre-Spanish Mexico City), as documented by Spanish missionaries; fifth-century B.C.E. Chinese philosopher-writer Lao Tsu; Lady Murasaki's eleventh-century Japanese novel, *The Tale of Genji*; Confucius (seventh century B.C.E.); the Sufi poet Rumi; the Chinese philosopher Mencius (ca. 300 B.C.E.); the prophet Muhammad and the Koran; the Indian ascetic philosopher Siddhartha; the Mayan sixteenth-century dance drama *El Rabinal-Achí*; the Chinese *I Ching,* or *Book of Changes*; the Mexican painted books, or Codices, of which there were once one thousand (all but thirteen were burned by the Spanish, who deemed them to be works of the devil); *Popol Vuh,* or *Book of the People,* a collection of poetry and creation myths of the Mayans; the Indian prophet Guru Nanak Dev (1469-1539); the Native American Coyote tales; and, to name a handful of greats in the modern era, Rabindranath Tagore, the great Indian writer (1861-1941); W.E.B. Du Bois; Pablo Neruda; Amos Tutuola; and the list goes on.

Multinational Unity vs. Bourgeois White Integrationism

1. "Integration" was the U.S. government (liberal ruling class) policy put forward as the "answer" to the struggles of oppressed nationalities, particularly those led by African Americans, to end forced segregation (the systematic separation and subjection of oppressed nationality peoples from the dominant white settler-colonial society). The U.S. federal government, with the support of the U.S. National Guard and federal troops and agencies, implemented forced integration. Why is this "forced integration"? The burden of "integrating" schools was the busing of oppressed nationalities to mostly or all-white schools and areas. Seldom was busing the forcible transit of whites to mostly or all-oppressed nationality communities since those schools were deemed inferior "quality" facilities. The burden of "integrating" was put upon oppressed nationalities. While many racist white communities strongly objected to these federal enactments, and the image of black children being escorted by armed national guardsmen into hostile schools is indelibly etched into our media consciousness, few white anti-integration protestors and purveyors of racist violence and invective were arrested and imprisoned. Integration has the presumption and effect of enforcing white assimilation: that white society is the "promised land"; that acceptance by whites and into white social settings is desirable and the goal of "freedom." As many Azanian liberation fighters asserted, the goal isn't integration but liberation. Liberation (i.e., national liberation) is the freedom and power to decide a people's destiny, to choose whether they want to integrate with their oppressors, or to ultimately exercise their most fundamental political freedom: the right to self-determination (up to and including the right to secession, i.e., political independence). The premise of integration/separation is that oppressed nationalities are free to choose. At this moment, however, oppressed nationalities can neither integrate nor separate. Both integration and separation are responses to white national oppression.

....

2. Internationalists and revolutionary socialists stand for revolutionary integration: the unity of the working class and oppressed

through voluntary union, and not forced social policies of integration that presume that social proximity between peoples is the solution to national inequalities and national oppression. Revolutionary integration is often referred to as "multinational unity." However, much of the U.S. Left, infected by white chauvinism, has an incorrect and white integrationist view of multinational unity, which I will discuss.

....

3. The main white chauvinist view is that "multinational" is a higher form of organizational relations (i.e., more revolutionary) than "national-in-form." This means that a mixed (and historically predominantly white) organization is more revolutionary than an all-African or all-Asian formation. However, given the legacy and social weight of white supremacy in the United States, majority or all-white groups are putatively white chauvinist. It never ceases to amaze me how white Leftists are constantly perplexed about why they can't attract or recruit more oppressed nationalities when they are majority or all-white. They try to scrutinize their organizational "culture" and dissect possible racism among their members. They fail to realize that their political line on the national question is the key. Some even give token lip service to the revolutionary importance of the national question and the national movements, but are superficial, never ever recognizing, much less upholding in theory and practice, the independent revolutionary character of the national movements. This failure in line results in a failure to accept national movement leadership, by holding on to the notion that the national movements should and need to relate to whites as a primary focus.

....

4. The cosmetic reforms that white chauvinist integration produces, such as trying to change organizational culture to be more sensitive to and inclusive of oppressed nationalities, presumes that a white home is the best home. Rather than shift the organization's base to organizing in the national movements (which is what the CPUSA did

in its revolutionary period following its adoption of the Comintern Resolutions), and attract the support of and recruit among poor oppressed nationality workers, predominantly white Left groups keep spinning their wheels in psychoanalysis about how they are being racist.

....

5. Integrationist multinational unity presumes that simply adding more oppressed nationality members to their ranks is building multinational unity. Multinational unity is not simply accumulating more "people of color" members, but uniting with people who have roots in the national movements and are leading militants within the national struggles. Increasing the membership numbers of oppressed nationality individuals who aren't recognized leaders and have no base in the national movements doesn't make for genuine multinational unity; it only means having more people of color who will accept white leadership and an incorrect or shallow line on the national question. While I don't mean to disparage those oppressed nationality individuals who are struggling in predominantly white organizations (e.g., sectors of the mostly white environmental movement or the mostly white anarchist groups), they have no base in the national struggles and therefore in some ways abdicate the responsibility of a Left presence in the national movements. It is also mistaken to assume that any struggle (e.g., environmental, gay liberation) or any political movement (e.g., anarchist) doesn't have a sector that is grounded in the national struggles (e.g., the anti-environmental racism struggle of Native peoples, Africans, and Asians).

‹ 315

....

6. Multinational doesn't mean mostly white. Indeed, four-fifths of the world is "dark." If we are to be true internationalists, multinational formations would be "Third World" (e.g., predominantly Afro-Asian, or Afro-Latino, or Latino-Asian, or Black-Native, or Black-Asian-Latino-Native). Europeans and whites would be the definite minority.

....

7. The fact that so many white Left groups are majority white is both a political error and a manifestation of the particular history of white-settler colonialism in the United States. There is no separate or special role for whites in the U.S. revolutionary movement. Indeed, given the legacy of white supremacy and racism, a mostly or all-white Left group is an expression of white supremacy. There have no doubt been genuine white revolutionaries (e.g., John Brown and so many others) who have played behind-the-scenes support roles and who have been at the forefront of antiracist struggles and have fought alongside (and a few even inside) the national movements (e.g., John Sinclair, Edna Silvestri, Pam Martinez, and others). While white Leftists are in the best position to struggle against the racism within the white Left and workers movements, contrary to the nationalist view that that's the only role white Leftists should play, all Leftists (be they white or oppressed nationalities) should and must be setting and developing the conditions to build the revolutionary struggle of the national movements, especially the working-class leadership of the national struggles. The nationalist advocated position that white Leftists should only organize among whites generally leads to tailing nationalism and usually the more reformist sectors of the national struggles (who would rather have whites as sycophant supporters). Thus so-called white Leftists become politically white liberals, mired in guilt from a faulty and flimsy political line on the national question, thinking their role is to acquiesce to the flavor-of-the-month leadership in the national struggles rather than addressing the political questions of developing the revolutionary proletarian leadership of the national struggles. White members in predominantly oppressed nationality organizations work to build the national movements and to build support for these movements among whites.

....

8. Building multinational unity among the working classes of oppressed and oppressor nations can only be based upon national equality, the elimination of all forms of national privilege, exclusiv-

ity, primacy, and rivalry. White privileges will have to be eliminated. The standard of living gap between the First and Third World will have to be closed.

． ． ． ． ． ． ． ． ． ． ． ． ． ．

9. Time after time, the discussion of the American Left has been a white presumption. Scholarly and analytical discussions of generic Leftist culture and history mean white folk music and the white Left. The failure to understand the national question in theory and practice has committed the white Left, both theoretically and politically, to see the main problem in the U.S. working-class movement as primarily a "divided working class" and not national inequality. "White-skin privileges" as a concept, while it recognizes material inequality, fails to recognize the system of national oppression as fundamental and essential to imperialism. National oppression includes oppressor nation privileges but is not limited to this as the main and dominant aspect of national inequality, which is superexploitation and land robbery. National oppression is systematic, pervasive inequality, privilege, and racism. The theoretical and political limitation of "antiracism" relies upon "racist" attitudes, ideas, behavior, and policies and not upon systemic exploitation and inequality. The legacy of white chauvinism in the U.S. proletarian struggle has produced two substantial and insidious errors: white guilt, which results in politically tailing nationalists and reformists in the national movements; and white chauvinism, the dominant aspect, which considers the national movements not revolutionary enough without whites.

< 317

． ． ． ． ． ． ． ． ． ． ． ． ． ．

10. Support for the "right to self-determination" in words, but denying certain or all oppressed nations the option of independence, as evidenced in the Revolutionary Communist Party's Chicano national question. Lenin repeatedly denounced such selective application of the "right to self-determination, including secession," as imperialist opportunism. The right is meaningless and hollow without the complete freedom of a people to decide its relationship to the

oppressor nation. Communists can disagree with how the right is exercised, but not with the right itself, including all of its options.

The White Oppressor Nation and "Whiteness"

Why is it in the interests of most whites to struggle against national oppression and to be anti-imperialist? For these two basic reasons:

One, political. To paraphrase Lenin, no people or nation can be free if they oppress another simply because the perpetuation of massive inequality requires tremendous amounts of resources devoted to oppressing entire nations and peoples. The oppressor nation inevitably faces the unremitting resistance of the oppressed, and the constant threat of revolt in all forms, at all levels.

Two, moral and ideological. One culture's mistaken view of another is its mistaken view of itself. The cultural and ideological distortions and lies an oppressor society maintains toward the oppressed is its own mythification. As Fanon put it, "It is the racist who creates his inferior." The oppressor culture is basically incapable of a realistic understanding of the world, since it must maintain a massive cover-up, prettification, justification, and denial of its iniquities. By diminishing another's humanity, it necessarily diminishes its own.

White Americans belong to the oppressor nation in the multinational United States. Its government currently sits in power in the ambiguous territory of Washington, D.C., which interestingly, with its black majority population, has been waging a struggle for statehood as it realizes its disadvantageous position as a "service" to the federal government with no benefits. White settler-colonialism, beginning with the arrival of Columbus and the European colonization of the Americas, proceeded differently in the rise of today's nation-states in the Western hemisphere. The territory of the United States grew from a small corner in what came to be called "New England" into the fifty states and several colonies and "protectorates" that exist today. The fiftieth state was the complete annexation of Hawaii after U.S. marines, in support of five white settler-colonial plantation families, overthrew the constitutional Hawaiian monarchy of Queen Lili'uokalani in the late 1800s.

The dominant America is the white oppressor nation with its white-oppressor nationality. There never has been one united America, one united nation-state, but rather a multinational state of one white oppressor nation and several oppressed nations, and even more oppressed nationalities (referred to in depoliticized terms as "people of color" or "racial or ethnic minorities").

While much detailed discussion and critique of nationalism was made at the beginning of this essay, it must be emphasized that white racist chauvinism, and not nationalism, is the primary aspect of the division and derailment of the U.S. Left and working-class movement. The history of the U.S. labor struggle, unfortunately, has been marred by consistent and constant betrayal of the struggle against national oppression in favor of oppressor nation workers' white-skin privileges. Oppressed nationalities are always the first to be sacrificed, while whites (as a nationality) are protected. A greater percentage of the labor aristocracy, of skilled and better-paid workers, is white.

The thesis expounded in *Settlers: The Myth of the White Proletariat* by J. Sakai is that there is no white proletariat, because white workers are objectively "bought off" and superprivileged as part of the white oppressor nation, similar to other settler-colonial societies such as Australia, apartheid South Africa, and Israel. However, in the United States both white and black workers are exploited, that is, neither group controls or benefits from the value of their labor power, although, owing to national oppression, this occurs with considerable unevenness.

‹ 319

The U.S. Civil War was the completion of the bourgeois democratic revolution, but only for the white oppressor nation (and its male populace). Enslaved African labor restricted the productive forces under capitalism. As Ted Allen explained (in a talk given at Red Bookstore, October 22, 1976) "slaves [couldn't] take complicated instruments as they could sabotage them; the products of slave labor went to the mills of England and were not used for American northern industry; and . . . the rate of industrial expansion was greater for the North."

Whites who choose to identify with and relate their lives to oppressed nationalities may garner disfavor, prejudice, and suspicions about "racist love" or "exoticism"; but their lack of "white identification and pride" is positive, and they risk a certain amount of ostracism from the oppressor nation society. For example, white female citizens who married Asian immigrants ("aliens ineligible for citizenship") from 1922 to 1936 lost their own citizenship and took on the political status of their oppressed nationality spouses. At one point in the early stages of white settler–colonial consolidation, the settler ruling class greatly feared the possibility of large numbers of whites defecting to live with Indians and adopt the Native way of life. There were many attractions to Native life, including the absence of hierarchy and increased democracy; the according of more status and power to women; the absence of religious-social discrimination and persecution; and the acceptance of racial mixture, since "half breeds" were not stigmatized as they were in white society. "Hernando De Soto had to post guards to keep his men and women from defecting to Native Societies. The Pilgrims so feared Indianization that they made it a crime for men to wear long hair" (Loewen 1995, 109). Indeed, today we in modern "civilization" are forced to adjust our attitudes and perspectives about "primitive" peoples and societies in view of all of the undesirable outgrowths and problematic features of "modern civilization."

Today, the consolidation of white supremacy has made the enjoyment of white privilege so "natural" that only deliberate and sustained acts by white antiracist "race traitors" will sever the indelible and pervasive physical identification so crucial to the maintenance of white supremacy. However, the more whites culturally and politically reject and oppose white supremacist values, ideology, culture, and privilege, the more fractious is their relationship to the rest of the white oppressor nation.

The racism of the "white Negro" (Norman Mailer) has been sufficiently exposed and discussed, namely, the cultural imperialist privilege of whites to take freely oppressed nationality resources (cultural identity, music, dialect, etc.), adopt them as their own, posture as hip, and never have to support the struggle against imperialism and for national liberation. This is why Paul Simon was targeted for violating the U.N. Commission on Apartheid's cultural boycott of recording and performing in then-apartheid South Africa. He both artistically and financially profited from the musical resources of Azanian musicians (even if they were paid far better than what they'd normally receive) and, while he claimed to "love" the culture, music, and people, could not find it in himself to commit to anti-apartheid politics. Above all else, Simon kept the lion's share of the royalties and payments from the *Graceland* recording. None of the Azanian musicians, while paid good first world fees, had any percentage rights or residuals to the music they so greatly contributed to and that dominated the aesthetics of the album much more so than anything contributed by Simon.

The work of Ted Allen, Noel Ignatiev, and others offers many valuable and interesting examples and processes about whiteness. However, their overall political framework of "antiracism" is formulated as "abolition of the white race," whereas a more correct stand would be "the abolition of race," which will only occur with the destruction of imperialist national oppression. Calls to commit "race treason" are incorrect and insufficient to completely destroy white supremacy and national oppression, and fail miserably at being of any political use to the national movements. They base their overall political framework about the construction of whiteness in the United States on promulgating white-black racial division in order to weaken and split the working class as a whole. This white-black paradigm, besides disallowing for other oppressed nationalities and nations, weakens any conception of national oppression and reduces black oppression simply to racism as an outgrowth of white ruling-class interests to divide and conquer. Such a framework reduces and oversimplifies the complexity of the construction of white supremacy and therefore the construction of U.S. imperialism and its domestic and international empire. The politics of antiracism is not necessarily anti-imperialist (in the premise that imperialism is made to be an outgrowth of white racism, and not, correctly, the reverse). Antiracism or "race treason" and "abolition of the white race" is oriented to whites and offers no program of struggle for the national movements; particularly overlooked is the struggle for land. It also chauvinistically presumes that the U.S. proletarian movement must be predicated upon overcoming "divisions" and thereby is nothing more than a call for integration with white workers. This view dovetails and supports the nationalist position that "white leftists should only or primarily organize and struggle with racist white workers." Implicit in this position is that communist or Leftist oppressed nationalities are dupes of integration and don't merit leading the national movements, thereby dismissing and discrediting the ideological and political struggle for socialism within the national movements. While tactically, white

Leftists working among whites might be appropriate and necessary, the overall role of white Leftists in terms of strategy and line on the national question is no different from that of the revolutionary movement as a whole: to build the revolutionary leadership and strength of the national movements against U.S. imperialism. There is no separate "line," "program," or "agenda" differentiated between whites and oppressed nationalities; however, there may very well be different tactical approaches.

The consolidation of white supremacy toward the end of the nineteenth and certainly by the beginning of the twentieth century was a historical process that combined creating a white majority population in the United States with the smashing of Reconstruction and the oppression of the New Afrikan nation, along with the final victory in the wars against the Native nations by the 1890s with the complete defeat and pacification of the Sioux and Apache and the end of their autonomy; the complete annexation of the Southwest territory and its incorporation into the United States; the colonization of Hawaii and other Pacific Islands (including Guam and other German colonies after World War I and many of the Micronesian possessions of Japan after World War II); the seizing of Puerto Rico and other territories after the Spanish-American War of 1898; the purchase of Alaska from Russia; and the complete disenfranchisement of Asian/Pacific Islanders in the United States.

The tremendous need for labor in the enormous growth of U.S. capitalism was unprecedented in the history of the world. Such a massive transportation of labor in turn greatly fueled Western European and American capitalist expansion by rapidly expanding a wide range of industries and businesses, including ship-building, private and state-sponsored labor procurement, financial investment, administrative and management services, as well as labor and goods security from extralegal pirate and marauding enterprises. The transcontinental transfer of labor began with the slave trade (which some estimate was in the hundreds of millions and which the great Guyanese Marxist Walter Rodney attributed to the underdevelopment of the entire continent of Africa) and extended to the importation of workers from around the world in the exploitation of two continents and thousands of islands (the "New World"). By the twentieth century, the competitive rise and industrialization of Western European nation-states with sufficient local proletarians limited the flow of immigrants from these nation-states to the United States, with the exception of the oppressed nation of Ireland. Fewer WASPS (white Anglo-Saxon Protestants) were migrating to the United States than in the first period of European settlement of North America. Eastern and Southern European newer nation-states, such as Italy, Greece, and Poland, provided the second wave of European immigration from Europe during the late nineteenth and early twentieth century. The third wave of Eastern European immigration was in the 1980s with the fall of the so-called Iron Curtain. While many of these "white" immigrants did face aspects of national oppression, they never became oppressed nationalities. The price for admittance into the "white" race or American white society was the de-ethnicization of the European ethnic immigrant. Europeans could also more easily intermarry among different European nationalities and blend into white American society. In Europe, the varying nationalities as part of the rise of nation-states were a mix of languages and ethnic groups.

‹ 323

"White" people became the majority by the twentieth century, and many were encouraged to "go West" and claim the territories taken from the Natives and the former northern territory of Mexico. The small and scattered Asian communities were razed to the ground and certainly by World War II, facilitated by anti-Asian laws that excluded or hindered Asian land ownership, the vast and profitable agricultural lands developed by Japanese American farmers were confiscated literally overnight. The Nikkei (Japanese Americans) were rounded up and herded into "relocation camps" (the white racist reasoning being to prohibit the potential activities of a "fifth column" as well as allegedly for their own protection against the racist anti-Japanese hysteria of World War II). With the purchase of Alaska and the growth of fishing and oil industries in that territory, and the colonization of Hawaii, white settlement was encouraged to these far and distant areas. The victory of Americana in the Western hemisphere required genocide, land theft, repopulation of the hemisphere by "white people," and the complete oppression of all others deemed "not white" (the range of classifications have shifted and varied, including "colored," "heathen races," etc., some including certain Europeans for a period of time, but all consistently applied to "people of color" as oppressed nationalities who aren't allowed to assimilate into American/white society). In its historical process, both in legal definitions of citizenship and in practical reality, for all intents and purposes "America" is synonymous with "white." Malcolm X clearly and sharply pointed out that New Afrikans are not Americans, but rather are "victims of America." He recognized the fundamental schism and conflicted reality of America: the simultaneity of an oppressor (dominant white) nation along with oppressed (not-white) nations and nationalities.

Can the white Left extirpate its white chauvinism? While it is possible for whites to be antiracist (as historical examples in certain bold and important cases such as John Brown have demonstrated), it is not possible for whites (including Leftists) to be nonracist. As I discussed earlier, even the self-avowed white "antiracists" can liquidate the national question and make white racist political errors and construct fundamentally white chauvinist–flawed analytic frameworks. I would add from my experience in the one majority white revolutionary socialist organization that on paper seemed to uphold the correct *general* positions on the national question, that it was white integrationism at its best, and white chauvinism as its worst in terms of specific and practical aspects on the national question(s).

324 ›

The weight of white supremacy and privilege has a history of over five centuries. As discussed earlier, the very meaning, identity, fabric, and social matrix of "American" is polluted and shaped by national oppression. Therefore "race" matters in everything "American" because everything American is thoroughly racist. The heroic history of antiracist struggle is not the dominant perspective or discourse in any aspect of American history, American studies or American anything (fill in the blank: music, art, literature, science, intellectual history, etc.). In theory, it is possible that a white majority Left organization or Leftist might have a correct position on the national question, but in practice this is not probable.

There is a reason why this has not occurred yet in the entire history of the U.S. Left with the exception of certain organizations and individuals from the national movements.

A number of groups that were once national-in-form, born of the great national movements of the late 1960s and early 1970s, quickly proceeded to liquidate the national question once they became Marxist-Leninist (e.g., the Revolutionary Workers League, the

Puerto Rican Workers Revolutionary Organization, the Black Workers Congress, the League for Proletarian Revolution, and others). This essay is not able to fully summarize why this process occurred, except to hypothesize that the majority-white U.S. Left may quite possibly have abetted this liquidation in its inadequate and incorrect (white chauvinist) positions on the national question. It is the experience of this author that the then–Workers Viewpoint Organization (WVO; a group that was notorious for liquidating the national question through its majority Asian-black-and-other oppressed nationality cadres) worked zealously in liaison meetings with many newly Marxist-Leninist groups to "win them over" to its political line, including temporarily influencing the then–Revolutionary Communist League (formerly Congress of African Peoples) and the then–August Twenty-Ninth Movement (from the Chicano Movement). The latter would break with the WVO and the Revolutionary Wing (a multilateral collection of local and national organizations taken over by WVO) and merge with the League of Revolutionary Struggle.

‹ 325

The League of Revolutionary Struggle was the merger of three nationwide Marxist-Leninist New Communist Movement organizations, all of which had long histories and deep ties in their respective national movements: I Wor Kuen from the Asian Movement; the August Twenty-Ninth Movement from the Chicano Movement; and the Revolutionary Communist League from the Black Liberation Movement. I united with the line and was a member of I Wor Kuen and the LRS from the summer of 1976 to the spring of 1989. It is my contention that for the majority of its history, the LRS and the IWK, in particular, held the correct line on the national question to the extent that it had. Its strengths, as well as its weaknesses and errors which led to its eventual demise, I discuss elsewhere (see *Legacy to Liberation*). In particular, the extent of its correct positions on the national question reflect a strong anti-integrationist and anti-assimilationist stand, and, unlike the rest of the Marxist-Leninist movement, the LRS vigorously upheld and built national-in-form organizations and led them. It boldly and consistently propagandized support for the right of self-determination for the Black Nation, the Chicano Nation, the Hawaiian Nation, the Aleutian Nation. How did it come to this correctness? Its majority oppressed nationality composition was a reflection of the particularly deep histories and ties of the respective member organizations, especially those of IWK to the Asian Movement. But other Marxist-Leninist groups had such histories and even brilliant leading theoreticians from the national movements, yet repudiated the national question and adopted liquidationist positions. I am not able to answer the specifics of how and why this happened, but I believe a key component must be an understanding of how internally, and what specific theoreticians, defended, upheld, and achieved unity around the vital importance and significance of national-in-form organizations. Until this is grasped, then the tendency to "integrate" and subordinate to the white Left will have both theoretical and practical vulnerability and susceptibility. The LRS collapsed eventually, not from nationalist deviations, as some have suggested, but from reformism, specifically the collapse and conflation with the Jesse Jackson/Rainbow Coalition component of the Democratic Party. Such reformism was perhaps more readily rationalized by the seductive rhetoric of "people of color political empowerment" put forward by Jackson and supported by our cadre. We should have known better, but because the majority of the leadership and cadre were enamored with electoral politics and careerist opportunities than they were with fighting reformism and defending revolutionary socialism, the LRS capitulated and soon split and dissolved.

In the final analysis, as the historical record has shown, the white Left, Marxist or otherwise, cannot accept subordination to oppressed nationality leadership. This was the problem in the integrationist Freedom Road Socialist Organization (FRSO), of which I was a member after the LRS dissolved. This remains a problem when white leadership figures vigorously fight other white Leftist leadership figures for liquidating the national question, but then quickly pronounce the debate about the existence of the black nation to be something that will be decided "in never-never land." It abounds and continues to be a problem with the FRSO, whose white leaders want to select oppressed nationalities to serve in distinguished leadership roles, more from tokenistic likeability than merit or political correctness. White leadership will not abdicate to oppressed nationalities unless they are "their" oppressed nationalities, namely the ones who don't overshadow or challenge basic white privilege and position. White leadership cannot accept that perhaps a movement or organization won't have any qualified whites, that the presence or absence of whites is politically irrelevant to correctness on the national question. This would violate any and all desires for integrationist "multinational unity." It would mean a new movement, one we have yet to experience and direly need to build if we are to end the rule of U.S. imperialism.

Specific National Questions in the United States

The application of "the right to self-determination" and "full equality" for oppressed nations and nationalities in the United States has been hotly debated. These debates center on several issues for the national question:

1. Do oppressed nations actually (still) exist?
2. The "right to self-determination" includes three possible options: secession, federation, and regional autonomy. How shall these forms be expressed in the respective national movement demands?
3. Is it practical and advisable to support the dismemberment of the United States?
4. How would a plebiscite be conducted as corruption-free from the machinations of the U.S. imperialists?

‹ 327

I do not purport to be able to fully address or discuss these important practical and programmatic questions in this essay, but choose to limit my focus to important features of the specific U.S. national questions in hopes of expanding our political understanding and achieving greater clarity on their interrelationship.

Imperialism in the United States currently operates through (forced) assimilation as its dominant method of rule rather than direct genocide or direct subjugation (legal discrimination, segregation, disenfranchisement, and denial of civil rights). While violence and brutal oppression continue, as a bourgeois democracy in the "post-Civil Rights era" after the dismantling of formal segregation and discrimination, the U.S. ruling class and its nation-state (government) function to "integrate" and "absorb" oppressed nationalities. Imperialist education, social institutions, and policies promote the idea that people within its borders are "all Americans" entitled to the same opportunities in a common pursuit of "the American Dream." Americanization is actually assimilation into "white" society and the adoption of a primarily Western European-derived heritage. Toleration and acceptance of "ethnicity" exists as long as it doesn't contradict or challenge the basic rule of imperialism and the apriority of U.S. borders. "Cultural diversity" is touted and promoted as long as it doesn't include territorial liberation, political self-government, or seizure and control of resources. Just as colonialism operated via native agents, imperialist assimilation requires token diversity to more smoothly and effectively disguise national oppression and inequality. Under imperialism, assimilation and integration are forced: a result of systematic and historical powerlessness to determine a people's own identity, resources, territory, and sociopolitical relationship to the United States.

328 ›

The Native American/Indigenous First Nations National Question

The construction of white settler-colonial society and the rise of U.S. imperialism began with the conquest of the indigenous/Native nations and peoples of the Americas. The U.S. socialist revolution and the fundamental essence of the national question must have the liberation of the oppressed indigenous nations as its cornerstone and foundation. The horrors of national oppression are most brazen with the genocide, annexation, and subjugation of the Native peoples across the Americas, from Alaska to South America. The Native nations represented the first national question, the first resistance movement to white settler-colonial rule and the system of capitalism, and represent the longest, continual struggle for decolonization and national liberation.

The last federally ordered mass execution in the United States was December 26, 1862, when President Lincoln ordered thirty-eight remaining Dakotas, reduced from the three hundred captured, all hung simultaneously. The ongoing war against the Native nations would continue for almost another half century, until the last formal surrenders to the U.S. army by the Apache. Simultaneous with these wars of conquest were the relocation, removal, and exodus of the Native nations that were not completely obliterated onto "reservations," euphemistically referred to as new "homelands." From the very beginning, the original white settler governments recognized the many Native nations via trade and treaty agreements, which have not been honored. As the famous Indigenous saying goes, The white man made many promises to Indian people, but he only kept one: he promised to take our land, and he did.

White chauvinist Leftists, including those who espouse the use of Stalin's criteria of nationhood, refute the existence of nationhood among Natives from a Eurocentric bias. The Native nations, they argue, don't resemble European or Western nation-states. They are more "tribal," "nomadic," less "stable." Never mind the fact that the Native nations themselves recognized mutual territories and had a different concept of national territory that allowed for fluid migration and common usage between various nations. The Eurocentrists (who claim to be using the supposedly Marxist criteria of Stalin) also argue that Native nations didn't have class formations (or at least those that they could recognize as being similar to Western capitalist nation-states) or have a common economic life, as demonstrated by a national market. They do concede that Native peoples share commonalities in their languages and cultures. But the mechanical and Eurocentrist position is that all four criteria need to be evidenced for nationhood to be conceded. Not that the Native peoples have to prove worthy of nationhood status to these chauvinists, but let me refute or at least point out the problems of such arguments.

Trade and exchange took place within and across Native nations. At the time of Hernando Cortés's arrival, Tenochtitlán (present-day Mexico City) had a population of 350,000, five times greater than that of London or Seville of that time. Certain South and Central American nations had vast cities and class stratification (from the Olmecs, Mayans, and Aztecs of the Yucatán Peninsula to the Andean Incans), but were decimated soon after the arrival of European conquerors. The North American Native nations also had stable communities, including major cities and trading centers (such as the Anasazi and the Pueblos in the southwest of the United States, the resident urban center near Cahokia, Illinois, or the mound-building Mississippian cultures of circa 700 to 1700), though for the most part these did not resemble European or Asian cities with large-scale population density, industrial factories, and commercial shipping and transportation. The population density in the northern Americas was far less than Europe, Asia, and northern and coastal Africa.

While it still remains an area of much-needed historical research and scholarship on the development and character of Native nation-states, it is abundantly clear that white capitalism did much to destroy the physical, economic, cultural, and social fabric of Native societies. In trading with Europeans, the consequences to Native nations was devastating and irreversible. On a physical level, Native peoples had never encountered European communicable diseases, which were introduced to the Western hemisphere via European domesticated animals such as cows, pigs, horses, sheep, goats, and chickens. Diseases passed between humans and livestock, such as anthrax, tuberculosis, cholera, streptococcosis, ringworms, and the various poxes, which had never been present in the Americas, became a wildfire that wiped out or decimated entire nations in a matter of a few years. This destruction was of a magnitude even greater than the bubonic and other plagues that swept Europe and is perhaps matched only by today's AIDS crisis in Africa and parts of impoverished Asia. The entire physical destruction and weakening of millions of Native peoples can in part explain the interrupted, arrested, and faltering process of capitalism arising in Native America. But the capitalism of the white settlers would become the death of the Native nations. Trading for a kettle instead of expending the time and labor needed to make a traditional watertight basket or skin container led to the atrophy of skills and deformation of Native productive forces and relations. A Native working class involved in mass production could not possibly develop under such a physical onslaught. The uprooting and forced migration of hundreds of thousands of Native peoples (e.g., the Trail of Tears in the 1830s) has had few historical precedents in any part of human history. Native mass production existed in agriculture, hunting, and crafts, and exchange was conducted via a market economy, first with other tribes and later with the Europeans. However, nascent Native capitalism was restricted by limited markets, since populated urban centers were far more distant from each other than in Europe, Asia, and other parts of the world, and since trade routes with other continental trading centers was not possible. The arrival of European colonization meant the conquest of a weaker Native protocapitalism by a much stronger and better-armed system.

330 ›

The colonization of the Americas meant both the physical and cultural destruction of the Native nations, as well as the appropriation of all the benefits of Native production, expertise, and resources. Native class and social relations were altered as the entire social fabric of Native society changed to fit white colonial expansion. Female political leadership was replaced by male in imitation of white social relations and because white male leaders wouldn't negotiate treaties with women. In the twentieth century, the U.S. government notoriously anointed its Native "leaders," deemed "progressives" who promoted even greater assimilation and accommodation with white society against the "traditionalists" who sought to defend Native sovereignty and cultural integrity. The current rise of Native capitalism via casinos is the latest distortion of oppressed nationality capitalism and class stratification.

While wars over resources and territorial claims did occur between Native societies, they were certainly less acute and severe compared with other societies with far greater imperial legacies.

‹ 331

The national oppression against the Native oppressed nations and nationalities is possibly one of the most brutal and horrific in the entire history of humanity. The physical aggression during the so-called Indian Wars is well documented. The effects today are reflected in numerous forms of oppression ranging from disproportionate rates in illiteracy, alcoholism, domestic violence, suicide, mental illness, poverty, income disparity, and in just about every social indicator. Cultural genocide was justified by the mindset of "Killing the Indian to save the man." Indian prisoners of war had to submit to cutting their hair in order to be fed. Native children were not allowed to speak their native tongue, deemed "the language of the insane." Dakota school children were physically beaten if they spoke Dakota. The wars against the Native nations by the U.S. white settler–colonial government took away their way of life, suffocated their spirit, and forced them to suffer as a defeated, beaten, disgraced people. The U.S. government and society banned their culture to exterminate their identity. Capitalism found a way to make money by placing a $200 bounty on scalps. By 1862, the Minnesota governor called the Dakota "the disappearing race." In forced labor camps, Native workers were paid 3 cents for beaded moccasins. Native women and children had to make at least five hundred moccasins a week to make $15 to feed a family (Berg). Thus the eventual and grotesque proletarianization of Native oppressed nationalities, energized by the liberation movements of both the Third and Fourth Worlds (the indigenous peoples of Third World nation-states, as well as the indigenous peoples of Western industrialized First World nation-states such as the United States and Canada), have been galvanized and amalgamated into a united front of indigenous movements both in the Americas and around the globe.

As research on Native social history emerges to help our understanding of the national development of Native nations and to further clarify the strategic issues for the Native national question in the United States, it is clear that new, larger confederations and nation-states were formed and took on the characteristics of what Lenin so powerfully described and argued for as rising "national movements." The beginnings of this First Nations/Native American/Indian national movement emerged with the amalgamation of smaller Native nations into larger ones that became "ethnic melting pots," which even included taking in whites and blacks as well as other Indians. New confederations and nations developed, such as the Creek, Seminole, and Lumbee. The Sioux and Apache were also a great amalgam of tribes that extended from the Southwest up to the Rockies, who united in fighting the U.S. aggression upon their lands and fought heroically down to a remaining few warriors who were eventually captured or killed. The modern-day Native American national movement includes the American Indian Movement (AIM), the League of Indigenous First Nations, and various Hawaiian sovereignty and independence organizations, among others. The slogan of AIM is "Many Nations, One Destiny" in its conception of the Native American struggle as a united front waging a struggle for national liberation and decolonization.

The New African (or Black Belt) Nation

The existence and significance of a "New African" or Black Nation is the touchstone of the debates and differences around the national question in the U.S. Left. The New Communist Movement that emerged in the early 1970s revolved its positions around either acceptance or rejection of the Comintern Theses, expounded and elaborated upon by African American communist Harry Haywood. The Comintern and Haywood both based their thesis for the Black Belt Nation upon Stalin's criteria for nations. In the 1950s, Haywood and a small circle of communists who rejected the CPUSA's liquidation of the national question, and the Black Nation specifically, issued a polemic "Toward a Revolutionary Position on the Negro Nation" to defend the assertion of the Black Belt Nation and to rebut arguments denying its existence and importance. Much of this polemic continues to be relevant in rebutting the various positions that argue against the Black Nation. I summarize this debate: The out-migration from the South has dispersed African Americans, making the population now primarily northern, urban and less cohesive and certainly no longer a concentrated territorial majority, but rather "minorities." Few argue that out-migration, similar to Third World immigrants coming to the United States and other affluent countries, is not forced migration. In the case of African Americans, job openings in Northern industries attracted workers away from the poverty and brutality of national oppression in the South (including racist terror, oppressive and discriminatory taxation, land confiscation, and robbery). Few would argue that life in the North was any "better." This forced exodus is common to imperialism, as the labor needs of the capitalist centers attract migrants from the superexploitation and crushing poverty of their homelands that have been pillaged for the profits of the imperialists. The number of counties in which blacks are a majority has decreased. Migration between the South and the North goes back and forth between generations, and black land ownership in the South is declining (due to robbery, cheating, fraud, and exploitation). These are all symptoms of national oppression. These are characteristics particular to the oppressed Black Nation.

Such an intensification of national oppression energized the black national movement. The Civil Rights Movement and the 1960s Black Liberation struggle arose both within the South and in the ghettos of the North. The black national movement has always embraced aspirations for land and nationhood (whether it be within the borders of the United States or seeking a new homeland elsewhere), from the beginnings of slave revolt and escaped slave societies to manifestos of black nationhood in the nineteenth century to Garvey's Black Zionism to black radical- and communist-formulated Black Belt national territory to the Nation of Islam's five-states demand, to the actual ownership of land in Mississippi and its armed defense by the Republic of New Afrika. The historical aspirations for land and nationhood are incontrovertible.

The oppressed Black Nation began in the South, after the period of formal slavery and during the rise of U.S. imperialism from the latter half of the nineteenth century and into the mid-twentieth century. Large numbers of enslaved Africans even became the majority of certain areas of the U.S. South, and, after the abolition of formal slavery, continued to live on and work the lands. After slavery, while blacks were never granted "40 acres and a mule" as promised by General Sherman's Special Field Orders, they nonetheless managed to come to own land, to build their own homes, and to farm. The period of Reconstruction ushered in an unprecedented level of black political assertion and economic activity, and black nationhood arose during this time. Few of the liquidation positions argue against or even address this historical process. But the smashing of Reconstruction, so powerfully analyzed by Du Bois and later by Haywood, thwarted black national aspirations and signaled the historical development of the Black Nation as an oppressed nation and black people in general both inside and outside the South as an oppressed nationality.

Despite out-migrations, and although they are no longer a concentrated majority in certain Southern areas, large numbers of African Americans still live there and many Northern blacks retain direct family relations to the South as well as connections to the land. The South has not lost its political importance as a region of severe poverty and national oppression. The struggle to defend black land ownership and to get back stolen property is unmitigated. Large out-migrations have occurred in many oppressed and colonized nations, including the massive dispersal of Palestinians from former Palestine, to a third of the Puerto Rican population residing outside the island, to the majority of Hawaiians now living on the U.S. mainland.

Black self-government had a nascent beginning during Reconstruction, and the number of black officials elected during that time has never been matched since. The smashing of Reconstruction postponed the completion of the bourgeois-democratic revolution until the 1960s, when the black national struggle rose to an even higher level of struggle and forced the dismantling of all vestiges of formal segregation and the inequality of Jim Crow.

The reparations movement is based upon an entire people's claims for recovery and recompense against both the U.S. government and corporations for the historical oppression and exploitation of slavery, the effects of post-Reconstruction dispossession of blacks from the land, and the consequences of oppressing an entire people and thwarting their social, political, economic, and cultural development. In a University of California–Berkeley study made several years ago, it was found that black income lost because of discrimination in the years between 1929 and 1969 comes to about $1.6 trillion (Gonsalves 2001).

While the legacy of slavery continues to devastate African Americans, the loss of black-owned property has been particularly acute. According to a three-part article on this subject by Todd Lewan and Dolores Barclay, "Investigation Shows Pattern of Violence: Blacks' Land Loss Hidden in History,"

> In 1910, black Americans owned at least 15 million acres of farmland, nearly all of it in the South, according to the U.S. Agricultural Census. Today, blacks own only 1.1 million acres of farmland and are part owners of another 1.07 million acres.... The number of white farmers has declined, too, as economic trends have concentrated land in fewer hands. However, black ownership has declined 2 times faster than white ownership, according to a 1982 federal report, the last comprehensive government study on the trend.

The variety of land confiscation techniques has ranged from direct terror and violence to force black families to abandon their homes to a myriad of financial and legal maneuvers to dispossess blacks of their land titles. The loss of black land, contrary to the white racist notion of using this argument to justify the liquidation of the national question and the specific existence of an oppressed black nation in the South, requires that progressives and revolutionaries support the reparations and land defense and recovery struggles of African Americans. National oppression cannot resolve or whittle away the national existence of an oppressed nation; just the opposite—it continually renews and intensifies the national movement. The struggle for black control over land remains central to the Black

Liberation struggle. The extirpation of black political control over a region or territory since the smashing of Reconstruction remains the political basis for black oppression and political powerlessness. Black electoral representation in the current U.S. political system is a dilution and diversion of black self-government and empowerment over its own resources and territory. It is but another effect of and ploy by imperialist integration/assimilation to undermine the national movement.

The key to understanding the Black Nation isn't statistics and demographics (though by all accounts, these support and verify national oppression and inequality), but politics. The Black Liberation Movement has never opted for integration. It continues, with nationalists and non-nationalist forces, to be a national movement fighting for liberation for an entire people, the basis of which cannot be won simply via "civil rights" or imperialist absorption via "integration," but which must be won through the exercise of political control over a region or territory along with its resources. It also requires an unremitting struggle for reparations (beyond affirmative action) to rebuild its nation, to restore its national culture, integrity, and dignity, and to correct hundreds of years of economic, social, and political oppression and inequality, with the concomitant effects of psychologically induced inferiority, whitewashing, and overall weakened national pride, identity, and consciousness.

The political assault on black political and territorial power began with the smashing of Reconstruction, with the state-sanctioned rise of white racist paramilitary forces, most infamously the Ku Klux Klan, which was formed in 1876. From 1880 to 1915, three thousand blacks were lynched. The KKK remains today a legal organization. It is well known that J. Edgar Hoover as long-standing director of the FBI targeted the Black Civil Rights and Liberation struggle with considerable vehemence and viciousness. Official state-sanctioned terror, intimidation, and harassment continue with police racial profiling, the use of excessive force against oppressed nationalities, unfair convictions and sentencing, and the overall warehousing of oppressed nationalities in the prison-industrial complex.

The New Afrikan Nation possesses all of Stalin's basic four criteria of nationhood, as argued by Haywood in response to the CPUSA's formal liquidation at its Seventeenth National Convention in 1959. As I

336 ›

have discussed above, though the territory has certainly been reduced via national oppression, and though African Americans may be dispersed throughout major U.S. cities, as long as one acre of black historically resided-upon land exists, then the nation exists, as well as its ongoing struggle for the return of stolen lands. Class development in the New African Nation, as in any imperialist oppressed nation, unfolds unevenly and in a stunted way, with all classes, including the bourgeoisie, suffering from national oppression. The black national bourgeoisie, as the bourgeoisie of an oppressed nation, is more like a petite bourgeoisie. Its ability for capital expansion is restricted and thwarted by the giant, mighty white imperialists' corporations. As the black bourgeoisie is disproportionately smaller than its white counterpart, conversely, the black proletariat among the Black Nation is far greater in proportion than white workers are to the oppressor white nation. In all of the oppressed nations, the working class is far greater in proportion to its national population than the percentage of white workers are to the white oppressor nation. One could argue that the proletarian base of the national movements is greater than that of the white oppressor nation, which perhaps also explains the greater militancy of oppressed nationality workers than that of the white workers, especially after the consolidation of white supremacist imperialist rule by the twentieth century.

‹ 337

The revolutionary elements of the American communist movement throughout the twentieth century have proved and defended the existence of an oppressed black (New Afrikan) nation. The liquidation positions have based their main refutations on out-migration and arguments for assimilation and integration. The political end result is to invalidate the Black Liberation struggle as nothing more than a figment of the aspirations of misguided nationalists, to disregard or diminish the struggle for land, and thereby to contain and restrict the "liberation" struggle to simply (primarily) uniting with white workers for anti-discrimination and economic demands with the goal of integration.

The Chicano Nation (Atzlan)

The existence of an oppressed Chicano Nation is well documented. The oppressed Chicano Nation emerged from the severance of the northern territories of Mexico in the mid-nineteenth century and the subsequent political and economic annexation and sociocultural absorption of this region and its people into the United States. The national rights supposedly guaranteed to the inhabitants of this territory by the U.S. government, including rights to the Spanish language, land ownership, cultural valuation, and so many others, have been completely denied and attacked by white settler–colonialism as the Chicano people were forged into an oppressed nation by U.S. imperialism. In recent years, the Chicano national question has deepened its relationship to the Native national question. The Chicano people and culture are an amalgam of the Spanish conquest of the indigenous peoples of Mexico. The current states of Texas, New Mexico, Arizona, Colorado, and California were shared by descendants of Mexico and by a number of Native nations, many of whom never accepted Spanish rule and continued to wage wars of resistance to the United States well after the absorption of these areas as states in the U.S. federated political system. Increasing numbers of Chicanos today are choosing primary identification with their Native heritage rather than with the Spanish-colonial aspect of their Mexican background. Increasingly, the concept of the Chicano Nation has become interconnected and united with the liberation of the Native/Indigenous Peoples as it is maintained that "Chicanos are indigenous": "we didn't cross the border, the border crossed us," as the saying goes. The struggle for Chicano liberation takes on an added dimension of deciding what the Chicano Nation's relationship will be to both the United States and Mexico. The massive infusion of Latinos from other Central and South American nation-states as a consequence of imperialism's underdevelopment and destabilization of oppressed nations contributes to the massive growth of the U.S. Latino population, which for the first time has exceeded African Americans. Many of the poorest Latino immigrants are of indigenous ancestry, oppressed and persecuted in their respective homeland nation-states from the respective legacies of their European settler–colonialism. In many ways, they share in the Chicano communities and struggles; in other ways, they are more kin to the heterogeneity of the Asian/Pacific Islander communities. The Chicano Movement must therefore simultaneously embrace Pan-Indian and Pan-Latino political and cultural dynamics. The programmatic demands in the struggle for homeland includes political and economic control over a wide territory of the Southwestern United States, perhaps as far north as northern Colorado across to northern California. As closer links are forged between the Chicano Movement and the Native Movement, the specific interrelationships of national demands and forms of self-governance and political expression will need to be developed.

Asian Pacific Americans

The various anti-Asian Exclusion Acts passed into law by Congress (e.g., preventing families from immigrating into the United States) had the effect of denying the development of community formation. Racist violence and legislation prohibited and restricted Asian property ownership. Asians were driven off the lands they worked and settled, and many of their innovations and contributions to American production were seized for the benefit of white profiteers. The rise of anti-Asian racism initially coincided with the need to scapegoat Asians during times of general economic downturn in the United States. In the post–World War II era of economic prosperity and U.S. world empire consolidation, a new form of insidious racism promoted the "model minority myth" of Asian "success" in order to divide APIs from other oppressed nationalities, and to foment jealousy and anxiety about Asian advancement. One of the most massive relocations and removals of a population in the United States was the Japanese American internment in concentration camps during World War II. Today, Arabs and Muslims are demonized as "terrorists" just as the Japanese were once targeted. Anti-Asian violence and hate crimes continue to escalate, the worst of any oppressed nationality group in the United States.

‹ 339

Asian Pacific Islanders do not have a claim to historical homeland territory in the United States. The lands that they did work and live on were part of the Chicano/Native nations, though most of the Asian settlements were not made at the direct loss of Chicano/Native habitation. The small communities of Truckee, Napa, Marysville, Placerville, and Stockton were in desolate or wilderness areas, remnants of mining towns and small farming communities. However, APIs are essential and critical to the economic development of the West Coast and Hawaii for U.S. capitalism. Their demands are for reparations (only partially won in the Japanese American redress and reparations struggle, without proper restitution for the value of their property and land, lives lost, and oppression and exploitation suffered); control over their own institutions and communities; support, expansion, and control of cultural representation and production (including language rights); abolition of unfair and discriminatory immigration legislation and treatment; fighting racist violence, racial profiling of street youth, and discrimination and persecution in employment and services.

One of the greatest struggles faced by API radicals and revolutionaries today is combating the internalization of the model minority myth within the API nationalities and the critical need to raise national consciousness and unity with other oppressed nationalities in fostering Afro-Asian and Third World consciousness and solidarity. The presence of Asian capital from the Pacific Rim has dramatically increased with overseas investments in the United States and Canada, much of which is oriented toward an Asian/Pacific immigrant market. This sets the conditions for increasing anticapitalist struggles of API workers and communities against petit-bourgeois API capitalists in anti-sweatshop labor organizing, in anti-gentrification housing struggles, and so on. With the rise of a significant petite-bourgeoisie in the API communities, the struggle for Leftist politics will undergo severe competition and contention from reformist and assimilationist forces. API Leftists also face difficulties with the increased anti-communism in certain API immigrant communities, where refugees and evacuees with negative experiences with socialism and communist forces in their former home countries have gathered.

Puerto Rico and Puerto Ricans in the United States

Internationally recognized as a "colony" by much of the world community, and with a continuous independence movement (albeit "small" in terms of current nonbinding plebiscites initiated and controlled by the United States), Puerto Rico's "commonwealth" status to the United States evinces the complexities of imperialist absorption via dependency. While disallowed certain national rights (such as controlling its own elections and implementing any real political independence), Puerto Rico "enjoys" paying no federal taxes to the United States, social security and welfare, free travel between the island and the U.S. mainland, and the "benefit" of being protected by the U.S. military. The pro-commonwealth mentality favors the status quo of forgoing national sovereignty for the "protections" and benefits of U.S. dependency as long as English doesn't supplant the Spanish language. Accepting "commonwealth" status reflects the insecurity inculcated now by several generations of dependency in the belief that Puerto Rico could not survive on its own, that it "needs" the United States. With such an inculcation of dependency has come massive welfare enrollment, the systematic disintegration of any indigenous economic activity, domination by U.S. corporations, and the ravaging of the island's ecosystem by U.S. military bombing exercises and sea dredging.

Due to the economic attraction of the U.S. mainland society, large numbers of Puerto Ricans travel back and forth between the island and U.S. urban centers, and large numbers of families are split between both. Differences have emerged within the Puerto Rican national movement based in both the United States and Puerto Rico around the positions of "the right to self-determination" and the specific call for "independence." The former tends to include the pro-commonwealth forces, which are aligned with U.S. imperialism, arguing that the Puerto Rican people have, via past "nonbinding plebiscites," overwhelmingly chosen commonwealth status (i.e., the status quo). Pro-independence forces criticize these "votes" for promoting the deception that "independence" would mean socio-cultural-economic losses and restricted bilateral travel. Anti-imperialist forces have stood for independence as the correct appraisal of Puerto Rico's true colonial status and to support the ongoing pro-independence movement that has been undermined and attacked continually by U.S. imperialism, including repression and jailing of its leaders and activists. The current upsurges against U.S. military occupation and maneuvers on the Puerto Rican isle of Vieques only underscore the colonial condition of the nation and the need for independence to remove U.S. political control.

For Puerto Ricans on the mainland, the right to return home to a truly free, independent Puerto Rico must be upheld. The struggle of Puerto Ricans in U.S. cities and mainland areas parallels the struggle of African American and other oppressed nationalities dispersed outside their national territories: it emphasizes the need to revolutionize these respective struggles in building unity across national movements. Puerto Ricans outside of Puerto Rico are an oppressed nationality in the U.S. mainland and struggle for full equality and empowerment, with common interests and struggles shared with other oppressed nationalities.

Postscript

1. How should the national question in the United States be resolved? What is the interrelationship between Native national liberation, the first and longest struggle against U.S. white supremacist settler-colonial rule, and that of the other oppressed nations and nationalities? The resolution of the national question cannot be predicted or guided as to which national struggles will erupt with the most velocity and ferocity against U.S. imperialism. However, Leftists must not stand opposed to the reconfiguration of the U.S. nation-state. Indeed, Leftists should welcome it as part of the general weakening and dismemberment of imperialism. Marxists stand for and must build the working-class leadership of the national movements, leading by example and emphasizing the need to unite with workers from all nationalities and with other national movements. The Marxists must wage an unremitting struggle against all forms of ideological and political chauvinism and opportunism that diminish or liquidate the national question. While it is the contention of some forces like the All-African People's Revolutionary Party that the Native national question must be the first to resolved, one cannot predict or control the outgrowth and outcome of the national movements, and Marxists must remain clear to lend full support to any national movement that has erupted to a level of challenging U.S. political rule by igniting, supporting, and leading a multiplicity of wars of independence. The liberation of indigenous nations is fundamental and integral to the overall question of the socialist revolution in the United States and the resolution of the national question(s). Currently, it seems that the Native Hawaiian struggle is at the forefront. Different forces are vying for sovereignty versus independence as part of the internal struggle to decide how to exercise the "right of self-determination."

All national movements must lend support to further such a victory of the Native Hawaiian nation over more than a century of U.S. colonial rule and imperialist domination.

The Black Liberation struggle has historically been the vanguard and spearhead for much of the U.S. Left and progressive development. Whether it will continue to play this role depends on the type of forces that vie for leadership within that movement and to the extent the black proletariat advances, gets organized, and exercises leadership. Perhaps the now numerically dominant Latino population will exert greater overall socio-cultural-political influence on the U.S. movement, expanding the multilingual capacity of the U.S. Left, making deeper ties and correcting its bad historical record toward the Native nations. Perhaps and perhaps not. The destiny of the U.S. Left depends in large part how much self-criticism it can make and the degree and lengths to which it will apply a program of rectification. The hope is that these "Notes" will provide a basis for such a self-criticism and exploration of a new way forward. ‹ 343

....

2. How does the U.S. national question(s) relate to the question of imperialism today in its international manifestations and consequences? The rise of nationalism is directly related to the rise of national oppression. The national question in the first half of the twentieth century has been primarily the rise of new nation-states and national movements in the context of anticolonial struggles. In the final decades of the twentieth century, the rise of nationalism and religious fundamentalism is a direct result of the failed socialist revolution (which stem from a combination of all-out anticommunist reactionary assaults supported and often engineered by Western imperialism and from the internal unraveling of much of the former Soviet bloc governments). Throughout the globe, U.S. economic, political, and military hegemony was firmly established following World War II. Socialist, communist, and nationalist independence movements and leaders were destroyed and killed by U.S.-CIA and Western European plots in cahoots with domestic reactionaries. From Noriega of Panama, to Saddam Hussein of Iraq, to the Taliban of Afghanistan, despots, dictators, and strongmen around the globe

were in the beginnings of their careers all clients and creations of U.S. geopolitical clandestine (and not-so-clandestine) operations to counter local communists as part of the then-superpower rivalry with the now-defunct Soviet Union.

....

3. What are the "new" forms of opportunism related to national question theory? Theories of "superimperialism" and "imperialist economism," which the Bolsheviks fought in the early twentieth century (proponents of which have included Rosa Luxembourg to Eric Hobsbawm), continue today with three assertions: one, that imperialism resolves the national question and therefore the national question will eventually diminish and cease to exist; two, all nationalism is bourgeois and reactionary; and, three, capitalism, having become international, no longer needs the nation-state (and therefore, the nation-state will decline and become obsolete).

344 ›

While corporations traverse the globe and transcend national boundaries, they are still headquartered in a nation-state and rely heavily upon a wide range of "services" and protections afforded by the nation-state. These include trade protections and tariffs against foreign competitors, political "aid" to influence market penetration, the availability of military force to open new markets and to construct neocolonies (as with the invasions of Grenada, Panama, Iraq, Kuwait, and Afghanistan). The nation-state has *not* become less relevant or useful to international capital, but has become even more important to facilitating capital penetration and dominance by ensuring compliant consumer populations, crushing competition and political challenges (such as by Leftists and progressives), constructing necessary infrastructure for the flow of goods and services, and developing culturally appropriate marketing and consumption. Indeed, the number of nation-states as seen in the membership of the United Nations has never decreased but always steadily increased.

Nation-states as entities are transient and malleable. Their borders constantly change and can never be construed as fixed, ordained, natural, or permanent. Indeed, the territory and border of the United States has gone through periodic adjustment to its current fifty-state configuration, with the last two official states, Alaska and Hawaii, not even sharing a contiguous border with the other forty-eight. Therefore, revolutionaries do not uphold the "closed borders" policies of any nation-state. While revolutionaries do defend a nation-state from aggression and threats of territorial annexation, as part of opposing imperialist aggression and expansion, we staunchly oppose all restrictions upon the flow of human labor and creativity (the former manifested in immigration exclusions and the latter in terms of protectionist measures such as copyright law, intellectual and scientific proprietorship, genetic patents, etc.).

. . . .

4. Finally, how do we explain the rise of Western Europe to capitalist preeminence and world domination? Are there "special" reasons for why Western Europe was the center of world capitalist growth and eventual hegemony? Or, to perhaps express this question more colloquially, if the Chinese invented gunpowder and firearms, why were the Europeans the ones to develop them so ably and with such venality (beyond the biological-environmental determinist explanations of Europeans being "ice people," predisposed to increased cruelty, competitiveness, and avarice)?

‹ 345

Prior to Columbus's arrival in the Americas, European society did not enjoy economic, social, military, or technological advantages over the rest of the world. Indeed, Europe was in the throes of internal rivalry between emergent mercantile-political centers and the rising bourgeoisie in struggles with the feudal aristocracy, as well as in external competition with several major economic-military powers, including the Ottoman Empire, South Asia, China, and major trading centers in north, western, central, and eastern Africa. James M. Blaut asserts that perhaps the only advantage that "Europe's mercantile-maritime communities enjoyed over the competing mercantile-maritime communities of Africa and Asia was location. European centers were some 5,000 miles closer to the New World than any competing non-European center, hence were much more likely to make contact with New World places and peoples first, and were thereafter certain to monopolize the immense fruits of plunder and exploitation" (Blaut 1993, 30).

Indeed, the concept of Europe did not exist prior to 1492. The tremendous riches from the Americas enabled European societies to harness their working class, and accelerated the rise and consolidation of the bourgeoisie, which spurred on the unification, integration, and consolidation of the Western European nation-states, enabling European powers to out-compete the rest of the world, not by chance but because European nation-states were colonizing nations with first and direct access to the Americas. Prior to the oceanic trade routes to the Americas, the great trade routes between Europe, Africa, and Asia were mainly continental. Several major centers were poised for bourgeois revolutions, such as the proto-capitalist regions of "Flanders, southeastern England, northern Italy, sugar-planting regions of Morocco, the Nile Valley, the Gold Coast, Kilwa, Sofala, Malabar, Coromandel, Bengal, northern Java, and south-coastal China" (Blaut 1993, 166). But the fortunes amassed from New World colonization and its attendant slave trade provided the infusion of new capital, generated new international markets and the re-exportation of products abroad, and stimulated new internal and external markets that fueled the European bourgeois revolution to accelerate and exceed all other global competitors. "Colonial capital, in a word, was new capital. Without it, the sluggish late-medieval economy of pre-1492 days would have continued its slow progress out of feudalism and toward capitalism (or something like capitalism), but there would have been no 17th-century bourgeois revolution" (Blaut 1993, 199).

346 ›

Blaut argues convincingly that the mere happenstance of locational advantage for Europe was the essential precondition for the accelerated rise of industrial capitalism in Western Europe. Other powers around the planet possessed many of the same protocapitalist conditions and features, but the capital accumulation afforded to the new European bourgeoisie greatly enabled its victory over feudalism and thereby "allowed the emergent capitalist class-community to mobilize state power toward its further rise, such that the entire society contributed to underwriting of colonial adventures and to the preparation of infrastructure such as cities and roads, which the state's police and military power could now be mobilized to force people off the land and into wage work, and to conscript people and resources for advantageous wars abroad" (Blaut 1993, 199). The ascension of European colonial dominance scourged the rest of the world like a juggernaut, deindustrializing India, depopulating Africa, addicting one out of four Chinese males to opium. "Capitalism became concentrated in Europe because colonialism gave Europeans the power both to develop their own society and to prevent development from occurring elsewhere. It is this dynamic of development and underdevelopment which mainly explains the modern world" (Blaut 1993, 206).

The "why" and "how" of European world colonization pivots not on technological or military development, nor sociopolitical uniqueness, and certainly not upon biological and environmental characteristics. There was nothing "special" about Europe other than the fact that it was situated far closer to the Americas and faced fewer obstacles, including distance, climatic adversity, and competition, over the Atlantic Ocean, whereas cross-continental land trade routes took longer, were more hazardous and vulnerable to marauders, were more logistically cumbersome, and faced far more competition. It was not any special venality of the Europeans that motivated them to exploit the already-existing slave trafficking of Arab and African merchants and ruling classes, purchasing slaves as "tools" of labor to work in the plantation systems in the Americas. The great "civilizations" of the non-European world were seeking advantages themselves to extend their empires. While Asian and African (as well as European) excursions and arrivals to the Americas had all transpired prior to Columbus, the cost, length of time, and hazards seemed to far outweigh any perceived gains at the time, and thereby precluded the evaluation of sufficient profitability. The travel by Columbus was relatively short in time, cost, and losses. Columbus made multiple voyages and faced very little resistance from the Natives he encountered. Repeated excursions would confirm an abundance of "discoveries" of staggering profitability (namely gold, silver, foodstuffs, and raw materials generated by large-scale plantations). Such profits incentivized dramatic European maritime advancements, which led to repeated voyages with replete returns and endless exploitation.

The rise of capitalism and the bourgeoisie is not something that could have been stemmed by moral human conscience or by political choice, as the power of capital and internal and external competition transformed European society. Every European man, woman, and child was assimilated, integrated, and implicated into the new and revolutionary bourgeois society and much of the population came to enjoy a new, better, and more democratic life. The power of such a massive socioeconomic transformation as the bourgeois revolution changed the entire planet. It made one part of the world and its peoples become gods living in paradise and the rest of the world become proletarian peons condemned to purgatory. The hell of the colonized makes for the heaven of the colonizer. In the era of imperialism, of domination by international finance capital replacing direct colonial occupation, the world is divided into oppressor nations and oppressed nations. The United States of America has become the epitome and embodiment of modern imperialism, as its very multinational character is composed of oppressor and oppressed nations and its foundation built upon national oppression.

REFERENCES

Africa Information Services, ed. 1973. *Return to the Source: Selected Speeches of Amilcar Cabral.* New York and London: Monthly Review Press.

Baraka, Amiri. 1982. "Nationalism, Self-Determination and Socialism." *The Black Nation: Journal of Afro-American Thought* (published by the League of Revolutionary Struggle [Marxist-Leninist]), 2, no. 1 (Fall/Winter): 5–10.

Berg, Kristian, producer. 1996. *Dakota Exile.* St. Paul, Minn.: Twin Cities Public Television.

Blaut, James M. 1993. *The Colonizer's Model of the World: Geographical Diffusionism and Eurocentric History.* New York: Guilford Press.

———. 1987. *The National Question: Decolonizing the Theory of Nationalism.* London: Zed Books.

Cabral, Amilcar. 1979. *Unity and Struggle: Speeches and Writings.* New York and London: Monthly Review Press.

Cheng, Lucie, and Edna Bonacich. 1984. *Labor Immigration under Capitalism: Asian Workers in the United States before World War II.* Berkeley: University of California Press.

Chrystos. 1995. *Fire Power.* Vancouver: Press Gang Publishers.

Communist Workers Group (Marxist-Leninist). Ca. 1970. *Our Tasks on the National Question: Against Nationalist Deviations in Our Movement.* Pamphlet.

Etienne, Mona, and Eleanor Leacock. 1980. *Women and Colonization: Anthropological Perspectives.* New York: Praeger Publishers.

Fernandez, Carlos. 1992. "La Raza and the Melting Pot: A Comparative Look at Multiethnicity." In *Racially Mixed People in America,* edited by Maria P. P. Root, 126–43. Newbury Park, Calif.: Sage Publications.

Finkelstein, Sydney. 1960. *Composer and Nation: The Folk Heritage of Music.* New York: International Publishers.

Forman, James. 1981. *Self-Determination and the African-American People.* Seattle: Open Hand Publishing.

Gonsalves, Sean. 2001. "The Opposite of Racism Isn't Colorblindness." August 21. Available at: http://www.hartford-hwp.com/archives/45/322.html.

Handyside, Randy, ed. and trans. 1969. *Revolution in Guinea: Selected Texts by Amilcar Cabral.* New York and London: Monthly Review Press.

Harmon, Chris. 1992. "The Return of the National Question." *International Socialism: Journal of the Socialist Workers Party (Britain),* no. 56 (September).

Haywood, Harry. 1975. *For a Revolutionary Position on the Negro Question.* Chicago: Liberator Press; written in 1957.

——. 1976. *Negro Liberation.* Chicago: Liberator Press; first published in 1948.

Ho, Fred, ed. 2000. *Legacy to Liberation: Politics and Culture of Revolutionary Asian Pacific America.* San Francisco: AK Press.

League of Revolutionary Struggle (Marxist-Leninist). 1979. "The Struggle for Chicano Liberation." *Forward: Journal of Marxism-Leninism-Mao Zedong Thought* (Getting Together Publications), no. 2 (August).

Lee, Butch, and Red Rover. 1993. *Night-Vision: Illuminating War and Class on the Neo-Colonial Terrain.* New York: Vagabond Press.

Loewen, Joseph. 1995. *The Lies My Teacher Told Me.* New York: Touchstone.

McAdoo, Bill. 1983. *Pre-Civil War Black Nationalism.* New York: David Walker Press.

The 1928 Comintern Resolution on the Negro Question in the United States.

The 1930 Comintern Resolution on the Negro Question in the United States.

Sakai, J. 1989. *Settlers: The Mythology of the White Proletariat.* Chicago: Morningstar Press.

Spickard, Paul R. 1992. "The Illogic of American Racial Categories." In *Racially Mixed People in America,* edited by Maria P. P. Root, 126–43. Newbury Park, Calif.: Sage Publications,.

Thiong'o, Ngũgĩ wa. 1986. *Decolonizing the Mind: The Politics of Language in African Literature.* Portsmouth, N.H.: Heinemann Press.

Matriarchy:
The First and Final Communism

I AM NOT an anthropologist, archaeologist, or any specialist in antiquity and early human social history and development. Therefore, my arguments in this presentation will be primarily theoretical and political, as an artist-activist, which is what I am, to analyze the questions of why womyn are oppressed, and what should be done to liberate more than half of humanity as part of liberating all of humanity. While I will draw upon scientific research and analyses made by historians and cultural anthropologists, my argument is not primarily made on the basis of being "scientific," or necessarily provable, but from a combination of scientific argumentation as well as advocacy, that is, I take a political stand motivated by the premise to eliminate all inequality, injustice, exploitation, and oppression and to create a new society.

I oppose and reject white supremacist, Eurocentric patriarchal capitalism and I declare myself to be for replacing this social system with its opposite: multicultural, internationalist matriarchal socialism. In this presentation, I shall argue that the first and longest form of human social existence was matriarchy—a female-centered, nonrepressive, egalitarian society—that lasted for tens of thousands

Presented as a speech on April 20, 2002, at Augsburg College, Minneapolis, Minnesota, cosponsored by the Global Women's Network, the Associated Colleges of the Twin Cities Women's Studies Department, KFAI Radio, and the Amazon Bookstore Cooperative.

of years—far longer than the current era of patriarchy. This system based on the rule of the mother ("mother-right") was challenged and eventually overthrown by patriarchy, a social existence predicated upon male hierarchy, domination, and class rule. From a Marxist perspective, the struggle to overthrow matriarchy was the first class struggle. The transition from matriarchy to patriarchy has been the longest class struggle, a historical process that began several thousands of years ago across many different cultures, and continues worldwide today with violent and tumultuous social struggles, aimed at trying to uproot and eliminate any vestige of female power and control. I will also argue that Marxism (i.e., the method of dialectical and historical materialism) is fundamentally "feminist." In its argument and advocacy to liberate humanity, its vision is quintessentially matriarchal, both locating the first early human societies as communal and projecting and struggling for communism, the final epoch of human social existence with the elimination of all classes and oppression.

‹ 351

Much criticism has been made of both the theory of Marxism and its practice worldwide on the subject of womyn's oppression and liberation. I will give a brief summary of these criticisms and objections, unite with many of them in the spirit of seeking to expand and deepen Marxism, which is not a dogma with fixed truths, but a science that is tested and transformed continually as a "work in progress" capable of self-criticism to strength its revolutionary practice and service to the liberation of all humanity.

First, the charges of sexism within the theory: the avowals that socialism automatically eliminates womyn's oppression and sexism; the overemphasis on womyn's liberation as an outgrowth of womyn increasingly joining the ranks of socialized industrial production; the overlooking of or deemphasis on forms of gender oppression specific to womyn, such as womyn's underpaid or unpaid labor, reproduction, sexist culture, rape and forms of violence against womyn, and so on; and the Eurocentric biases of its historical analysis in primarily focusing upon family structures and gender relations among Western European and white settler-colonial societies.

Second, the sexism within the movement: of male domination and sexist leadership of Left and revolutionary organizations in which womyn are relegated to the typical "female" tasks and roles subordinate to and supportive of male leadership, from cleaning the office to making coffee to secretarial duties. Other criticisms include: heterosexism, male majority leadership and underrepresentation of womyn's leadership, machismo and macho culture, and failures to take up issues and struggles effecting womyn.

In the debates between feminism and Marxism that have ensued in the New Left since the 1960s, uneven progress and development has taken place in the arduous advance on "the woman question" both in theory and in practice. I will only briefly summarize what I believe to be some of these advances (albeit uneven) before I delve into the argument and analysis of matriarchy.

In practice, the struggle against sexism internal to organizations unfolded in a great many Left and revolutionary groups. For example, in the early days of the Puerto Rican Young Lords Party a male central committee member was removed for sexism. The central committee leadership body of a group I formerly belonged to, the League of Revolutionary Struggle (Marxist-Leninist) (1978 to 1990) was unique in the U.S. Left for being both majority womyn and majority oppressed nationalities ("people of color"). The LRS organized seven nights a week of child care for its cadres who had children. While justifiable criticisms of the movement have received much attention, particularly by academic feminists such as bell hooks and Michelle Wallace and many others about the "macho New Left," I believe an overall objective evaluation of this era and the movement as a whole must affirm, as Kathleen Cleaver, former Black Panther central committee member and the only womon to be on this leadership body, has done: that the movement politicized and drew in thousands upon thousands of womyn into revolutionary political struggle, challenged previous gender roles, and did effect massive and broad social change, including gender relations and revolutionary theory on gender liberation.

Much of the antirevisionist Marxist-Leninist party-building movement of the 1970s and early 1980s was homophobic and heterosexist, united around the core view that homosexuality is a form of "decadent deviancy of bourgeois society." Homosexuals were not allowed to join these organizations until they gave up being queer. These groups expectedly earned the scorn and aversion of many queer progressives, radicals, and revolutionaries.

The various socialist states that emerged in the twentieth century liberated the masses from brutal oppression and made tremendous advances compared to the previous prerevolutionary societies, including in the area of womyn's rights and gender equality, such as the universal right to divorce, rights to education, suffrage, universal child care, the elimination of prostitution, female infanticide, and many of the most brutal forms of womyn's oppression. While advances were certainly made, patriarchal practices, sexism, and male domination persisted, and were confronted with varying degrees of criticism and uneven efforts to uproot them. As these revolutions have unraveled or retreated, as we have seen in the former Soviet Union and East European states, and as capitalism spreads in China and Cuba, there has been a dramatic resurgence of gender inequality, commercialized sexism, prostitution, and trafficking in female infants.

Major advances to Marxist theory on the "woman question" resulted from the criticisms by feminist theory. Marxist theory in turn has expanded the understanding of the systemic and historical roots of womyn's oppression, including affirming the great importance of Engels's contribution on the family as a changing socioeconomic unit shaped by particular class relations, and not a fixed biological entity. Marxism has come to recognize the complexity and breadth of patriarchy as it manifests in male privileges and manifold forms of gender oppression beyond the concept of womyn's underpaid labor in production and her unpaid labor in performing free domestic work and services as wife and mother. Leopoldina Fortunati (1995) has contributed the concept of womyn's role in capitalist society as "reproducing labor" by: first, reproducing children who will be the future workers; second, providing the necessary labor and support services for male workers to live and return day after day to work as exploited workers; and, third, providing for themselves to live and return day after day to work as superexploited workers, and to return home night after night to work for their families. Engels's (1978) critique of the nuclear family continues to be disregarded in large parts of the socialist movement, and particularly by socialist states. Just as socialist states have not "withered away" in this past century, so too has the nuclear family become institutionalized and entrenched, with its concomitant gender roles for womyn as primary homekeeper.

Marriage and monogamy have become institutionalized in much of the socialist world instead of the free love, polyandry, and the sexual polymorphisms that should have happened in sexual relations.

One important area in which Marxists have advanced their understanding is their view of prostitution and prostitutes. Prostitutes have come to be viewed as sex-workers, though criminalized by bourgeois society. Prostitution is an outgrowth of womyn's oppression, since prostitutes are criminalized while their clients are usually not. Furthermore, Marxists no longer dismiss or mistakenly place prostitutes as part of the lumpenproletariat, a declassed criminal sector that preys upon the working class. Prostitution is part of the sexual exploitation of womyn and its criminalization is part of the social oppression of womyn.

While political trends for lesbian separatism are still espoused, most of the feminist movement and the Left have come to see that patriarchy is not the product of male culture or intrinsic to the biology of men, but rather a sociohistorical construction. To identify the root source of patriarchy as the biological and innate characteristics of men allows no possibility for revolutionary change, ignores the class contradictions of womyn exploiting womyn as well as men exploiting other men, and argues that the overriding, fundamental interest that men share as men is to protect their privileges. This position has not only been shown to suffer from a shortsighted cultural/historical bias that projects present realities upon past societies, but it also incorrectly accepts the premise that patriarchy is natural, permanent, and a universal truth for all societies throughout time. And nothing could be further from the truth.

Indeed, the opposite is true. Human society began as matriarchy and the solution to end all exploitation and oppression, especially that of womyn, will be matriarchy.

Both male and female Leftists bristle when I mention "matriarchy." The usual reaction is, "Why do you support female supremacy or womyn oppressing men? Why can't we be for male-female social equality?"

To which I reply matriarchy is the *opposite* of patriarchy, not its inverse. Matriarchy in early human development, and in my vision of its revolutionary future, is the just and rightful return to the producers what they've been denied: the fruits of their labor. In other words, if womyn, according to the United Nations Commission on Women, bear 100 percent of the world's children, grow 70 percent of the world's food, do 60 percent of the world's work, but earn 10 percent of the world's income and own less than 1 percent of the world's property, which is the system of patriarchy, then matriarchy would be the opposite or overthrow/reversal of this injustice. Womyn would have the return of their productive and reproductive labor. This would mean a womyn-centered social order, or the turning upside down of the world social pyramid whereby the producing majority would rule over the nonproducers.

Let me briefly digress and explain why I prefer not to use the term "feminist" and prefer "matriarchal" or "womyn-centered." "Feminist" came from and is primarily the identifier of the mainstream, white "bourgeois" womyn's movement that primarily seeks to redress and reform the unequal status of womyn in capitalist society. While radical and revolutionary and socialist feminists have challenged the monopoly on the usage and meaning of feminism, even these proponents have been plagued with national chauvinist, white racist, and imperialist biases and baggage. In the perspective of many progressive and revolutionary Third World womyn, feminism will always mean white womyn. A white womon identifies and benefits from the position of being white first and foremost. Feminist sisterhood doesn't extend to ending imperialism and the privileges of white settler-colonial society. Feminism seeks equality with white bourgeois men, to reform capitalism and to include white womyn as equal participants along with white men in the system of imperialist privilege and power.

As European colonization was expanding around the world, many of the womyn-centered societies—deemed by the Western colonizers as "primitive"—were what cultural anthologists term matrilineal and matrifocal, which are concepts that also do not encompass, embody, or express the full power and status of womyn in these societies. The colonizers forced their so-called civilized values, ideas, attitudes, and social practices about gender upon these so-called primitive peoples. But as we've now come to recognize, "primitive" societies were more socially advanced as far as gender and social equality and sustainable development. It was writer-activist Alice Walker who promoted the usage of "woman-centeredness," a term that isn't beholden to the political history and traditions of the white mainstream.

Most anthropologists concur that matriarchy preceded patriarchy as the first form of human social community, starting anywhere from 1 to over 3 million years ago. Most anthropologists will also concur that about four to eight thousand years ago, patriarchy emerged with the beginnings of "civilization" (i.e., the rise of large-scale stable communities supported by agriculture, which led to surpluses, which in turn gave rise to developed state structures and class divisions). Even the most die-hard apologists for patriarchy, who argue that man is genetically favored or predisposed to hunting, greater physical strength, and sexual dominance, will admit that the vast period of early human history was characterized by woman-centered social groups, namely the matriarchal clan.

Early human society worshipped womanhood (Mother Earth), and a plethora of goddesses across cultural groups were associated with nature, creation, and life. The scientific research from which I will argue the characteristics of matriarchy are drawn from a variety of sources, including Engels (1820-95), Lewis Morgan (1818-81), the Swiss anthropologist and cultural historian Johann Jakob Bachofen (1815-87), and contemporary Leftist anthropologists and social scientists such as the late Evelyn Reed (1905-1979), Maria Mies, the late Eleanor Burke Leacock (1922-87), and others.

Humans are distinguished from animals by the following characteristics:

1. The opposable thumb, which gives humans the ability to grasp tools, though primates share this trait.
2. Humans are omnivores and therefore can select from a diversity of food sources, while primates are for the most part herbivores.
3. Humans possess an enlarged brain relative to body mass and thereby are more intelligent.
4. Humans have vocal organs and therefore have the capacity for speech communication, which primates share as well.

5. Humans have sexual intercourse to reproduce as well as for pleasure and are capable of sexual activity 24/7. The restrictions humans observe about sexual activity, such as not mating with their parents, siblings, and children, are cultural and not necessarily biological inhibitions.

6. The most fundamental difference that separates humans from even primates is our ability to create cultural and social institutions via social cooperative organization at a complex level, which enables humans to develop technology, including the mastery of fire, and artistic expression (the ability to imagine that which we cannot yet create).

Even in the animal world, females are far from being the secondary sex. On the contrary, it is the male who is the expendable sex, whose role is for sex while the female is for maternity, to nurture, protect and raise the young. In early human society, "mother" was not an individual biological identity but a social and functional term. All womyn are "mothers," i.e., the providers and protectors of the clan.

‹ 357

Evelyn Reed's (1975) comprehensive study of matriarchy found the following characteristics shared by early human societies across the planet:

1. The original human social organization was the matriarchal clan and not the family.

2. Womyn were the procreators of new life and chief producers of the necessities of life.

3. Early society was organized around the collective production of life's necessities and communal possession of property, with the concept of property still very minimal.

4. Womyn were the leadership of the "humanization and socialization of our species."

5. Therefore, womyn were the centers of society, the organizers and leaders of social life.

Reed traces the creation of social taboos against incest and cannibalism as womyn-originated and implemented social limitations placed upon competition and aggression, to delimit the maternal clan or "sister-brother matriclan."

The myth of male superiority commonly derives its argument from the purported superior physical strength of the male and his heightened characteristics for competition and aggression that purportedly stem from his role as hunter in early history.

For hundreds of thousands of years human society was based upon food-gathering and hunting. Only 8,000 years ago did agriculture and animal husbandry (the raising of livestock) begin. Maria Mies's highly important book *Patriarchy and Accumulation on a World Scale* (1998) refutes the male-as-hunter archetype. Mies reveals hunting to have been a marginal activity and of far lesser social importance to early human society for the following reasons:

1. The most reliable food sources weren't animals but vegetables.
2. The food from gathering accounted for the vast majority of the caloric intake of early humans, rather than meat-eating.
3. Food gathering and early horticultural activity produced much greater benefits for the labor expended.
4. Hunting was not very fruitful, required the need to chase animals over vast areas with uncertain results and expended much time and caloric energy.
5. Gathering utilized more members of the community, fostered community ties and relations among generations (older people could still contribute), and generated more socially useful byproducts.

In early human society, physical strength was not that markedly different between the sexes as it has evolved into under patriarchal society. Patriarchy has perhaps enabled men to receive better and more food as well as cultural, social, and psychological advantages such as greater athletic training, occupations that emphasize physical strength and skills, and a general "masculine" identity that favors physical size and strength. Womyn, conversely, have been acculturated and socialized to accept "femininity," which preferences "sexual beauty" over physical prowess. Yet even under the most extreme patriarchal oppression, womyn, particularly laboring womyn, have not been physically inferior to men.

In her studies on enslaved African womyn in the United States during the antebellum era, Jacqueline Jones points out that black womyn always worked at physical labor as arduous as men's work; that black married womyn have always worked in proportionately greater numbers than white wives; and that black slave womyn weren't allowed to be solely housewives but were expected to do a slave's work in men's physical labor as well as to do all the work and duties of a female domestic worker both for her master and for her husband and family. She was a veritable "slave of a slave":

> female field hands were a common sight ... together with their fathers, husbands, brothers and sons, black women spent up to fourteen hours a day toiling out of doors, often under a blazing sun. In the Cotton Belt they plowed fields; dropped seed; and hoed, picked, ginned, sorted and moted cotton. On farms in Virginia, North Carolina, Kentucky, and Tennessee, women hoed tobacco; laid worm fences; and threshed, raked and bound wheat. (Jones 1985, 15)

‹ 359

In Jones's study, everywhere black men toiled, so did the womyn, with the addition of work they were expected to do as womyn.

While it is generally accepted that men's physical size was on average greater than womyn, rarely is size equated with strength, stamina, and dominance. It has almost nothing to do with social, economic, and political power, in either early or modern society.

Instead of physical strength, many other values associated with mothering and womyn's production were much more critically important to these early human societies. The mother or female was the producer-procreatrix. Because human birthing and nurturing required that the females remain close-knit for much longer durations than animals, gathering was more efficient and suited for human sustenance. And gathering generated the creation of technology and human activity far beyond the skills and technology used in hunting. Females, as Reed (1975) points out, were the first craftsmen, creating vessels for cooking that were leak-proof and fire-proof; the first fire-users through domesticating and controlling fire for cooking and home warmth; the first doctors and pharmacologists; the first chemists; the first artisans; the first farmers; the first inventors of tools; the first to create textiles; the first to tame the cat to keep food vermin-free; the first homebuilders; the main haulers of goods, belongings, and equipment (as womyn carried firewood, water, food, and building materials); the first teachers, the first linguists; the first historians. More than simply biological mothers, womyn were the mothers of invention.

Nigerian anthropologist Ifi Amadiume has argued for the matriarchal foundations of early west African society and makes the point: "Mother-focus/matrifocality covers the importance of women in kinship terminology, domestic arrangement and their central role in the economy as producers and providers. As soon as all these aspects of women's contribution in society are taken into consideration, one begins to recognize the limitations of analysis based on the simple dichotomy of matrilineal and patrilineal."

In other words, more than simply tracing lines of descent or sexual/marital relations, which tend to be reductive and not able to convey the real power and centrality of womyn to these societies, the term *matriarchy* more fully conveys the power held by womyn and their centrality to society. No evidence suggests that matriarchy was marked by the exploitation and oppression of men. If anything, matriarchal society was far more egalitarian and inclusive, and far less repressive and stratified. Matrilineal rules of succession may be evident in strongly patriarchal societies (e.g., ancient Egypt under the pharaohs). But patriarchy has never shown the egalitarianism and inclusion that was matriarchy.

Matriarchy offered the following features:

1. In primitive communalist society, there was no forced or alienated labor, male or female.
2. Work and social life were far more interdependent.
3. There was no sexual jealousy. Indeed, matriarchy was the "universal stage of promiscuity" (Bachofen 1967) with the extended family organized strictly by the mother and her children without regard to paternity, transitioning after several millennia into a "matriarchally controlled family with acknowledged fathers, and replaced finally by the patriarchally controlled family." Polyandry was the norm; people had sex with whomever they pleased. Should a more fixed pairing be chosen, the male would enter the womyn's clan. Either gender could leave or find other sexual partners without much reprisal, sanction, or risk.

4. Greater sexual freedom and range of sexual practices were an outgrowth of an uninhibited view of sex. It is now commonly acknowledged that what we today called transgender, bisexual, and homosexual practices and preferences were known among a number of North American indigenous peoples, including the "berdaches" of the Lakota Sioux and Cheyenne peoples west of the Mississippi. Among the Navajo and Mojave peoples, there were men who wore womyn's clothing and did the work of womyn, accepted as part of the natural identity of the community without any sort of stigma or ostracism. As Margaret Cruickshank has pointed out: "particular sexual practices did not place a person into a special category. Acts were homosexual; people were not" (1992, 5).

5. Due to the low technological level, no consumerist economy existed and the notion of individualism as understood today was nonexistent.

‹ 361

6. Those who toiled the most had the greatest influence.

7. Men were assistants to womyn.

8. There was virtually no internal group social violence or predation (crime, domestic violence, rape); however, evidence does suggest there was intergroup violence (such as warfare or raiding), but never on a massive scale of destruction and always as a last resort after other exogamous forms of negotiation, trade, exchange, and diplomacy were exhausted.

9. No state existed; neither did institutional coercion.

10. Though still highly debated, there may possibly have been more leisure time (though this very well may have varied across groups). Studies of rainforest cultures show that since the struggle for necessities was relatively easier than in harsher climates and topographies, these cultures had more time for artistic, recreational, and other leisure activities.

11. The concept of the family was one of sister-brother and not father-centered. The concept of individualistic or private families or activities or property did not exist. Everything was common: from residence, food, motherhood, children,

child-rearing and sexual partners to common suckling of infants.

12. There was greater co-existence with the natural world; a respect and deep spiritual connection and relationship with natural forces; and a veneration of nature as Mother Earth that mandated responsible behavior from humans toward all of her creations. Even the killing of animals for food required some form of spiritual contrition for or ritualized showing of respect to the slain creatures.

All these features of the matriarchal society were opposed and overthrown by the rise of patriarchy, which we will now analyze.

Father God vs. Mother Earth

362 ›

Even such a masculinist cultural historian as Amaury de Riencourt (in *Sex and Power in History*) acknowledges the overthrow of womyn:

> At some point ... men gradually substituted male god for the former Mother Goddess when they discovered the connection between sex and procreation, and their biological paternity. This patriarchal revolution, which swept the whole world some 3,500 years ago, was preceded in the collective unconscious by the mythological metamorphosis known as solarization, the victory of the male sun god over the female moon goddess. In turn this implied the collapse of the female-oriented cyclical fertility cults and the rise to supremacy of the male concept of linear history. (1979)

In a massive cultural paradigm shift, creative power was transferred from the female womb to the male brain (symbolized by Athena's birth from Zeus's forehead), valorizing male-dominated culture over female-intrinsic nature, and male-inspired ideas over female-created life itself. From the biblical Eve, to the Greek Pandora, to Aristotle's philosophic rationalizations, the female becomes depicted as inferior or as an incomplete male. But what is so artificial and contrived about such a problematic concept as male progeniture is that parthenogenesis in the natural world is still female in origin; as Helen Diner points out: "thread worms, wheel animalcules, plant lice and many branchiopodia as well as diverse types of wasps and butterflies are all virginal mothers" (1965, 4).

The overthrow of womyn or mother-right, while acknowledged by virtually all anthropologists worldwide, and depicted through myth, legend, and art throughout the world's cultures, was a struggle of immense historic proportions that traversed eons and unfolded unevenly across the globe. When it first began is not as important as why and how it happened.

Most scholars trace the beginnings of patriarchy (the rise of father-right or the father-family) to about 8,000 to 4,000 years ago. The beginnings of widespread and large-scale agriculture and livestock herding, the presence and growth of surplus and its attendant struggle for private accumulation, led to the rise of classes and the need for the militarist state to protect the nascent ruling classes. These ruling classes utilized new technological developments, such as metallurgy to create weapons with more destructive capabilities. They also seized control of scientific knowledge, such as biology to control the reproduction of livestock and of womyn, to serve the nonreproductive father-family.

‹ 363

The transition to patriarchy is marked by the following struggles, much of which were violent and vicious:

1. Men taking over agriculture and livestock husbandry as hunting becomes a sport, since food becomes a function of male-controlled domestication.
2. Under matriarchy, men as hunters specialized in killing skills and technologies. Men's monopolization of the means of violence positioned them to compete more aggressively for the surpluses created by the inventions and techniques innovated by womyn. External and internal predation intensify simultaneously.
3. Over centuries of battle and struggle, womyn are removed from the control and authority they held in society from the centrality of their position in production; the corner is turned as womyn are excluded from the means of violence.
4. The male-centered and -created state is an instrument of class rule to suppress the original producers and creators

of human society, womyn. Womyn become the first class overthrown by the rising patriarchal ruling-class state.

5. Polygamy and monogamy arise simultaneously and coexist as a function of male supremacist privilege. Father-right asserts that the father's sons would inherit his property and the females, including his wife, sisters and daughters, would have no rights.

6. Social relations become increasingly endogamous and narrower. Eventually, in Western European capitalist society, the bourgeois heterosexual nuclear family develops, with enforced monogamy for the wife and sexual chastity and purity expected for womyn, and anything-goes-sexuality for the men (the double standard), as long as profit-making isn't impeded. The working class in these Western societies is socialized to adopt and imitate the bourgeois family values and structure, though in reality many aren't able to and thereby suffer from neuroses, denial, guilt, inadequacy, shame, and a host of other psycho-sexual-cultural dysfunctions.

7. Sexual freedom for women is commodified into prostitution. Sexual fantasies are commodified into pornography.

8. With the degradation of Mother Earth, human exploitation and domination over the natural world, from the atmosphere to the oceans to the gene and atom, accelerates with irreversible devastation.

9. Predatory systems develop from slavery, feudalism, and other forms of tribute-extracting societies, to modern-day industrial capitalism. Concomitant with such a voraciously exploitative system are genocide, colonialism, imperialism, the intensification of internal social conflict, increasingly destructive external warfare, and irreversible ecocide.

Most anthropologists agree that about 3,000 B.C.E., the one-father patriarchal family and the complete overthrow of mother-right were achieved in all major "civilizations" around the planet. As Reed (1975) put it, in this new concept called family, "the father has total control of his wife and children, the line of descent is from father to son, and the mother's brother has vanished." However, the consolidation of patriarchy would take several more millennia as womyn would resist and fight against their downfall and degradation.

Private wealth became possible with ever-increasing surplus production, which was generated from the inventions of matriarchy. Men, through their monopolization of the means of violence, rose up against their mothers and sisters. Why couldn't womyn control their sons and brothers and husbands? Why did men choose aggression and competition over the surplus instead of greater communal sharing? Dialectical and historical materialists, that is, Marxists, don't accept biological-driven explanations or innate cultural arguments of men being by nature equated with aggression and competitiveness. As scientists, we acknowledge the limitations of our present capabilities to fully explain matters that extend far before the scientific historical record. *Why* men overthrew womyn may yet not be answered, but we have achieved a clearer understanding of *how* this happened.

‹ 365

Evelyn Reed notes:

> The essence of male sexual dominance in our society, which is founded upon the father-family, is the husband's exclusive possession of his wife who, by law, must restrict her sexual activities to him alone.... The sexual freedom of female apes and other animals who mate at their own will and with any number of males they choose testifies that, in nature, males do not dominate females. Male domination is expressed only in relation to other males.... There is no "father-family" in the animal world; males do not provide for a pregnant female or for her offspring. (Reed 1975, 53)

The war on mother-right and the legacies and vestiges of matriarchy continued with the rise of expanding patriarchal states, with their state-sponsored religions, and the ever-intensifying class stratification of the globe with the colonial expansion of Western European bourgeois capitalism. Entire societies, cultures, and nations had to be forced to submit to Western capitalist dominance, and the world's peoples, cultures, and societies had to be fitted, either by force or by conversion, to the economic profit of the colonial world powers.

Religions as we know them today are all patriarchal. Mother Goddess belief systems have been virtually wiped out. Capitalism and Christianity are codependent twin evils that sought to conquer and

colonize the entire biosphere. Christianity pre-dated capitalist hegemony as feudalism rose from the ashes of the Roman Empire. Christianity officially served European feudalism as a religious mantra
that served to unite Europe against the rest of the non-Christian/
non-European world, to seize their lands and wealth, and to justify
the colonization of the earth. "The aim of European Christianity was
acquisition of property, which meant overturning pagan systems of
matrilineal inheritance" (Reed 1975, 623).

A series of papal decrees from 1031 to 1051 ordered priests to abandon their wives and to sell their children, turning over their property
and monies to the church upon death and not to any family heirs.
Eventually, differing Christian sects broke away from the Roman
Catholic church as rising competing capitalist circles demanded
greater independence from church control for their unrestricted
pursuit of profit and wealth. These new circles were tired of sending
parts of their profits to papal coffers. The rise of Protestantism and
other more pragmatically focused sects conformed to the needs and
interests of the new, rising European bourgeoisie who dared to defy
the sanctified birthrights of the monarchy and the dominance over
land and wealth held by a papal feudal theocracy. All men were equal
in the eyes of God, proclaimed these Christian breakaway faiths, and
therefore had an unrestricted right to compete and to profit without
having to give a portion of their surplus to either royalty or Rome.

The Christians brought the Devil to the "New World" and the Devil
was them. So-called primitive peoples did not subscribe to the mono-
theism and anthropocentrism of the Europeans. While the Aztecs
and Incans had entrenched and established hierarchical religio-
political ruling-class structures, they shared the same polytheism
and animism as the other more tribal peoples in the Americas. It
was not possible for these societies to regard even their enemies as
subhuman or without a soul. It was not possible for them to regard
nature as not a living being for which they, as humans, came from
and belonged to. The Europeans, however, slaughtered and enslaved
them as if they were logs to be felled, and their land and ecology nothing more than objects from which money could be made.

As Ward Churchill and other "indigenists" have pointed out, for
indigenous peoples, a "feminine" nature is to be loved and venerated.
For the predator cultures, a "feminine" nature is to be dominated,

controlled, and conquered. Thus, the interconnected triple struggle to save the planet, indigenous peoples, and womyn is the struggle to stop ecocide, genocide, and matricide.

As the conquerors raped the societies, cultures, resources, and womyn of the world, the effects of their colonization would profoundly change the world and consolidate patriarchal capitalism as a world system in the following ways:

1. The European colonizers did not recognize the leadership and political authority of womyn leaders and in many instances created male puppet leaders with whom to sign treaties, thereby eroding forever the power and leadership of womyn and changing gender relations and wreaking havoc upon the social structures of indigenous peoples.

2. The colonizers imposed cash crop production and destroyed indigenous economies that were often womyn-centered and controlled, thereby replacing interdependency with dependency upon the outsider's economy and making womyn dependent upon men.

‹ 367

3. The indigenous people, under the onslaught of this brutal juggernaut, lost their culture, their indigenous technology, medicinal knowledge, and way of life, which was often kept and managed by womyn.

4. Contact with the colonizers brought diseases and drug addiction (such as alcohol), and sometimes brutal physical genocide of outright slaughter by the colonizers. No better example illustrates this than the practice of scalping, which whites took from a traditional native war ritual in which the "small piece of flesh taken from the head of a man was a substitute for killing the man or decapitating him." (Reed 1975, 231). The Europeans took this ritual of indigenous warfare that granted humanity to captives and turned it into a sport and attached a cash reward to create a profit incentive that resulted in mass genocide. Not only were the buffalo gunned down en masse from passenger trains by whites as a sport, so too were native peoples slaughtered simply for sport and money.

5. Horrific terror and abject squalor reduced once-proud

peoples to shame and self-hatred. This cultural genocide led to spiritual decimation and cultural prostitution, including pandering to white New Age commercialism, supporting Disney's *Pocahontas,* and building casinos as a choice for progress.

6. The world lost, perhaps permanently, an environmentally sustainable way of life practiced by generations of indigenous societies, that was often the responsibility of its womyn, as the assumption of technological progress and superiority committed an unremittant, unforgivable, and irreparable ecocide through the murder of Mother Earth.

However, the clash between indigenous societies and the colonizing capitalist societies has always been resisted, especially by the indigenous womyn. Such acts of resistance include the underground female cultures of resistance held by the Andean *puna* (which upholds womyn as the purveyors of culture) to the countless native womyn who hid their children from baptism, to the womyn warriors who compose the majority of the armed rank-and-file and leadership of the Zapatistas, the Tupac Amaru, the FARC (the Revolutionary Armed Forces of Columbia) and other forces, as well as the millions of womyn active in nongovernmental and grassroots organizations and movements throughout the Third World who struggle for womyn's rights, indigenous self-determination, and ecological defense.

Whether patriarchy originated in one part of the world first or in multiple sites may never be clearly answered. However, it spread to all major continents, with the possible exception of Australia until the arrival of the Europeans. But wherever advanced ruling-class "tributary" states arose, they were all patriarchal: from the Eastern Asian dynasties of Japan, Korea, and China; to the great kingdoms of the Indian subcontinent; to the western Asian empires of Persia and the Ottomans; to both the eastern and western coasts of Africa and the great central African kingdoms; across the oceans to the Incans, Aztecs, and Mayans of South and Central America. But it was in Western Europe and in its settler-colonial offshoots in North America that patriarchal capitalism arose and eventually brought its white racist, patriarchal class system to every part of the planet. As part of Eurocentrism, we have a preponderance of scholarship focusing on Western European historical, socioeconomic, and cultural development. The Afro/Asian/Oceanic/pre-European Americas have not received as much attention, especially cases in which matriarchal legacies may have persisted more strongly despite the dominance of patriarchal class formations—particularly in small, relatively isolated societies that were late in contact with Western colonialism, such as in the Pacific Islands and aboriginal cultures that retain the gathering and hunting mode of production. But all great "civilizations" and empires were intensely patriarchal, as a popular feudal Chinese saying bears witness: "A woman is born and serves her father as daughter; when she marries she serves her husband as wife; and when she gets old, she serves her son as servant." Her role of mother (once honored as the source of power throughout the early human world) was no longer acknowledged.

‹ 369

We know in looking at the world historical record that wherever Christianity and capitalism arrived, the old laws of mother-right were destroyed and the wife soon was deprived of everything. The overall position of womyn quickly fell as a consequence of this destruction of matrilineal inheritance. In ancient societies, the only way for men to get property was to seek a matrilocal marriage with an heiress from another land, as his sisters inherited his family home and its belongings. "'Matrimony' used to mean the feminine equivalent of 'patrimony': inheritance of property in the maternal line. Matrimony came to be synonymous with marriage only because marriage was a way for men to gain control of property" (Cruickshank 1992, 21). Furthermore, "the English word 'heir' came from *here,* cognate with the Greek word for a female landowner, *here* or 'Hera.' The Magna Carta referred to a *here* as a person of either sex. Later Church laws listed *heres* as exclusively male" (Cruickshank 1992, 20).

Private wealth could only occur from surplus. Surplus could be obtained either internally, from greater productivity, or externally, through predation and the plundering of resources and wealth, that is, through conquest, confiscation, slave or conscripted labor, and exacting tribute. The acquisition and holding onto of surplus required the use of force: to ward off other aggressors and competitors and to suppress revolts by the conquered, enslaved, and have-nots.

Furthermore, mechanisms needed to be developed by the surplus accumulators to fend off internal competitors, and, more important, the proponents of matriarchal communalist and egalitarian positions who would demand that the surplus be shared and not monopolized.

Through male control over the state, laws stripped womyn of property and citizenship, and forbade womyn to do business with a bank (she could not even make a small deposit without her husband's permission). A systematic campaign against womyn was unleashed by the forces of patriarchal class rule, through force and violence, the enactment of laws, vigilante terror such as the anti-witchcraft pogroms, and countless womyn-hating cultural "diatribes against womankind," to enforce the power of fathers-brothers-sons over mothers-sisters-daughters worldwide.

All positions of power became majority male and masculinized, especially in the control of violence, force, and coercion, principally the military and police. While today womyn are partially integrated into the police and armed forces of certain countries, these institutions remain patriarchal instruments, thoroughly masculinized. An army or police in a matriarchal revolutionary socialist society would be entirely different in character and role from what it is under patriarchy. If womyn held most of the guns, do you think domestic violence would have any social support? Even in the early stages of class society, which still had many influences of matriarchy, a captured enemy would often be adopted rather than enslaved forever as chattel property. I'm not saying that womyn are innately predisposed as mothers and nurturers to not be as inclined toward violence. However, the skills and culture of motherhood valued and promoted in a matriarchal society would be capable of utilizing a myriad of nonviolent and noncoercive methods in responding to the plots of patriarchal capitalist restoration.

Iris Young writes:

> While women in precapitalist societies were by no means the social equals of men, all the evidence points to the conclusion that our situation deteriorated with the development of capitalism. In precapitalist [European] society women dominated a number of crucial skills and thus their labor and their knowledge were indispensable to the family, the manor and the village. In many craft guilds of the

16th and 17th centuries women were members on equal terms with men, and even dominated some of them. Women engaged in industry and trade. Precapitalist culture understood marriage as an economic partnership; men did not expect to "support" women. The law reflected this relative equality of women allowing them to make contracts in their own name and retain their own property even in marriage. (Young 1981, 59)

The consolidation of capitalism in the West ushered in the modern-day ideal of the bourgeois nuclear family. The bourgeois male is the "breadwinner," the economic engine of the family in its quest to increase its wealth and accumulations. His wife is a "housewife," who is expected *not* to be involved in any direct economic activity, but to be a housekeeper and to raise the children of her husband. The bourgeois nuclear family is a single household with expectations of monogamy between husband and wife. However, monogamy is one of the endemic contradictions in capitalist society, along with many other double standards and hypocrisies. In reality, capitalist monogamous marriage is restricted, explicit monogamy for the wife and implicit sexual freedom for the father-husband, who, while legally married to only one wife, could indulge himself with mistresses of all ages and classes. Lastly, the bourgeois nuclear family institutionalizes the father-to-son transfer of property inheritance.

‹ 371

Besides being stripped of legal rights and property ownership, womyn in bourgeois society had to be "housewifed" or domesticated, restricted from remunerative economic activity both inside and outside the home. However, the reality for millions of working-class womyn, though inculcated with this bourgeois nuclear family ideal, has been quite the opposite. Working-class families could not realistically survive with the father as sole wage-earner; in many families, womyn and children joined adult male workers in industrial production. In the example of 1866 France, Helieth Saffiotti (1978) notes that womyn were 30 percent of the industrial workforce, and, though never totally marginalized, womyn were coming to be "defined as a secondary labor force which served as a reserve of cheap labor." For the next century, womyn's labor came to serve the new expanding industries and the void filled by men fighting in the two world wars. These included new occupations such as textiles, nursing, sales work, clerical and administrative, telephone operators . . . the rise of the so-called pink-collar ghettos. Such "women's jobs" were typically paid less than what came to be denoted as "men's jobs." The sexual division of labor under capitalism has marginalized and devalued womyn's occupations while those of men are given greater pay and importance.

As an economic unit, the family provides both formal (i.e., paid) labor and informal (un- or under-paid) labor to the capitalist. The working-class male worker is exploited for the profit extracted from his productive labor. The capitalist derives his profits from the wealth of the products created by his workers, whose wages are just barely enough to support the worker and his family. Working-class womyn, whether married, single, or unmarried family providers, are doubly exploited, both at the workplace and for their contribution to the reproduction of surplus value in informal sectors of the economy. The unpaid labor of maintaining the working class allows the capitalist to keep overall wages lowered. By paying womyn less than men, capitalism extracts greater profits, ensures a reserve of surplus labor, and divides men and womyn with sexism. Patriarchy keeps womyn oppressed and keeps the profits generated from this social condition flowing to the capitalist ruling class. As discussed earlier, Marxist theory has been making greater strides into the critique and analysis of the reproduction of surplus value from womyn's role as wife-mother, unpaid reproducer of the family, household worker, child-care provider, and sex provider, and how patriarchal oppression maintains bourgeois male control of society.

As the amount of capitalist production has increased, wave upon wave of consumer goods and services floods the market, demanding the wages of the masses of workers to purchase this glut of goods. The family has increasingly been a unit of consumption (father, mother, kid, car, TV, microwave, refrigerator, summer home, family vacations, cell phone, SUV, personal computer, etc.). After World War II with U.S. world hegemony established and affluence increasing within America, the housewife became a major demographic profile for advertising. The day-time soap opera and talk show was created as a cultural form through which products could be marketed and sold to the housewife. Soap operas and their advertisers continue to target housewives, but as American prosperity has declined, these programs have expanded their target to attract her children, the highly lucrative "youth niche market."

Ecocide, Genocide, and Matricide: The Killing of Mother Earth and the Dire Need for Matriarchal Socialist Revolution and Eventually for Matriarchy as the Final Communism

The revolutionary movements around the world, even at their patriarchal worst, have always adopted slogans that at least convey a proclaimed and professed commitment to womyn's liberation, including slogans such as "Women Hold Up Half the Sky," or "Unleash the Fury of Women," or "Women Are Half the Revolution," or "There Can Be No Revolution without the Revolution of Women." But nowhere have I seen T-shirts or banners, worn either by men or womyn Leftists, that declare, "Matriarchal Socialism Is the Only Socialism!" except in a small national collective in the mid-1990s that I belonged to, the short-lived ORSSASM, which stood for the Organization of Revolutionary Socialist Sisters and Some Men. During the early 1990s, several revolutionary socialist feminists formed Revolutionary Sisters of Color (RSOC), though this group was not united around socialism. ORSSASM was unique: it was majority "women of color," but it had some men as members, including me; while it was united around socialism, it had a very diverse socialist composition, including Marxist-Leninists who believed in the single vanguard party, former revolutionary anarchists who came out of the split and breakup of Love and Rage, and radical socialist feminists and lesbians. While most of the members were young, in their twenties and thirties, almost all of the womyn rejected marriage and the concept of monogamy (though they were willing to practice it in individual cases) and, of course, the nuclear family—only a small minority had children. They began a serious re-study of Marx and Engels on the theory of the state, private property, and the family and they critically examined the problems of patriarchy in socialist countries and movements with an avowed position that "patriarchal socialism is unacceptable, therefore we call for and will build matriarchal socialism as the only possible way to get to communism, the fullest and final liberation of womyn, which will be matriarchy." In a break from all other Left groups that professed and called for a generic "society without class and gender divisions and equality between the sexes," ORSSASM correctly and scientifically understood that womyn not only are a numerical majority of the world's population (therefore unequal in an abstracted democracy), but will remain the procreative power of the species (as females are in the natural world) while being social equals with men (meaning that biological or individual advantages should be directed toward the common good). But the transitional stage of socialism, where the injustices and inequalities of the past patriarchal class societies are corrected, should be firmly matriarchal as a form of super-affirmative action, or the implementation of the position that "the last shall be first, the first last" (without subscribing to Christianity). ORSSASM, before it dissipated from lack of revolutionary organizational leadership, engaged in a year and a half study of the question of matriarchy. Rather than publish a political manifesto, it decided to create a more popular educational tool, the Sheroes/Womyn Warriors calendar, which has been published annually since 1998, and for the 2003 edition has been significantly revised and expanded. This propaganda/cultural tool has been popularly received, and at the same time has earned the ire and castigation of many white male purported radicals, who whine and complain about the proposition of matriarchy. Should we be surprised?

The goals of a revolutionary matriarchal socialist society include:

1. To de-genderize every sphere of social life, particularly institutions of power that have been dominated by men.
2. To valorize "feminine" skills and interests such as education, child care, cleaning, cooking, and nutrition.
3. To demilitarize society by placing the forces of repression and violence under the command of womyn and the working class as a whole; and to promote womyn's self-defense, including training and the bearing of arms. As quickly as possible, to destroy all forms of chemical, biological, nuclear warfare, and to eliminate all technology used for warfare and intelligence gathering, and to destroy all conventional firearms, battle cruisers, nuclear submarines, fighter planes, tanks, and so on. To prevent the restoration

of the patriarchal bourgeois-controlled police and military-
state, a socialist state would create a people's militia in
which all citizens may serve and work primarily not
in repression and social control, but in community service
to eliminate poverty and inequality, disaster relief, and
protection of the environment. The main function of any
control or repressive aspect of the state would be to out-
law exploitation and restrict the privileges of the former
ruling class. Such decisions would be under the command
of matriarchal leadership bodies based in communities
of oppressed nationalities and working-class people.

4. To promote a massive campaign for anti-sexism, particularly among men.

5. To promote a massive cultural campaign for womyn's
self-worth independent from male approval.

6. To abolish all unequal and sexist laws against womyn
and to repeal all heterosexist laws and policies, such as
anti-sodomy, anti-gay families and marriage laws, and
laws that privilege the nuclear family.

7. To erode the primacy put on the nuclear family (though it
still may be an option for many or some people), to socialize
household work, to make child care a universal right along
with health care, housing, education, and the right to basic
income; to support new and different forms of sexual relationships, partnerships, and living units as alternatives to
the nuclear family.

8. To ban the private ownership and commodification of seeds,
life forms, and the human genome; to promote biodiversifi-
cation, organic farming, sustainable development, global
redistribution of wealth and resources, and anti-consumerist lifestyles; to stop the use of nuclear energy and thereby
halt nuclear waste; to encourage zero population growth
through the promotion of family planning, socioeconomic
equity, non–chemical dependent birth control, and greater
gender liberation overall.

9. To provide massive reparations to indigenous peoples, to
carry out every treaty (since the U.S. government has never
honored a single one) since the arrival of the Europeans,

to redraw the U.S. borders to allow for the restoration of indigenous self-government, and to make first allocations of public monies to the poorest and longest oppressed of the peoples in the U.S.

Many tasks and challenges will confront the struggle to create a matriarchal socialist society. But without such a society, womyn will continue to be oppressed. With or without the support of men, womyn can and will shape and lead the matriarchal revolution. Where men will be in this society depends on what they do to help or hinder its birthing.

REFERENCES

Amadiume, Ifi. 1987. *Male Daughters, Female Husbands: Gender and Sex in an African Society.* London: Zed Books.

———. 1997. *Reinventing Africa: Matriarchy, Religion and Culture.* London: Zed Books and St. Martin's Press.

Bachofen, Johann Jakob. 1967. *Myth, Religion, and Mother Right: Selected Writings of J. J. Bachofen.* Translated by Ralph Manheim. Princeton, N.J.: Princeton University Press.

Cruickshank, Margaret. 1992. *The Gay and Lesbian Liberation Movement.* New York and London: Routledge.

de Riencourt, Amaury. 1979. *Sex and Power in History.* New York: Dell.

Diner, Helen. 1965. *Mothers and Amazons.* New York: Julian Press.

Engels, Friedrich. 1978. *The Origin of the Family, Private Property, and the State.* English translation. New York: Pathfinder.

Etienne, Mona, and Eleanor Leacock. 1980. *Women and Colonization: Anthropological Perspectives.* New York: Praeger.

Fortunati, Leopoldina. 1995. *The Arcane of Reproduction: Housework, Prostitution, Labor and Capital.* New York: Autonomedia.

Jones, Jacqueline. 1985. *Labor of Love, Labor of Sorrow: Black Women, Work, and the Family from Slavery to the Present.* New York: Vintage.

Leacock, Eleanor Burke. 1981. *Myths of Male Dominance: Collected Papers on Women Cross Culturally.* New York: Monthly Review Press.

Mies, Maria. 1998. *Patriarchy and Accumulation on a World Scale: Women in the International Division of Labour.* London: Zed Books.

Morgan, Lewis Henry. 1974. *Ancient Society, or, Researches in the Lines of Human Progress from Savagery through Barbarism to Civilization.* Edited by Eleanor Burke Leacock. Gloucester, Mass.: P. Smith.

Reed, Evelyn. 1975. *Woman's Evolution: From Matriarchal Clan to Patriarchal Family.* New York: Pathfinder.

Sargent, Lydia, ed. 1981. *Women and Revolution: A Discussion of the Unhappy Marriage of Marxism and Feminism.* Boston: Southend Press.

Saffiotti, Heleith. 1978. *Women in Class Society.* New York: Monthly Review Press.

Young, Iris. 1981. "Beyond the Unhappy Marriage: A Critique of the Dual System Theory," in *Women and Revolution,* edited by Lydia Sargent, 43-69. Boston: Southend Press.

Momentum for Change: Lessons for the East Coast Asian Student Movement

THANK YOU FOR THIS HONOR of presenting the keynote address at your tenth anniversary conference. Ten years ago, while a junior at Harvard, I participated in the founding conference of the ECASU on April Fool's weekend, 1978. A historic step was made as close to three hundred students from more than two dozen campuses united and organized themselves to build an Asian student movement that would advance our struggle for respect and equality in this society. Like you, we did all-nighters to do outreach, plan housing, get funding, plan the workshops, and struggle with the direction of this network.

Your theme, Momentum for Change, is very appropriate. After a decade, many changes in the character of Asian students on the East Coast reflect parallel changes and challenges to our communities. Not only has active participation in Asian American student groups and conferences such as this one doubled from ten years ago, but also we find a greater diversity of Asian/Pacific nationalities, with more Korean, Southeast Asian, East Indian, and Filipino/Pacific Americans. We also find Asian students in greater numbers more active and organized than a decade ago; on some campuses there are almost half a dozen different Asian student clubs. My address to you will look at some of these changes and the new challenges for not only the Asian

Presented as the keynote speech for the tenth anniversary of the East Coast Asian Student Union (ECASU), Cornell University, Ithaca, New York, 1988.

student movement but for the Asian American Movement as a whole as we step into the last decade of the twentieth century.

The ECASU was an outgrowth of momentum that began in 1977. Throughout the 1970s, Asian students held annual conferences. These were one-shot, annual events (what we called "identity" conferences). They were a way to bring Asian students scattered across East Coast campuses together to meet each other, to socialize, to share experiences in workshops to learn about basic Asian American history and current issues, and to affirm a common identity of being Asian in America. But in 1977, at Yale University, a small working conference set forth the idea of forming an organized network of Asian campus organizations on the East Coast. This embryonic network was called the "Intercollegiate Communications and Liaison Committee"—a lengthy name, referred to as ICLC for short.

The ICLC's main focus was to help build the anti-Bakke movement among Asian students. This momentum took place in the context of the mid-to-late 1970s, a period of growing retrenchment and rising conservatism, as U.S. society took concerted steps to wipe out the gains won from the protests and struggles of the preceding decade, the 1960s.

‹ 379

A chief ideological and political slogan was "Reverse Discrimination"—a charge made by Alan Bakke, a white man, who blamed special admissions programs for minorities as discriminatory against white males; in Bakke's case, denying him admission to medical school. But for all of us at this time in history, we knew this dangerous lie had to be opposed. The notion that we were "discriminating against whites" is absurd. In fact, at Harvard, when I entered as a freshperson in 1975, Asian Americans weren't recognized as a minority and were excluded from minority programs and events. Harvard had only 4.5 tenured black faculty (the .5 comes from a professor who was in semi-retirement), and almost no tenured Asian American faculty in the undergraduate college—with most appointments of Asian American faculty being in West Asian languages and lower-level teaching posts in the sciences and math departments. We had no Asian American courses, except for student-created independent study courses, and certainly no special recruitment and admissions for Asian Americans.

The "reverse discrimination" onslaught was the historic challenge to Asian and minority students of the 1970s. The ICLC was formed to better organize and prepare us for this battle to defend the minimal gains made from the earlier decade. To do this, we had to educate Asian students about our history of oppression and resistance, which included our own contemporary history as Asian American students. We put together slideshows, speaking events, and some activist-leaders traveled to different campuses to do this work. In our East Coast meetings, we recognized that a broader, more permanent network needed to be built beyond one issue, beyond annual identity conferences/get-togethers—a movement that would set the direction for our and succeeding generations of Asian students. ECASU was born.

Part of organizing ourselves required us to understand where we, as Asian American students, came from. Our legacy begins in the period of the late 1960s: the era of the Civil Rights Movement that quickly leaped into the Black Power rebellions and revolutionary upsurge that swept across America. The militant sit-ins, boycotts, demonstrations, building-takeovers led by black students both in the South and in the North were an example to students of color and progressive white students. Make no mistake: students sacrificed their academic standing, and even their lives (as in the case of Kent and Jackson State, to name only two), to change society; to oppose the racist, imperialist war in Southeast Asia, to fight for minority admissions and Black studies departments, among a host of other demands.

At Cornell, the African American students seized campus buildings, bearing guns, and, with national media attention, demanded black student services, affirmative action, and Cornell's first Black studies department. Elite Ivy League schools that had only a handful of minority students were forced to recruit and admit greater numbers. If you look at any one of these schools, you will see a huge jump in the number and percentage of minority students in the matter of one year from 1968-1969.

At San Francisco State College, in 1968, the first ethnic studies department (that included Asian American studies) was won after a massive student strike that was met with violence hurled by the police unleashed by the then college president, the banana S. I. Hayakawa. Hayakawa, a Japanese American, sought to divide the minority students by pointing to the Asians as "quiet and hardworking" and a "model minority" that the Black students should emulate, rather than to rock the boat.

In a matter of a couple of volatile years, from 1968 to 1970, dramatic changes were made in the U.S. higher educational system. Prior to 1968, at a public university like the University of Massachusetts at Amherst, there were more African students from Africa and more East Asian students from Asia than there were black American or Asian American students enrolled. When I entered Harvard in 1975, my freshman class had about sixty to seventy Asian American students, compared to four in 1968, and now compared to about two hundred for the entering class of 1992. At Harvard, for us to win Asian American minority recognition from the administration, twenty Asian, black, Chicano, Puerto Rican, and white students refused to leave Dean Archie Epps's office until our demands were met. After that, Asian Americans were included in recruitment and admissions plans, and invited to minority prefreshmen and freshmen orientations. We also became conscious of the need for what we then called "Third World Unity."

‹ 381

Even though I have only touched on this historical background, you can see that it took a spirit of defiance, of struggle, a willingness to take whatever steps were necessary to win justice and equality, to force open the heretofore exclusive, white male country club doors of these institutions.

But once we got in, we found that our fight had only begun. More complex questions confronted us. Some of the minority faculty members we had fought to be hired vacillated, and those who maintained their backbone and commitment to their communities found themselves not getting tenure. We found that admissions committees we had fought to establish had the least committed people appointed to them. Demands for a Third World Center were thwarted by "race relations" committees or foundations ruled by the administration with token student representation. It was not enough to get these programs in place; we now had to fight to control them. Before many of us had a chance to catch our breath, we were charged with "reverse discrimination."

ECASU was born in this period of the late 1970s—of threats to the small democratic gains won from the late 1960s. Out of the founding

ECASU conference at Princeton in 1978, we united around four core principles that I believe still guide the Asian American student movement. These principles are:

1. Build and strengthen Asian student organizations as broad, democratic organizations, taking up the interests of Asian students by integrating social, cultural, political, and educational activities.
2. Promote the unity of Asian peoples, among different nationalities and from various backgrounds.
3. Build, learn from, and support an Asian American student intercampus network.
4. Fight the oppression of Asian people and strive for unity with Third World people as part of the progressive movement.

These principles expressed a vision of our role as part of the Asian American Movement working to change the larger society. While respecting the broad and diverse interests, heritages, and backgrounds of Asian American students, we believed unity to be essential to advancing our common struggles for dignity, justice, and equality in American society.

Today, along with the Asian American student organization, there are organizations of Chinese, Korean, and other Asian/Pacific nationalities. These specific nationality student clubs aren't contradictory to the AASA or Asian American coalition type of group. Asian American identity is the collective experience of all of the distinct nationalities of Chinese, Japanese, Filipino, Korean, East Indian, and so on, with different languages and cultural heritages and different generations of immigration to the United States. Yet, the consciousness of being "Asian American" is relatively recent, a product of the late 1960s that recognizes the fundamental commonality of our experience and destiny in America—a people of color, oppressed, struggling for respect, equality, and justice. Hence, an Asian American studies department or program is not a singular academic discipline, but intrinsically interdisciplinary. What holds it together, or makes it cohesive, is studying the Asian American experience from the perspective of those who live it, distinct also from the mainstream

experience and perspective. Asian American studies are also mandated to serve the community, a mandate to which we, the community and the students, must still hold these departments and faculty
accountable.

Most of the first Asian American studies departments were established on the West Coast, where there is a much greater number and
concentration of Asian/Pacific Islanders. With the exception of City
College of New York, there hasn't been any established Asian American studies until recently. There is a great need to understand the
many issues of our identity, history, and heritage, a burning desire
and hunger to know who we are, our worth in this society, and our
direction and destiny. So the ECASU and individual member ASOs
took it upon ourselves to fill the voids. That's how the annual Asian
Awareness Month began: a coordinated campaign among East Coast
schools initiated by the ECASU to plan and put on programs and
events that address and promote our cultural heritage, history, and
current issues: to educate Asian Americans, as well as the larger
campus, about who we are. Other campaigns were also launched that
have greatly impacted upon Asian students on the East Coast, reach-
ing out to hundreds, such as the college days held in the community.

‹ 383

We recognized that we couldn't rely on the admissions offices to
earnestly recruit our younger brothers and sisters, especially from
inner-city schools instead of the traditionally elite private and prepa-
ratory-type high schools. We also knew that admissions policies and
criteria had to be changed to genuinely allow for a culturally diverse
student body instead of WASP and affluent color clones. The docu-
ment/study done by the ECASU admissions task force, published
in *Bridge* magazine, remains an important indictment of continuing racism in university admission practices, quoted nationally by
educators, activists, and other Asian American students challenging
similar patterns of quota ceilings and anti-Asian biases in the higher
education system.

ECASU has a proud record of accomplishments. In addition to
what I've just cited, look at what's been done:

ECASU and individual ECASU campuses have continually supported critical issues of the Asian American communities, such as
redress and reparations for Japanese Americans interned in concentration camps during World War II; support for the struggles

of restaurant and garment factory workers; protests against racist stereotyping in the media (films such as *The Return of Fu Manchu, Year of the Dragon, Big Trouble in Little China, Charlie Chan,* and many other examples); protests against anti-Asian violence such as the Long Huang Guang case in Boston; the ECASU Asian American studies campaign has helped to bring about Asian American studies courses on many campuses; ECASU women activists helped to generate greater attention on Asian American women's experiences, which has led to new Asian American studies courses addressing Asian women; and, to my joy, last summer, ECASU and the AARW in Boston produced Genny Lim's play, *Paper Angels*—and audiences were ecstatic! Back in 1978, we knew that someday, Asian students from coast to coast would formally link up. And that time is now!

The next decade for the Asian student movement, as well as for the larger Asian Movement, will pose new and more complicated challenges, as well as exciting promises for a generation prepared to meet them. By the twenty-first century, the Asian/Pacific population in America will be over 10 million, or 4 percent of the total U.S. population. But in certain regions, like California, our presence will be far greater. However, as we grow, as history teaches us in the example of the nineteenth century, white supremacy will seek to restrict us, to deny us equality, pointing to us as a threat.

Let's look at the contemporary images of and ideas about Asian Americans. Basically, white racism reacts to us as a yellow peril horde, a foreign invasion. Though these yellow peril images of the Exclusion Acts period of the nineteenth century still hold, the contemporary variety is more complex and subtle. We are still stereotyped as not real Americans (it still surprises some whites to find that American-born, third-generation Asian Americans can speak good English); we clan together in ghettos as if it was a matter of our choice; we are overrunning campuses, classrooms, and neighborhoods and taking away white jobs. Unlike the blatant, stinking yellow coolie image of yesteryear, the modern image is more insidious because it is promoted as a positive stereotype. Of course, I am referring to the Model Minority Myth.

The model minority myth is the *main* stereotype of the 1980s. Though certainly other stereotypes coexist, it is the model minority myth that is being given fullest media attention and is guiding current social policy. The model minority myth does not praise Asian Americans: it attacks us and denies our demands for affirmative action. And it is extremely dangerous because it has Asians believing in it, going along with it, aspiring to be model minorities.

Images abound: of Asian whiz kids taking over computer science departments, or amazing cellists and concert pianists herding into Juilliard practice rooms, or Asian female news reporters and anchors coming across the airwaves on the evening news every night; or the gray-suited Japanese businessmen buying up American real estate and taking over American factories, etc., etc. ad nauseum.

It's true that more and more Asians are entering new fields that they previously did not have access to, some with a fair amount of public visibility. For example, Asians fill the lower-level clerical and technical ranks of San Francisco's City Hall, which has come to be called a "Chinatown ghetto." Or we can't help but notice those attractive, articulate newswomen. And, yes, according to the Southern California Korean Grocers and Liquor Retailers Association, the number of Korean-owned grocery stores, small liquor outlets, delicatessens, and convenience stores in the L.A. area is now about 3,000, an increase of 1,500 to 2,000 since 1982. And, yes, according to the *New York Times,* the Chinese American population in New York City is now at 300,000, growing at 1,400 per year, with a number of financial institutions and backs that are (quote) popping up like bean sprouts (unquote). And it is true that Asian families put a heavy emphasis on their kids doing well in school, particularly in the sciences, and middle-class parents like to have their kids playing European classical music rather than avant-garde jazz saxophone. But the fundamental question is: have Asians made it, outdoing the whites?

Often the explanation for these super characteristics of Asians is cultural: it's the stern, disciplined Asian family that produces obedient, hardworking, straight-A students; or traditional Asian culture makes them conformists, good team players, loyal, but also indistinguishable and not too exciting. Cultural explanations are tricky. They are conveniently offered to explain "positive" stereotypes but also to explain our limitations.

Here's the double standard: Asians make good workers, they're reliable, honest, and loyal, but they also don't make good managers or leaders or decision-makers. Asians aren't assertive, they have poor communication skills, and they don't fit in socially, like playing golf with the ol' white boys—qualities judged for leadership and executive material. Often in the job world, it is not enough to simply perform well on the job for promotion and advancement. Often subjective factors are more important—mingling, acting whiter than white, playing politics. Many Asian immigrants especially don't feel comfortable interfacing and socializing in a white environment.

How successful are the most successful Asian Americans? The number of Asian American CEOs is miniscule. I can only think of Gerald Tsai, of American Can Corporation in Connecticut—that is, CEOs of established, mainstream American corporations. The case of An Wang is always brought up, but Wang is the CEO of a company that he started, after having worked for years in the established corporate world. People like Wang realized that they couldn't go any further and ventured out on their own. The An Wangs are Asian American entrepreneurs of their own companies, which doesn't discount discrimination, but actually confirms it. Asians in decision-making, leadership levels are still extremely rare, except when they head their own companies. People like An Wang couldn't become CEOs of the traditional corporations and had to start their own. This applies to successful fashion designers, architects, merchants, and other businesspeople, as well.

Has the model minority myth really helped us, have we made it? Yes, there has been some access to broader fields, but the presence of Asian Americans is still quite limited, and most aren't making it. The traditional WASP, male-controlled and dominated institutions—the real power of America, such as investment banking, corporate law, politics, the board rooms of major corporations, educational institutions, and entertainment and communications conglomerates—remain as they were at the beginning. The American power structure, which includes the boards of trustees of higher educational institutions, has learned from the 1960s. Now in the 1980s, a chief way to disarm discontent and disturbance is through tokenism to show that the bootstraps do work if pulled up hard enough. This ideological ploy gets immigrants to work harder for a lot less and to accept their suffering silently. It also conveniently blames failure for not making it as lack of effort and not enough pulling up of your own bootstraps.

So we see the vicious cycle, the catch-22 of it all: when Asians do well in a certain field, they are penalized, charged with taking over universities. But we must remember our history: ten years ago, Asian students were taking over university officials' offices to simply get in.

How do we fight the model minority myth? Well, first we mustn't believe in and accept it. We need to expand the struggle for Asian American empowerment: to report the news from our perspective, to tell our own stories, to create our own images, to define and analyze our own experience.

Back in 1978, when we first began to form ECASU, we recognized that Asian American students had to move beyond identity conferences. That affirming identity is important and necessary only because we, as Asians, are an isolated minority in a very white environment. ECASU was formed to *organize* Asian students, to unite and thereby strengthen the larger movement for Asian American political and economic empowerment. Feeling good about being Asian is inextricable from the status and conditions of the majority of Asians in America, and not by how far a few have advanced and how comfortable they have become. Individually, we might believe that we might have overcome discrimination, but as I have tried to show in refuting and attacking the model minority myth, what matters is the overall lack of real political and economic power for most Asian Americans.

Asian American students come together for a variety of reasons: to socialize, to affirm their heritage, their sense of who they are, and their self-worth. And all these reasons are indications that we are indeed a minority—we still lack the power to define, to share equally in American society. Political and economic empowerment means control of our communities, asserting our political representation in areas of our concentration, and the development of our resources and institutions. By Asian American empowerment, our communities will determine how our land will be used (for housing and services, rather than speculation and outside encroachments); we will build and expand social services, cultural organizations, promote training and diversity of employment and business ventures; foster bilingual/biculturalism; do everything for our communities that needs to and should be done for us to exercise full equality and control of our lives. As an Asian American student, more than ever, your generation has the responsibility to contribute as much as you can to the further empowerment of our peoples, to make sure that future generations will reap benefits from our long history of struggle and to propel us, better organized, more united, to win greater victories. The critical issues for organizing in our communities—in issues of housing, workers' rights, community land development, greater electoral representation—require the active involvement of and support from Asian students. Your heightened consciousness and organization can only strengthen our collective empowerment for equality and respect in this society.

The recognition of moving from feeling good about one's identity to empowerment motivated me to choose my life work and to compose and perform original, innovative music that evokes our heritage and spirit, our aesthetics focused to free all people from exploitation and oppression.

A people without a sense of history and culture do not have an identity. Asian American identity is a question because society never allows us to select and promote our own images and cultural expression—we assert our cultural identity as a form of struggle against the myths, distortions, lies, and stereotyping.

But too often, as a symptom of an oppressed people, we don't value our own culture and identity, but adopt the standards, values, and mentality of the dominant culture. And the internalization and acceptance of the model minority myth contributes to self-denial and white-washing.

Asian Americans need to be more conscious consumers of their own culture besides cuisine. We need to study and become aware of the continuum of Asian American folk culture, literature and art, and thereby support the growth and development of our own contemporary forms of expression that will inspire and empower us, not confuse and eviscerate our spirit.

Racism in American culture, as I have posited, is today more complex and sophisticated. Instead of the obviously offensive whites in yellow make-up in popular media, Asian American actors are being hired to carry out the same function of a Fu Manchu, a Charlie Chan, a Hop Sing, or a Susie Wong. That's why it was so important to oppose Michael Cimino's *Year of the Dragon.* There's no excuse, even though Tisa Chang, John Lone, Dennis Dun, Victor Wong and the air-brained Ariane (as Tracy Tzu, what else, the Asian female reporter) are featured.

Our own cultural work must be strong and deeply rooted in our own standards and heritage and not be superficial, appealing to the "lowest common denominator" with delusions of a "crossover" dream in a mainstream market. While important as "firsts" with mainstream distribution, there's a tendency among some Asian American media and performing artists to do light comedies that imitate white pop or commercial formulas—more fluff than real stuff. While they aren't stereotypic, neither are they very inspirational or insightful. Often the notion that what makes something Asian American culture (music, plays, literature, etc.) is that it must have references to Asian food—this borders on perpetrating another narrow and trivial image that panders to white acceptance and fuels the model minority perception of Asians. It is ironic that the title of the self-proclaimed "premier Asian American/Pacific Rim magazine" is *Rice*.

‹ 389

The campaign of Asian students on both coasts to develop and institutionalize Asian American and ethnic studies is critically important.

While a visiting lecturer and artist in residence at Stanford during this past winter quarter, I taught the first Asian American literature and culture course there. I have found that many of this generation of Asian American young people don't know a thing about the literature, music, theater, and visual art forms created by their forebears in America. Sure, there are East Asian studies to learn about classical Asian art, calligraphy, and so on. But the culture of Asian America is the expression of our identity and experience in America, with roots to the traditional and folk forms of our ancestral Asian homelands, evoking all of the complex questions and contradictions of our lives here in America.

Unfortunately, most Asian American studies departments and intellectuals have not paid enough attention to the performing arts and narrowly deal with literature (mostly from the limited point of view that Asian American literature is in English and published by white publishers), ignoring the significance of oratory and the folk culture of poetry, storytelling, songs, and drama.

This is staid academic snobbery that some of our professors and program heads have adopted, like their white ivory tower counter-parts: if it can't be shelved in a library, then it's probably not worth studying.

Working for Asian American or ethnic studies is part of making an impact upon the entire university for a more multicultural curriculum. But it's important to have a solid base for which students can gain this knowledge, and continue to fight all cultural biases throughout the educational system, including curriculum, testing, arts programming, support services, and programs.

Furthermore, students need to demand that Asian American studies professors remain relevant to the needs of the Asian American students and the larger Asian American communities and not withdraw into the insular, removed world of academia. In many cases, the ASOs were at the forefront of the tenure battles of the 1970s. Complacency needs to be combated.

The complexity of racism and discrimination today poses new challenges, and demands great clarity from us. While gains have been made by Asian Americans, we must guard against tokenism—a tiny handful of "firsts" who are held up as success-story examples of how Asians have made it. Real barriers are broken when the majority of Asians advance—the collective empowerment of our communities that is both the struggle to gain access into all spheres of American society as well as the right to build our own institutions, to define our own culture and community life, to make our most innovative and original contributions to this society. The 1960s were a battle for access to higher education; the 1970s were a period of defending and expanding the gains; the 1980s and beyond will be the real test of real empowerment waged against a mounting campaign to stereotype Asian Americans via the model minority myth. This current period has required us to sharpen our opposition to the model minority myth. Anti-Asian violence is on the rise, along with the gutting of affirmative action and social programs. The anti-Asian backlash is mounting. Amid all the propaganda of Asians making it, anti-Asian flyers are being circulated in Bensonhurst citing the Asian "takeover" of the neighborhood. *Rolling Stone* magazine (February 11, 1988) insults Korean Americans as fanatical, violent workaholics with "Kim Chee breath" and "Kim Chee farts." Asian American students, activists, intellectuals, and artists need to vigorously unite and move forward for greater political and economic empowerment—which, in the cultural and intellectual areas, necessitates building our own institutions.

The workshops for this conference will help to clarify and guide you as activists to your role in the struggle for Asian American empowerment.

Art and Culture—Creating literature, performing arts, media, and visual work that inspires pride in our heritage and resistance will combat the passivity and conformity promoted by the model minority myth. Raising our cultural expression and awareness and consumption contributes to the struggle to build our own institutions and to portray ourselves as ourselves.

Asian American Studies—Studying and analyzing the entirety of our experience (history, culture, politics) will enable us to redefine the American experience to be a multicultural one, and clarify the tactics and strategy of our struggle.

‹ 391

Asian American Admissions and Financial Aid—We need to assert control of all university policies that affect the composition, character, and quality of higher education to which we are entitled.

Civil Rights and the 1988 Elections—We need to shape a national political agenda that addresses the issues impacting on Asian Americans tied to a larger political strategy for social change.

Third World Unity/Expanding Our Sphere of Activism—How to unite with other peoples of color to advance our common struggles for greater representation and control over student government, budgets, performing arts, and all areas of the education system.

Asian American Sexism—Why are we divided? How do we advance equality for Asian American women, develop leadership among Asian American women, and uproot sexism in all of its manifestations?

Developing Leadership/Organization Building—What qualities, abilities, and characteristics are important to lead? How do we build broad, democratic organizations and raise consciousness? Without strong organizations, we will lack empowerment.

These workshop topics address the broad important issues that are our Momentum for Change.

Thank you.

Flags, Falsehoods, and Fascism:
As Long As Imperialism Exists,
Chickens Will Come Home to Roost!

THE EVENTS OF September 11, 2001, involved an attack on two mighty symbols of American imperialism: the World Trade Center in New York City, symbolizing primarily the strength of U.S. finance capital, and the Pentagon, the headquarters of U.S. military command. A third attack was interrupted and its intended target remains unknown. A great number of civilian lives and small businesses were lost and destroyed in the New York attack, the tragic and unfortunate consequence of what has been branded "terrorism." Leftists can expect the U.S. corporate media and ruling-class leaders to whip up jingoism, patriotism, national chauvinism, and support for military campaigns. The U.S. Left can expect escalating difficulties and challenges posed by the tidal wave of flags, falsehood, and fascism that, in my perspective, are to be expected and, given the current direction of U.S. imperialism, will only continue in greater intensity and devastation to both the Third World and to the people of the United States.

To accept in any way the U.S. ruling-class spin and actions to the events of September 11 as a legitimate response to "terrorism" is to succumb to vile opportunism; that is, the Left and revolutionary movement conceding to imperialism by confusing its stance and goals with that of the world's biggest capitalist power. And, the U.S.

Presented as a speech for the forum "Perspectives on Radical Social Change and Revolution," held at the University of California–Los Angeles, February 9, 2002.

Left would be harming and defeating itself in a period when, more than ever, the devastation and havoc created by capitalism needs to be staunchly fought.

Yes, the acts of September 11 were terrifying, heinous, inhuman, and massively criminal. However, to call them "terrorist" (the generally accepted legal and political definition being the use of violence primarily upon a civilian population for political goals) only plays into the hands of the U.S. ruling class and its military and government, which has been both one of the biggest terrorists of the modern era and probably the greatest sponsor of terrorism across the globe for the past one hundred or more years.

The term "terrorist," according to Anthony Simpson, "was first used to describe terror by the state, when the Jacobins launched their 'Reign of Terror' after the French Revolution." He cites the modern meaning accorded by the *Oxford Dictionary* of "a member of a clandestine or expatriate organization aiming to coerce an established government by acts of violence against its subject[s]" as first used in 1947 in a reference in the British Annual Register to the blowing up of the King David Hotel in Jerusalem: "the latest and worst of the outrages committed by the Jewish terrorists in Palestine." Simpson notes that "when the Israelis established their state the next year, few people cared to use that word about their founders."[1]

The U.S. Left plays into the hands of its ruling class by accepting the imperialist version of history and politics. Before I discuss what I view as the needed strategy and course for the U.S. Left, I must oppose the opportunism within our movement on the issue of September 11.

....

1. In opposing the U.S. ruling class's push for a "war on terrorism," some on the U.S. Left argue that the attacks of September 11 should be viewed as criminal acts and not automatically assumed as acts of war. They correctly argue that no real proof has been offered, no convincing case has been made of the motives, means, and evidence of the perpetrators, who also remain uncertain. In other words, except for an undisclosed report revealed to and cosigned by British Prime Minister Tony Blair, there is no smoking gun, no confession, no admission of guilt, and, at best, even in the eyes of legal novices,

no physical evidence and only the flimsiest of circumstantial "evidence" pointing to Al-Qaida and its leader Osama Bin-Laden. These U.S. Leftists and liberals who caution about a rush to judgment, who call for calm but concerted and vigorous investigation and pursuit, and who advocate for the use of international legal, investigative, and law enforcement measures, with military deployment only after confirmed culpability, however, were easily ignored, and were ineffective in mitigating or tempering the military juggernaut that has been unleashed abroad and the escalating repression domestically. But more critically, the danger and incorrectness of this opportunist position is its reliance upon imperialism to follow its own laws, which it hasn't done and will never do.

....

2. Carl Davidson, a longtime Leftist and personal friend since we were comrades in the League of Revolutionary Struggle in the 1980s, has the view that the U.S. Left must stand for the safety and security of American civilians and unite with the fears of a great many of this country for their rights to life, safety, and property. He believes that a broad peace movement must be based on recognizing that Americans face an "immediate and present danger." Davidson unquestioningly accepts the U.S. ruling-class guilt placed upon Bin-Laden and Al-Qaida, for which he is taken to task by many for uniting with U.S. imperialists on this assumption. In condemning the attacks as horrific "crimes against humanity," Carl Davidson tries to maintain a Leftist position by acknowledging the America of empire as distinct from the American people.

However, Davidson equates the "theocratic fascists" of Islamic fundamentalism as being just as bad as U.S. imperialism, indeed, probably worse, because to Davidson, they are on the rise. In my reading of Carl, his position borders on "class collaborationist" as he views Al-Qaida specifically and terrorism generally as the main danger to the peoples of the United States. This is reminiscent of the position taken by the former October League, of which Carl was a leading member before he joined the LRS, that read the 1970s-80s People's Republic of China position on the then-USSR as the "main danger" to the peoples of the world, which (and for which I believed the October

League was rightly criticized) led them to mute their criticisms of, and in some cases to side with, U.S. imperialism.

American civilians, whether ensconced in U.S. suburbs, working in U.S. embassies around the world, or simply going on tourist vacations, will always face threat to their lives and property so long as U.S. imperialism exists, because much of the exploited and oppressed world will resent, hate, and target anything American. The social chauvinism of the bankrupt French communist party during the 1950s sided with French colonialism during Algeria's struggle for independence against France. That struggle included mass protests, uprising, guerrilla warfare, and, yes, even so-called terrorist attacks like Algerian women carrying bombs in their purses in suicide attacks upon French discos and cafes in posh European enclaves in occupied Algeria. See the film *The Battle of Algiers* by Italian Leftist filmmaker Gillo Pontecorvo. The revisionist Communist Party of France condemned the terrorists and refused to support the Algerian struggle. This is social chauvinism: socialism in words, national chauvinism or oppressor nation patriotism in deeds.

‹ 395

....

3. The U.S. Left must not confuse or conflate its independent political interests and class outlook in any way with that of American imperialism. We must never accept national chauvinism, that is, adopting the stand and view of our ruling class as ours. We are not patriotic. We don't apologize for or defend the actions of the ruling class imperialists. We don't rationalize or justify any policies on behalf of the ruling class. So, when someone asks us, "What would you do if you were president or running this country?" we would decline to answer this question and say, "The first thing I'd do is dismantle the imperialist military and end the capitalist system; then I'd make reparations to all the people of the world and ask for their forgiveness for the crimes perpetrated by the United States." I would not acknowledge that this government is *my* government. While I am of this country, I don't stand with its capitalist interests and I didn't make nor do I want this system we must live under.

....

4. Why is the U.S. system and government hated, especially by many in the Muslim world? As many in this audience are aware, the U.S. government funded and supported the rise of bin Laden, Hussein, and many dictators around the world during the era of U.S.-U.S.S.R. global rivalry. The CIA funneled $2 billion to the Afghan mujahideen in the 1980s and bin Laden was hailed as a freedom fighter, while during this time, Mandela and the anti-apartheid forces were labeled as terrorist. To offset Soviet maneuvers in the Middle East, and to maintain U.S. access to oil supplies in that region, in 1990 the United States established permanent military bases in Saudi Arabia. According to Noam Chomsky, this was comparable to the Russian invasion of Afghanistan in 1979, except that Saudi Arabia is "way more important" as the home of the holiest sites of Islam. The act compounded the animosity against the United States from years of backing of regional dictatorships, its subversion of democratic and progressive movements, its policies and continual military sorties that devastate civilian populations such as in Iraq, and its unremitting support for settler-colonialist expansion by Israel and oppression of the Palestinians. Add to all of these U.S. troops, military personnel, and destructive armaments, the growing presence of U.S. corporate and cultural invasion with Hollywood movies, malls, and consumerist garbage and arrogance that insults, defames, and tramples over traditional cultures and lifestyles.

. . . .

5. As long as U.S. imperialism rules, chickens will come home to roost. The five top corporations on this planet are all U.S.-based: General Motors, Wal-Mart, Exxon Mobil, Ford, and Daimler-Chrysler; all five are bigger than the gross domestic product of 182 countries.

. . . .

6. The U.S. "holy war" is one of asserting capitalist fundamentalism upon the entire planet. Bush's rhetoric is just as maniacal, evangelical, and terrifying as any jihad cleric's. Bush and his alliance are the twenty-first-century version of the Crusades phrased as a mission to "conquer all evil." To focus on the minor and lesser terrorists and de-

flect attention from the world's biggest terrorist (U.S. imperialism) is precisely what the imperialists want. But millions have died from U.S. military actions and tens of thousands die daily from First World prosperity, affluence, and global economic destruction.

There is so much historical evidence about the crimes of atrocity by the United States that I won't take the time to dwell on them in the short time allotted to my presentation. I will cite one example: the destroying of the El Chorillo neighborhood in Panama when U.S. military forces were ostensibly hunting Panamanian president Noriega, in which the official count of 500 dead was probably more in the range of 5000 people killed, according to Yale University professor John Gerassi.[2] It was common knowledge then that Noriega wasn't even hiding in that neighborhood, but the pretext allowed the United States to murder many Panamanian nationalist activists who lived in that neighborhood.

‹ 397

....

7. The United States has repeatedly defied all bodies on international law when it chooses to. In the 1980s, the International Court of Justice, the World Court, and the United Nations Security Council and General Assembly ordered the United States to stop its "unlawful use of force" against Nicaragua. That is, all these world bodies found the United States to be engaged in international terrorism, ordered the United States to stop these crimes, and to pay huge reparations. But the United States used its veto in the U.N. Security Council to thwart Nicaragua's case. Then Nicaragua went to the U.N. General Assembly, where technically there is no veto. The entire body of the U.N. General Assembly condemned the United States and passed a resolution condemning international terrorism (though it did clearly exempt violence used in resistance to colonial and racist states). But the U.S. "no" vote, first joined by Israel and El Salvador, then the next year only by Israel, made it clear the United States was not going to abide by any laws or world mandate. The United States is the only state on record to be condemned by the World Court for international terrorism and it vetoed a U.N. Security Council resolution calling on states to observe international law. To the United States, laws aren't to be followed in a world ruled by force.

....

8. Let's be clear, September 11 didn't "cause" the warmongering and hyper-militarization that has since dramatically increased. It was clear that George W. Bush, as soon as he was selected by the Supreme Court to be president, was determined to complete the New World Order planned and begun by his daddy George Herbert Walker Bush during his presidency.

September 11 has given Bush the pretext to further the military hegemony of U.S. imperialism and the economic colonization of the vital oil pipeline territories of Central Asia to Europe. NATO, once an alliance against European communism, is now a pact for aggression, expansion, and intimidation against Eastern European, Western Asian, and Pacific Rim states. Afghanistan borders Iran, India, and even China, but more importantly the Central Asian republics of the former Soviet Union: Uzbekistan, Turkmenistan, and Tajikistan. These republics border Kazakhstan, which borders Russia. All these republics are in the pathway of the oil-rich Caspian Sea. Afghanistan is needed as a base of operations to dominate the Central and South Asian republics, which will enable U.S. control over the oil pipeline between Europe and Asia.

Since September 11 Bush wants to increase the U.S. military budget by $48 billion. Already the United States supplies 40 percent of the world's weapons and maintains a military presence in 140 countries. It is no surprise that Britain is the second-largest arms exporter at 25 percent of the legal market.[3] The United States is also the largest manufacturer of the horrific biochemical weapons, including the variety of anthrax found in the recent U.S. mail.

Genuine revolutionaries oppose terrorism because we believe that revolution, if it is to be real and effective, must be based upon and supported by the masses of people and not the adventurist acts of a small group. Terrorism, whether it be bank robberies, bombings, or any use of violence that harms civilians, will alienate mass support, and strengthen repression by the enemy. Revolutionaries primarily function in the realm of political activism to destroy the credibility and influence of the ruling class and its state upon the masses. Only once this is accomplished in a massive way can effective war be waged against the state forces. Acts of resistance to repression, racist violence, and state attacks, including armed rebellion, are *not* forms of terrorism. In the late 1960s and 1970s, some U.S. Leftists engaged in armed attacks upon police, money appropriations (the Leftist euphemism for bank robberies), airplane hijackings, and other so-called criminal acts. Many of us in the movement criticized and rejected these actions, but nonetheless will defend these Leftists against the imperialist state because they received very harsh sentences because they were politically Leftist. Our commitment to demand amnesty for many political prisoners comes from recognizing that they are prisoners of war, from the Puerto Rican struggle for national independence or the New African independence struggle or ongoing struggles to defend their nationhood as indigenous First Nation peoples.

September 11 did not begin a new era for the U.S. imperialist ruling-class agenda. If anything, it revealed the weaknesses of the right wing, which is using the attacks of September 11 to reinvigorate itself. It was clear before September 11 that the U.S. right wing was unraveling. Not since the Vietnam War had the Democrats been in the Oval Office for two terms. Clinton moved the Democratic Party more to the right, and co-opted much of its conservative but non-extremist base. As many of us have always known, instead of two parties contending for national office, in reality we have one party with two wings. But from a combination of the Democrats moving rightward and the Republicans embroiled in their own internal cleavages, during the 1990s we saw the weakening of the right-to-life movement, the implosion of right-wing militias and white supremacist groups, the many scandals and internal fractures of the Christian fundamentalists, and the fall from grace of Newt Gingrich and his "Contract with America." However, the U.S. right wing wasn't going to allow Al Gore to be president, using the daddy Bush-stacked Supreme Court to rule against the U.S. popular vote (which Gore won by over 600,000) and the popular vote of Florida (which at best was never counted).

....

The "War against Terrorism" has intensified the War at Home with mounting attacks upon civil liberties as Americans are made to accept "less" freedom for more "security." Military tribunals, secret trials, no trials, unilateral imprisonment, increased surveillance, racial/ethnic profiling, sweeping state powers to arrest and indefinitely "detain" with no charges or evidence, academic hit lists sponsored by the American Council of Trustees and Alumni (chaired by the terror of the National Endowment for the Humanities Lynn Cheney, the vice president's wife, and Senator Joe Lieberman, Al Gore's vice-presidential running mate) against tenured faculty they deem dissident, and the building of public consent against protest and dissent, all in the cause of fighting "terrorism." With these expanded powers of "domestic security," civil disobedience, marches and demonstrations, boycotts, and other protest actions could be deemed terrorist acts.

Any and all compromise, accommodation, acquiescence, or intimidation to the military and economic aggression in the world by U.S. imperialism and its attendant domestic repression must be staunchly opposed by the U.S. Left. As this forum reflects, we of the U.S. Left must build our own alliances and united fronts across the political and ideological spectrum of anticapitalist, antiracist, antisexist, antihomophobic forces, including Marxist-Leninists, socialists, anarchists, nationalists, greens, radical feminists, queers, and others.

We must aggressively expose the jingoism, warmongering, and national chauvinism being whipped up from political spin-doctors to popular cultural propaganda in such films as *Black Hawk Down* and anti-Arab racism propagated in films like *The Mummy.* We need to sink deep organizational roots among workers, oppressed nationality communities, and in the varying social movements, intensify all forms of struggle and demands for social and economic justice, equity, protection of the environment, and opposition to all forms of chauvinism and racism and consumer-commercialism.

We need to develop and deepen revolutionary theory and ideology, especially in refuting postmodernism (the highfalutin' justification of hyper-individualism and political inactivity) and enriching Marxism through such ideological struggles. We need to demonstrate both theoretically and in practical political struggle that Marxism is *the* revolutionary theory in a dialectical and historical materialist application to issues of environmental sustainability, to indigenous cultures and sovereignty rights, and to the struggle to realize matriarchy, the true communism.

Marx preferred not to use the term "Marxism." The method of dialectical and historical materialism is the only philosophy that rejects divinity, biological superiority, and social hierarchy as unchangeable and permanent. Contrary to some criticism of Marxism as being anti-ecological, pro-technology and industrialization; as anthrocentrist and anti-nature; as culturally Eurocentric and not global; creative Marxist activists and theorists are daily disproving these allegations by proving that without changing the relations and means of production, that is, systemic change, then everything else—be it changing values, changing ideas, changing governments and officials, changing policies—is merely superficial and not total.

All of this requires the role of revolutionary party building. I don't believe that in the United States we've had a genuine Marxist-Leninist party because such a party would manifest as a worker-grounded, majority-oppressed nationality and womyn membership and leadership. Such a party would not liquidate the right of self-determination by denying the existence of oppressed nations in the United States, including the New African Nation, Atzlan, Hawaii, and the indigenous nations. Such a party would not hold sacred or respect the borders of the U.S. imperialist nation-state; would never go along with any ethnic minority to be interned in concentration camps; and would never hold a sectarian stance toward non-Marxist revolutionaries it disagrees with, such as revolutionary anarchists, revolutionary nationalists, and other Left political trends. Such a leading revolutionary party would have united many of the leading revolutionaries across the social movements, have a political line with influence far beyond its immediate base areas, have its own radical media and cultural institutions, and be strong enough to withstand being hijacked into electoral politics by winning over large numbers of people to see the inherent bankruptcy of the U.S. electoral system and want to replace it completely. In other words, while it may engage in some electoral work as a tactical matter, it will always reject the bourgeois electoral system which is *not* a system of one person-one vote or proportional representative democracy, whereby if the greens won 4 percent of the vote, they should hold 4 percent of the seats in

‹ 401

office. Rather, the U.S. imperialists would never have to respect the popular election results so long as it has the system of the Electoral College and as a class monopolizes the media and the means of violence and repression.

Two critically important tasks must be engaged dialectically today: building broad Left unity and building a revolutionary party. We cannot afford to neglect or deny either of these two basic tasks.

NOTES

1 Anthony Simpson, "To Defeat Terrorists, Their Grievances Must Also Be Addressed," *International Herald Tribune,* December 22-23, 2001, 6.

2 John Gerassi, "Will Tears Ever Stop?" (September 2001). Nuclear Age Peace Foundation, http://www.waging peace.org/articles/2001/09/00_gerassi_tears.htm.

3 William Takamatsu Thompson, "Militarism, Racism and U.S. Imperialism: Centering the Race-Class Dialectic," *diʌ/content* 4, no. 2 (December 2001): 4.

Report from the Front Lines:
A Dialectics of the Future

Bill V. Mullen

HISTORY OF THE PRESENT ILLNESS: *The patient is a 50-year-old gentleman found to have a sporadic case of adeno-carcinoma of the colon, rectosigmoid, and underwent surgery 8/29/06. Presenting symptomatology was lower GI bleeding and diarrhea. He underwent an R0 resection of a pathologic T4 B N1 (1/22 lymph nodes replaced by metastatic carcinoma with extension into surrounding mesenteric adipose tissue. The proximal and distal margins are negative for tumor, but no specific comment on circumferential margin status. He completed twelve cycles of adjuvant modified FOLFOX March 2007 under the care of Dr. Dilip Patel. Treatment was complicated by grade 2–3 neuropathy from January until June 2007. He also had what sounds like an allergic reaction possibly to the oxali-platinum, which was successfully managed by swelling oxali-platinum infusion rate. He has persistent grade-1 neuropathy, but this does not interfere with his musicianship. He is a professional saxophonist.*

   —November 14, 2007
   INITIAL BETH ISRAEL MEDICAL ONCOLOGY
   CONSULTATION NOTE on medical condition of Fred Ho

Every day in war has pain and suffering. That is why we should and must avoid wars of all kinds unless they become absolutely necessary (to save our lives, including saving the

planet, which sustains human life). If those who made the deci-
sions to go to war actually themselves had to experience di-
rect pain and suffering, such decisions would not be easily or
readily made. There is extreme volatility (very bad and very
good days) to a general malaise and trauma (constant fatigue,
weariness, exhaustion). It is important to NEVER *allow one-*
self to have doubt, depression, despair. All of my great circle
of friends never allowed me to feel isolated, letting me know
that I could call on someone for help of any kind, or that people
would regularly come and visit and talk with me.

—Fred Ho "Cancer Diary #11: The Fatback Fan Club"

ON AUGUST 4, 2006, Fred Ho was diagnosed with a "sporadic case
of adenocarcinoma of the colon," more commonly known as colon
cancer. Fred was in typically superb health at the time of his diagnosis. He has lived a life free of cigarettes, alcohol, and fatty foods,
disciplined by years of martial arts exercise, ocean swimming, hik-
ing, and rigorous, body-shaking practice on his baritone saxophone.
Since the day of his diagnosis, friends, lovers, family, comrades, and
a legion of concerned people have refracted back onto Fred the love,
joy, and will to live and fight that has marked every day of his life on
this earth. As I write these words, Fred is recuperating in his Brooklyn home from a second round of medically necessary chemotherapy
and radiation initiated by discovery of a second tumor in his body in
the fall of 2007. He continues to be surrounded by friends and family both in New York and via his "Cancer Diary," a brilliant, intimate,
and hopeful sequence of electronic ruminations posted regularly to
his homepage, www.bigredmediainc.com, and to his MySpace page,
http://www.myspace.com/fredhomusic. Fred's diary has also been
posted as an Autonomedia site at http://www.autonomedia.org/
cancerdiary, and he has appeared on New York's WBAI radio program
Health Watch to talk about his illness as a sign of environmental assault on the human body, the cancerization of the green world. Since
his diagnosis, Fred has bravely fought to demonstrate that it is the
body that carries the literal weight of capitalism, swamped by its carcinogenic, toxic, profit-seeking, and diseased assault on the human
condition:

The death of cancer will only come about when the very conditions of toxicity that give growth to cancer cells have been eliminated. What we are faced with is how systemic the conditions of toxicity are: engendered and enhanced by all the "things" that are accepted as "natural" to capitalist-industrial society (sadly, imitated and not thoroughly challenged or countered by many socialist societies, both present and collapsed). The constantly expanding exposure to many forms of electromagnetic radiation, the shredding of the natural ozone layer that protects us from the sun's harmful UVA and UVB radiation, the pollutant poisons we dump into the air, earth, and bodies of water, the fluorocarbons emitted by refrigerators and carbon-burning cars, the saturation of chemicals in our food, the nutritional degradation of our food, the toxic chemicals that permeate our dry cleaning, shampoos, etc., our overall weakened immune system from nutritional deficiency, overreliance on chemical vaccines and treatments—and the list goes on and on and on because all of these are manifestations of modern, industrial, capitalist existence. It is more profitable to "manage" than to cure/solve. The one basic fundamental of capitalism: it is a system that has created the power to feed, clothe, house everyone and to remake or destroy the world; but at the heart of it all, it is a system that creates more problems than it solves.

‹ 405

—"Cancer Diary #12: The Cell of One's Sound," March 8, 2007

I FIRST SAW FRED perform live at the Brooklyn Academy of Music in 1997. I attended a performance of the *Journey Beyond the West: The New Adventures of Monkey!* I was beginning research into Afro-Asian political and cultural connections. The event was transformative for me in several ways. It introduced me to the person who was and is the leading, living, practicing authority on Afro-Asian cultural politics. More than that, it introduced me to an enormously generous man whose loyalty to his friends was matched only by his loyalty to revolutionary art and politics. Like everyone who had come to Fred before me, I quickly learned that Fred's life, art, and words are antidotes to the fear and despair created by capitalism, racism, sexism, and homophobia. Fred's mind and body are tonics to the political and environmental threats people face every day in their struggle to build a better world. That is why I think of the book you have just finished reading as an anatomy of hope. It tells us how to live and think and breathe (Fred Ho is nothing if not about the art of breathing) the air of love and change. Fred has aptly described his life as dedicated to producing music and art that has not yet been said or thought. He has lived a *utopian* life in the best sense of that word: a life lived as an exemplar of what is possible. Fred Ho's life is itself a revolution, his body a battering ram against injustice:

> *Anything that implies or complies with material accumulation for me will be resisted with all my might. I have* EVERYTHING I NEED AND WANT IN LIFE *and if I die today, I'd be satisfied with what I've contributed and created as templates, precursors, exemplars, and experiments for a new society. A lot more needs to be done, and every day I have more to live will be devoted to figuring out by example and experimentation* HOW *to make the impossible. Sun Ra said something that strikes at the necessity of uniting imagination and revolution:* "Everything possible has been done and nothing has changed. What we need is the impossible." YES: *impossible ideas and activities.*

—Fred Ho "Cancer Diary #13: These Shall Be Our Power"

SINCE FALLING ILL, Fred and his music have been the subject of several tributes organized by friends and fellow artists. On October 25, 2007, the World Music Institute hosted a twenty-fifth anniversary celebration of Fred Ho and the Afro Asian Music Ensemble in New York. The performance, appropriately titled "Revolutionary Earth Music," was attended by an overflow crowd. On December 16, 2007, the Museum of the Moving Image in New York hosted the world premiere of a new documentary film by Kamau Hunter and Jose Figueroa, *Urban Dragons* (2007, 90 minutes), examining the role and presence of Blacks and Latinos in the martial arts in the United States. The event was organized as a "Fighting Fred Ho" tribute in honor of Fred's masterful choreographic work in martial arts.

Those of us who have benefited from Fred Ho's magnificently lived life of words and music, song and dance, interpretation and analysis, adoration and critique must see this moment of his life as a reflection of what each of us yet must do. Today is the day to join (or start again) the struggles in your home, your neighborhood, your barrio, your street to tear down the barriers of hate and fear that keep us immunized from possibility. Think of your politics as in symbiotic relationship to Fred's life and illness. *Use* this book as a healing map. Copy pages from this book and post them on public walls. Download Fred's music from his MySpace page and send clips to people who need to be reminded of what revolution sounds like. Read to children from the book of Fred. Make someone somewhere every day aware what a future with Fred Ho in it will be. Fight for someone in his name. We love you, Fred.

"From Banana to Third World Marxist" was first published in *Boyhood, Growing Up Male: A Multicultural Anthology,* edited by Franklin Abbott (Freedom, Calif.: Crossing Press, 1993), 195-99; second edition published by the University of Wisconsin Press, 1998.

"Beyond Asian American Jazz: My Musical and Political Changes in the Asian American Movement" was first published in San Francisco as "Power and Responsibility: Politics, Identity, and Technology in Music," *Leonardo Music Journal* 9 (1999): 45-51.

"What Makes 'Jazz' the Revolutionary Music of the Twentieth Century, and Will It Be Revolutionary for the Twenty-first Century?" was first published by St. Louis University in *African American Review* 29, no. 2 (1995): 283-90.

"Musical Borrowings, Exchanges, and Fusions: New/Experimental Genres" was first published as "New and Experimental Genres" in *Garland Encyclopedia of World Music, Volume 3: The United States and Canada,* edited by Ellen Koskoff (New York: Routledge, 2000), 334-36; reprinted with permission.

"Highlights in the History of 'Jazz' *Not* Covered by Ken Burns: A Request from Ishmael Reed" was first published in Berkeley, California, in *Shuffle Boil* 5/6, edited by David Meltzer and Steve Dickison (2006): 63-66.

An earlier version of "The Damned Don't Cry: The Life and Music of Calvin Massey" was published in *Unity* newspaper, Oakland, California, February 15, 1985.

"How to Sell but Not Sell Out: Personal Lessons from Making a Career as a Subversive and Radical Performing Artist" was first published in New York in *Movement Research Performance Journal,* no. 12, "Dollars and Sensibility," Annie Rachelle Lanzillotto, guest editor (1996): 18.

"Big Red Media, Inc., a Composer/Musician–Driven Production Company: Doing It Yourself" was first published in *Sounding Board,* the newsletter of the American Composers Forum (Summer 1998): 1.

"An Asian American Tribute to the Black Arts Movement" was first published online in *Critical Studies in Improvisation* 1, no. 3, edited by Ellen Waterman (2006), at www.criticalimprov.com. It was later published by Michigan State University Press in *CR: The New Centennial Review* 6, no. 2, edited by Scott Michaelson and David E. Johnson (Fall 2006): 141–89.

"Asian American Music and Empowerment: Is There Such a Thing as 'Asian American Jazz'?" was first published in *Views on Black American Music,* Seventeenth Annual Black Musicians Conference and Festival, University of Massachusetts-Amherst (1989), 27–31.

"Interview with Amy Ling" was first published in *Yellow Light: The Flowering of Asian American Arts,* edited by Amy Ling (Philadelphia: Temple University Press, 1999).

"Bamboo That Snaps Back! Resistance and Revolution in Asian Pacific American Working-Class and Left-Wing Expressive Culture" was first published in *Left of the Color Line: Race, Radicalism, and Twentieth-Century Literature of the United States,* edited by Bill V. Mullen and James Smethurst (Chapel Hill: University of North Carolina Press, 2003).

‹ 409

"Tomoe Tana: Keeping Alive Japanese American Tanka" was first published in *Asian Week* newspaper, San Francisco, June 17, 1988, 18.

INDEX

FRED HO is a one-of-a-kind revolutionary Chinese American baritone saxophonist, composer, writer, producer, political activist, and leader of the Afro Asian Music Ensemble and the Monkey Orchestra.

DIANE C. FUJINO is associate professor and chair of Asian American studies at the University of California, Santa Barbara. She is the author of *Heartbeat of Struggle: The Revolutionary Life of Yuri Kochiyama* (Minneapolis: University of Minnesota Press, 2005).

ROBIN D. G. KELLEY is professor in the departments of American studies, ethnicity, and history at the University of Southern California. He is the author of several award-winning books, including *Yo' Mama's DisFunktional! Fighting the Culture Wars in Urban America* (Boston: Beacon Press, 1997).

BILL V. MULLEN is professor of English and the director of the American studies department at Purdue University. He is the author or editor of several books, including *Afro-Orientalism* (Minneapolis and London: University of Minnesota Press, 2005) and, with Fred Ho, *Afro Asia: Revolutionary Political and Cultural Connections between African Americans and Asian Americans* (Durham, N.C., and London: Duke University Press, 2008).